PROBLEM SOLVING STRATEGIES AND INTERVENTIONS FOR

MEN

IN CONFLICT

Edited by

Dwight Moore and Fred Leafgren

American Association for
Counseling and Development
5999 Stevenson Avenue, Alexandria, VA 22304

American Association for Counseling and Development
5999 Stevenson Avenue
Alexandria, VA 22304

Cover design by Sarah Jane Valdez

Library of Congress Cataloging-in-Publication Data

Problem solving strategies and interventions for men in conflict
    Dwight Moore, Fred Leafgren, editors.
        p.   cm.
    Includes bibliographic references.
    ISBN 1-55620-067-6
    1. Men—Counseling of—United States.   2. Men—United States—
Psychology.   I. Moore, Dwight.   II. Leafgren, Fred.   III. Title: Men in
conflict
HQ1090.3.P75   1990
305.31′0973—dc20   89-39498
                                                                    CIP

Printed in the United States of America

CONTENTS

PREFACE

Men in our culture are in conflict. This book addresses the special issues with which men deal in this time of conflict. Our goal is to bring new information to the growing body of knowledge of men's issues. Our book attempts to be practical as well as challenging regarding men and their needs.

The metaphor we use throughout the book is that of men on a journey. Along the path of the journey each man makes in his life, he confronts challenge, grief, hope, peace, and conflict. We believe that this metaphor of a journey is familiar to most men. The events and faces may be different along the way, but we share the common experience of venturing out on our own, confronting our fears, joining with others, grappling with responsibility, and learning to nurture.

Audience

This book is a compilation of our current knowledge of issues that affect men in the late 20th century. As such, men, and anyone who "journeys" with men, will find this book relevant. Specifically, the book is intended for counselors at all educational levels, social workers, community therapists, private practitioners, clinicians, teachers, hospital workers, and Employee Assistance Program workers. Anyone who works directly with men's emotional well-being will find this book illuminating and thought-provoking.

Overview of Contents

We have segmented the book into five sections. They are:

> Personal Growth and Societal Expectations
> Sexuality, Family, and Marriage
> Multicultural Concerns
> Techniques and Treatments
> Where Do We Go From Here? Ideas for the Future

In the first section, Personal Growth and Societal Expectations, Fred Leafgren in chapter 1, "Men on a Journey," explores men in the context of their culture and identifies the positive impact counselors can make both on the lives of these men and on the culture.

Ron May in chapter 2, "Finding Ourselves: Self-Esteem, Self-Disclosure, and Self-Acceptance," explores how men's self-esteem is developed, methods of intervention, strategies for change for men who have low self-esteem, and an approach to developing an awareness of feelings. He is specific in his suggestions concerning the need for men to self-disclose, develop community, confront their own homophobia, and find their fathers.

James M. O'Neil in chapter 3, "Assessing Men's Gender Role Conflict," provides concepts to assess this conflict and a diagnostic schema to use in counseling, psychotherapy, and educational programming.

Thomas M. Skovholt in chapter 4, "Career Themes in Counseling and Psychotherapy With Men," identifies how the culture prepares men for the work world. He cites case studies that illustrate career dilemmas that men face.

In the second section, Sexuality, Family, and Marriage, chapter 5 by Phil Colgan, "Dimensions of Pleasure: Sexuality, Men, and Counseling," is a radical departure from traditional conceptualizations of male sexuality. The author looks at meaning, mission, power, structure, and resources in men's sexuality, which is broadly defined in a context of relationships.

Vincent Ciaramella takes a family systems approach in chapter 6, "Men and Marriage." He writes about the complementary relationships and the triangles that couples develop. He addresses the "balance of fairness" in which conflict is reframed to be understood as the process of filling unmet expectations. He makes specific suggestions for men who are contemplating marriage.

Ron Levant in chapter 7, "Coping With the New Father Role," addresses the significant cultural change that fathers currently are experiencing. He examines the "new father and the new American family" and discusses the implications for individual men. He outlines a "fatherhood" course.

Patrick McKenry and Sharon Price in chapter 8, "Divorce: Are Men at Risk?" discuss divorce as a process, the adjustments associated with divorce, relationships with former spouses, life as a divorced single man, social supports, living single, dating, sources of stress, and parenting difficulties. They also cover interventions, divorce therapy, group approaches, divorce mediation, and services for fathers and their children. The chapter provides a listing of self-help materials as well.

Stephen Parker and Ted Thompson write "Gay and Bisexual Men: Developing a Healthy Identity." Chapter 9 addresses the elements of healthy identity formation specifically applied to gay and bisexual men. The authors discuss therapeutic approaches particularly germane to gay and bisexual clients.

In the third section, Multicultural Concerns, Courtland C. Lee begins with chapter 10, "Black Male Development: Counseling the 'Native Son.' " He takes an incisive look at a program to help young Black men develop a sense of identity. He describes specific steps that enable African-American men to explore the thoughts, feelings, and behaviors associated with being Black.

Fernando J. Gutierrez in chapter 11, "Exploring the Macho Mystique: Counseling Latino Men," presents case studies and explores how issues affect Latino men at different developmental stages in their lives. He also discusses how counselors can assist their clients navigate through this developmental process.

David Sue in chapter 12, "Culture in Transition: Counseling Asian-American Men," focuses on the family structure and values of traditional Asian Americans, counseling approaches based on these values, the impact of differences in acculturation and ethnic identity, and special problems Asian men face.

The fourth section, Techniques and Treatments, begins with Patrick Dougherty's chapter 13, "A Personal Perspective on Working With Men in Groups." This is a look at Patrick's own experience as a psychotherapist with men in groups. Patrick is not a linear thinker and, therefore, examines the circular nature of men's journeys into emotions and intimate relationships.

Dwight Moore is the author of chapter 14, "Helping Men Become More Emotionally Expressive: A Ten-Week Program." It provides step-by-step descriptions of readings, experiential activities, and group process for a 10-week group designed to increase emotional expressiveness. This model has been tested and found to help participants increase their ability to express feelings.

Roger Grusznski and Gunnar Bankovics in chapter 15, "Treating Men Who Batter: A Group Approach," describe a particular program that helps men understand their behavior, control that behavior, and develop alternatives to deal with their underlying emotions and tension. This particular program has been highly researched and found to be successful for those men who complete it.

Dennis Elsenrath in chapter 16, "Counseling Suicidal Men," outlines the causative factors in suicide, focuses on male relationships, and looks at special populations at risk of suicide. He then thoroughly discusses assessment of suicidal intent and myths concerning suicide. Finally, he suggests resources and approaches for suicide prevention.

The final section, Where Do We Go From Here? Ideas for the Future, begins with Sam Femiano's chapter 17, "Developing a Contemporary Men's Studies Curriculum." He traces the history and development of men's studies, discusses the goals for a men's studies curriculum, and outlines specific objectives that would meet such goals. He concludes with a specific curriculum outline of a course on American masculinity.

In chapter 18, "A Survey Report: Men Counseling Men," Richard W. Thoreson, Stephen Cook, Peter Shaughnessy, and Dwight Moore report on an extensive research study of male members of the American Association for Counseling and Development. The research focused on issues and concerns of male counselors.

Fred Leafgren in chapter 19, "Being a Man Can Be Hazardous to Your Health: Life-Style Issues," emphasizes the significance of the social, occupational, spiritual, physical, intellectual, and emotional dimensions of men's lives.

In chapter 20, "The Journey Continues," Dwight Moore, Stephen Parker, Ted Thompson, and Patrick Dougherty take a new look at some of the emotional components involved in a man's developmental experience. This chapter is meant to stimulate thinking about the men we work with in helping relationships.

CONTRIBUTORS

Gunnar Bankovics received his BS from the University of Minnesota. He is a licensed social worker and a family court counselor in Hennepin County Court Services in Minnesota. He has worked as a therapist in the Domestic Abuse Project.

Vincent Ciaramella received his BA from Maryknoll College, his MA from the City University of New York, and his MS and PhD from Fordham University. He works for Ackerman Institute for Family Therapy and is a counselor supervisor on the NYC Board of Education. He is a family therapist in private practice in Yonkers, New York.

Philip Colgan received his BA from St. Ambrose University and his MA from the University of Iowa. He is in private practice as a licensed psychologist and certified sex therapist. He is also a member of the clinical faculty of the Program in Human Sexuality in Minneapolis.

Stephen Cook received his BA from Texas A & M and is a doctoral candidate at the University of Missouri-Columbia, working as an assistant to Richard Thoreson. He has an emerging interest in men's issues and has assisted with projects for the AACD Committee on Men.

Patrick Dougherty received his BA from Metropolitan State University and his MA from St. Mary's College. He is a licensed psychologist with a private practice in St. Paul. He is also among St. Mary's graduate school faculty.

Dennis E. Elsenrath received his BS from Slippery Rock State College, his MS from Westminster College, and his EdD from Indiana University. He is a co-founder of the National Wellness Institute, a licensed psychologist, and an associate professor of psychology at the University of Wisconsin-Stevens Point, where he is currently teaching with an emphasis in health psychology.

Sam Femiano received his BA and MA from the University of Toronto, his ThD in theology from the Institute Catholique de Paris, and his EdD from the University of Massachusetts. He is a clinical psychologist in private practice in Northhampton, MA, at the Center for Changing Men. He is currently involved in men's issues, particularly through the Men's Studies Association where he serves as co-chair.

Roger Grusznski received his BA from the University of Wisconsin-Madison, his MS from the University of Wisconsin-Oshkosh, and his PhD from the University of Minnesota. He is the Clinical Program Coordinator for Child and Adolescent Mental Health at Riverside Medical Center in Minneapolis. He worked as a therapist for the Domestic Abuse Project prior to his current position.

Fernando J. Gutierrez received his BA from Michigan State University, his MS from Purdue, and his PhD from Boston University. He was born in Cuba and works as a consultant to Black and Latino community agencies. He is the director of the Growth Center in San Jose, California.

Fred Leafgren received his BS from the University of Illinois and his MA and PhD from Michigan State University. He is the Assistant Chancellor of Student Life at the University of Wisconsin-Stevens Point. He is co-director for the National Wellness Institute, and an associate professor and consultant on wellness and psychological type. He presently serves as co-chair of the AACD Men's Committee and has been actively involved in the ACPA Committee for Men.

Courtland C. Lee received his BA from Hofstra University, his MS from Hunter College, and his PhD from Michigan State University. He is the Director of Counselor Education and an associate professor at the University of Virginia.

Ronald F. Levant received his BS from the University of California and his EdD from Harvard University. For 13 years he was on the faculty of the Counseling Psychology Program at Boston University, where he also served as the director of the Fatherhood Project. In 1989 he joined Rutgers University as an associate professor of counseling psychology.

Ron May received his BS from the University of Wisconsin-Stevens Point, his MEC from the University of Missouri-Columbia, and his PhD from Michigan State University. He is Director of Counseling at the University of Oregon and is chair of the Standing Committee for Men of the ACPA. Over the past decade, he has worked with men's issues as an author, researcher, educator, and psychotherapist.

Patrick C. McKenry received his BA, MA, and PhD from the University of Tennessee. He is a professor of family relations and human development and adjunct professor of Black studies at Ohio State University.

Dwight Moore received his BA from Colgate University, his MA from Michigan State, and his PhD from the University of Minnesota. He has been the chair of the Men's Committee for AACD for the past 3 years and currently is co-chair with Fred Leafgren. Dr. Moore is a consulting psychologist in Vancouver, B.C., with Wilson Banwell, Inc., specializing in organizational consultation on issues of health and stress with executives.

James M. O'Neil received his BA from LeMoyne College and his MA and PhD from the University of Maryland. He is a professor of counseling at the University of Connecticut and a licensed psychologist in private practice in South Windsor, Connecticut. He has a long-standing commitment to men's issues and research in this area.

Stephen Parker received his BA from the University of Minnesota and his MA from the College of St. Thomas. He is a licensed psychologist at Northland Therapy Center in Minneapolis.

Sharon J. Price received her BA from MacMurray College for Women and her MA and PhD from Iowa State University. She is a professor and acting head of Child and Family Development at the University of Georgia.

Peter Shaughnessy received his BA from the State University of New York at Albany. He is a doctoral candidate in the Department of Educational and Counseling Psychology, specializing in counseling psychology, at the University of Missouri-Columbia. He has been helpful to the AACD Committee on Men and has an emerging interest in men's issues.

Thomas M. Skovholt received his BA from St. Olaf College and his MEd and PhD from the University of Missouri-Columbia. He is a professor at the University of Minnesota in counseling and student personnel psychology, a diplomate of the American Board of Professional Psychology, and has a private practice in Minneapolis. He has been involved with men's issues for most of his professional life.

David Sue received his BS from the University of Oregon and his MS and PhD from Washington State University. He is the director of the Clinical Counseling Program, and a professor at Western Washington University. He is also an associate at the Center of Cross-Cultural Research.

Ted Thompson received his BA from Morehouse College and is in a doctoral program at the University of Minnesota. He is a licensed psychologist and a family therapist in private practice in Minneapolis.

Richard W. Thoreson received his BA and MA from the University of Minnesota and his PhD from the University of Missouri-Columbia. He is a professor in the Department of Educational and Counseling Psychology at the University of Missouri-Columbia. He is working on an extensive survey of male counselors in AACD and has been a long-standing member of a men's support group.

Personal Growth and Societal Expectations

*Men's journey in life is highly dependent upon the culture that
can both facilitate and restrict human growth and development.*

Chapter 1
MEN ON A JOURNEY

Fred Leafgren

Man's journey begins at birth. In many instances, this journey has
its beginnings in a family that has expectations about the life of the
individual even before birth. All men may be created equal according
to the constitution, but they are not all born into equal circumstances in
terms of socioeconomic, racial, or family environments. Some individuals
will not experience the traditional family environment. Nevertheless, the
journey begins.

The journey is a multifaceted one throughout men's lives. It is a
journey of physical growth and development from birth to infancy, the
childhood years, adolescence, young adulthood, age 30 transition, middle adulthood, mid-life transition, age 50 transition, culmination of middle adulthood, and late-adult transition. It is also a journey through the
educational system of our country from kindergarten, elementary school,
junior high school, senior high school, and for many, technical/vocational
training, college, and professional training.

Men's journey is also one of psychological development. According
to Erikson (1959), the journey includes developing basic trust, autonomy,
initiative, identity, intimacy, generativity, and integrity. At the same time
men are on a journey to learn how to achieve, to succeed, to control, to
maintain power, to compete. It is a journey of belonging, a journey to
maintain safety and security, a journey to establish self-esteem, social
identity, sexual identity, relationships, and values. The individual must
also cope with such issues as basic competence, intelligence, temperament, physical strength, stamina, health, and physical appearance. These
are the givens in each man's life, the basic ingredients that give him the
opportunity to build his life. The various elements of the journey are
woven together like a fine tapestry, each making its own unique contribution to the total personality that emerges.

Throughout this journey, there are peaks and valleys. There are
successes and failures. Some expectations are met and others go unful-
filled. William James, in *The Principles of Psychology* (1890), proposed that:

> In its widest possible sense, however, a man's self is a sum
> total of all that he can call his, not only his body and his psychic

3

powers but his clothes and his house, his wife and children, his ancestors and friends, his reputation and work, his land and horses, and yacht and bank account. All these things give him the same emotions. If they wax and prosper, he feels triumphant but if they dwindle and die away, he feels cast down. (p. 291)

Effects of Cultural Expectations

The cultures in which men live affect their lives enormously. The impact of the culture on men's lives is much greater than most of us are aware. Cultures establish norms, expectations, and goals for how we live, why we live, and what we ought to be accomplishing. Cultures in which we live influence everything that happens. We know that cultures can encourage and support positive human growth and development. Cultures can also discourage and restrict human growth and development. We remain largely unaware of the aspects of the culture that affect us positively and those that affect us negatively. There is a basic assumption that whatever the culture promotes is positive. Living in the culture blinds our objectively viewing its impact because we are so enmeshed in it. We are like fish that do not know water exists until they are out of it. Eric Fromm (1955) maintained:

The statement that man can live under any condition is only half true; it must be supplemented by the other statement that if he lives under conditions which are contrary to his nature and to the basic requirements for human growth and sanity, he cannot help reacting; he must either deteriorate and perish, or bring about conditions which are more in accordance with his needs. (p. 19)

Fromm further reported that psychiatrists and psychologists were beginning to recognize that contemporary American society as a whole may lack sanity judging by the problems of mental health and well-being. He raised major concerns about the culture and society in which we live. He concluded that our culture and society results in individuals' living lives of massive maladjustment in terms of the optimal human condition, even though they may be adjusted to the culture and society in which they live.

Men often face a paradox in coping with their culture. On the one hand, the more successful they are in meeting cultural expectations, the more harm they may be doing to their basic human needs, motivations, and the essentials for living mentally healthy lives. On the other hand, failure to meet cultural expectations can produce havoc in self-worth and self-esteem. Cultural norms, the expectations of others, the standards of society, all become gauges that many men use to determine a sense of worth. Failure to meet these expectations can diminish their self-esteem in significant ways and have massive detrimental effects on their emotional health and well-being. Men's need to validate themselves by cultural standards is a powerful force in their lives. Most men are unable to separate themselves to any significant degree from cultural role expectations. Most men are unable to listen to their internal self and use that as a standard by which to gauge their well-being, their worth, the value of their existence.

Men who are Black, Native American, Hispanic, or Oriental experience additional forces on their journey that press on them to meet the expectations of the American culture. A traditional culture that sets the expectations may also, through a variety of barriers, prohibit some men from achieving the expectations so highly valued for White men. Further confusion may exist because of differing expectations of the specific cultures of non-Whites.

Men validate their maleness in American society through achievement-oriented behavior such as winning in sports, winning in physical fighting, winning intellectually, winning financially, and winning in achieving power. Involvement in friendships and intimate relationships or investing in the welfare and concern for others are not behaviors associated with developing a masculine identity in our current traditional culture.

Cultural expectations for men to remain strong and to live up to the traditional male role deny boys, young adults, and adult men the opportunities to express important facets of life that deal much more with intimacy, gentleness, caring, and the opportunity on occasions to be weak and in need of help. The article "Men in Transition" (Hayes, 1988) reports that "for adolescents who are just assuming the masculine role, this is easier said than done. At an age when conformity is so strongly valued, adolescents currently face conflicting messages about the behaviors that are expected of them as men" (p. 3). Certainly the Rambo supermasculine macho image is being held up to adolescents at the same time they are introduced to characters such as PeeWee Herman, who is at the other end of the behavioral continuum. Imitating Rambo may be applauded, whereas imitating PeeWee Herman is likely to result in rejection. If a young man decides he wants to bake a birthday cake for a friend, he should not have to be the victim of disdain by his peers because this activity doesn't fit expectations.

Some men find it difficult to accept and to follow the traditional male role because of their basic temperament or family modeling. Even those men whose basic temperament enables them to assume the characteristics most closely associated with the typical masculine role can still experience problems because they are unable at times to accept any other style of behavior and instead try to maintain, at a very high cost, the rigidly determined role expectations for masculinity. Any behaviors that may suggest a weakness become associated with a loss of masculinity, and consequently, a loss of worth and value.

Many men can experience themselves only in terms of these fixed role expectations and are unable to view themselves as they really are. As a result, they lose spontaneity, they lose aliveness, they become artificial, their laughter is forced, their communications are less genuine. They live with these major defects at a horrendous cost to their own emotional and physical well-being.

Gloria Emerson's book, *Some American Men*, describes her interviews with several hundred men during a 6-year period. She found them caught between conflicting expectations. "At a time when women want men to love, raise babies and remember our birthdays, it is also required that they be the ones who rescue people in burning buildings" (p. 14).

Stereotypical Male Role Behavior

Boys and men are trained from childhood to be goal-oriented. They are raised to be productive and to do things with purpose. Boys and men often have trouble communicating personal concerns and issues. They can communicate about sports, cars, work, and other activities. They do not communicate about feelings, goals, attitudes, and values. Frequently women request men with whom they are intimate to sit down and talk about their relationships. The most common response by the man to the woman's request is, "What is there to talk about?" Men have little training or modeling in conversation about personal and intimate matters in their lives. They are encouraged to keep feelings hidden and emotions from showing, with the exception of aggression and anger.

R. C. Brannon (1976) identified several general dimensions of stereotypical male role behavior. He summarized these four brief phrases: (1) no sissy stuff (representing a need to be different from women); (2) big wheel (representing a need to perceive oneself as superior to others); (3) sturdy oak (representing a need to be independent and self-reliant); and (4) give them hell (representing a need to perceive oneself as more powerful than others, accompanied by a willingness to use violence if necessary to accomplish this objective).

Such a model of male role behavior denies both the complexity and reality of men's unique human potential because it is based on external standards. According to Sidney Jourard (1971), however, the fundamental psychological needs of men are essentially the same as women's. These are: (1) to know and be known; (2) to be mutually interdependent; (3) to love and be loved, and (4) to find purpose and meaning in life. Thus, men who fulfill their socially stereotypical male role by behaving in ways that are expected are in conflict with men who attempt to behave more in accordance with their basic psychological needs. When men give priority to psychological needs, they may be classified socially as unmasculine. Stress can result when men do not get the support of the culture and society in which they live.

Men are in conflict and they need help. Men tend to judge themselves by their role in society much more than women do. Often a feeling of tension results because men feel that they are not living up to expectations. A man's self-image depends most heavily on his achievements; for many men this becomes an oppressive idea, engendering strong feelings of failure and inadequacy.

Interventions

This book focuses on men's issues and the specific dilemmas they face in their life journey in a modern society. It is also the purpose of this compendium to identify intervention strategies for the helping professionals—such as counselors, social workers, and psychologists—so they can enable men to solve problems and cope more effectively.

In contrast to men, many more women participate in the counseling process and avail themselves of the opportunities for change. This continues despite evidence indicating that men's needs are significant. Ironically, the very culture that creates men's needs for assistance establishes barriers that prohibit men from seeking the assistance they need. That women consult therapists much more frequently than do men does not prove that men have fewer problems. It more likely demonstrates how men deny evidence of problems.

Men have a great potential for change. One of the first requirements for change is a desire to change. Without the desire to change, change is not likely to occur. When men are made aware of the possibilities for richer, more fulfilling lives, they are often interested in making changes. This awareness may come through reading books on men's issues. It can come through involvement in men's groups. There may be a precipitating crisis or life event that will generate a call for help. Men may be encouraged and supported by a close friend who will serve as a support or mentor to them. Relationships with their children may help men recall their own youth and their own experiences in the process of growing up, and make them aware of the need for changes in their own lives.

What means can we use to help men avail themselves of change processes and begin to cope in more positive and effective ways with their needs? I suggest several proactive methods. I believe we need to use our organizational structures in business, organizations, and institutions to introduce workshops, training sessions, and skill programs that provide opportunities for people to better understand themselves and their relationships with others. We can present programs on physical fitness. We can present programs that focus on emotional well-being. I believe that many men are increasingly accepting programs related to their place of employment. When it is expected that they will engage in such workshops to enhance their job satisfaction and potential, we find many more willing participants. Because men identify so closely with their careers, facilitating their development through specific programs associated with their employment is a natural way to get men involved in personal growth experiences. Once into these experiences, many men recognize their benefits and are eager to proceed with the growth and change process.

In the 1970s, the Chicago Men's Gathering group was organized to facilitate men's growth through awareness and through consciousness raising. The Chicago Men's Gathering also provided men an emotional support system and encouraged men to participate in self-exploration and growth. This is only one of many groups that have been formed in communities to support men's growth and awareness. Again, such groups can provide considerable insight to facilitate growth and change in men's lives.

Institutions such as churches, YMCAs, or other organized groups can promote and provide opportunities for men's growth and awareness by sponsoring and facilitating organized programs and men's groups. Again, forming such groups in structured programs provides men an opportunity to seek out proactive experiences without specifically having to acknowledge their need for help.

Medical clinics and family health care centers can set up programs to promote involvement with health issues, both emotional and physical. Such programs give men an opportunity to explore change and growth.

Colleges and universities can offer programs on men's health issues to students. These institutions can also provide programs to members of the community. Institutions possess excellent resources to facilitate men's issues and men's awareness and change. Employee assistance programs in any organization can provide specific programs and services to address men's concerns and men's issues.

Films and television programs addressing men's issues can be excellent sources for increasing men's awareness. Films and videos are available on topics such as parenting, divorce, suicide, sexual relationships, stress, physical health, careers, power, love, and marriage. All these topics contribute to increasing men's awareness. They can also be used to support dialogue in men's groups.

Effecting Cultural Change

The good news is that people can and will change their cultures with assistance. It is not realistic to expect that a single force, no matter how dramatic, will totally alter the existing culture. Change is more likely to occur through a gradual system where, as people change, they modify their culture, thereby increasing the possibilities for further change. The dedication and commitment of professionals working with individuals over time can affect not only the lives of those individuals, but also the support, norms, expectations, and goals that their cultures provide. The authors in this book are not only changing people but they are also altering cultures. These professionals are making significant contributions to the lives of men and the cultures in which they live.

I have introduced the concept of change. Professional counselors are definitely change agents. Change comes about in clearly defined ways. One of these is through the imitation of others. Professional counselors serve as role models, and clients imitate professionals in many ways. The degree to which clients will imitate must not be overlooked. It's a powerful force in the therapeutic process and a powerful change agent.

Change also comes about through affiliation and identification. If our clients do not find appropriate individuals or groups with whom to affiliate and identify, the anticipated and suggested changes in their life may never be realized. Their present condition is often a result of difficulties they are experiencing that are supported by individuals with whom they are associated. Family system therapy has identified the need for total environmental change, not only the individual's need to change in a system unwilling to accommodate the behaviors.

A third means of effecting change is through communication, which includes both instruction and consultation. The typical therapeutic process involves both in varying degrees. The client has an opportunity to learn from the therapist new options available and means of achieving these options. Acting on these new ideas not only in the counseling session but in the larger world results in change.

A fourth way to change involves managing environments. Therapists can identify the opportunities and means available to make changes in the community, organizations, and businesses. This is where therapists can affect significantly the larger cultural arena. For example, teaching men that it is okay to be in touch with their feelings and to express these feelings must be communicated to the larger society so that such expression is safe and supported.

Change can also come about as a result of interventions. These interventions need to facilitate harmony between the client and his environment. If the individual's needs cannot be met in the environment, interventions are appropriate. The interventions can be individual and may lie outside the therapeutic process. It is important that interventions be made in positive ways to facilitate change in cultures and environments that restrict and discourage optimal human development. It is important that interventions be made to effect desperately needed changes to enhance the well-being of individuals.

The sixth method by which change is brought about is enforced obedience. This method of bringing about change may be the one most onerous to therapists and the one with which we least identify. Nevertheless, it is a means by which change can be effected. We all recognize instances in our professional lives when it is has served us well. Therapists are familiar with setting limits in the counseling relationship.

Men on their journey are affected in powerful ways by the culture in which they live. It is the interaction between men and their culture and environment that determines happiness and fulfillment. Can the culture and environment produce the healthy child, the healthy human being? Do we know when our culture and environment are supporting or thwarting the individual's development? George Vaillant (1977) wrote, "at each stage of a man's life he responds to challenges with characteristic style and adaptation. Often he changes and grows; other times he fails and retreats. There still remains much to be learned about men and change and growth. There remains much to be discovered about the optimum conditions favorable to men and their lives" (p. 34). As counselors, we can make a significant contribution by fostering men's optimal development on their journey. The chapter authors in this book have identified issues that men in our culture are facing today. The authors, all counselors themselves, share the strategies they use in facilitating men's development to greater productivity, health, and happiness.

Jean Houston (1973) wrote:

> We are undergoing perhaps the most critical revolution in history, comparable to when man moved from being a hunter and random forager to agricultural society. Man is radically questioning what it is to be man, and it might be in part because for several hundred thousand years, he has been man the worker, whose reality is completely structured in terms of getting food into his stomach and a roof over his head . . . . We are now in the first or second generation of a different type of man; man the player, man who has the leisure and the freedom to explore all those potentials he has kept on the shelf all those hundreds of thousands of years. (p. 16)

This chapter offers interventions for counselors to help clients to develop more fully the emotional, expressive, and relational aspects of their lives.

Chapter 2

FINDING OURSELVES: SELF-ESTEEM, SELF-DISCLOSURE, AND SELF-ACCEPTANCE

Ron May

This chapter will focus on some of what we have learned about self-esteem, self-disclosure, and self-acceptance in the lives of men. A brief summary of male development will emphasize how the real self is easily lost and how difficult it can be to recapture. More importantly, the chapter will discuss specific strategies for helping men to develop an appreciation of their masculine selves, become aware of and express their real feelings, and accept themselves as both vulnerable and capable.

Development of the Male Self

Theoretical Views

A variety of developmental theorists have conceptualized the development of the male self. Psychodynamic theorists tend to emphasize gender identity development during the first years of life. Chodorow (1978) suggested that male and female differences are largely influenced by differences in parent-child interaction patterns. Although all infants begin life with a primary emotional attachment to the mother, sons must separate from this relationship to achieve their masculine identification. The male infant seeks out the father for continued nurturance and protection. Merton (1986) and others found that the frequent lack of an emotionally available father creates a condition referred to as "father hunger." This subconscious yearning is believed to result in behaviors that attempt to make an emotional connection with the father. The behavior patterns may range from being passive and approval-seeking to macho and attention-seeking. From this perspective, the self-concept becomes a collection of the son's projections of behaviors that would build a connection with the father.

11

Rubin (1983) also addressed the emotional deprivation that results from the separation from the mother. She hypothesized that repressed anger covers an inner experience of abandonment and betrayal. Rubin suggested this anger may be the source of patriarchal contempt toward women.

To protect himself from the pain of the separation from his mother, the young boy is believed to develop a set of defenses aimed at providing a type of character armor (Gilligan, 1982; Rubin, 1983). Ego boundaries become firm and fixed. Feelings of vulnerability and dependence are denied. When threatened, the young boy learns to communicate messages such as "I need no one" or "I can do anything." The rigid use of these defenses thwarts attempts either to discover the real self or to make emotional connections with others.

Based on her research on moral development, Gilligan (1982) also offered a more positive view of gender differences. As a result of these early dynamics, male development emphasizes separateness and independence whereas female development emphasizes attachment and connection. Gilligan stressed that each of these "voices" are equally valid and useful, though one voice may be more appropriate for a particular situation. Furthermore, each gender is viewed as capable of developing the other perspective. Gilligan's description of male development includes identification through roles and positions, self-esteem resulting from individual achievements, conceptualizing with a distinct and rational cognitive style, and ethics based on principles of justice.

Social learning theorists (Bandura, 1977) emphasized the application of learning principles to the development of gender identity. Boys learn to seek rewards for exhibiting male sex role behavior and to avoid punishment for demonstrating female sex role behavior. The anxiety associated with punishment leads to a rigid adherence to traditional roles. Lynn (1966) emphasized the role of mothers and teachers as socializing agents. He viewed their socialization as including a devaluing of femininity as a reflection of our social values. Hartley (1959), on the other hand, stressed the impact of peers and older boys in the learning of sex role behavior.

Implications for Change

Understanding male development enables one better to appreciate men's resistance to self-exploration and to design more effective interventions for promoting change. Several lessons can be gained from the developmental literature. First, important turning points in a man's emotional development occur early in life—before trust, memory, and language are fully developed. The issues tend to be unconscious and preverbal. Consequently, trust building is critical in helping men to explore their lives. Activities designed to build trust should precede exercises involving more significant emotional risks. Nonverbal exercises are helpful for addressing important issues for which conscious recollections are not available.

Second, most men have relied on a strong set of defenses to protect themselves emotionally throughout their lives. Many of these defenses have been widely criticized in recent years as men's roles have been reexamined. However, it is important to validate the fact that these defenses may have served a man well in protecting him from greater hurt and pain. At the same time, it is useful to acknowledge the limits defenses set for experiencing vulnerability and emotional connectedness in a man's adult life. Again, it is important to go slowly, to acknowledge the process of defending oneself, and to let participants freely choose to let go of their defenses.

Third, much of a man's sense of self has been learned. What has been learned can also be unlearned! Men benefit from understanding the process of their own socialization. Workshops and support groups can provide new norms and role models for promoting a healthy discovery and expression of the male self.

Fourth, the masks men develop often result from a fear of femininity. O'Neil (1982) stated that this fear is a primary driving force behind his concept of "gender role strain." Men must receive permission for developing their more feminine parts as well as their masculine parts. Such change, however, occurs only when men confront their societal attitudes that devalue women. Consequently, interventions designed for personal development also need to include an element of social consciousness.

Fifth, men need to understand and appreciate that which is uniquely masculine. Gilligan's work has led to considerable insight in understanding gender differences in perception, values, and reasoning. The male "voice" she described is a valuable resource for responding to many life situations. Yet, many men tend initially to deny their masculinity in their search to become the "the new male." Masculine expressions of instrumental caring, role identification, and individual achievement can serve as a foundation for expanding a man's expression of his humanness.

Finally, a man's relationship with his father often proves to be the missing link in developing his self-concept. Even when a father was not emotionally available, the resulting feelings of anger, grief, and emptiness must be acknowledged. Only in working through these feelings is a man able to develop an attitude of forgiveness that allows him to incorporate the positive experiences of his father-son relationship.

Strategies for Change

Carl Rogers (1961) described self-concept as the collective perceptions of one's self that an individual has deemed worthy of positive regard from others. Unconditional positive regard tends to produce self-concepts that are congruent with one's organismic strivings. However, conditional regard leads one to deny and distort one's own experience to fulfill conditions of worth.

The literature on male sex role socialization in our culture clearly identifies conditions of worth for men (Farrell, 1974; Goldberg, 1977; Hartley, 1974). Our review of theories of male development describes the resulting formation of emotional defenses and a sense of alienation from the real self. Efforts to enhance men's self-esteem, promote men's self-disclosure, and increase men's self-acceptance must create an awareness of these conditions of worth and encourage a rediscovery of self with unconditional positive regard.

The remainder of this chapter will discuss specific program interventions for promoting these changes. These interventions will be presented through topics that are considered critical and, in some respects, sequential for developing a healthy sense of masculinity.

Developing an Awareness of One's Masculinity

Many men display little awareness of gender role strain and do not seek out opportunities to explore their masculinity. Yet, these men may still benefit from a consciousness-raising experience. The purpose of this experience might be to develop an initial awareness of sexism by presenting information typically avoided or denied. Such programs might be presented in business forums, workshops, health classes, social science courses, student organizations, or living units in residence halls or Greek houses.

Several excellent films are available for these types of presentations. "Men's Lives" (Hanig & Roberts, 1974) was one of the first such films produced. This Academy Award-winning documentary examines the male mystique as two men revisit their high school to interview former teachers and childhood heroes. "An Acquired Taste" (Arlyck, 1982) portrays the filmmaker's review of the school, work, and media influences that have shaped his life as a man as he reaches his 40th birthday. "Stale Roles and Tight Buns" (O.A.S.I.S., 1988) explores male stereotypes by reviewing images of men in media advertising.

Because these films are visually appealing and entertaining, they tend to be well received by a wide variety of audiences. Follow-up discussions with trained facilitators maximize the benefits of viewing these films. Discussion topics may include emotional reactions to the films, identification of stereotypes, and personal experiences associated with topics presented in the films.

Other men may respond more readily to factual material. Numerous statistics can be shared that are likely to lead less aware men to question their well-being as men. For instance, compared to women, men: tend to have at least 8 years less life expectancy (Harris, 1976), are twice as prone to severe cardiovascular disease (Harrison, 1978), are four times more likely to be alcoholic (Chafetz & Demore, 1972), and are more likely to commit suicide (Weiss, 1974). Being exposed to these health-related risks causes some men to question the strains of the male role. Applying these risks to their own life-style is apt to develop a greater awareness of gender role strain.

Still another approach to reexamining self-concept lies in the use of psychological inventories. The Bem Sex Role Inventory (Bem, 1974) consists of 60 items that equally represent traits rated as desirable for a man, woman, or neutral. Using a median split method derived by Spence, Helmreich, and Stapp (1975), Bem revised her original scoring procedure and now considers those scoring above both the masculine and feminine means to be androgynous, and those below both means to be undifferentiated.

Using the same scoring format, the Personal Attributes Questionnaire (Spence & Helmreich, 1978) uses items chosen for social desirability and prevalence in either gender to determine levels of androgyny. A short form of 24 items is available with a 0.90 reliability correlation between forms.

A 56-item instrument based on Murray's need theory is the PRF ANDRO (Berzins, Welling, & Wetter, 1978). Masculine items reflect ascendancy, autonomy, and risk taking, whereas feminine items reflect nurturance, affiliation, expression, and self-subordination.

These inventories all measure androgyny, but another instrument assesses attitudes toward the rights and roles of women in society. The Attitudes Toward Women Scale (Spence & Helmreich, 1972) uses a 15-item rating scale to measure these attitudes on a liberal-to-conservative continuum.

These inventories can be used in a variety of formats to promote personal development. One such method involves having participants anticipate their scores prior to completing the instrument. These ratings can then be compared to the actual test results. Discrepancies between "perceived" and "real" scores can provide useful material for examining a man's self-concept in relation to his masculinity, level of androgyny, and attitudes toward women.

A more informal assessment method for gaining self-awareness involves time management studies. Participants are asked to monitor and record how much time they spend each day in various activities. Categories can be developed to address specific issues in men's lives. A review of the result of these personal surveys may produce insights into time spent at work versus at home, with others versus alone, or in intimate relationships versus pastimes and activities. Choices made about spending time can be interpreted as values and life-style decisions. A greater awareness of these decisions allows men to review and possibly change them.

Developing an Awareness of Feelings

Being aware of one's emotions is one of the crucial components of self-exploration. However, an awareness of feelings in the here-and-now is a most difficult task for many men. The psychological defenses around vulnerability and dependence developed early in life form a sort of crust around a man's feelings. Years of socialization serve to harden the crust. Attempts to soften this crust and to penetrate these defenses must be taken with great care.

Most men respond to questions about their feelings with a rational statement about their cognitions. Thus, a starting point is to help men to differentiate between the processes of thinking and feeling. Once this differentiation is made, men can strive more intentionally to access their feelings. In fact, the most common need I have heard expressed in workshops is to help participants to "develop access" to themselves. Once men have had an emotionally intimate experience, their sense of isolation from themselves and others becomes less tolerable. These men then need to learn to access their feelings.

Programs designed to facilitate emotional awareness need to set a tone that conveys comfort and safety. I find it helpful to have soft music playing as participants enter the room and are introduced to one another. Much of the "new age" music is ideal for this purpose. It helps if the room has soft lighting, carpeting, comfortable seating, soundproofing, and a sense of privacy.

The manner in which the facilitators and the program are introduced also can be used to promote a trusting environment. Facilitators can model self-disclosure and awareness of feelings as they present themselves. An overview of the content and process of the program reduces anxieties about what lies ahead. A sense of personal safety is also enhanced by giving attendees permission not to participate in activities that feel too uncomfortable.

A variety of structured activities can be used to develop a greater awareness of feelings. Visual imagery exercises encourage personal awareness by eliminating the risks involved in interpersonal contact. Participants can be instructed to get in touch periodically with feelings throughout the exercise. I have found the meditations and imaging of Virginia Satir (1985) to be particularly effective. Her scripts convey a strong sense of self-affirmation, personal freedom, and universality. Stevens (1971) also provides a useful handbook of awareness and focusing exercises.

The creative arts offer many possibilities for enhancing self-awareness. Many popular songs arouse powerful emotions associated with issues in men's lives. Simon and Garfunkel's (1965) "The Sounds of Silence" and "I Am a Rock" address personal isolation and loneliness. Mary Travers's (1971) "I Wish I Knew How It Would Feel To Be Free" beckons the listener to express feelings and dreams. Bette Midler's (1978) "The Rose" delicately resonates with the potential for human growth. In addition, "men's music" artists such as Geof Morgan (1980, 1982, 1985) and Gary Lapow (1982) address in their lyrics men's issues like success and achievement, sexuality, power and control, homophobia, and violence. After listening to these songs, it is important to provide some opportunity in dyads or small groups to share feelings and experiences the music elicits.

Drawings and paintings provide another creative avenue for gaining access into one's emotional world. Instructions for such exercises might be to draw "yourself," "you in your family," "you with other men," "you at a pleasant moment," or "you at a painful time." Such exercises promote both awareness of and the sharing of these inner experiences with others. Because these exercises can elicit unexpectedly strong emotions, it is important to provide follow-up support after the program.

Another visual mode involves sharing old photographs. In a men's group I facilitated, each member used a session to discuss his relationship with his father. Members introduced their fathers by sharing old photographs of their times together. This sharing brought on a range of feelings, from broad smiles to painful tears.

Other methods of emotional arousal may be more interactive. Role-playing can be used to strengthen connections to important affective experiences in difficult interpersonal interactions. Virginia Satir developed a variety of sculpting techniques for enhancing the potency of these role plays (Satir & Baldwin, 1983). Role plays also can be videotaped and reviewed to gain a more objective perspective of oneself in interpersonal situations. Kagan's (Kagan & Krathwohl, 1967) Interper-

sonal Process Recall provides a nondirective method for reviewing videotaped interactions. Frequently, participants become aware of feelings
during recall sessions that were beyond their awareness during the initial
interaction.

Learning to Self-Disclose

Once a man becomes more aware of feelings, the task becomes one
of sharing these feelings with others. Such self-disclosure is difficult for
most men. Expressing emotions contradicts the messages of our socialization to be invulnerable and in control. Jourard (1971) believed the
tendency for men not to self-disclose leads them to be "less insightful
and empathic, less competent at loving, and more subject to dispiritation
than women" (p. 28). He also felt that stress associated with withholding
emotion contributed to health problems and reduced longevity.

However, men can learn to self-disclose (See chapter 14). The safe,
comfortable environmental conditions described earlier also are important for programs designed to promote self-disclosure. Similarly, a trusting interpersonal atmosphere also needs to be developed. Some men
find it easier to self-disclose immediately following an emotionally arous-
ing exercise as described in the previous section. Dyads and small groups
provide a relatively safe context for these disclosures. One such exercise
asks participants to have a "heart-to-heart talk" with another group member immediately following the playing of Gary Lapow's "Tell It From
the Heart" (1982). The self-disclosure is facilitated both by the music
and the granting of permission to break social norms.

Structured exercises also can be useful for enhancing self-disclosure.
The completion of sentence stems such as "I am . . ." or "I feel . . ."
offers one such approach. A particularly effective adaptation asks participants to write down 10 responses to "I am . . .", pin their paper to
their chests, and then mill around the room nonverbally. When conducted at the beginning of a workshop, this exercise serves to introduce
the participants to each other, to begin the process of self-disclosure,
and to make valuable observations of how men tend to identify themselves.

Nonverbal and physical touching exercises, although they involve
more risk, can be effective. Back rubs and massages can be used to
express compassion and affection without words. When participants are
engaged in conflict or painful issues, having two participants hold hands
while looking directly into each other's eyes enhances immediacy and
direct communication.

Confronting Homophobia

As men begin to interact more intimately, homophobic fear will inevitably arise. For groups of men who have not confronted this issue, it is most important to address the topic and encourage participants to discuss their feelings. Homophobia typically represents projected fears rather than actual threats. Consequently, it is important for participants to own their fears and to work through them. If gay participants have disclosed their sexual orientation, opportunities arise for learning to accept affection and intimacy from gay men without the contact becoming sexualized.

In general, internalized homophobia is a primary obstacle for many men in exploring their emotional lives. These men may feel guilty or ashamed for homosexual thoughts or acts they have experienced, however fleeting or benign. Avoiding this guilt or shame, however, may mean avoiding any self-exploration at all.

Consequently, homophobia becomes an important topic to address in any men's programming. I have found the best intervention to be direct interpersonal contact with a gay man. For instance, participants might interview a gay man to learn his sexual history. Hearing a gay man talk lovingly about his partner helps straight men to identify with these men. The opportunity to ask questions directly serves to dispel misconceptions and prejudices. Most importantly, the direct contact usually instills a feeling of comfort and trust that overcomes the homophobic reactions.

Exploring Gender Roles

For young, straight men, self-esteem is most clearly at stake in relationships with women. However, traditional dating rituals serve only to reinforce sex-role stereotypes and covert, manipulative, and often coercive interactions. Recent concerns with acquaintance rape have led to a wide variety of program interventions in this area. Typically, these programs attempt to accomplish several goals: (1) to promote more open, honest, and direct communication, (2) to support each individual's autonomy for making choices to become sexually involved and the assertive communication of these choices, and (3) to develop a better understanding of the other person's needs, values, and perceptions. Sample interventions will be discussed for each of these goals.

One intervention for improving communication begins by taking a look at typical dating rituals. Small same-sex groups are instructed to brainstorm behaviors used by the opposite sex to communicate sexual attraction. After reconvening, the group shares the lists and identifies themes for describing these behaviors. Invariably, the brainstorming and the sharing of lists involves a lot of joking. However, groups often become more sober as the themes are identified. The most common themes describe dating behaviors as manipulative, dishonest, covert, and coercive. The implications for developing healthy relationships are obvious. This exercise often leads to participants' sharing their personal anxieties in dating interactions and the negative effects on their self-esteem.

A similar intervention involves brainstorming sex role stereotypes for men and women. Small mixed-sex groups are used in this exercise to develop lists for each gender. Again, the lists are shared and combined in the large group. The identification of themes usually reflects expectations for women to be submissive and compliant and for men to be initiating and dominant. Discussions can emphasize how these stereotypes infringe upon individual autonomy and choice. Discussions of alternate, more healthy dating interactions might emphasize a woman's right to refuse sexual involvements as well as a man's not needing to feel responsible for initiating sex as a way of proving his manhood.

The research of Gilligan (1982) and others has demonstrated striking gender differences in values, perceptions, and ethics. Yet, many young men and women display little awareness or understanding of these differences. This lack of understanding often has painful consequences for both individuals and relationships. An intervention entitled "Everything You've Ever Wanted to Know About the Opposite Sex, but Were Afraid to Ask" serves to bridge the gap. A double fishbowl is formed with a small inner group consisting of an equal number of men and women. The participants of the inner group take turns asking questions of the opposite sex. For instance, one fraternity member asked why all of the members of the sorority knew about his date with one of the members the previous evening. The sorority members quite simply explained the close connective, relational climate of their house. Yet, they were able to understand how the young man experienced this event as an intrusion on his sense of privacy and separateness.

Finding Our Fathers

A man's search for his self inevitably leads him to his father. Although research often cites the emotional unavailability of fathers, a son's need for his father's attention, nurturance, and approval does not cease mearly because these needs have not been met. Various authors (Herzog, 1982; Merton, 1986; Osherson, 1986) refer to this condition as "father hunger." The resolution of one's father hunger is an important step in becoming one's own man.

One workshop designed around this topic is entitled "Finding Our Fathers" (May & Eichenfield, 1989). The workshop begins with a brief introduction followed by the "I am . . ." milling exercise described earlier. Two mini-lectures are then presented providing overviews of men's issues and father-son relationships. Then, a visual imagery exercise is conducted adapting a Satir (1985, p. 31–33) meditation. The participants are invited to revisit their earliest happiest and most painful memories of their fathers. As the memories are shared in the group, common themes of father-son relationships are identified and discussed. The imagery exercise often elicits significant grief issues associated with losses experienced with fathers. The remainder of the workshop helps participants to experience these losses, learn to forgive, and to incorporate the positive aspects of their relationship with their father.

Developing Male Friendships and Community

No individual workshop or program is sufficient for promoting a man's discovery of his real self. Traditional roles are well established through years of experience in a culture with a particular set of values and norms. Changes in male consciousness are more likely to occur with the support of a culture whose values and norms promote growth. Such cultures are becoming more available through men's groups, men's networks, and other communities supporting a new definition of masculinity. Whereas our societal norms typically have created competition and emotional distance between men, these cultures promote inter-dependence and cooperation. A brief list of these networks by the author is summarized elsewhere (May, 1988).

As a man's sense of self becomes more whole and integrated, these changes begin to transform men's relationships and social existence. Relationships that cannot integrate these changes begin to lose meaning. With a growing sense of compassion and nurturance, men become sensitized to the pain and suffering in their world. This sensitivity ideally is actualized in social and political commitments that support human values.

Conclusion

A man's search for an authentic sense of self can be a long and arduous journey. The traditional male role promotes a sense of alienation reinforced by a firm set of psychological defenses. However, new views of masculinity provide options for men to recapture the emotional, expressive, and relational aspects of their lives. In doing so, living their life in accordance with their basic human experience reestablishes a sense of self-esteem. The courage to disclose their experience to others provides a healthy avenue for self-expression. And finally, self-acceptance despite societal pressures develops a sense of personal integrity.

When men are conflicted by their gender roles, what specific domains need assessment and exploration?

Chapter 3
ASSESSING MEN'S GENDER ROLE CONFLICT

James M. O'Neil

Men face difficult times in the 1990s, particularly those men who have not liberated themselves from restrictive gender roles. Men's gender roles have been implicated in family violence, rape, and child sexual abuse (Finkelhor, 1984; Finn, 1986; Russell, 1984). These serious problems have received much attention in the media, and the public has become sensitized to men as abusers. Consequently, men feel blamed and on the defensive about sexism and their gender roles. Blaming men for sexism and labeling them as oppressors has not resolved the anger between the sexes, advanced equality, or decreased victimization. "Male blaming and bashing" reached its all-time high in the 1980s and did not prove to be an effective strategy for constructive change.

Men now need to analyze feminists' positions on changing gender roles. In the 1970s and 1980s women feminists argued that men should change their conceptions of gender roles. They rightly asserted that men's gender role values were patriarchal, oppressive, and discriminatory toward women. Men reacted to these assertions in a variety of ways. Some men denied the existence of sexism, others became angry, and some began the liberation process. Charges that men were oppressors also brought men together collectively. A national men's movement began that was committed to men's liberation and new conceptualizations of masculinity. Men's studies has also emerged as a new discipline committed to nonsexist study of men and masculinity (see Femiano, chapter 17 of this text, and Kimmel, 1987). Men's studies aims to understand men's socialization and conflicts with gender roles.

Men's studies, from a psychological perspective, investigates men's gender role conflict over the life span. Many men have difficulty labeling emotions resulting from changed gender roles and experience gender role conflicts internally, along with confusion and limited support. Many men are unaware of their gender role conflicts or become bewildered by their failure to adapt to women's "new voices" (Gilligan, 1984). Definitive analyses of men's gender role conflict are needed if the restrictive

23

and oppressive aspects of masculine behavior are to be understood and changed. How sexism violates men has become an important issue because many more men want a new, positive sense of their masculinity.

Counseling, psychotherapy, and preventive programs can help men with their socialized sexism and assist them in redefining their conceptions of gender roles. Professionals working with men need innovative methods to assess men's gender role conflict. When men are conflicted by their gender roles, what specific domains need assessment and exploration? What do therapists and programmers need to know about men to make comprehensive assessments and develop therapeutic interventions? What are men's personal experiences of gender role conflict and how do these experiences affect men negatively? In this chapter, information is presented to help answer these questions, thereby promoting more effective interventions with men.

Few paradigms exist that explain how men behave and feel when they experience gender role conflict. More precise conceptualizations are needed to explain men's gender role dynamics. This chapter provides concepts to assess men's gender role conflict as well as a diagnostic schema to use in counseling, psychotherapy, and educational programming. Specifically, a diagnostic schema is presented that defines four critical assessment domains. These domains are defined in the next sections. Implications for using the diagnostic schema are given at the end of the chapter.

Prerequisite Knowledge to Assess Men's Gender Role Conflict

The most valuable asset to implement gender role assessments is a strong theoretical and research background in the psychology of gender roles. The psychology of gender roles is emerging as a respected area of scientific and human inquiry, and practitioners should begin to incorporate the psychology of gender (Basow, 1986; Doyle, 1983, 1985) into their assessment of male clients. Four important assessment concepts relevant to men's struggle and change are: gender roles, gender role conflict, gender role transitions, and gender role themes.

Gender roles are behaviors, expectations, and values defined by society as masculine or feminine. Gender roles are embodied in the behavior of men and women and culturally regarded as appropriate to men or women (O'Neil, 1981a, 1981b, 1982). These roles are learned through gender role socialization and may change with the demands of adulthood and aging (Moreland, 1979, 1980). Gender roles are core dimensions of a person and, therefore, central to understanding human behavior. Gender role development occurs through gender role social-ization. This process includes how people acquire, internalize, and re-define values, attitudes, and behaviors associated with gender roles (i.e., masculinity and femininity).

Gender role conflict is a psychological state in which gender roles have negative consequences on the individual or on others. The ultimate outcome of this conflict is the restriction of the person's human potential or the restriction of someone else's potential. Gender role conflict occurs when rigid, sexist, or restrictive gender roles, learned during socializa-tion, result in the personal restriction, devaluation, or violation of others or self (O'Neil, 1981a, 1981b, 1982). One outcome of gender role conflict is gender role strain. This occurs when psychological or physical tension is experienced as a result of the expectations and norms of masculinity, femininity, and androgyny. Garnets and Pleck (1979) operationally de-fine sex role strain "as a discrepancy between the real self and that part of the ideal self-concept that is culturally associated with gender" (p. 278). They believe that sex role strain is an intrapsychic process that can lead to poor psychological adjustment, particularly low self-esteem. Pleck's (1981) sex role strain (SRS) paradigm is based on two theories of sex role strain including self-role discrepancy theory and socialized dysfunctional characteristics theory. The discrepancy theory implies that individuals suffer negative consequences when they fail to live up to gender roles. The latter theory suggests that socialized gender roles produce dysfunctional personality characteristics in people.

Numerous ways of conceptualizing gender role conflict support the development of a diagnostic schema. Gender role conflict can be ex-perienced in part as a cognitive process—how we think about gender roles and our values related to masculinity and femininity. It can be experienced in part as an affective process—how we feel about our gender roles and the conflicts we have with ourselves and others. Gender role conflict can be experienced in part as a behavioral process—how we act, respond, and interact with ourselves and others. Finally, gender role conflict can be experienced both as a conscious and unconscious process. This implies that some gender role conflicts are in our awareness and others are repressed beyond our conscious awareness. How we think, feel, and behave because of our gender roles can affect our overall human development.

Awareness of gender role conflict may stimulate reevaluation of gender roles in a person's life and lead to gender role transitions. The literature provides some conceptualizations of gender role transitions, and models of gender role change are slowly emerging (Block, 1973, 1984; Giele, 1980; Moreland, 1980; Levinson, Darrow, Klein, Levinson, & McKee, 1978; Rebecca, Hefner, & Olenshansky, 1976). These tran-sitions are events and nonevents in a person's gender role development process stimulating changes in gender role values and self-assumptions. Transitions occur when demonstrations, reevaluations, and integrations of masculinity and femininity take place over the life span (O'Neil & Fishman, 1986; O'Neil, Fishman, & Kinsella-Shaw, 1987). The demonstration, reevaluation, and integration of masculine and feminine values may occur during crises or during the normal maturation process. Struggles to integrate new gender role definitions may occur as roles change. Good examples of gender role transitions are when men: leave home permanently; become fathers or spouses; lose their jobs or personal confidence; become interpersonally dysfunctional, divorced, or sexually impotent; lose a parent, child, or lifetime dream. In all of these situations men reevaluate their gender role values and struggle with themes directly related to their masculine self-concepts. Gender role transitions may produce confusion, anxiety, and threat. But, these transitions also can open up internal parts of the man, expand his self-definition, and promote personal exploration and growth.

Gender role transitions are not completed in a vacuum but in the context of certain gender role themes (O'Neil & Fishman, 1986). A gender role theme is defined as a developmental and human issue involving the demonstration, reevaluation, or integration of masculinity and femininity. Each man struggles with different themes depending on his early socialization, gender role values, and coping styles. Some of men's gender role themes include: success, achievement, and competence; control, power, and competition; strength, personal worth, and status; provider role, parenthood, and mentor; health, aging, and loss of power; and intimacy, sexuality, and emotionality. Many of these themes can be determined by assessing men's cognitions, values, fears, emotions, and behavioral patterns, as discussed in the next section.

Diagnostic Schema to Assess Men's Gender Role Conflict

Few explicit schemas exist to facilitate systematic assessment of men's gender role conflict in counseling, psychotherapy, and preventive programming. Table 1 depicts a four-part diagnostic schema (A-D) that gives structure to assessing men's gender role conflict. Four assessment domains are shown in Table 1 and presume prerequisite knowledge of men's gender role conflict as described above. In assessment domain A, men's cognitions and gender role values are assessed as the "masculine mystique." Assessment domain B implies assessing men's fears and emotions about gender roles, such as the fear of femininity. In domain C, men's behavioral patterns of gender role conflict are evaluated. Finally, in domain D, men's personal experiences of gender role conflict are appraised in certain situational contexts.

TABLE 1

Diagnostic Schema to Assess Men's Gender Role Conflict

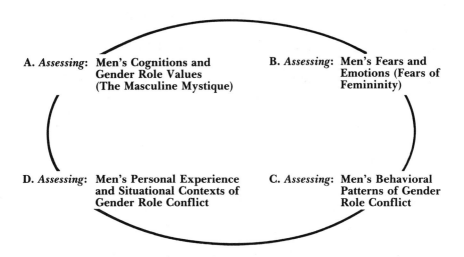

A. *Assessing*: **Men's Cognitions and Gender Role Values (The Masculine Mystique)**

B. *Assessing*: **Men's Fears and Emotions (Fears of Femininity)**

D. *Assessing*: **Men's Personal Experience and Situational Contexts of Gender Role Conflict**

C. *Assessing*: **Men's Behavioral Patterns of Gender Role Conflict**

The relationship between the four domains is interactive and complex. In this analysis, no focused attempt is made to explain how cognitions, emotions, or specific behavioral patterns actually produce the experience of gender role conflict. However, the assessment domains in Table 1 do imply that men's cognitions, values, fears, and emotions about gender roles can result in behavioral patterns and personal experiences of gender role conflict in certain situational contexts. Each of the assessment domains in Table 1 are discussed below, and specific applications are summarized after each section.

A. Assessing Men's Cognitions and Gender Role Values: The Masculine Mystique

Men's cognitions of gender roles are thought patterns about masculinity and femininity in the contexts of personal, professional, and family roles. Men's values result from these internalized cognitions and give meaning and order to their life. Masculine thoughts and values are learned during early socialization and over the life span. Researchers have yet to determine how these cognitions and values are affected by biological-hormonal antecedents and the effects of sociopolitical environments. Clearly, individual differences in men's cognitions and values are based on many factors such as age, race, family background, and socioeconomic levels, to name a few. Yet, numerous authors have hypothesized a commonality in men's thoughts and values as the masculine mystique (Dubbert, 1979; Farrell, 1974, Mayer, 1978; O'Neil, 1981b, 1982).

The masculine mystique represents what men think about men's and women's gender roles and specific values about masculinity and femininity. These values define optimal masculinity in our society and are based on rigid sex role stereotypes and beliefs about men, women, masculinity, and femininity. The masculine mystique is a sexist set of thoughts and attitudes about women, men, and life in general. Dubbert (1979) presented an excellent historical analysis of the emergence of the masculine mystique in America from the early 1800s to the present.

Overall, the masculine mystique implies that men are superior to women and masculinity is superior to femininity; power, control, and dominance are essential to prove masculinity; emotions, feelings, vulnerability, and intimacy are to be avoided because they are feminine; and career successes and sexual potency are measures of masculinity (O'Neil, 1981b, 1982). Implicit in these values is the implied inferiority of femininity compared to masculinity. These masculine values can have negative consequences for men, women, and children. These values violate women because they devalue women's feminine attitudes, values, and behaviors. They violate men by denying them the opportunity to express their feminine side, therefore denying them important parts of themselves. Failure to accept these values or live them out can produce self-devaluation or ridicule from others. In varying degrees, the masculine mystique devalues femininity (i.e., sexism), overvalues masculinity (i.e. hypermasculinity), and produces fears about emotions and femininity.

Applications

Therapists and educational programmers can assess men's cognitions and values related to the masculine mystique. Therapists can probe clients' gender role values and thought patterns as part of the overall assessment process. Specific attention to how clients learned these values and from whom can help link early socialization experiences to present conflicts. Programmers can present the masculine mystique as the typical gender role ideology and stimulate discussion and dialogue in both large and small groups. Discussion of how specific cognitions and values reinforce hypermasculine, macho, and unhealthy behavior can be the first step in assessing men's gender role conflict.

B. Assessing Men's Gender Role Fears and Emotions:
The Fear of Femininity

Men's fears and emotions have been taboo topics for men because they are anthithetical to the masculine mystique. Fears and emotions destabilize men's facades of strength and power. Yet, men do experience many feelings and fears during early development and over the life span. Fears and emotions related to control, power, failure, and weakness are dynamic issues in many men's lives. What men feel, what they fail to feel, and how they manage fear are critical in understanding men's gender role conflict. One concept that epitomizes men's fears and emotions is the fear of femininity.

The fear of femininity is a strong negative emotion associated with feminine values, attitudes, and behaviors (O'Neil, 1981a, 1982). These emotional reactions are learned primarily when gender identity is being formed by parents, peers, and societal values. David and Brannon (1976) indicated that parents are concerned about how well boys conform to the masculine role. Fathers are particularly concerned if their sons manifest feminine qualities. Many boys learn to avoid stereotypical feminine qualities because of expressed displeasure or ridicule from parents and peers. Consequently, male socialization can produce: (1) a life-long aversion to qualities stereotyped as feminine; (2) constant strivings to be masculine; (3) an inexpressive male image that prohibits expressions of emotion; and (4) emotional and physical distance between men because of feared homosexuality.

Men's fears of their feminine sides and of women have been noted in the literature for many years (Boehm, 1930; Hays, 1964; Horney, 1967; Jung, 1953, 1954; Lederer, 1968; Menninger, 1970). These analyses of men's fears rely primarily on a psychodynamic perspective. Jung's archetype in men, the anima, is a well-known concept relevant to men's difficulty in integrating their feminine side. Reviews of mythology (Lederer; Johnson, 1977) provide substantial evidence that the threat of femininity has been part of men's experience over the centuries.

When a man fears his feminine side, he really fears that others see him as stereotypically and negatively feminine (weak, dependent, submissive) rather than positively masculine. Being considered a wimp is emasculating and fear-provoking. This is not an unreasonable fear because femininity is subordinated, depreciated, and maligned in our hypermasculine society. Men who express their feminine side fear they will be restricted, devalued, and violated by others. The cost of showing stereotypical feminine qualities can be disrespect, failure, and emasculation. These are high costs for a man wanting to fulfill the masculine mystique over the life cycle.

Applications

Men's fears and emotions can also be assessed, providing a deeper context for issues and conflicts. Helping clients face fears about femininity and women who represent feminine values can be useful. For example, probing early childhood memories of mother and father as representations of femininity and masculinity can elicit valuable information. Helping men face their emotions about their mothers or other feminine forces in their lives can be crucial for change and growth.

During workshops and groups, leaders can try specific approaches related to feelings. Self-disclosure (Beck, 1983) and emotional expression by the leader can help create an environment where feelings can be shared. Structured exercises can be used to stimulate deeper fears and unexpressed pain (see chapter 2). For example, the simple act of asking men to draw on newsprint a situation where deep feelings were experienced but not felt can be powerful. Collective discussion of these situations can elicit deeper experiences of men's gender role conflict and specific patterns of behavior.

C. Assessing Men's Behavioral Patterns of Gender Role Conflict

The first two assessment domains (A & B) provide a basis for assessing men's behavioral patterns of gender role conflict. In other words, assessment of men's cognitions, values, fears, and emotions can facilitate a behavioral analysis of men's gender role conflict. In an earlier set of papers (O'Neil, 1981a, 1981b, 1982; O'Neil & Fishman, 1986) the masculine mystique and fear of femininity were hypothesized to be related to six patterns of gender role conflict and sexism as shown in Table 2. The six patterns represent the behavioral manifestation of men's cognitions, values, fears, and emotions as discussed in the earlier sections. The six patterns are: (1) *Restrictive Emotionality*—Having difficulty expressing one's own feelings or denying others their rights to emotional expressiveness; (2) *Homophobia*—Having fears of homosexuals or fear of being a homosexual, including beliefs, myths, and stereotypes about gay people; (3) *Control*—A need to regulate, restrain, or to have others or situations under one's command; *Power*—A need to obtain authority, influence, or ascendance over others; *Competition*—Striving against others to win or gain something; (4) *Restricted Sexual and Affectionate Behavior*—Having limited ways of expressing one's sexuality and affection to others; (5) *Obsession With Achievement and Success*—Having a disturbing and persistent preoccupation with work, accomplishment, and eminence as a means of substantiating and demonstrating value; (6) *Health Care Problems*—Having difficulties maintaining positive health care in terms

TABLE 2

Patterns of Gender Role Conflict and Strain Emanating From Men's Gender Role Socialization and The Masculine Mystique

From: *Personnel and Guidance Journal, 60*, 203–210, 1981.

of diet, exercise, relaxation, work, and stress. Recently, empirical research has also documented the existence of some of these patterns (Davis, 1988; O'Neil, Helms, Gable, David, & Wrightsman, 1986; Snell, 1986; Thompson & Pleck, 1986) and some have been shown to affect men's help seeking (Good, Dell, & Mintz, 1989).

Application

These patterns of gender role conflict are not an exhaustive list of men's problems. Yet, they do provide an operationally defined set of behaviors that can be useful to men seeking answers about their conflicted thoughts and feelings. Table 2 has been illustrated in the literature (Basow, 1986) and used with individual clients and in workshops (Croteau & Burda, 1983; O'Neil & Roberts Carroll, 1988) to organize conceptually the complexity of men's socialization. Often a cognitive understanding of men's behavioral patterns can stimulate more finite conceptualizations of men's personal experiences of gender role conflict in certain situational contexts, as discussed in the next section.

D. Assessing Men's Personal Experience and Situational Contexts of Gender Role Conflict

How men's thoughts, feelings, and behavioral patterns are experienced personally in situational contexts is critical to a comprehensive assessment of men. The personal experience of gender role conflict is defined as the negative consequences of gender roles for the individual man and for other people. The situational contexts of gender role conflict are defined as how and from whom the conflict emerges for an individual man.

Table 3 depicts three personal experiences of gender role conflict and three situational contexts of its occurrence. The 3×3 diagram shows 9 gender role conflict assessment cells. On the left side of Table 3, the personal experiences of gender role conflict are shown as devaluations (D), restrictions (R), and violations (V). These outcomes define men's private pain and conflict over gender roles. Across the top of Table 3, three situational contexts of gender role conflict are shown including conflict (1) within oneself, (2) caused by others, and (3) expressed toward others. Gender role conflict *within oneself* is defined as thoughts, feelings, and behavioral patterns that produce negative emotions and consequences for an individual man because of his own conflict. Gender role conflict *caused by others* is defined as thoughts, feelings, and behavioral patterns that produce negative emotions and consequences in a man because of someone else's conflicts. Gender role conflict *expressed toward others* is defined as a man's thoughts, feelings, and behavioral patterns that produce negative emotions and consequences and are expressed toward others. These three situational contexts demonstrate that gender role conflict can exist within a man, emanate from others, or be expressed toward others.

The nine assessment cells in Table 3 can be used to assess men's personal experience of gender role conflict in different situational contexts. For example, self-devaluations would be Cell D_1, whereas devaluation from others or devaluation of others would be Cell D_2 and D_3, respectively. Likewise, restrictions and violations within self, from others, or expressed toward others are represented by Cells R_1, R_2, R_3 and Cells V_1, V_2, V_3, respectively. Specific examples of men's personal experience of gender role conflict are described below as devaluations, restrictions, and violations using the nine cells in Table 3.

TABLE 3

Diagnostic Schema Assessing the Personal and Situational Contexts of Men's Gender Role Conflict

PERSONAL EXPERIENCE OF GENDER ROLE CONFLICT	SITUATIONAL CONTEXT OF GENDER ROLE CONFLICT		
	Conflict Within Self	Conflict Caused By Others	Conflict Expressed Toward Others
D. DEVALUATIONS	D_1	D_2	D_3
R. RESTRICTIONS	R_1	R_2	R_3
V. VIOLATIONS	V_1	V_2	V_3

A. Gender Role Devaluations

Devaluations are experienced when there is a discrepancy or deviation from expected gender role norms. Devaluation implies a lessening of status, stature, and self-esteem and may occur after the fear and anger is turned inward, causing depression and isolation. Gender role conflict can occur from devaluing oneself (Cell D_1), being devalued by others (Cell D_2), or by devaluing someone else (Cell D_3). When men feel unable to emulate the values of the masculine mystique, they may devalue and blame themselves (Cell D_1). Self-devaluation may occur when a man has failed on the job or in an intimate relationship. The failure may be of little consequence, or a major error or loss. Devaluation may also occur when a man's success expectancies cannot be met in a work setting or when he is not a responsive father or spouse because of work overload, stress, and exhaustion. Difficulties, lost career dreams, and unemployment all can trigger gender role devaluations in men's lives. Devaluations may also occur from others, particularly from competitors, parents, and family members (Cell D_2). Devaluations by mothers and women are particularly painful and can engender defensiveness, withdrawal, and sometimes even violence. Men also devalue others when they do not meet the expected gender role norms (Cell D_3). Men devalue women who deviate from the feminine stereotype of attractiveness or who assume a traditionally defined masculine career role. Devaluation of other men occurs when the stereotypes of the masculine mystique are violated.

B. Gender Role Restrictions

Restrictions are experienced when men confine themselves or others to rigid gender role norms that cause a violation of personal freedom and human rights. Gender role restrictions occur when masculine and feminine norms or expectancies limit flexibility in work, family, and interpersonal patterns. Restrictions limit options, deny needs, and often represent manipulative control and an abusive use of power. The cost of frequently restricting oneself or others are feelings of guilt and powerlessness. Cells R_1, R_2, and R_3 represent how gender role restrictions can occur within oneself, from others, or toward others.

Men's restriction of themselves (Cell R_1) occurs in a number of different ways. Men's restriction of emotions, self-disclosures, and overall communication is a typical complaint of women about men. Men can also restrict themselves by devoting too much time to work, thereby restricting their roles and effectiveness as responsive spouses or nurturing fathers. For example, workaholics tend to avoid intimacy and have difficulties processing the complexity of interpersonal exchanges. Restrictions also can be experienced as role conflict or overload. Many men are stretched between demanding jobs and family responsibilities. Some men feel restricted by their work schedule and are unable to find time for leisure and relaxation. Men also feel restricted by inflexible masculine norms set by others at work (Cell R_2). Many work settings are competitive, and there is pressure to succeed and compete. This pressure can produce conflict and combat between coworkers, resulting in dysfunctinal relationships. A restrictive range of emotional expressiveness (O'Neil, 1981a, Skovholt, 1978) can limit men's understanding of complex work dynamics or discourage personal relationships with others.

Gender role restrictions expressed toward others (Cell R_3) can be difficult for men in their relationships. Men have restricted women in their personal and career growth for centuries. Restriction and control of women are the most blantant forms of sexism and the essence of men's oppression of women. Some men who are interpersonally restricted try to control individuals or environments, causing tension and resentment. Emotionally restricted men do not express their feelings and pain and may express emotions inappropriately. Outbursts of anger, family conflict, and violence can result.

C. Gender Role Violations

Violations are experienced when men harm themselves, are harmed by others, or harm others trying to meet the gender role stereotypes, norms, and ideals of masculinity. To be violated is to be abused and victimized because of gender role conflict. Men violate themselves (Cell V_1) by overwork, excessive stress, and abuse of substances to dull emotions and painful life experiences. Unexpressed emotions, fear, and anger can be internalized, causing chronic depression, self-hate, isolation, and serious health problems. Men are also violated by others (Cell V_2) both at work and in relationships. Preretirement men often feel violated by their employers when they are asked to retire early to make way for the younger and more energetic (masculine) men. Many men feel violated by the organizational politics of work settings. Power plays, manipulations, and back stabbing can culminate in violation of individual workers. Extreme manipulation may lead to demotions, aggressive behavior, and unemployment. These kinds of violations can produce work stress, health problems, and even early death. Other men feel violated by women who manipulate them in response to complicated gender role dynamics. Men's violations of others have been a central topic in the media and the women's movement since the 1970s (Cell V_3). As mentioned in the introduction, men's gender roles have been associated with violations such as rape, sexual abuse, and family violence. The degree to which gender roles contribute to these violations is unknown, yet both theory (Finkelhor, 1984; Russell, 1984) and research to show causal relationships (Finn, 1986). What has not been explained is how gender role conflict stimulates men's violence and the complex psychological dynamics with others. Gender role violations represent the most severe kind of gender role conflict because direct harm is inflicted on oneself or others.

Application

The nine cells in Table 3 provide the most personal, psychologically rich, and situationally specific way to assess men's gender role conflict. The personal experience of being devalued, restricted, or violated provides an operationally defined vocabulary to describe men's deeper experience of gender role conflict. The three situational contexts describe possible ways for men to understand how these conflicts occur in themselves or with others. Often clients need an emotinal vocabulary and a situational focus to label their gender role dynamics before actual changes can occur. In men's groups and educational programs, Table 3 can be used to stimulate participants' personal feelings of devaluation, restriction, and violation. Discussions of how other people stimulate these dimensions and how men actually express them toward others can be provocative and educational.

Implications of a Diagnostic Schema to Assess Men's Gender Role Conflict

A diagnostic schema assessing men's gender role conflict has been presented in this chapter. Four critical diagnostic activities are implied by the diagnostic schema in Table 1. Practitioners can use the diagnostic schema with individual men in counseling, with men's groups, and in educational programs.

The schema in Table 1 does not suggest an ordered process of assessment using assessment domains A through D. Therapists and programmers can make assessments of men in any order that is conducive ato decreasing resistance to the exploration process. Some men may first want exploration of their thoughts and values, others may seek knowledge of their specific patterns of gender role conflict, and others may want to disclose their personal experience of gender role devaluations, restrictions, and violations. Therapists and programmers can complete an overall assessment of the domains in Table 1 and proceed with approaches that best facilitate a working alliance and growth.

Programmatic efforts and therapeutic interventions are more likely to be successful if they are based on conceptualizations of men's and women's socialization and needs assessment data. Assessment schemas are useful to the extent that they help men discover the complexity of their socialization experiences. Helping men look inside themselves to ascertain how they think, feel, and have personally experienced gender role conflict is crucial.

Recently, I have used the metaphor of the gender role journey as a nonthreatening description of the exploration process (O'Neil, 1986; O'Neil & Roberts Carroll, 1988). The gender role journey is the process of examining how our gender role socialization experiences have promoted our growth or how sexism has affected our lives negatively. In other words, the journey involves reevaluating how masculinity and femininity have affected us in the past and present. This process can be both a retrospective analysis of early family experiences as well as a future projection of self. I have used biographic sketches of famous men's and women's gender role journeys to legitimatize personal exploration and growth (O'Neil & Roberts Carroll). For example, presenting John Lennon's gender role transformation (O'Neil, 1988) by using biographical sources, music, and video footage can give men vivid examples of how to process their own gender role journeys. Practitioners can alternate between carefully prepared schemas and affectively charged media that describe both the costs of socialized sexism and the possibilities for personal transformation.

Cognitive understanding of gender role conflict without affective awakening is usually insufficient to promote lasting change with men. Likewise, affective awakening, without cognitive understanding of the emotions experienced, also may be insufficient. Interventions that carefully organize both cognitive and affective experiences are more likely to stimulate the empowerment that men need to make real life changes. Diagnostic concepts provide an organized way to understand the process of change cognitively. The charged, emotional media can help men translate these understandings into deeper feelings that block growth and behavior change. Individual checklists and small group activities that help men assess their thoughts, feelings, and behavioral patterns can help focus discussion and collective explorations.

The diagnostic schema needs further development and extension. Specifically, the schema's components all imply focused assessments of men's early gender role socialization and experiences with mothers, fathers, and siblings. Future conceptualizations could isolate the factors that contribute to men's gender role conflicts at an early age and hypothesize how these factors contribute to men's difficulty over the life span. Furthermore, the diagnostic schema does not address women's gender role conflict. Future conceptualizations could explicate how women's gender role conflict can be assessed. This conceptualization would be particularly useful for marriage and family therapists working with men and women simultaneously. Therapists and programmers are also encouraged to apply specific therories of counseling and psychotherapy to the diagnostic schema in Table 1. More specific analyses are needed to demonstrate how behavioral, psychodynamic, and cognitive theories relate to the assessment paradigm.

Therapists and programmers can be pivotal in helping men make comprehensive assessments of their gender role conflict. These assessments can empower men to develop a healthy sense of their masculinity. Gender role assessments are important if men are to enter the 1990s with a new, positive sense of strength and convictions that mute the societal blame that typified the 1980s.

Acknowledgments

I am deeply appreciative of comments and critique of this chapter by colleagues and friends. The following individuals gave generously of their time and talent in revisions of this manuscript: Dwight Moore and Fred Leafgren (editors of this book), Paul Heppner (University of Missouri-Columbia), Michael Blier (Georgia State University), Glen Good (University of Southern California), and Mark Hall (Traumatic Stress Institute, South Windsor, CT). Darlene Eichacker (Tolland, CT) provided expert word processing services and completed redrafts quickly and efficiently. I am grateful to the Research Foundation of the University of Connecticut, which provided a grant to prepare this chapter.

In counseling and therapy with adult men, work themes are prominent because work—defined as performance and mastery in competitive situations—is such a major element of adult male identity and self-esteem.

Chapter 4

CAREER THEMES IN COUNSELING AND PSYCHOTHERAPY WITH MEN

Thomas M. Skovholt

Performance and Mastery Route to Male Self-Esteem

Painting a picture of men's lives often results in a work-dominated landscape. This occurs because a central adult role for men involves performance and mastery in competitive situations. Men's identity is a result of this role. For example, the first question at a gathering, "What do you do?" directly ties identity to occupation. Also, the traditional last names for many men—Smith, Joyner, Haymaker, Slater, Farmer—tie identity directly to occupation-based performance. To a significant degree, self-esteem is a direct result of this mastery. The individual achieves this self-esteem through two forces: first, through the reinforcement of others—men who look up to the winners of male races (i.e., the top salesman at a battery and tire store); women who seek and reward such men (i.e., the female attraction to successful men in public arenas such as politics and music); and children who treat successful men as major or minor heroes (i.e., congressmen), and, second, through self-reinforcement that results from internalized expectations. Those who succeed at this race are privileged members of most human societies. Lack of success at this male role often leads to painful consequences because there are few other established routes to self-esteem for men aside from the performance and mastery route. This sentiment was captured succinctly by a 53-year-old male client who recently suffered a career setback. He explained his great distress when he said, "If you don't work hard and get success, there is nothing else."

Sports

Because the adult male self-esteem arena is narrowly defined and centered on mastery and successful performance, boys at a young age begin preparing for this arena. The sports field is a childhood and adolescence practice field for male adult life. There, the central task is to compete over and over again against other boys using a set of rules that produces clear winners and losers. Although skill development in a particular sport, such as hitting a baseball, is often the focus of effort, a less obvious focus is learning the rules, attitudes, and behaviors of the adult male world. Being able to hit a baseball or make a free throw has little value in the adult world because fewer than 1/10 of 1% of adult men are employed as professional athletes in the United States. Rather, the knowledge of the rules, the proper attitudes, and the right behaviors are critical when young men enter the work world that is the playing field of adult life. Thus, learning how to cooperate to reach a common goal is a constant theme in team sports. Emotional intimacy and intense connectedness to teammates is often as dysfunctional as the other end, extreme individualism. So, as adults, men often cooperate well together but also report that they have no best friend in the female sense of that term.

A central attitude taught on the playing field is that the "game is not over 'til it's over" and that one should be optimistic and hopeful. A related behavior is to learn a sequence that involves trying hard-losing-trying hard. This is an important behavior to learn for the world of work because it is easy to try after success and to quit after failure, but it is difficult to try after failure. Yet, because the adult work world is extremely competitive, failure is a natural event. At work, it will occur and reoccur for men. So, in childhood, it is extremely important to learn the difficult behavioral sequence of trying-losing-trying. Proper emotionality is also taught. Expression of the vulnerable emotions is punished (i.e., crying) and expression of the hardened emotions is tolerated or rewarded (i.e., an outburst of anger). Hence, the playing fields of male childhood teach that the keys for adult male success are cooperation with colleagues, emotional toughness, trying until the end, and "getting up after you fall down."

In adulthood, the proving ground shifts from the playing fields of childhood to the playing fields of adult life. However, the playing fields of childhood continue to be powerful in symbolic and metaphoric ways. On Memorial Day weekend every year, millions of Americans watch a drama as the announcer states, "Gentlemen, start your engines," and the Indianapolis 500 begins. It is a very male event—there are clear winners and losers; there is a need for a kind of courage that can result in physical harm; there is cooperation with others in terms of the rules of competition, but little emotional intimacy; expressions of vulnerability are uniformly condemned and punished; and winners are praised as heroes whereas losers are forgotten. At the Indianapolis 500, male self-esteem and identity are tied directly to external performance. It is skill, effort, tenacity, courage, and endurance that matter. Appreciation of beauty, empathy for others, a need for connectedness, strong intimacy skills, shying away from pain—these are dysfunctional.

Other sporting events communicate similar expectations. The National Basketball Association Playoffs, the World Series, the Super Bowl, and the Stanley Cup finals capture the attention of millions of Americans on an annual basis. These visible sporting events provide excitement and entertainment. Yet, perhaps their essential function is to reinforce basic assumptions and values within the culture regarding the essential sphere for adult men and the way men are judged within this sphere. Accolades go to the winners of very visible, very difficult, very painful, very demanding, and intensely competitive contests. Men and women in the audience, and with TV this includes millions of Americans, continually receive powerful messages about men's roles. The messages are given in an indirect way so that they enter the individual psyche as unarticulated assumptions about life. This is a powerful way of communicating, one that psychotherapists often attempt to use with their clients because it tends to minimize resistance.

The Military and Other Career Choices

Military training provides a second layer of socialization for male adulthood and the world of work. Military training is an intense indoctrination process that aims to turn young civilians quickly into highly disciplined, highly docile, and highly effective warriors. As part of the process, a number of traits are encouraged: aggressiveness, teamwork, low empathy for suffering, single-mindedness, and obedience to authority. Although perhaps dysfunctional in intimate relationships, all of these traits later can be adapted to the work world of performance and mastery in competitive situations (Skovholt, Moore, & Haritos-Fatorous, 1989).

Besides the military, a variety of other career arenas such as politics, business, the arts, government, and science, constantly present their highly successful performance and mastery male models to the public (e.g., an astronaut, orchestra conductor, corporate CEO, Nobel Prize winner in science). These men are usually received positively by the public. Young boys learn early to attempt to "be like them."

Role Models

In addition to these career socialization processes, male roles are learned in other ways. Older men within a family such as fathers, older brothers, uncles, grandfathers and great-grandfathers, or community express the proper male role, thereby helping to establish the stage for male adult identity and self-esteem. These are all visible models for a young man to copy and identify with on external and internal levels. Perhaps the actual jobs of these older relatives do not fit with the modern occupational world. Yet the major theme remains to be copied. The essential message is often that adult men are expected to work at a job outside the home for the decades of their adult life. Whether the job is loved, hated, intrinsically satisfying, or boring is much less relevant than the expectation that a man will work. A long-term nonworking male adult violates this strong male principle and is usually shunned and rejected.

Women's Expectations

Farrell (1986) discussed women's expectations of men in his examination of the most popular magazines, novels, and television shows women read and watch. This popular literature demonstrates that women are frequently attracted to men who are successful and reject men who fail. For the most part, the criteria center on mastery in the male adult work world where money, power, and status dimensions are central. Farrell found this pattern even in the advertisements in a magazine like *MS.* as well as in magazines with higher subscriptions such as *Better Homes and Gardens* and *Family Circle*.

Women will often talk about sensitivity, understanding, caring, and communicating when describing desired male characteristics. However, Farrell suggested that traditional performance criteria are a prerequisite. ". . . Alan Alda is loved not because he's sensitive, but because he's successful and sensitive. I call this the Alan Alda Syndrome" (Farrell, 1986, p. 137). Women's expectations are, of course, of crucial importance in men's lives. One aspect of this relates to men's dependence on women. Gilbert (1987) illuminated some of the important elements of this often misunderstood and unrecognized male dependence.

Counseling Interventions

You might find descriptions up to this point an over-generalization and an overdone caricature. You may be aware of many exceptions to this portrait; you may know many men whose career issues and personal values are at odds with this characterization; you may know many women whose career issues and personal values challenge this description.

You also may be aware of the privilege that men enjoy who possess and express these traits. And, indeed, this portrait of the male role does produce privilege for men who carry it out successfully. One need only look at lists of American corporate leaders or the wealthiest Americans. The membership in these groups, predominantly male, makes others envious. Yet it is important to remember that our work—therapy and counseling—is about human distress, disappointment, loss, inadequacy, and insufficient knowledge. People usually do not seek us out because things are going well. None of us run a joy clinic, a place where people come when life is going well. Rather, our occupational world is a world of negative emotions and our focus is on limits in life roles and stressors individuals face. Consequently, this chapter is geared to looking at the limits of traditional male traits and characteristics.

Although there is much controversy about gender roles (e.g., what they are, if they are changing), I contend that the portrait I have painted thus far does present a set of unarticulated assumptions that guide, like an underwater rudder, the adult lives of men. Knowing about these career themes enables the therapist or counselor to be proficient in staying with and navigating the therapy and counseling process with men in individual work and men and women in marital and family work.

Case Studies

Now I would like to present cases that illuminate this major theme and the subthemes that will be described later.

Clem, the Unemployed Father

Clem, 34, was highly depressed when he began counseling. In 5 years, he had experienced a series of disasters in his work life. At 22, he began his own business of repairing machinery in a small town in a rural area. He worked hard as a newly married father with a young child. After a year, the business failed because the economy of the agricultural area was so poor. After much discussion, he and his wife, April, decided to move to a major urban area to find a better job. They moved, but the job search went poorly for Clem. Finally, out of desperation, he tried a sales job because mechanic positions were scarce. He failed miserably at the sales job. By this time in the family, there were three children and money was very scarce. The stress in the family worsened and marital conflict became severe. Clem moved out on his own, began an affair with a woman he had met, and also began drinking excessively.

By the time Clem began counseling, he was suicidal and very depressed about his failure to support his family and fulfill his role as the primary breadwinner. He realized that moving out, the affair, and the drinking were simply ways of coping with his own sense of failure.

Counseling focused first on suicide prevention. The guilt and depression Clem felt concerning his breadwinning failures also were addressed, and he was helped to reframe and expand his own definition of himself and his self-worth. The next step involved a trait-factor focus on career and occupational issues. He was given information on his abilities, interests, motivational patterns, and the work world. In addition, counseling involved job-hunting skills.

At the end of counseling, Clem was employed again—as a truck mechanic making a wage below his aspirations. But he had a better psychological understanding of his disappointment and a much stronger support system. He understood more clearly that the trigger for his distress was his inability to fulfill his own and his wife's expectations for his role in the marriage and the family.

Henry, the Graduate Student

Henry was a 31-year-old Black male graduate student attending a research university on a fellowship in economics. He had grown up in the Delta region of the South and had attended a local Black college. He had done well in college, not by design, but as a result of being interested in economics and having good and helpful relationships with his professors. In his senior year, he was presented with a graduate school fellowship because of his high undergraduate GPA. He decided to accept the fellowship although it meant attending a university 600 miles away in an area where there were few minority students. He decided to attend and began the next fall. Gradually it became clearer and clearer to him that he did not fit in. He felt lonely, isolated, frightened, and insecure. He was angry because the school seemed disinterested and sometimes hostile to minority students.

Henry entered counseling at the university counseling center because he had been offered a second fellowship to continue for a doctorate, but he dreamed mostly about quitting school and returning to his small hometown where he had grown up. Issues of racism were prominent for him in counseling, but expectations for him as a man also emerged as a theme. He liked the status that could come with a PhD, but he did not want the pressure and the expectations for performance. He was a gifted student and loved the field of economics. Yet, he felt alone and needed better mentoring if he was to learn the credentialing and professional mazes he was expected to pass through. Counseling focused on all of these issues as part of helping him decide whether to go on for a doctorate.

Larry, a Disabled Tree Trimmer

Since his late teens until his mid-40s, Larry, age 52, had worked as a tree trimmer for a small firm that specialized in this work. He prided himself on being willing to do the more hazardous and difficult elements of the job. However, he became disabled one day when he fell while working on a large tree. Although he recovered physically from most of the injuries, he was barred by his physician from continuing to work as a tree trimmer. This brought on a period of crisis for Larry because his work as a tree trimmer was very important to him in terms of his own definition of himself. Larry had never been highly proficient at other activities such as art, outdoor skills, athletics, or school, or very successful in relationships with women.

Larry had gravitated to the job as tree trimmer at a local firm and gradually had developed an expertise and an identity. It did provide an income for his family, and, along with his spouse's income from a job as a waitress, they were able to care for their one child. Larry was devastated by the loss of his occupation and his identity as a person with a meaningful job. His recovery from the accident was gradual, and the acceptance of the fact that he needed to find a different job was also gradual. While he worked to make the transition to other employment, a problem that had developed in his life became even more severe. On several occasions over the course of his marriage, he had become involved in altercations with his spouse and had been physically abusive toward her. Now with Larry's unemployment and his self-esteem even more tenuous, the abusive behavior accelerated. During one of the episodes, Larry's spouse called the police and he was arrested and put into the Workhouse and court-ordered to a domestic abuse program. Larry began this program as a way to eliminate his unacceptable aggressive behaviors and also to learn more about himself and his own psychological makeup. Following the domestic abuse program, he began individual counseling for self-esteem and alternative careers. From this counseling, he gradually was able to develop an interpersonal pattern that eliminated the violence. In time he began working as an assistant at a used rent-a-car agency and found that the income from this, along with his Worker's Compensation, nearly matched his former salary as a tree trimmer.

Seth, Dual-Career Man

Seth, age 29, and Mary recently completed graduate programs, he in sociology and she in law, and moved to a new city. During graduate school, Mary was pregnant and had their first child. After the move, she became pregnant with a second child. Both Mary and Seth were very career-oriented, but also committed to family. In the new city, Seth began a job as a research associate in a large survey research company. He felt a great deal of anxiety about this new position and a good deal of pressure to perform well. He realized that Mary, too, would feel as much pressure to perform and do well in her job. He wanted very much to be an equal parent and homemaker and assumed that role by picking certain hours of the week when he was responsible for homemaking tasks, meal preparation, and child-rearing. One of Seth's major difficulties was the lack of male models with whom to identify and talk about this kind of career and family pattern he was attempting. He had other male friends who were committed to being good parents, husbands, and workers, but there were few older men that he knew who, as younger fathers, had been invested in child rearing as well as working and who had spouses that were professional women. Hendel (1989) made this point in his research on highly involved fathers; that is, that they cannot use men of the older generation as models and are left, in some ways, without role models for being involved fathers in the newer sense of this term.

Seth experienced a good deal of satisfaction in his new role. However, he did feel many other emotions as well. These included guilt for not being good enough at any of the roles he was trying to play—worker, husband, father, and friend. It seemed that he was always going quickly to the next thing. Also, he was ambivalent about these roles. Although he cared about the child-rearing, he felt that his work environment gave him no credit for being a good father and he was punished, in fact, in comparison to other men who were single or older or who were not invested in being fathers. Confusion was another emotion he felt, partly because he couldn't find a mentor, especially a male mentor, who was supportive of the way he was living his life in a dual career with his spouse. He felt quite alone at times.

Counseling was helpful to Seth in understanding the normality of his reactions and in helping him find support for the way he was attempting to live his life. He also received a variety of stress management and communication techniques that helped make his hectic life-style less stressful and more satisfying.

Philip, Premed Student

Philip, age 19, came to the university counseling center during the fall quarter of his sophomore year asking for assistance because he was failing a chemistry course. Having grown up in a family where academic achievement and professional careers were highly valued, Philip always dreamed and planned on entering medicine as a career field. He had a good deal of family support for this career choice, and he carefully prepared throughout high school by taking a college prep program so that he would be optimally prepared. Now, in his sophomore year, he was doing poorly in a critical course in the premed curriculum. He was highly distressed when he entered counseling.

His first request was for assistance in order to complete the course. He wanted study skills or anything else that would help him do better in chemistry. He was eager to go along with any requests from the counselor that would help him improve as a chemistry student. At this point, Philip was not interested in looking at any other career choice. He did not seriously want to explore his values or whether a high-status, pressure-filled professional career was something he wanted. His sole desire was to get some assistance in order to be more successful in completing the course as part of being accepted into medical school.

The counseling with Philip was aimed, first of all, at anxiety reduction and academic achievement. He continued to come for a number of sessions during the term to work on these areas. It seemed that the counseling was helpful because his grade did improve in this course. However, it only improved to B- from a low C. Philip terminated the counseling relationship at the end of the term except for one return visit during the second semester. A year and a half later, he returned during his senior year. It seemed that Philip continued to push to be admitted to medical school. His grades were marginal, as was his medical school admissions test. He came back to the counselor more open to possible optional career areas. The counseling focused on a number of different themes: his own sense of failure, alternative routes to medical school in the future, other health care fields as alternatives, the role of his family in his career choice, and his own identity as a person. At the end of this counseling, Philip decided to go on for a master's degree in zoology at a regional university in the hope that his additional training in the sciences would make him more attractive to medical school. He also indicated that he now saw other possibilities for himself in the future if medicine didn't work for him. He was a bit less frantic about the future. Now it seemed that there was more than medical school or nothing.

Discussion

A review of these cases reveals the embedded nature of male role themes. A major theme is this: Performance and mastery in work situations—and the corollary commonly called breadwinning—remains a core ongoing experience for adult male identity. In this regard, Pleck (1987) said, ". . . fulfillment of the breadwinner role remains a central objective for the majority of adult men in the United States" (p. 25). Following are some subthemes that emerge in the previous case studies.

Career and Life Planning

Educational and occupational choices are extremely important in men's lives because, outside the home, employment takes up much of a man's time, energy, and commitment. For most men, these choices are not made in isolation but rather conjointly with a spouse or partner and often within the larger context of children, extended family, and community. Thus, career and life planning, a more encyclopedic term, can be used to describe this larger arena. The career and life planning process is becoming increasingly complex and increasingly difficult because of all the relevant variables to consider, such as personal values, job requirements, and developmental family life stages (O'Neil & Fishman, 1986). Making wise choices in planning one's life means that one must acquire a wide variety of career and life planning skills. These include decision-making skills, developmental stage concepts, values clarification ability, trait and factor data, occupational information, holistic planning models, and a lifelong process framework.

Given the importance and complexity of this work, men will continue to need competence in this area. Both self-directed career planning (Bolles, 1988) and professional career counseling services (Kinnier & Krumboltz, 1984) will continue to be valued for this purpose.

Performance Failure Distress

If much of the male equation is occupational success = self-esteem, then some men do well in the self-esteem area. How about the others? Repeatedly studies suggest that occupational aspirations are not matched by available jobs. "Most [men] work in jobs where they cannot live out the 'American Dream' as portrayed by the media. The number of individuals in professional white collar occupations account for only 15% of all employed men, or 8% of the total male population" (Harris, cited in DuBois & Marino, 1987, pp. 70–71). Also, there will continue to be a surplus of college graduates, and those graduates who will often end up in low-paying jobs will be part of the following equation: high levels of education = low pay = serious job dissatisfaction (Wegmann, Chapman, & Johnson, 1989). The gap between expectations and reality is an especially severe problem for men with less than college educations who have been in blue collar career ladders or who had aspired to be in these career ladders. "Well paid jobs which used to be open to persons with relatively little formal education, however, seem to be disappearing with particular speed" (Wegmann et al., p. 19).

In addition, the labor market is changing rapidly, with jobs being created and jobs disappearing. The experience of unemployment can be stressful and traumatic. Robert Farrer Capon (1987) wrote about being fired:

> For a while, admittedly, the shock of being let go numbs a man, enabling him to function as if nothing life-threatening were happening. And often nothing is—at first. Money, from either severance pay or unemployment benefits, enables him at least to subsist; moreover, his lifelong conviction that he is a marketable commodity has not yet been contradicted by rejection. For a few days or weeks, he actually enjoys his leisure. But then (assuming he is not snapped up at twice the salary), the bloom slowly begins to fade. Desired jobs are not offered; offered jobs turn out to be deeply undesirable . . . A hundred fears come together in the anguish of a man's being out of work: failing to provide, losing an outlet for his talents or his masculinity, being deserted by his friends, destroying his future. . . . But every item in that mixed bag is, appropriately or inappropriately, tied to the grand, almost sacramental fear of being without money. (pp. 179–180)

Performance failure distress is a major theme in the lives of many men. If the goal of adult male life is to compete and win in the sphere of a narrow, hierarchical ladder, then failure is inevitable. Failure can occur in many subarenas, such as an inability to get an apprenticeship in the trade one desires, finishing at a less-than-expected rank in a military training school, missing a promotion, having one's play rejected, being demoted, and losing the business or farm to foreclosure. The emotions of performance failure distress often involve depressive effects. Suicidal thoughts can be the outcome of male performance failure. For example, a major symbol of the stock market crash of the 1920s is the picture of men on Wall Street jumping from the windows after the market fell. More recently, displaced farmers have suffered enormous performance failure distress. For example, a rural career counseling hotline at the University of Missouri was flooded with calls from farm families in Missouri. Themes expressed in the calls revealed great difficulty in coping. Grieving, frustration, denial, passivity, and cynicism were some of the emotional themes expressed by callers (Heppner, Johnston, & Brinkhoff, 1988).

Singlemindedness

Successful achievement often results from a concerted focus on a narrow sphere with much energy, a belief in one's ability, and some luck.

This is the formula many men use in their adult work lives. This strong external focus on achievement can produce what Fasteau (1975) called the male machine. It is a style criticized in the early men's literature (David & Brannon, 1976). Of course, the successful male machine is also greatly admired by a society where money-power-status is the most desired male commodity.

Are there any negative consequences? An obsessive and excessive occupational style has been called workaholism. The individual may lose track of himself in an emotional/psychological sense and become insensitive to the needs of others in his life such as spouse, children, extended family, friends, coworkers, and neighbors. He may neglect his own physical health. Some writers suggest that this style partly explains the short male life expectancy versus the longer female life expectancy (Farrell, 1986).

Losing one's life to work can result from this pattern. Although the material benefits and sense of achievement from an obsessive work orientation can be significant, one loses time. Many men regret the loss of the chance to be with their young children because of work. Then when the children are teenagers or have left the house, the father may slow his work obsession and desire more involvement. Unfortunately, by this time, the children may be focused on independence and autonomy. One client told me how his physician father felt so much regret at the time of his death because he had worked all the time and missed being involved with his family. Yet, the modeling, expectations, and rewards of singlemindedness will continue to attract many men in adulthood.

Ambivalence About Career and Life Goals

As the road map for women's lives expands and changes, does the adult road map for men's lives also expand and change? The most accurate answer seems to be yes and no. Men are increasingly conscious of alternatives to singleminded breadwinning and some of the costs associated with this route. For example, diminution of personality has been suggested as a cost of external success. Many intrinsic pleasures such as expressing one's creativity must, at times, be sacrificed for job success. Yet men often do not choose these other routes. Some of this may be due to the lack of clarity regarding alternatives. Friedan (1981) said:

> The trouble is, once they disengage themselves from the old patterns of American masculinity and success—John Wayne, Lindbergh, John Kennedy—men today are just as lost for lack of role models as women are. (p. 140)

Also, it seems that clearly superior alternative routes do not exist. Most of the high-status occupations have been traditionally held by men. The energetic movement of women into these career fields (e.g., law, business, ministry) is not being equalled by men's moving in another direction. All the possible male moves seem to offer mixed results— some advantages and some disadvantages.

For example, one alternative is to voluntarily step off the treadmill or to avoid stepping on it in the first place. Men are doing this in order to devote their time, energy, and talents to jobs where the pay may be low but interest may be high, such as social causes or the arts. Perhaps a more central reason is that some men simply do not want the intense pressure and stress that performance and mastery in competitive situations entail. It may be too difficult, painful, and unpleasant. Others want more time for family, wanting the intense meaning that can come from parenting in a deep and personal sense.

Working Equitably With Women

Perhaps the infusion of women into the labor force is the single most important social event of the last half of the 20th century. Women are radically altering the sexual composition of many occupations, such as business management, medicine, the Protestant ministry, and law. For some men, working as equals with women is a welcome process that is natural and easy. Working for a woman boss is also a positive experience for some men.

For other men, however, the infusion of women into traditional male occupational territory produces unease and disquiet. The sex segregated friendships and play periods of childhood provided a forum where boys learned to compete with boys. But competing with women may seem strange for some men. They may attempt to romanticize work relationships, find themselves expressing sexist attitudes, or experience difficulty in losing at work to women who perform at a superior level.

Being Included in the "American Dream"

If meaningful work is an essential component of adult male identity, what happens to those men left out of the dream? Racism, lack of opportunity, and other demographic factors seem responsible in the lives of many men who are severely underemployed or unemployed. A wide range of behaviors seem to correlate for adult men with the inability to have a meaningful job. These include health deterioration, interpersonal violence, and family trauma (Skovholt & Morgan, 1981). Rollo May (1972), in searching for the causes of violence, suggested that a sense of pow-

erlessness is the correlate in violent behavior. It seems that when a core
of identity and self-esteem—in this case, the work role—is removed from
an individual, severe stress and high levels of shame may result.

Balancing Work and Family

There is enormous pressure on contemporary couples to juggle
career and family (Gilbert, 1988; Hansen, 1984; Hansen & Minor, 1989).
Although women experience the bulk of this stress, men also are stressed
by it (O'Neil, 1981). For example, a Gallup Poll found that 32% of men
versus 35% of women experienced a great deal of work-family conflict
(cited by Hansen & Minor). Men will continue to experience a variety
of work-family conflicts because of their gradually increasing family role.
Pleck (1979) predicted such a change in 1979:

> An increased family role is the single most important man-
> ifestation of change in the male role in contemporary history,
> just as increased labor force participation is probably the most
> important change in the female role. (p. 485)

Themes related to the balance between work and family will be
prevalent in counseling and therapy with men in future years. For example, Mott (1987) described his own experience:

> My wife's announcement was not dramatic. She marched
> into the house after work and said, "They want me for the Paris
> job. . . . But within days of letting "Sure, that sounds great" slip
> out, I succumbed to second guessing, reluctance and terror.
> Then it struck me where my fears came from. The man in the
> family—me—was putting his career at the mercy of his wife's.
> In the starkest psychological terms, I was following her and
> abdicating my traditional male role. I grew up believing that I
> would be the breadwinner and those little girls across the school-
> house aisle would be housewives and mothers, not professional
> competition or providers. Although I have embraced the notion
> of career women for the last ten years, the move opened mental
> cubbyholes in which the idea of a working woman just didn't
> seem right.
> I'm actively challenging my assumptions about traditional
> male roles and forcing myself to live the beliefs about women
> that I've held for the last ten years. . . . (pp. 90–92)

Male Resistance to the Counseling/Therapy Process

Male socialization is at such odds with the client role that a term—
male resistance—can be used to describe the set of discontinuities that

makes counseling/therapy difficult for men. Given the significant level of male emotional distress (Pleck, 1987), male underutilization of counseling/therapy is surprising yet explainable when considering the male roles (Bruch & Skovholt, 1982; Good, Dell, & Mintz, 1989).

In addition to male-role versus client-role discontinuities, the lack of an alternative future is another source of resistance. Men often do not envision alternatives to old ways of gaining approval. If performance, mastery, and breadwinning are not central, what can be? It seems that— as with a tree—there is only one root system, and this root system, this way to obtain substance, is buried deep in the soil of the external success dimensions. The male client may experience counseling/therapy as an attempt to cut off his one root system without offering alternatives. Hence, counseling/therapy may be slow and difficult for many male clients. Counselors and therapists who develop an understanding of male resistance will be better able to help these clients.

Conclusion

In counseling and therapy with adult men, work themes are prominent because work—defined as performance and mastery in competitive situations—is such a major element of adult male identity and self-esteem. It seems to be a key to life satisfaction and positive relationships with others. Although some men travel through this maze of expectations with grace, skill, and luck and reap great rewards, others get caught at one point or another. They become our clients in counseling and psychotherapy. And it is there that many of the themes discussed here become important when we attempt to reduce negative emotions and negative cognitions and increase positive behaviors of the individuals who come to us.

SEXUALITY, FAMILY, AND MARRIAGE

Healthy integration of sexuality within psychological health remains elusive for many male clients. This chapter addresses the meaning, context, and emotional significance of sexuality.

Chapter 5

DIMENSIONS OF PLEASURE: SEXUALITY, MEN, AND COUNSELING

Philip Colgan

The importance of this chapter lies within the reader. Although much has been written about male sexuality, not enough has been digested and absorbed by most to produce anything but confusion. The male client presenting concerns about sexuality is beset both by a bewildering array of objective informational sources and by his self-perceptions, his relationships, and his world.

Extensive discussions of sexual counseling have focused on biomedical aspects (e.g., *Journal of Sexuality and Disability*) and psychological aspects (e.g., *Journal of Sex Education and Therapy*). Thus, although much excellent material concerning such diverse topics as sex roles, gender identity, sexual behavior, sexual performance, and sexual dysfunction is available, clinical experience still suggests that satisfactory integration of sexuality within psychological health remains elusive for many male clients.

What seems to be lacking is a coherent discussion of the meaning, context, and emotional significance of sexuality. Consequently, this chapter approaches this problem with two important ideas. The first is the concept that sexuality embraces all of the issues described above and yet implies more. A working hypothesis of this chapter is that sexuality is best described as a phenomenological experience whereby one makes sense of his desires for human relationships in the context of his life—past, present, and future. The chapter begins with a discussion of these issues.

The second important idea lies in a conceptual map for both client and clinician to use in approaching, understanding, and resolving concerns about male sexuality. The map can be used both in diagnosing and treating sexual issues in a contextual approach. The chapter concludes with some suggestions regarding clinical practice in working with sexuality and men.

Sexuality in Context

Because the beast with two backs (Othello, I, i, 116) has no voice, all discussions of sexuality merely approximate internal experience. Within these approximations, however, some basic principles seem to describe the experience of healthy, mature, integrated sexuality.

1. Integrated sexuality—involving the ability to know and love oneself and the ability to give and receive love from others—is a cornerstone of self-esteem.
2. Although the ways of expressing sexuality may vary from person to person, or within the person at any given time in life, the meaning of sexuality lies in the phenomenological sphere of expanding one's self-understanding beyond that customarily available through thought, emotion, or action alone.
3. Consequently, sexuality is transcendent. Like all mature, developed notions of man, sexual expression allows one to become larger than oneself, to be more than one usually is. What is transcended, then, is the aloneness of the self. Sexuality allows man to move momentarily from physical, emotional, and cognitive isolation.
4. Sexual behavior—desire, arousal, release—is but the observable structure, form, or process of transcendence. Tumescence is a metaphor.
5. As a corollary, sex can be viewed as an emotion (Everaerd, 1988). It has three components: (a) neurophysiological-biochemical; (b) behavioral-expressive, and (c) feeling-experiential (Izard & Blumberg, 1985).
6. Consequently, psychological sexual development is based largely on experience. Life experiences related to sexuality—feelings, thoughts, behavior—become the clinical "baggage," both good and bad, that influences further psychosexual development via therapy.

Sexuality, then, is both noun and verb. Sexuality is a bridge. And sexuality bridges. What is bridged is a gap between self and other. As bridges come in many forms, so too does sexuality. Sexuality may be expressed as a silent, yet knowing glance across a crowded room. Sexuality is expressed in a wedding ritual of two people jointly lighting a third candle from two still-burning tallows. Sexuality is expressed in tender moments of affection following genital sexual play. In all cases, a combination of thought, emotion, and action enables the individual to briefly become connected with something larger than self, even while participating in its creation.

The Map

Given the above, it would seem that a useful map for understanding the multiple roles of sexuality in a man's life may come from sexology. Only recently, however, has the field of sexology begun conceptually to address the experience of sexuality as more than the sum of physical, emotional, and cognitive factors (e.g., see Derogatis, Lopez, & Zinzeletta, 1988). Help comes from the progenitor of psychology—philosophy.

The map develops a paradigm for understanding sexuality in terms of Aristotelian physics. This paradigm, in turn, suggests strategies for intervention.

In his *Physics* (Book 2, Chapter 3, 194B–195A), Aristotle explained four components that together cause an entity to be what it essentially is. These essential causes are very briefly summarized as:

Material—the raw materials or natural resources; the fundamental building blocks.

E.g., A house is made of bricks and wood.

Formal—the structure, or form of the combined material components.

E.g., Bricks and wood are assembled into a form.

Active—that which infuses the project with energy to effect its completion as an entity; that which effects, or influences, things to be as they currently are.

E.g., A builder uses his energy to create the structure.

Final—the purpose, function, or mission of the entity.

E.g., A house provides shelter.

Using Aristotle's categories, we can use 20th-century psychological terms to interpret sexuality as having four components:

Material: the basic building blocks; in human sexuality, a man's natural resources: his mind, heart, and body.

Formal: the structural features; in human sexuality, the interaction of a man's mind, body, and heart observable in his sexual behavior and interpersonal communication.

Active: the energy or power that influences the current state of affairs; in clinical terms, the affective, cognitive, and behavioral energies with which the man constructs his sexuality.

Final: the purpose for his activation of sexuality; the mission of his sexual desire and sexual expression. As described above in Platonic terms, his reach for transcendence. (see Plato, *Symposium*, 209C–211C)

If we think of the components described above as a repetitive cycle, it becomes apparent that the final cause is both end point and starting point. The French description of orgasm, "Chaque petit mort est une

naissance" [Every little death is a birth], says it well. Sexuality is both
process and product.

Working Backward

This section will elaborate on the components of sexuality, or the
map, described above. This is preparatory to describing their use for
clinical intervention with men presenting sexuality concerns.

Fundamental to effective intervention, in this view, is the heuristic
of "working backwards." The concept of working backwards comes from
the field of intelligence research, especially information-processing approaches. Compared with means-end analysis (the customary approach
to sex therapy), working backwards offers a more efficient and therefore
useful heuristic for problem solving.

Working backwards is simply described: "One begins with the goal
and seeks an operation from some intermediate state that would lead
directly to the goal" (Kail & Pellegrino, 1985, p. 68). In other words,
start with where you want to arrive. Work backwards through the map
step by step to the beginning.

Working backwards is a way of conceptualizing the components of
problem solving. It becomes a procedure for using the map. To encourage the focus on working backwards, Aristotle's hierarchy of components will be discussed in reverse order, starting with Final Cause, or
Mission.

Final Cause or Mission

Most descriptions of healthy, mature, and integrated sexuality view
sexuality as an important foundation for the twin goals of self-esteem
in the way of self-respect, and self-esteem as the way to give and receive
love. The purpose for developing healthy sexuality, then, is not merely
as a goal in itself, but more importantly to remove sexuality from the
sphere of "problems" and place it in perspective as a cornerstone of self-
esteem.

From semiotic theory, or the science of language and its symbols,
linguists teach that certain statements can serve two functions simultaneously (see Greimas, 1987). Similarly, from psychoanalytic theory, psychologists commonly hold the belief that the same may be said for any
given behavior: It can serve two functions simultaneously. I will refer
to one function as explicit and the other as implicit. One is apparent;
the other is apprehended. Using this understanding, one can subdivide
a statement of Mission to describe two purposes—one explicit, one implicit.

In terms of sexuality, it may be said that the explicit mission of healthy sexuality is pleasure—physical, emotional, mental. Within this is perhaps the implicit reason for healthy sexuality: Employing the ability to transcend the isolation of the self, physically, mentally, and emotionally. Via transcendence, one achieves an awareness of self in relation to others, an awareness that surpasses ordinary understanding. The desire for transcendence, like all great and mature emotions, is developed both in self-love and in love for others. Transcendence may be stated as the implicit mission of healthy, mature, integrated sexuality.

Active Cause or Energy

In this paradigm, action is viewed as a description of energy or power. In matters of sexuality, power becomes the psychic and physical energy that gravitates toward satisfying human connections. Power in this regard does not refer to control over others. Rather, it is an energizing term.

Formal Cause or Structure

In sexuality, the form or structure is the process of cognitive, physical, and emotional arousal that leads to transcendence. Traditional forms of sex therapy attend to the structure of sexual behavior. Historically, the basis for sexology lies in science. Kinsey, Pomeroy, and Martin (1948) reported their observations regarding sexual behavior. Masters and Johnson (1970) continued and expanded this work in what we have come to know as sex therapy. Included in this is attention to those parts of the process of arousal and release that commonly afflict people—the sexual dysfunctions.

Material Cause or Resources

In sexuality, a man's resources are his mind, his body, and his heart. As noted above, the resources of mind and body are being attended to, and continue to receive attention crucial to our understanding of the effects of drugs—illicit, medicinal, and recreational—and of various disabilities, some one or more of which will probably affect us all eventually. Matters of the heart, however, are often ignored in the definitions and treatment of sexual concerns. The only apparent reason for this is simply a matter of state of the art: Only now is sexuality being approached in terms of emotion research (Everaerd, 1988).

In discussions of sexuality, especially as applied to clinical practice, these resources within the individual describe both his physical self and his phenomenological understanding of himself, with the accompanying history of sexual behavior, attitudes, and knowledge. Some of these accretions are impediments to healthy sexuality. These are later referred to as limitations. This is the "baggage," both good and bad.

The next section will describe problems encountered in each of these categories. The goal is to help the clinician evaluate problems within the dynamic hierarchy of components. In successful sexuality counseling, satisfaction generally refers to developing mature, healthy, integrated sexuality, enabling the man to be more at home with himself (self-esteem), and to be more at home with others (intimacy) (Colgan, 1987).

Sexuality Problems

This section focuses on developing the concepts of the map. The purpose is to further elucidate clinical situations in which accurate problem identification can lead to greater clinical success.

Problems of mission are among the most difficult for clients to identify. This is understandable because the concept of mission attached to sexuality has not received sufficient attention in either the popular or the professional press. Even when a man knows that "something is missing" or that "sex seems empty," still he may not have the words that would help him articulate the nature of the problems.

The professional can help in such cases by leading the man to develop his own language about the intrinsic role of sexuality in his life. Sexuality, in this context, is an embodiment of conscious or unconscious statements about the self. The therapeutic goal in clarifying problems of meaning is to help the client uncover the explicit or implicit self-definitions embodied in his understanding of himself and his sexuality.

Some clinical examples of such self-definitions include: "I am a lovable person." "I am a generous person." "I am a loving person." Conversely, a man may find also what Jung terms the "dark side" (Jung, 1959). Statements that reflect the dark side of sexuality might include: "I am a greedy person." "I am an animal." "I am a controlling person."

Clarification of these issues is not directed toward immediate amelioration of the concerns a man feels. Nonetheless, without clarification, therapy is apt to be misdirected.

As noted above, the explicit meaning may be that the purpose of healthy sexuality is pleasure, both physical and emotional. The physical has been adequately explored in many publications (e.g., Masters & Johnson, 1970). Emotional pleasure has been vaguely referred to in the current jargon of "intimacy" (Colgan, 1988). But, just as many professionals are confused about what constitutes intimacy, so too clients are often confused about the meaning of emotional pleasure.

Once again, the difficulty arises from inadequate language to describe sexuality as a physically and emotionally transcendent experience. Consequently, expect confusion. What is transcended? How can that which is rooted in the physical become something beyond the physical? Is this what people mean when they say "spiritual"? Is this mixing up sex and love?

To clarify, consider the concept of ecstasy. Ecstasy is defined as a state of exhalted delight in which normal understanding is felt to be surpassed. The origin of the word is Greek, ekstasis, from existanai—to displace, drive out of one's senses. Ecstasy, then, is akin to having a nonphysical experience even while sensually awake and alert.

Ejaculation is commonly thought of as the physical moment of ecstasy for men (Kaplan, 1974). But sex researchers have added to our understanding of the subjective experience of orgasm. Bohlen (1981) documented the distinction between objective, measurable physical changes that accompany ejaculation and the subjective, personal, nonobservable qualitative experience of orgasm. In test-retest clinical trials, men's perceptions of the duration, intensity, and pleasure associated with orgasm varied whereas objective physical changes associated with ejaculation did not.

These observations give credence of our understanding that ecstasy—or transcendence—is not only a physical but also an emotional experience. Orgasm is perhaps one of the easiest (outside of drugs), but by no means only, way of reaching a state of transcendence. The physical sensation of release is associated with pleasure on a level beyond our normal understanding.

The sensation of becoming larger than oneself—or transcending the self—is not limited to orgasm. If transcending oneself can be viewed as joining with something larger than oneself, then transcendence is available to us in other ways. For example, joining with another in the creation of mutual pleasure can be subjectively defined as a transcendent experience.

Disorders of transcendence are most easily seen when men include emotional power and control over others as part of their sexuality. The rapist, the child molester, the man who uses emotional manipulation to gain sexual favors, can all be viewed as using domination as an acceptable route to becoming something larger than themselves. In less extreme examples, men who do not wish to join with another to achieve an awareness of self beyond the usual—that is, for example, men who do not love their parents—will have problems of mission connected with sexuality as well.

Problems of energy or power surface through the rubric of sexual desire. Note that power is defined as an energy term, not a reference to domination. In this sense, sexual power encompasses two complementary impulses in integrated sexuality: the urge to take and the urge to give. The urge to take is defined as lust. "Lust" includes the desire to take the pleasures life offers, pleasures of the flesh exhibited in a robust relish of sensual pleasures. These include stimulation of all physical senses—the succulence of a strawberry, the beauty of a sunset, the roar of the ocean, the aroma of hot pastrami, the silky fur of the dog. Lust then, is the animal urge.

Love is the human urge. Love in all its forms—brotherly, romantic, erotic, love of hearth, homeland, friendship, higher power—is understood as both a state of being and a state of becoming. In loving relationships, people give, people share, people accommodate, and people tolerate.

Love and lust combined result in a willingness to partake of and share the physical and emotional pleasures of life. As such, the power of an individual's sexuality within close relationships may be stated as "I will demand of your time, your interest, and your body only what you freely offer" (Brantner, 1987).

A power failure—lack of potency in positive responses to the gifts of aliveness—may indicate psychopathology (e.g., Meyer, Schmidt, Lucas, & Smith, 1975); emotional disorders such as depression (LoPiccolo, 1980) or anhedonia (Schover, Friedman, Weiler, Heiman, & LoPiccolo, 1980); learning deficits (Wolpe, 1969); or organic factors (Stuntz, 1983).

Problems of form or structure emerge when the process for attaining meaningful human contact is either dysfunctional or misguided. This is the area for traditional sex therapy, which focuses on sexual dysfunction. Sex-focused therapy has evolved from achieving goals of education and increased awareness (Masters & Johnson, 1970), to more refined combinations of psychodynamic and behavioral approaches (Kaplan, 1974), to more eclectic individual and relationship combinations (Sollod, 1988).

Sex therapy is a subspeciality of sexuality counseling. Generally, resolution of problems of structure is best left to those with specialized training in sex therapy. In some cases, however, providing accurate sexual information can resolve sexual concerns (Annon, 1977). In any case, the general practitioner can utilize general principles of problem identification and referral for sexual dysfunctions.

Problems of resources include those that interrupt the man's natural ability to coordinate his body, mind, and heart to achieve meaningful human connections. As noted above, matters of his body are primarily the province of his physician. The clinician, however, needs to be fully apprised of the limits to physical resources the client experiences. Attention, however, to general matters of physical maintenance—eating and exercise patterns, for example—are optimally approached in the therapeutic relationship. Resources for the mind abound in the present culture. Bibliotherapy, communication classes, seminars, and men's retreats are all helpful ways to stimulate self-awareness, sexuality attitude reassessment, intellectual curiosity, and communication skills development.

Matters of the heart are more difficult for male clients to approach. In mainstream United States culture, men are encouraged to inhibit affective verbal expression (see Moore & Haverkamp, 1989, for a discussion of these issues). Instead, a premium is placed on expression of emotion through action, often aggressive action (Miller, 1983). As a result, even when directly questioned about feeling fear or anxiety, boys are more likely than girls to lie and keep their feelings secret (Lekarezyk & Hill, 1969). It is not surprising that, as adults, men self-disclose less than women (Cosby, 1973). And it is not difficult to understand that the male client may well have trouble recognizing and utilizing the emotional resources at hand in life as well as in therapy.

Limitations to resources may surface in an initial assessment of early learning experiences and later developmental experiences concerning sexuality in all forms. Additionally, such problems of resources (again, the "baggage" a man carries) may surface during the course of therapy. This is especially true, in my experience, of traumatic, shameful, or abusive events of the past (see Brown, 1988, for a discussion of these issues).

Treatment: Using the Map

The sections above describe a map for both accurate assessment and understanding of sexuality problems. Using the map is the focus of this section. In therapy, the map is used as an instrument for problem clarification both at the beginning of therapy and at any time the focus of therapy seems lost. Failure to conduct a thorough diagnosis and loss of direction in sexually focused therapy have been cited as major determinants of therapeutic failure (Chapman, 1982).

Conceptually, the map is both hierarchical and circular. Both uses for clinical work will be illustrated below. Primary to both utilizations, however, is a clear understanding that without clarity in the mission statement, therapeutic interventions at other junctures are apt to fail.

Both client and therapist work best together for problem resolution when the statement of purpose is jointly understood and approved. Arriving at a mutual understanding of the goal of therapy alleviates many future disappointments. Again, stating the obvious may seem pedantic. Yet explicit statements of the therapeutic goals, and their intrinsic meaning to the individual client, begins or refines the process of skill development in communication. Masters and Johnson (1970) noted that communication problems may be responsible for 50% of the problem in sexual dysfunction.

Using the map hierarchically means starting at the top and working backwards, clarifying concepts as one moves. For example, if the purpose of sexuality is to be a well-adjusted person, the purpose of therapy may be to develop specific skills that, when incorporated, will lead to more satisfying sexual adjustment. Understanding and directing the client's energy expenditure can help the therapist focus on relevant material and not waste time on tangential quests.

Once the purpose is clarified, the next components—structure and resources—can fall easily into line. Structure becomes the best method for achieving the goal; the resources of the client in the way of motivation, time, money, willingness, and so forth can be aligned with structural demands. Limitations to resources for satisfying the mission can be addressed.

Therapeutic use of the map is, again, circular and hierarchical. Whenever the focus of therapy seems vague to either therapist or client, reference to the map can help to clarify the therapeutic goal. Circular use means going right to the top; restating the mission can clarify direction of energy expenditure. Current topics or homework in the therapy sessions, then, can be redesigned to be more specifically goal-directed.

Hierarchical use of the map is indicated in the direction taken for problem resolution. Simply put, work backwards. If a man believes he has a problem within resources, his impulse will probably be to address limitations of resources. Problem resolution, however, more likely lies at the level above resources, that of structure. Changing the structure may mean reallocation of resources, thereby addressing the resource problem.

Clinical examples will clarify these uses of the map. [Note: all clinical examples have been developed by the author for teaching purposes, and as such, do not reflect individuals.]

Clinical Examples

Joe is a 48-year-old stockbroker who develops a close relationship with a female colleague. Although it's not a sexual relationship, Joe feels increasingly drawn to her, and he reports experiencing a "meeting of the minds" unlike that which he experiences with his wife. In his confusion about his feelings, Joe has begun to have difficulty maintaining an erection with his wife. He feels bewildered, angry, and guilty. He has begun to believe that, although he loves his wife, he must leave her to pursue his attachment to the coworker. He interprets his impotence as a sign of lagging interest in his wife. He initiates therapy to resolve his feelings: Should he leave his wife and start a relationship with his coworker? Or should he be content with his lot and say goodbye to what feels to him like his best chance for happiness?

Conceptual analysis: Personal mission: Have a happy life. *Purpose of therapy*: Explicit—resolve feelings; Implicit—make value choices about what constitutes happiness. *Energy*: anxiety about his feelings of confusion and guilt; desire to do the "right thing." *Form of intervention*: Self-discovery via one-to-one therapy, initially; probably incorporating marital counseling in the future, all supplemented by bibliotherapy. *Resources*: the therapist; Joe himself; outside influence in the way of reading, seminars, conversation with others; perhaps his wife; perhaps his coworker. *Limitations to resources*: an irrational need for perfection in his own progress; awareness of his own mortality; 48 years of learning; current responsibilities to job and family.

Primary therapeutic intervention: Understand the nature of the problem. A problem defined (as above) as one of values clarification involves a question of purpose: How should Joe conduct his life? The solution requires Joe and his therapist to examine the question as one of meaning. What does it mean to him to have found this "meeting of the minds" with his coworker? Why is this happening at this stage of his life? What will it mean to him to leave his wife? Answering these questions will (in this example) clarify that Joe has discovered a new lease on life via his experience of having an intimate (notice, nonsexual) relationship with a coworker.

He may begin to see his marriage as the source of his dissatisfaction with life. If this is the case, then leaving the marriage for another relationship seems to be attempting to solve a meaning problem by attending a structural issue. This can only bode failure, as the energy expended in problem solving will have been misguided.

Secondary therapeutic intervention: If structure (marriage) is dissatisfying, move to next level up (energy) for problem solution. Is Joe willing to focus his energy on making his marriage more satisfying? If yes, then the therapeutic goal has shifted to focusing on marriage involvement. If no, then the therapeutic goal focuses on marriage dissolution. Thus, therapy goals shift toward the application of energy to address the newly stated mission.

Two other brief clinical examples of intervention at the level of problem identification will solidify the reader's understanding. [Note: these are simplified for teaching purposes.]

1. *A case involving therapeutic intervention at the level above problem identification*: Psychogenic erectile dysfunction seems to be related to anxiety about sexual performance (a structural problem). *Intervention*: Redirect client's energy to focus on pleasure (an energy investment), not on sexual performance, that is, tumescence (a resources issue). *Note*: this would require both client and therapist to share an understanding that

pleasure is the mission for the client's healthy sexual adjustment (a meaning statement).

2. *A case involving redirection of therapy by reviewing the mission statement*: Attempts to help a homosexual client develop a positive social network have resulted in frustration. Reevaluation of the mission statement reveals that the client actually wants a primary pair-bond, not a social network. He silently viewed the social network as a structure for achieving his goal, rather than as a mission statement in itself. Therapy is redirected toward the real goal.

Use of the map in sexuality counseling is, of course, effective only within general guidelines of sound therapeutic practice. These are extensively discussed elsewhere, and need not be reviewed here. Guidelines specific to sex therapy are available in other sources as well. In addition to these, however, I would suggest the following:

1. A familiarity with the transference and countertransference issues of interpersonal boundaries is a necessary foundation for a satisfying and effective clinical practice with sexuality issues (Colgan, 1988).

2. Counseling people on issues of sexuality can proceed only to the therapist's level of self-understanding (Maddock, 1975). This does not require the therapist to "have it all together." Rather, this is to indicate that therapists who are aware of their own strengths and limitations are more effective.

3. As a corollary, a phenomenological understanding of sexuality requires the therapist to respect the individual's idiosyncratic understanding of himself and his relationships (Colgan, 1988).

For further resources, the clinician is encouraged to receive specialized training in sex therapy. Seminars ranging from general principles to specialized interventions are widely available. Contact either the American Association of Sex Educators, Counselors, and Therapists [435 North Michigan Avenue, Suite 1717, Chicago, Illinois 60611] or your professional organization for specific information concerning lectures, workshops, supervisory opportunities, and training institutes.

Summary

This chapter has reviewed clinical concepts of sexuality counseling with men. Discussion has specifically been directed toward understanding sexuality in the phenomenological realm of the individual. As such, male clients addressing issues of sexuality will benefit by the clinician's close attention to the meaning, context, and emotional significance of sexual expression. Intervention strategies based on a conceptual map of the experience of sexuality have been suggested. Finally, although specific suggestions are beyond the scope of this chapter, the clinician is encouraged to apply the principles of sexuality therapy, as discussed, in the context of the helping relationship.

Acknowledgment

The author gratefully acknowledges the contributions of G. Leonard Weirs (and Richard Kott) to this chapter.

Relationships are, by definition, reciprocal so that context and interaction become the key elements for any understanding.

Chapter 6
MEN AND MARRIAGE

Vincent Ciaramella

Making a relationship work is the most difficult of psychological tasks. It requires the use of all one's personal skills. It is complex because all intimate relationships, especially marriage in Western culture, require a transgenerational fluency: the ability to understand and articulate the "legacy" of our parents and grandparents. We never enter a relationship except as "emissaries" from our family of origin. Carl Whitaker, one of the four or five original thinkers in family therapy, once gave a talk in which he said, "I don't believe there is any such thing as an individual. We are all merely incomplete parts of a family."

This "diminished position" ascribed to the individual is simply another passageway for understanding the reality of human behavior. This family systems approach presents a construct that maximizes the possibility for change. It is optimistic because it relies heavily on our human ability to influence the transactions among ourselves. It places each of us on the path of responsibility for the state of the relationship we find ourselves in, and at the same time empowers us in our quest for intimacy through a balance of fairness and trust.

The Balance of Fairness:
The Give-and-Take of Relationships

It is difficult to speak of men in relationships entirely from a gender perspective. Relationships are, by definition, reciprocal so that context and interaction become the key elements for any understanding. The writing of Ivan Boszormenyi-Nagy, a leading family therapist, is extremely helpful in formulating an understanding of a reasonable model of intimate relationships.

Boszormenyi-Nagy speaks of the relationships of peers, mates, lovers, or friends in which there is an expectation of an equitable "give-and-take." He goes on to say that a relationship stays viable only as long as people manage to achieve a balance of relatively reciprocal contri-

71

butions between them. The commitment of the relationship manifests itself through each partner's doing his or her fair share of the work of the relationship. This work includes not only the daily chores of shopping, cleaning, child care, and so on, but also the emotional work necessary to maintain a bonding or closeness. If this is not the case, the relationship becomes one-sided and exploitative and cannot be sustained.

The key elements in Boszormenyi-Nagy's give-and-take are the attention to fairness and equity in a relationship. This ethical dimension, not often considered in current psychological practice, seems inherent to our everyday intuitive assessment of how individuals should relate. It is probable that without the elements of trust, fairness, or justice in a relationship, a partner may perceive a negative entitlement, that is, a kind of permission to behave in an exploitative manner toward a partner: "I have every right to do what I'm doing given the way I have been treated." It is also possible that transgenerational issues, cutoffs from parents for example, may have serious consequences for the marital couple because concerns about loyalty affect the balance of fairness.

When this cycle of unfairness and negative entitlement exists in a relationship, a kind of cancer invades the balance between the partners. Naturally, the converse is true. If there is an equitable balance of fairness in the relationship, then a merited entitlement or expectation of caring from the partner is earned, thereby expanding the mutuality of the relationship.

Men experience and may even actively practice negative entitlement in a number of ways. Three easily discernible forms are: emotional disconnectedness, overinvolvement in a career, and a cultural/familial imperative.

As part of his training to be a man, a boy quickly learns that rational, objective, logical thought is much preferred to emotional acknowledgement. A man in a group was asked to interview his father about emotions and family emotional expressiveness. When he approached his father with this task, his father said, "Your mother handles that sort of thing."

A second area of negative entitlement is overinvolvement in one's career. A man perceives that a successful career will bring recognition from his family and community. A middle-aged executive recently mused that his children faulted him for not being available to them when he believed he had "given all they ever wanted."

Third, men are occassionally burdened by a cultural imperative that places him in a position where the expectation is that his partner will "do for him." It is an expectation that comes more from a kind of family imprinting rather than a conscious arrogance.

For Boszormenyi-Nagy, relationships finally succeed on the basis of their long-term resources rather than on short-term behavior patterns. Clearly, it is impossible for any of us to avoid some element of exploitation of our partner. What is devastating to a relationship is "consistent unilateral usage" over a period of time.

"Marriages founder or succeed on the question of whether or not people can develop the capacity to be responsible for the consequences of fairness and trust" (Boszormenyi-Nagy & Krasner, 1986, p. 336). In any given relationship individual men will need to reevaluate their "entitlements." "Have I 'earned' this entitlement?" "Has it been earned in a context of fairness?" "Am I contributing to an equitable balance in the 'give-and-take' of this relationship?"

We have all seen children debating in the schoolyard whether a particular arrangement or exchange between them is fair or not. "It's not fair for you to bat two times in a row." Perhaps instinctively children grasp this primary concept of the balance of fairness as the key element in a functioning relationship. As adults, we seem often to lose sight of this essential truth. We have another opportunity to rediscover it in the intimacy of an adult relationship.

Mate Selection

It is not uncommon to hear a man say, "She's different now than when we were first married. I had no idea she was so attached to her mother or that she was so angry a person." These kinds of statements imply that the spouse practiced a kind of deception in order to hide certain personality characteristics or traits. Perhaps they were hidden to achieve a goal such as entrapment in the relationship.

My observation is that each of us "deserves" the spouse we have chosen. As I review the many couples I have worked with over the past 15 years, it becomes evident that, almost invariably, a kind of fit demonstrates itself. Although this fit may not and usually is not particularly evident, especially to couples who are experiencing serious problems, it is always present.

I began with the premise that both men and women select mates in a persistently directed and informed manner. By persistently directed and informed I mean that mate selection comes out of the jagged edge of our personality. The shape that our personality takes has been informed and continues to be influenced by the ebb and flow of our family of origin. Our efforts, then, driven by our own existential incompleteness, are to make a fit with that jagged edge. Imagine here a piece from a puzzle. The search is for another piece that will fit into the contours. This process of seeking a fit is instinctual and unconscious. In practical terms, we seek a mate who complements our own stage of psychological complexity. We seek a person who "fits" our inner structure. In effect, couples too far apart don't marry. This is not to say that people of vastly different backgrounds don't marry one another. What I am saying, however, is that the couples fit together in some way, and on some level are fulfilling personal, and, perhaps, familial goals.

According to Prosky (1979), "Some basic complementary pairings are:

1. the good one and the bad one, the warrior and the peacekeeper; the martyr and the meanie;
2. the pragmatist and the dreamer, in which one person performs at the level of basic necessity and the other adds the color.
3. the pursuer and the distancer, in which one person constantly feels neglected and demands more attention and the other asserts his right to privacy and space around him.
4. the overt controller and the covert controller, in which one person is seen as the authority and lays down the explicit laws and sanctions and the other, seen as the weaker, wields power through covert manipulations and punishments.

. . . the fact that intimate relationships are reciprocal means that no matter how much it looks like it, there is never a villain and never a hero. Each is in fact, a bit of both" (p. 25). The terms *reciprocal* and *complementary* are fundamentally interchangeable for our purposes. They mean "a reciprocal giving and taking of instruction, the reciprocal asking and answering of questions, the reciprocal asserting of an agreeing to statements, all of these reciprocal relationships being characterized by inequality stemming from the participants occupying a one up and a one down position" (Bodin, 1981, pp. 277–278).

Clearly complementarity does not imply that one partner is always one up and the other one down. It is likely that these roles swing depending on the issue. Yet, the relative position vis-à-vis power in the description of complementarity misses the point. It is precisely the appearance of helplessness of the martyr that organizes the meanness of the meanie, and vice versa. Each "grows fat" on the relative positions each adopts.

An example of this can be seen in a marital case in which a long-suffering wife puts up for years with the drunken behavior of her husband. She picks him up out of the gutter, endures his insults, and makes excuses for his behavior. Each incident is followed religiously by the husband's sincere repentence for several days following the binge. See how they dance together! Each giving gifts to the other. The husband giving his wife the gift of martyrdom. The wife giving her husband the gift of unbridled indulgence. Power, or one up or one down, is not the point; *mutual empowerment* is closer to the reality.

So the superorganized man may choose a less-than-ordered woman, or the laid-back man chooses a more responsible woman. If a variety of conditions exists in a functioning relationship, each partner will teach the best of his or her personality to the other. In a problematic relationship, the differences eventually become even more exaggerated, leading to even greater distance between the couple. In other words, if there is trust and parity in the relationship, individuals will be open to learning about what they lack. In a recent conversation with a friend, he indicated that he had learned from his wife how to compliment people without feeling manipulative or fawning. This is a functional relationship. If the relationship had been problematic, he might have seen her suggestions as demanding and controlling.

In an intimate relationship, the issues of individuation and fusion emerge in this balancing of identities, or complementarity. Individuation is a process by which one achieves a sense of self-completion, particularly as it relates to one's family of origin. Fusion is an incomplete or nonexistent emergence of one's self as a discrete individual. Individuals in relationships continually search for a dynamic balance between individuation and fusion. Individuation in the case described above is being loved for who one is, and fusion is becoming so like a part of the partner that one is lost.

McGoldrick presented a caution as she observed issues of complementarity becoming a block to individuation and a doorway to fusion. It is not contradictory to see the compulsion of complementary forces acting in our interpersonal actions, while at the same time valuing one's personal sense of existential separateness. "There is a vast difference between forming an intimate relationship with another separate person and using a couple relationship to try to complete one's self and improve one's self-esteem. The natural human desire to share one's experience often leads to this confusion between seeking closeness and seeking fusion in coupling" (Carter & McGoldrick, 1987, p. 213).

Bowen (1978) would say that the root of this problem of seeking completeness through fusion with another is related to incomplete differentiation from one's family of origin. A distinction is now being made between the general interactional force of complementarity which, again, in itself is neither productive or destructive, and Bowen's observation of the dynamics of fusion, which he observed as a destructive method of "completing" oneself. It is clear, however, that incomplete, unhappy adult relationships with parents almost always fold back onto the marital relationship of the adult child.

A young couple in treatment described how each partner operates a separate enterprise within the marriage. Each keeps separate accounts. Monies are never mixed. He tells her, "Don't pay a cleaning person, you pay me with your money and I will clean our home." Her family absentmindedly forgets to set a place for him at the table during a recent visit. His family talks about how she takes advantage of his good nature. Neither partner has been able to claim adulthood in their respective families, thus making impossible the creation of a new family. In fact, this couple can never "divorce" because they have never been "married."

Suggestions For Men (Couples) Contemplating Marriage

Given what we know about the impact of the family of origin on marriage, let us review some suggestions for men who are contemplating marriage.

1. Be aware that instituting a serious relationship directly after a serious loss increases the possibility of marital failure. Serious loss changes the fundamental shape of our puzzle piece and, given the interactive systemic forces operating in every family, one cannot predict the new shape the family may take. The loss, for example, may cast the individual into a different role, which may either enhance or detract from his ability to sustain a serious relationship.

2. Be aware that the more significant the differences between each spouse, such as religion, education, social class, ethnicity, age, and so on, the more risky the relationship.

3. Choosing a geographic comfort zone that incorporates a relationship with both families of origin increases the chances of success. This zone needs to be far enough away so that primary loyalty to one another can be built, yet close enough to find support and familiarity with one's psychological history.

4. Be aware that marriage is not a useful vehicle for distancing from family-of-origin problems. Sequence here is crucial. One must first establish a sense of self, however imperfect, before one can establish an intimate relationship. It is incredibly more difficult to use a marriage relationship as the vehicle for individuation.

5. The new relationship must have a sense of its own resources—financial, physical, and emotional. An overdependence on outside resources increases the possibility of triangulation (see next section).

6. A reasonable period of acquaintanceship should precede the marriage. As a general rule, a reasonable period of acquaintanceship facilitates the negotiations that must follow the fall-out from unresolved issues of complementarity.

7. The wedding should be seen as an event that includes not only the marrying couple but the extended family and friends as well.

8. Each spouse should make every attempt to take care of unfinished business before the wedding, such as cutoffs from siblings or parents (adapted from Carter & McGoldrick, 1989, p. 231).

Men and Triangles
What Are They—How Can You Avoid Them?

There are solutions to marital problems that lead to resolution and there are solutions that delay an immediate crisis, sometimes for a long time. Solutions that result from the formation of a triangle are pseudo-solutions in that they protect all the participants from a major pain or intense anxiety by moving their focus to a new terminus. The appearance of this new terminus is the basis of triangulation. Imagine a triangle with the husband on one angle, the wife on another, with the third angle containing the person or issue being triangulated. This triangle is the smallest relationship grouping. A partial description of an emotional system described by Murray Bowen is the following: "The triangle describes the dynamic equilibrium of a three person system" (Kerr & Bowen, 1988, p. 135).

As anxiety increases in a two-person system, the involvement of a third element prevents a crisis by dissapating it throughout the system. This construct then reduces the possibility of the two-person relationship crisis. The newly stabilized three-element unit can now proceed, having achieved what may become a long-term accommodation.

An example of triangulation might be the following. A man feels his partner is not responding to him sexually. From the woman's perspective, the man's self-absorption is sufficient enough reason for her to withdraw. As she withdraws, the man's anger grows, and the couple's anxiety level rises to a level that threatens the stability of the relationship. At this point, the couple moves toward a method of dealing with this stress: the incorporation in the circuitry of a readily available element. This element may be a somatic complaint, overinvestment in a job, an affair, or a child, to name a few examples. In our example, the couple chooses to triangulate a somatic complaint, the headaches of the woman. The headaches immobilize her and provide a cover and explanation for her lack of sexual interest. Similarly, they give the man permission to overinvest in his work, and provide an area in which he can comfort his sick wife and assuage his guilt for being absent so often from the family. An evaluation of the workings of this triangle reveals that each partner helped to create this solution and each benefited both immediately and also helped to stabilize the relationship. Yet, the underlying, basic relationship dilemma remains unsolved by the triangle.

Although the formation of a triangle often offers a kind of solution to a problem, there remains a vague awareness on the part of all the participants that something is not quite right. A kind of twilight discontentment exists in the midst of the triangle.

Detriangulation is risk taking. It means giving up a proven device for a less-than-secure outcome. One half of the couple must take a risk and move out of the triangle first by reevaluating and reworking his or her actions to determine how to earn merited entitlement within the relationship.

Second, the partner must move toward the other partner directly, not through the circuitry of the third element. For most men, this means reevaluating their investment in work or in an affair, for example.

The therapist's best chance to help comes out from an appreciation of how systems operate. Thinking systemically permits the helper to speak from a more neutral metaposition. "In essence, neutrality is reflected in the ability to define self without being emotionally invested in one's own viewpoint or in changing the viewpoints of others" (Kerr & Bowen, 1988, p. 150).

Every human relationship remains imperfect. It is not suggested that as one earns merited entitlements from a partner and rejects triangulation through straightforward communication, the couple will reach some sort of utopian joining. An intimate relationship exists as a living organism with each element having discrete functions yet being operationally joined. Functional couples are greater than the sum of their parts. The interactional life of a functioning couple produces a new dimension, a transactional spirit that is an intermingling of unconditional trust.

Men and Marriage Counseling

Most would agree that the overwhelming number of couples who seek marriage counseling present the female partner as the person more invested in seeking help. Somehow talking to a therapist about a problem in the marriage seems to come easier for women. They seem naturally less threatened by the process. What then often is presented to the therapist is a rather flexible, committed woman and a more detached, somewhat distant man. This constellation may induce the therapist into an unconscious alliance with the woman, cementing the outside position of the man.

Often the therapist will be induced into working with the more committed wife. The therapist, who may be either male or female, may decide to see the wife separately. If there is anything that will induce a crisis even more quickly in an already stressed marriage, it is the involvement of one half of the marriage in a "therapeutic" process. This can serve only to unbalance the relationship further. Thus, the therapist may be seduced into becoming part of a system that has already decided how its members are to be arranged and how it will deal with the stress of the relationship.

The point is that whatever causal factors society or even individuals may ascribe to men's greater difficulty in accepting "talking" help, these male "characteristics" are used by all the participants in a marriage system. This is not a denial of male or female differences, either physiological, psychological, or societal in origin. Rather, it is simply a statement that whatever these characteristics are, they are adopted by the marital system, and all members are thus equally responsible for the actions that result.

For example, a couple comes into treatment with the man not at all sure this is going to work. He is less verbal, more distant, with the woman presenting the more reasonable and emotionally complete explanation of the marital difficulty. It would be natural for her story to be better received. Were this to occur, however, there would be a consequent escalation of martial difficulty or a premature ending of the treatment. One can safely state that the couple used this male/female difference as their way to have a "nontherapy," and, in the process, got the therapist to assist in the creation of this "nontherapy."

Special care must then be exercised by the helper not to go along with this marital dance. A direct effort must be made to engage the man. Compliment the man for allowing his wife to be seen as the more cooperative spouse: "What an unselfish position you are taking." At the same time, you're complimenting the wife for working so hard: "You work so that your husband doesn't have to risk too much of himself in this marital work." If the therapist takes this position or something akin to this, it becomes impossible to be seduced into this family game of keeping the man distant and protected.

Conclusion

It is a truism that only through relationships can one stimulate personal growth. In trying to think about men in relationships, our emphasis has been placed on the man—not in terms of gender differences, but rather, how the family system cooperates to incorporate all gender differences, both male and female.

Given the culture we operate in, marriage is clearly the most useful vehicle for stimulating intimate relationships. It provides both men and women a structure to increase intimacy and personal growth. It is an imperfect institution peopled with imperfect marriage partners.

Marriage has existed in many historical forms. In Western culture an evolution of this institution in a technological society has resulted in a change in the very nature of the contract of marriage. Both women and men face new problems as the structure of marriage continues to evolve.

In the midst of this change exists the relationship of two people in context. Each has a history that contributes to a systemic balance. This chapter elevates the couple in relationship by saying, "What goes on between you is what you deserve. Change it if you choose to!"

This chapter provides an outline for a course to facilitate fathers' commitment and interaction with their children.

Chapter 7
COPING WITH THE NEW FATHER ROLE

Ronald F. Levant

Is There a New Father Role?

A lot has changed with regard to families in one short generation. The modal family of the 1950s, with a breadwinner husband and a homemaker wife, has been all but replaced by a plethora of new family forms. Only 9.8% of the population are married couples with children under 18 in which the husband is the sole breadwinner (U.S. Bureau of Labor Statistics, 1985). Single parent households, stepfamilies, and families where both parents work are the more common family forms today. Some of the factors contributing to this change include the development of the birth control pill in the late 1950s, which served to separate the pursuit of intimacy from the responsibilities of parenting; the explosion of divorce rates beginning in the 1960s, which more than doubled by 1979; the sharp increase in the employment of women in the 1970s, to the point where over half of all mothers of children under 6 are employed, and the reduction in the American standard of living to the point that membership in the middle class now requires two incomes.

All of this has served to generate considerable confusion regarding the roles of men in families. On the one hand there are some indications that the father's role has changed, and countless articles appear in the popular press touting the "new father," a parent who is personally involved in the day-to-day rearing of his children; on the other hand data suggest that the father's role has not changed all that much, and the airways are filled with television "talk" shows that decry the lack of male involvement in family life.

Changing Norms for the Father Role

Indications exist that there has been a significant change in the father's role. This phenomenon was illustrated in the popular 1979 film

81

Kramer vs. Kramer, in which Dustin Hoffman poignantly portrayed the struggles that some men were going through as they confronted their limitations in such areas as maintaining a home and caring for children. These men made some rather painful and difficult choices that limited their careers. This film seems to have tapped a heartfelt dimension, one that shows up in attitudinal studies that find that men's family roles are more significant to them psychologically than their paid work roles. These data include men's self-ratings of their psychological involvement in family and work (Erskine, 1973; Lein, Durham, Pratt, Schudson, Thomas, & Weiss, 1974; Pleck & Lang, 1978), and of the relative contributions of family and work experience to their sense of well-being (Andrews & Withey, 1976; Pleck & Lang).

This same deeply felt dimension is also being tapped by the advertising industry in the current trend of depicting men in nurturing roles in order to sell various products. A recent two-page magazine ad for Team Xerox shows a little girl looking out through a lace curtain. The caption reads:

> Sara really didn't expect her daddy to show up for her birthday party. His work never seemed to let up and his office wasn't exactly built for speed. But lately, he's been doing something about his office. He brought in Team Xerox. . . . The products and people of Team Xerox not only helped him get his office up to snuff, but also gave him one very important side benefit. The birthday party his daughter never forgot.

Ads like these are becoming more common and are being used to sell products such as insurance, credit cards, diamonds, film, and even soap. The point is that Madison Avenue is spending a lot of money promoting products by appealing to a nurturing spirit in men, which it most certainly would not do if it did not have reason to believe that such a spirit exists and is fairly widespread.

Other evidence that supports the view that the father's role has changed comes from the workplace and includes anecdotal and empirical accounts of the ways in which men are making compromises in their careers for the sake of their families. There are several manifestations of this trend. The first is increased father involvement in seeking child-care services, whether in the form of direct dependent-care financial assistance, "cafeteria style" benefits packages that include some child-care assistance, on-site child-care, or child-care information services (Catalyst, 1988).

The second manifestation is alternative work schedules, such as flexi-time, flexi-place, compressed 4-day work weeks, permanent part-time work, and job sharing. Although these job designs are still primarily used by women, the elderly, and the very young, men are increasingly utilizing them to balance work and family responsibilities. The third manifestation is resistance to relocation. Employees on management tracks are increasingly refusing to relocate, citing family needs as the reason (Catalyst, 1983). As a consequence, relocation policies are changing at many firms in order to respond to the family needs of their employees. The fourth manifestation is paternity leave, which is a new concept reflecting the importance that men place on being with their families during and shortly after the birth of their child. New evidence indicates that large numbers of fathers find some way to take time off from work, if not through formal paternity leave, then through sick child leave and the like (J. Pleck, personal communication, November 3, 1988). This phenomenon also shows up in the dramatic increase in the proportion of fathers attending the births of their children, which has risen from 27% in 1974 to 80% in 1984 (Lewis, 1986).

Traditional Norms of the Father Role Resisting Change

On the other hand, evidence exists that although the father's role has changed from what it used to be in the 1950s, it has not changed that much. In the middle and late 1960s, the time budget indicated that husbands' participation in family work was low (1.1 to 1.6 hours/day) compared to that of their wives (7.6 to 8.1 hours/day for housewives and 4.0 to 4.8 hours/day for employed wives) and that husbands tended to increase their participation only slightly (0.1 hour/day) in response to their wives' employment (Robinson, 1977; Walker & Woods, 1976). This had improved by a small amount by the mid 1970s due to husbands' doing more and wives' doing less. Using measures comparable to those used in the earlier studies, Pleck (1985) found that husbands put in 1.8 hours/day, housewives put in 6.8 hours/day, and employed wives put in 4.0 hours/day. This study was repeated in 1981, allowing an even more direct comparison of changes over time. In this later study, Juster and Stafford (1985) found a 20% to 30% increase in the amount of time husbands put into family work; however, husbands' participation in family work remained only about a third of that of their wives. Thus, men are doing more family work, but the lion's share of the responsibility still falls to women.

Reconciliation: The Culture Versus the Conduct of Fatherhood

We are in the midst of an era of social change in which certain aspects of men's roles are changing faster than others. LaRossa (1989) pinpointed the issue with his distinction between the *culture* of father-hood (the shared norms, beliefs, and values about fathering) and the *conduct* of fatherhood (what fathers actually do). We are living in an era in which we feel strongly that men can be involved, nurturing parents; but yet the men who are trying to enact this role find themselves falling short of the idealized model.

Various explanations have been put forward to account for this disparity between the culture and the conduct of fatherhood. Cowan and Bronstein (1988) identified the following factors: Mothers may be ambivalent about sharing the parenting role, and in subtle ways make it difficult for their husbands to be more involved; parenting programs and services have, in general, not been designed to accommodate fathers; and employers and legislators are not enthusiastic about men using work time for family concerns. Although I think all of these factors play a role, I would like to advance the hypothesis that *that the primary factor is the fact that men who are fathers today were simply not prepared for the role.* Their fathers—their primary role models—were cut from traditional cloth, and enacted the good provider/chief disciplinarian paternal role. Moreover, as boys, the current generation of fathers was socialized to be like their fathers. They did not play with dolls, nor mind their younger siblings, nor go to home economics classes, nor offer babysitting services to their neighbors.

More fundamentally, the current generation of adult men did not as boys learn psychological skills that are basic to being able to nurture and care for children. These skills include the ability to be empathically attuned to the feelings of others, and the ability to access and to become aware of their own feelings. While their sisters were taught to be sensitive to the feelings of others, boys were taught to be aggressive and com-petitive. If boys were ever taught anything about attentive listening, it was in the service of listening to one's opponent closely in order to identify the flaw in his position (Farrell, 1986). In regard to their own feelings, boys were told that "big boys don't cry," or, in sports, that they should learn to "play with pain," exhortations that served to train them to be out of touch with their own feelings, particularly those feelings on the vulnerable end of the spectrum.

Many fathers struggling with the new father role can receive sig-nificant aid from some form of remedial education, which helps them develop both the knowledge about parenting and the psychological skills that they need to enact the involved parent role. Later in this chapter, one such course (the Fatherhood Course) will be described. Before we get to that, it is necessary to take a closer look at the kinds of family contexts in which today's adult men are expected to enact the new father role: the working parent family, the post-divorce family, and the re-married family.

The New Father and the New American Families

In this section, we will consider the three family types most common today, with particular reference to the demands on the new father. Of necessity, the coverage will be brief, with the aim of highlighting the particular difficulties for today's father. Readers may wish to explore these topics in greater depth through some of the publications listed in the section on additional resources.

The Working Parent Family and the New Father Role

The working parent family, which includes both the dual career and the two paycheck family, is one of the most common family types today. Over 50% of couples now consist of two breadwinners. The growth of this family type parallels the rise in the employment of women, which increased from 26% of all women over 18 employed in 1960 to 30% in 1982.

The working parent family, while increasing role options and opportunities for life experiences for many men and women (particularly the dual career variant), brings with it a host of problems not encountered in the husband-as-breadwinner-wife-as-homemaker model. The major problem, for both men and women, is the lack of time. Indeed, the lack of time was the cover story in a recent issue of *Time* magazine entitled, "The Rat Race: How America Is Running Itself Ragged" (Michaels & Willworth, 1989). The lack of time results as two people try to manage their career or job and their family. The result is role overload and role strain.

The stresses on the working parent family are exacerbated by the lack of external supports and the existence of impediments. First and foremost, there is difficulty in finding child care, affordable, high-quality care, whether in the form of day care for preschoolers, after-school care for school-age children, or sick child care. Second, there is the lack of flexible workplace policies that might facilitate the balancing of multiple roles, policies such as flexible scheduling, parental leaves, flexible benefits, and family-sensitive relocation policies.

Another problem for working parents is role-cycling—that is, the process of transitioning between the demands of one role to the demands of the other. An example is the executive who comes home in the evening after a typical but very difficult workday, and whose wife is teaching a class that evening. Role-cycling requires that he shift gears from a fast-paced, perhaps aggressive, mode of functioning, to a softer, nurturing style as he prepares his children's dinner and hears about their concerns of the day.

There is also the problem of conflict between one's external role and psychological factors such as self-concept, identity, values, and moral commitments associated with gender issues. For women, a prominent issue is guilt over not fulfilling the homemaker role, guilt that may in fact be reinforced by her own mother reminding her (as the mother protests her daughter's work role), "But I was always home for you." A parallel issue for men is conflict over not fulfilling the good provider role. This can take many forms, from feeling competitive with, or inadequate in relationship to, his wife because of her earning power, to resenting his children for "holding him back."

The key to a workable family life lies in the parents' ability to hear each other's concerns in a nondefensive manner, to articulate their own complaints without blaming the other, and to work together in a flexible and creative way to find solutions to their conflicts. Many men living in a working parent family are at some disadvantage in working out the arrangements for a reasonably harmonious family life because they lack the requisite communication and negotiation skills. For these men, participation in a course that provides training in the psychological skills of listening and negotiation could be helpful.

Gilbert and Rachlin (1987) advised couples, particularly dual career couples, attempting to work out a set of balances in their family to seek "equity" rather than "equality." Given the psychosocial distance most parents are trying to traverse in the mere space of a generation, attaining a completely "50/50" split of all the household, child care, and paid work responsibilities is unrealistic for many couples. However, it is often quite possible to achieve a set of arrangements that both parents feel is *fair*. Equity is a more modest and ultimately more practical goal than equality.

The Post-Divorce Family and the New Father Role

We are living in the era of the "Divorce Revolution." The divorce rate climbed from 2.1 divorces per thousand population in 1958 to 5.3 in 1979, increasing more than 250% during this period. Since 1974 there have been more than one million divorces every year in this country. Fully one third of the children born in the 1980s are expected to live in a single-parent home at some time before they are 18 years of age.

The modal post-divorce family is a female-headed household with a noncustodial father who is required to provide financial support and is entitled to reasonable visitation with his children. This family form accounts for 9% of the post-divorce families; the rest consist of a smaller portion of couples with joint physical custody, and a larger portion of father-headed households. This section will focus on visitation father-hood. For an in-depth study of custodial fathers, see Greif (1985).

The reality of visitation fatherhood is bleak. Visitation tends to be maintained for the first 2 years, and then falls off. Furstenberg, Nord, Peterson, and Zill (1983) found that fewer than half of a national sample of children of divorce had seen their fathers once in the preceding 12 months. Child support was maintained better than visitation, but it too dropped off over time. The children pay a heavy price for this (Kelly, 1988), but the fathers suffer as well. Ambrose, Harper, and Pemberton (1983) found that all but one of their sample of nonvisiting fathers had developed a mental health problem since the divorce.

Many, if not most, divorces are characterized by ongoing conflict between the former spouses. This conflict must be resolved or set aside in order to facilitate continuing contact between the children and their noncustodial father. Noncustodial fathers are at a particular disadvantage for dealing with post-divorce conflict because of the shift in the balance of power in favor of their wives. As mentioned above, men of this generation have not, in general, been prepared to be good listeners or flexible negotiators; in fact, as boys they were trained to resolve conflicts through the exercise of power, in the form of physical strength, verbal facility, or a superior strategy. I would advance the hypothesis that many men call it quits with visitation because they cannot tolerate feeling so powerless in the face of unremitting conflict.

Numerous problems bring these issues to a head: experiencing passive resistance or outright hostility to his visits from his ex-wife; feeling left out of his child's upbringing ("feeling like a distance uncle," as one man put it to me); or feeling like a social director (which is common among men who have only weekend visitation). Many non-custodial fathers need to learn a new way of functioning and a new set of skills to make visitation work. They need to learn to modulate the one emotion they have been permitted, even encouraged to have—anger. They need to learn to become aware of and find constructive ways of expressing those other feelings they have not been allowed to have, the feelings on the vulnerable end of the spectrum: hurt, disappointment, rejection, sadness, shame, fear, helplessness, and even powerlessness. They need to learn how to see things from their ex-wife's point of view (and recognize, for example, that one reason she may be resisting visitation is because her time with the kids has decreased significantly due to her having to work outside of the home). Men need to learn to find ways to give their ex-wife some credit as a parent (which may help defuse that part of her hostility that stems from feeling undermined). These are not difficult skills to learn, but the stressful circumstances following divorce do not make learning easy. However, the alternative is far worse.

The Remarried Family and the New Father Role

Because the modal post-divorce family is female-headed, the typical remarried family consists of a mother with her children, who have been living together for some years as a single-parent family (and have drawn together closely during the process), and an outsider—the stepfather. He may have children of his own, living with his former wife, and with whom he has visitation. Then there is his stepchildren's father, who has visitation with them.

Remarried families are on the rise, due to the high divorce rates and the tendency of 80% of divorced adults to remarry within 3 years of their divorce. By the time this book is published, 25% of all children under 18 are expected to have lived some time in their childhood in a stepfamily.

Many of the problems that stepfathers confront have to do with establishing themselves in their new families. Many people approach second marriages with unrealistic expectations, hoping for instant love between themselves and their stepchildren. These expectations often result from attempts to compensate for feelings of failure regarding first marriages and lead to trouble very quickly, for the stepfamily is laced with visible loyalties and strung with impermeable boundaries. A stepfather must wait as long as 2 years before he is let into the family. It is not only the children with their loyalties to their biological father and to the former nuclear and single-parent families who will take their sweet time to accept their stepfather; his wife will also have some difficulty letting him into a co-parental role. This latter, somewhat paradoxical phenomenon often manifests itself in discipline encounters in which the stepfather attempts to set the limit, the child complains to the mother, who then sides with the child.

To make stepfamilies work, a stepfather needs to be realistic about the difficulties and should negotiate his role explicitly with his wife, preferably before the wedding. He also must be prepared to experience a lot of painful rejection; hence the comments made above about the visitation-father's needs for self-awareness and skills in processing vulnerable feelings apply to the stepfather as well.

By this point, it should be obvious that the comment that "being a father today is difficult" is a gross understatement. I mentioned earlier men's lack of preparation for an involved parenting role, even under the best of circumstances. But when one takes into account the stress and complexity of modern families, the urgent need for remedial education becomes quite clear. To give the reader some guidance as to how to help men become "new fathers," I will turn now to a discussion of the Fatherhood Course.

The Fatherhood Course

The Fatherhood Project at Boston University has been offering a course designed to help men become better fathers. Simply called the Fatherhood Course, it meets one evening per week, and teaches fathers communication skills, particularly learning to listen and respond to their children's feelings, and to become aware of and express their own feelings in a constructive manner. In addition, it teaches fathers about child development and child management. The course uses a skill-training format, in which fathers role-play the particular skills in relationship to situations that have emerged in their own families, with videotape used to provide instant feedback. In addition, each father receives a workbook containing exercises that can be done at home, including interactional exercises to do with his children.

The course is a psychoeducational group that can be used for prevention (with high-risk fathers). But most often it is used to facilitate the adult development of men as parents. It is thus informed by life-span developmental psychology.

The approach to fostering father's development comes from: (1) the cognitive social development literature, which describes how social perspective-taking in parents develops through a stagewise sequence; and (2) the Rogerian literature on the characteristics of effective relationships in counseling and parenting, which highlights the importance of empathy. Both literatures are utilized to help fathers learn to take their child's perspective with increasing degrees of empathic sensitivity, and to balance their child's and their own perspective on the father's role. Thus, fathers learn about the important issues with regard to the cognitive, social, emotional, and moral development of their children, such as how fathers may act as "gatekeepers" for their sons' and daughters' sex role attitudes and behaviors.

The program is designed to fit men's traditional learning styles. It is not held out as counseling, and men are not initially required to talk about their feelings (although most eventually do). Instead, it is offered as an educational program with an opportunity to develop skills. When men first walk into the room, hardware is immediately in evidence in the form of video equipment, which may provide a sense of familiarity, in terms of men's traditional relationship to machines. Furthermore, they are told that we will teach them to be better fathers in a manner comfortable to them, in much the same ways they might have learned to play a sport such as football or tennis.

The outline for the course is detailed in the Leader's Guide (Levant & Doyle, 1981a). The course is usually co-taught by the author (a father) and an advanced doctoral student in counseling psychology (who may or may not be a father himself) who has had training in parent-child interaction and in leading structured groups. The first half of the course focuses on listening and responding to children, beginning with a session on nonverbal parental behaviors that can facilitate communication, such as staying at eye-level with the child and maintaining an open-body posture. In the next session fathers learn about responding reflectively to the content of a child's message. In the third session, fathers learn about listening empathically to a child's feelings. The fourth session is devoted to review, integration, and practice.

In the second half of the course, fathers work on speaking for themselves, beginning with a session on increasing their awareness of the thoughts and feelings that emerge that interacting with their children. This is one of the most difficult sessions because many men have been socialized to tune out most of their feelings. We begin by developing a lexicon of the full spectrum of feelings. Fathers are then taught to tune in to their feelings through watching and discussing immediate play-backs of role-plays in which feelings were engendered. By pointing out the nonverbal cues and asking such questions as "What were your feelings, Don, when you grimaced in that last segment?", fathers learn to access the ongoing flow of emotions within. Next comes a session on learning to express thoughts and feelings in a nondefensive, open manner. In the segment on acceptance, the fathers examine their own personal sensitivities in order to become more accepting of their children's feelings and behavior. The final session is devoted to termination and includes a graduation ceremony.

The program includes didactic and experiential components. A typical format for a session is as follows: (1) introduction and definition of the particular skill to be covered in a brief lecture; (2) demonstration of the skill using videotaped and live examples, usually role-plays between the two instructors; (3) discrimination training, in which the instructors role-play parent-child situations, demonstrating varying degrees of skillfulness—and with the fathers rating and discussing the role-played examples; (4) practice of the skill in role-play exercises, using videotape for immediate feedback; and (5) consolidating and transferring the skill to the interaction with their children through homework assignments from the Father's Workbook (Levant & Doyle, 1981b). Fathers are expected to spend 1 hour per week on homework, including readings, paper-and-pencil exercises that progress from asking the fathers to discriminate between good and poor responses to asking them to formulate their own good responses, and interactional exercises. Completed assignments are discussed in class each week.

The in-class role plays in which the fathers participate serve several important functions. They are drawn from the discussion of the previous week's homework, in particular, from the interactional exercises between father and child. It is not uncommon that several fathers will have experienced difficulties in carrying out these exercises with their children, and it is also likely that these difficulties will reflect long-term problems in the father-child relationship. By selecting the role plays in this manner, several purposes are served. For one thing, difficulties are attended to, so that hurdles are overcome and motivation remains high. It is highly possible in such short-term structured groups for unsatisfactory experiences with the homework to lead to discouragement, which can be expressed either in the form of dropping out of the group or participating at a pseudomutual level. For another, by focusing on the longer-term issues as they have emerged during the homework, we work on the structural problems in the family, but do so in a way that an optimal balance between safety and depth is achieved. Ostensibly we are working on the fathers' difficulties in learning the skills—but in the process, the fathers enact the difficulties in their relationships with their children, which then become available for modification. An additional benefit of focusing on such longer-term issues is that a climate of engagement and genuineness is created in the group.

The role plays are performed in two different ways. At times we have the father role-play himself, while another participant plays the child. In these cases, the goal is to have the father learn the skills and apply them to his interaction with his child. At other times the father role-plays his child. In these instances the intent is to help the father develop an appreciation of the child's point of view, and also to learn how his child experiences him. This latter learning can be quite profound in helping fathers modify their approach to their children.

The fathers who participate in the course come from all walks of life, from laborer to plumber to lawyer to stockbroker. Their ages have ranged from the late 20s to the mid-50s, with their children's ages ranging from early infancy to young adulthood. About half the men are married and half divorced, with a few of them remarried and working out a "reconstituted" family. Those who are divorced have custody arrangements ranging from visitation to joint custody to sole custody.

Though the men are successful in the workplace and fulfill the "good provider" role, they experience dissatisfaction with their relationships with their own fathers, or articulate a desire to not make some of the mistakes with their children that their fathers made with them. Others feel inadequate with their children, and marvel at how well their wives "do it" when it comes to simple tasks such as getting 10-year-old Timmy to bed. Mom can do it with four words, yet for Dad it is often a half-hour struggle that usually ends in tears and frustration. Some are very uncomfortable with feelings, both their own and their children's. Others get caught in the "anger trap" and become ensnared in unproductive repetitive patterns of testing and punishment.

Many assume at the onset that they know how to communicate with their children. Two fathers in particular, who thought their communication skills were adequate, were shocked to see videotaped replays of role-playing sessions. One saw himself towering over his child, the other talking from behind a newspaper. Another noted, "The idea that being a father is a learned skill never occurred to me."

About halfway through the course, after fathers have had some success at mastering the skills, some report that they are finding the skills useful not only with their children, but with their wives, and others at the workplace as well. For example, one father said:

> I found the lessons in practicing communication particularly valuable. I would add the concept—the one most people miss—that communication is generally undervalued and completely misunderstood in our society. I think that people must feel as though they are doing fine, when in fact they are not dealing with the emotional level at all, in many, many cases.

And another observed:

> Like I said in the beginning, not only family members, but I'm using the listening skills in my job. I'm taking those same skills that we developed, and applying them so that if I'm talking to an employee, and the employee is having a problem, I try to develop some trust with that person, establish eye contact, and respond to his statement by saying the statement back to let him know that I'm listening.

The Fatherhood Course has been evaluated (Levant & Doyle, 1983). Experimental group fathers, their wives, and one of their children were compared to control group families before and after training on several paper-and-pencil measures. Fathers' communication skills were assessed using the Sensitivity to Children Scale (in which fathers are presented with vignettes of children's behavior and are asked to respond with written statements to what they would say if the child depicted were their own) and the Porter Acceptance Scale (a multiple-choice instrument). Fathers' and mothers' views of their actual and ideal families were assessed using the Family Concept Test, a multiple-choice test that gives measures of family satisfaction (correlation between the parents' real and ideal family concepts) and family congruence (correlations between husbands' and wives' real, or ideal, family concepts). And children's perceptions of their fathers were assessed using interviews and the Kinetic Family Drawing Test, in which the child was asked to draw a picture of his or her family doing something together.

The evaluation found that training resulted in an improvement of fathers' communication skills—specifically, a significant increase in overall sensitivity, a significant reduction in the use of undesirable responses, a trend toward increased use of desirable responses, and a trend toward increased acceptance of the child's expression of feelings. In addition, a complex pattern of findings of fathers' and mothers' real and ideal family concepts suggested that, as a result of the course, fathers underwent a cognitive restructuring, changing their views of the ideal family.

Changes also were seen in children's perceptions of their fathers, with significantly more experimental than control group children perceiving positive changes in their relationships. A telling example was the change in one boy's pre- and post-course Kinetic Family Drawing. Before the course began the child drew a picture of a roller coaster, with the tracks filling 90% of the page. At the very top was a tiny little car. In the front seat was the boy, legs and arms akimbo, in the next seat was Mom and then Dad, and in the last seat was his brother, who appeared to be falling out of the car. After the course was over, the boy drew a picture of a spaceship running diagonally across the page in which the cockpit filled about 40% of the page. Seated at the control was Dad; next to him, Mom. At opposite sides, looking out the window, were he and his brother. From a clinical perspective, this sequence of pictures suggests a remarkable transformation of family structure and emotional climate.

Conclusion

This chapter first asked the question of whether there is a new father role. Both the evidence for such a new role and the evidence against it were presented. These conflicting lines of evidence were reconciled using LaRossa's (1989) distinction between the culture and the conduct of fatherhood: There is a change in how fatherhood is viewed in the contemporary United States toward a more nurturing role; however, the men who are trying to enact this role find themselves falling short of the cultural ideal. The author then advanced the hypothesis that the major factor producing this shortfall is that men who are fathers today were not prepared for the nurturing father role.

The second part of the chapter took a closer look at the kinds of families in which today's adult men are expected to enact the new father role: the working parent family, the post-divorce family, and the remarried family. In a very brief review, some of the more prevalent difficulties fathers face in each of these family types were highlighted.

Finally, after having made what I hope is a convincing case for the need for services for fathers, particularly fatherhood education, one such service (the Fatherhood Course developed by the author at Boston University) was presented in some detail. The course is unique in that it was designed specifically for men, and has been successful in engaging men.

In today's world, men are asked to "provide for their families" as well as actively father their children. They have been trained to do the former but not the latter. I have described a fatherhood course which provides fathers both the skills and support for effective patenting. Given the stress and complexity of modern families, the urgent need for remedial education to engage men to cope optimally as fathers becomes quite clear.

A number of authors in this book have alluded to the negative effect produced by the "absent father." It is my hope that the father can become reengaged in the family in expressive, nurturing, and educational ways as well as in financial and protective ways.

---

1. The material in the section, "The Fatherhood Course," is reprinted from Levant, R. F. (1988), Education for fatherhood, In P. Bronstein and C. P. Cowan (Eds.), *Fatherhood today: Men's changing role in the family*. New York: Wiley Interscience. Copyright © 1988, John Wiley & Sons, Inc. Reprinted by Permission.

The traditional view of the male role assumes that men derive their major life satisfaction from extrafamilial endeavors . . . yet men may be at equal or greater risk for the negative consequences of divorce.

Chapter 8

DIVORCE: ARE MEN AT RISK?

Patrick C. McKenry and Sharon J. Price

The divorce rate has more than doubled in the last 20 years to the extent that two thirds of all first marriages today are likely to end in divorce (Martin & Bumpass, 1989). Although divorce has become almost commonplace, even termed by some as a normative life transition, there is not a lot of knowledge to guide men through the transition. What we do know is focused on women as it has been widely assumed that women, with custody of children and fewer economic resources, are at greater risk for any ill effects of divorce. In addition, American society has not readily responded to the many needs of divorced individuals, especially those of men. The traditional view of the male role assumes that men derive their major life satisfaction from extrafamilial endeavors, that they are not as emotionally upset by the termination of relationships, and that they are self-sufficient and strong enough to take care of their own problems without the assistance of others. Yet research suggests that men may be at equal or even greater risk for the negative consequences of divorce and are often less able to cope with the emotional consequences. Social changes such as greater participation of women in the labor force, increased alternatives to traditional marriage, the rising standard for individual happiness in marriage, and the declining stigma of divorce have been related both to recent high divorce rates (Cherlin, 1981; Weitzman, 1981) and confusion for men who are attempting to deal with such radical change in traditional gender role prescriptions.

Divorce as Process

Divorce is perhaps best conceptualized as a developmental process that begins long before the actual physical separation. Kessler (1975) spoke of a marriage dying by inches, a little at a time, beginning early in the marriage. Although men and women may respond differently to divorce, there are no indications they experience the basic grief/loss adaptation process of divorce differently (i.e., denial, mourning, anger, and readjustment). Several authors have developed models that describe this developmental process in some detail, including Kessler, who has developed a six-stage paradigm:

1. *Disillusionment.* This initial period of marital instability is characterized by disenchantment with the marriage, fault finding with the spouse, and the realization that real differences exist in the marriage.
2. *Erosion.* This stage is described as the period of emotional divorce; focus is on taking rather than giving; and anger and hurt are openly expressed. Stress related to this stage may be evident in physical symptoms including migraine headaches, anxiety, or impotence.
3. *Detachment.* At this point the individual no longer invests in marriage and thoughts shift to the future, such as fantasies about what life would be without the spouse, assessment of the financial situation, and evaluation of the potential for future relationships.
4. *Separation.* This period of actual physical separation is the time of most stress (Weiss, 1975). Separation is a public declaration that a marriage is not working and a time of learning new roles and behaviors. Men especially will experience dramatic change in their life-styles at this time.
5. *Mourning.* The individual at this stage feels sad about the "death of the marriage," and may also feel angry, hurt, lonely, and helpless. Although anger is generally focused toward the former spouse, a common response during this period is depression as the result of blaming oneself.
6. *Recovery.* At this point, the individual accepts that the marriage is over, and a degree of objectivity about the marriage and the former spouse develops. Divorced persons at this stage concentrate on personal growth by either engaging in a "second adolescence,"—an almost vengeful pursuit of sex, travel, fun, or clothes, or exploration and hard work—curtailing their previous anxious floundering and recommitting to their life goals.

Divorce Adjustment

Much research on divorce adjustment has centered on the question of who is most adversely affected by separation and divorce, men or women. Research findings are presently inconclusive, but some evidence suggests that men are at greater risk for emotional disturbance, especially during the separation stage. The person who initiates the divorce typically has the advantage of having worked through the divorce process for some time prior to the actual decision. In most cases, it is the women who are the initiators, which means that men usually have more difficulty accepting the divorce, experience greater loneliness, are angrier, and report higher stress (Buehler, 1987; Spanier & Thompson, 1984). This phenomenon has been referred to as the "abandoned male" syndrome stemming from the growing number of women who are initiating divorce today because more options are available to them (Myers, 1986).

Men are also thought to be more vulnerable to marital separation because of their tendency to deny or suppress feelings. Men often use buffers such as work or excessive social activity to avoid dealing with emotional problems (Chiriboga & Cutler, 1978; Wallerstein & Kelly, 1980; Weiss, 1975). Men's greater discomfort as a result of separation suggests that men may be less prepared to cope with object loss and, contrary to popular belief, experience greater difficulty in recovering from attachments (Krantzler, 1973). Also, androgynous behaviors have been related to less divorce-related distress (Bloom & Clement, 1984; Chiriboga & Thurnher, 1980), and women are typically more androgynous than men. This is consistent with Bem's (1977) work, which has found that androgynous role behaviors are more adaptive, especially during times of major stress.

In addition to greater separation-related stress, some evidence also indicates that the total divorce experience may constitute a more severe emotional impact for men (Albrecht, Bahr, & Goodman, 1983; Weiss, 1975) because they exhibit more symptoms of emotional and physical disturbances than do divorced women (Bloom & Caldwell, 1981; Gove, 1973). In addition, men have been found to take longer to adjust to divorce and experience lower levels of adjustment (Price-Bonham, Wright, & Pittman, 1982). These gender differences have been attributed to men's tendency to deny their dependency needs and their feelings about the loss of their children, friends, home, possessions, and sometimes status. (It should be noted that although men may fare less well in some respects in the short term, long-term differences between men and women may be minimized because of the greater economic assets of divorced men and their greater likelihood to remarry.)

Relationships With Former Spouses

Traditionally, it has been assumed that divorce meant complete termination of any relationship with the former spouse. Today, however, it is increasingly viewed as "normal" or appropriate for former spouses to maintain regular contact, particularly if they have children. This acceptance of a post-divorce relationship between spouses is reflected by the terms we now use to refer to these relationships, such as *former spouses* instead of *ex-spouses*, and *binuclear family* (Ahrons, 1979) instead of *post-divorce family* or *broken home*. This post-divorce relationship is still difficult for former spouses because of the lack of societal norms and role models (Ahrons, 1980), and couples often have difficulty determining where their former-spouse relationship ends and their parental relationship begins (Roberts & Price, 1985/1986). In addition to the co-parental relationship, most divorced persons experience some feelings of attachment toward their former spouse, and this may be greater for men than for women (Gertsel, Reissman, & Rosenfield, 1985; Price-Bonham et al., 1982). This complex bond, which does not necessarily decrease with time (Kitson, 1982), may be manifested through recurrent thoughts and images of the former spouse, attempts to contact or learn about her, feelings of missing part of oneself, loneliness, and even panic (Berman, 1985; Bloom & Kindle, 1985; Weiss, 1975). In some cases, the attachment even may result in continuation of sexual relations. This attachment to a former spouse also may result in ambivalent feelings—the desire to reconcile and yet feeling angry because of the former spouse's role in the production of separation distress (Spanier & Thompson, 1984). Although some authors have contended that these former spouse attachments are dysfunctional in terms of readjustment to a new life-style (Krantzler, 1973; Kressel & Deutsch, 1977), others contend that the continuation of a former spouse relationship is desirable, primarily because of the fact that it facilitates a closer relationship between the father and his children, and it is generally maladaptive or less comfortable to maintain animosity toward a former intimate (Daniel, 1977; Wright & Price, 1986).

Historically, it was assumed that a man would be linked to a former spouse primarily for economic reasons in fulfilling his traditional role as the good provider. Today, however, in the era of changing sex roles and "no fault" divorce, this assumption has been seriously challenged. Criteria used in determining alimony awards have shifted from "fault" reasons to the needs of the wife and the ability of the husband to pay (McCubbin & Dahl, 1985). In general, only women with custodial responsibility for children, those who need transitional support to become self-supporting, and those who are incapable of becoming self-supporting are viewed by the courts as deserving of alimony (Weitzman, 1985). It cannot be assumed, however, that older women and younger women with children automatically will be awarded alimony. Rather, only 15% of all men are required to pay their former wives alimony, and this is often a "transitional" or temporary award for an average of 2 years (Weitzman, 1985). Also, it should be noted that the alimony awards are typically small—the mean award in 1983 was approximately $3,000.

Furthermore, few husbands pay the decreed award on a regular basis; less than half of women due alimony payments in 1985 received full payment (U.S. Bureau of the Census, 1987).

Fathers are still legally viewed as having the primary financial responsibility for their children as determined through court-mandated child support awards. However, only about one half of the children awarded child support actually receive it (U.S. Bureau of the Census, 1987). Several reasons have been put forth to account for the failure of so many divorced fathers to pay the decreed child support awards. Some contend that fathers cannot afford to pay, but several authors have refuted this claim as fathers seldom are ordered to pay more than a third of their income for child support, and many fathers are better off financially after the divorce than while married (Weitzman, 1985). Some noncustodial fathers' feelings of emotional distance from their children as well as remarriage make it economically and psychologically burdensome to support two households (Wallerstein & Kelly, 1980). Also, because of the lack of societal norms regarding divorced fathers' roles and presence in the divorced family, there may be a lack of clarity regarding their obligations. Then, too, the lack of strong enforcement mechanisms to guarantee that court-ordered child support is paid is an obvious factor. Interestingly, divorced men have indicated that even though they are not complying with child support, they state that they could and should be doing so (Haskins, Dobelstein, Akin, & Schwartz, 1987). This would suggest that men who are not fulfilling their support obligations are experiencing much guilt.

Life as a Divorced Single Man

The establishment of a new life-style may be more problematic for some men than going through the divorce itself (Spanier & Casto, 1979). Divorce usually involves extensive changes in family ties, friendships, leisure activities, and sexual behaviors (Hetherington, Cox, & Cox, 1976).

Social Supports

Family members, especially parents, are generally very supportive in providing temporary financial assistance, housing, and a wide range of services including emotional support and child care (Albrecht et al., 1983; Spanier & Casto, 1979). Men, however, receive less support than women probably due to the fact that they usually do not have custody of their children, typically have greater economic resources, and are socialized to seem self-sufficient (McKenry & Price, in press).

The reaction of friends to divorce ranges from genuine concern to disinterest (Krantzler, 1973). Friends are often important sources of social support, but it is not unusual for divorced persons to find their pre-divorce friendships decline in interaction and importance. This change may be the result of friends "taking sides," lacking knowledge of how to incorporate a single friend into their couple-oriented world, being threatened by divorce, or merely feeling awkward (Spanier & Thompson, 1984; Weiss, 1975). In addition, divorced persons themselves may be responsible for the decline in these friendships as they move out of the neighborhood, work longer hours to meet increased economic demands, or prefer to socialize with other divorced persons (Hunt & Hunt, 1977; Spanier & Thompson, 1984; Price & McKenry, 1988).

Divorced men maintain more contact with married friends than do divorced women, and these friends tend to be very helpful (Gertsel, 1988; Hetherington et al., 1976; Milardo, 1987). This is probably because married friends are often developed through occupational roles. In addition, men without partners are viewed by society as more lonely and emotionally helpless and thus in greater need of support. Because men do have more trouble establishing social relationships, they are more likely than women to use organized activities such as continuing education, athletics, or hobbies to form friendships (Albrecht et al., 1983; McKenry & Price, in press).

Living Single

Men experience more difficulty in living a single life-style after divorce than do women. They are less well socialized to function autonomously and are often reluctant to master the skills necessary for independent living because these activities are not viewed as part of the socially defined male role (Johnson, 1977). Thus, the more androgynous man should be at an advantage in adapting to life as a single person.

Men may be particularly vulnerable because they have been both emotionally and physically dependent to a significant extent on their former spouse to manage their lives. Also, they have been socialized to be "strong," that is, to manage all their responsibilities without help. This show of independence may, however, be a disguise for withdrawal and inability to reorganize one's life, and indicates that such individuals are at high risk for personal distress and a reduced level of functioning (Weiss, 1975).

Dating

Perhaps the most important factor in improving the self-esteem of divorced men and women is the establishment of a satisfying intimate relationship (Hetherington, Cox, & Cox, 1978). Dating is an important step in this process and serves a variety of other functions including socialization to the "world of the formerly married," self-appraisal, companionship, and therapeutic support (Hunt & Hunt, 1977).

The "double standard" works as an advantage for post-divorce dating men. They more often feel it appropriate to initiate dating, and seldom have the responsibility or problems associated with child custody (Price & McKenry, in press). Men also have more resources to spend on dating, have fewer age constraints in selecting partners, and a man's attractiveness is not so highly related to physical appearance as is a woman's (McKenry & Price, in press). Yet divorced men do tend to exhibit fears that prevent them from establishing long-term relationships. These fears include rejection, loss, and damage to self-esteem. Some divorced men try to place limits on their feelings to avoid emotional commitments for fear of making "another" mistake (Hunt & Hunt, 1977). Also, men may feel awkward in a youth-oriented dating world, and they also may have difficulty adjusting to the more sexually assertive role of women (Weiss, 1975). In terms of sexuality per se, divorced men report satisfaction with their sexual experiences, and their sexual activity is highly correlated with their overall sense of well-being (Spanier & Thompson, 1984).

Fathers

Sources of Stress

Fatherhood seems to compound men's vulnerability to negative consequences of divorce. For the vast majority of fathers (approximately 90%), divorce means the loss of physical custody of their children. The threatened loss of their relationship with their children is, in fact, a chief complaint of men in the midst of divorce crisis (Jacobs, 1982). The father's own emotional reaction and eventual adjustment to divorce is inevitably intertwined with that of his children. Almost all children experience divorce as a major crisis event, regardless of whether it was anticipated or how "friendly" the divorce may have been. Parental divorce generates an emotional loss response in children that lasts at least 2 to 3 years (Hetherington, Stanley-Hagan, & Anderson, 1989). Although some children are remarkably resilient, many others are still dealing with divorce-related issues into adulthood (Wallerstein & Blakeslee, 1989).

Because of the father's own emotional instability, he is often not in a position adequately to comfort his children, provide a clear, rational explanation for the divorce, or generally to parent effectively—a phenomenon that has been termed a "diminished capacity to parent" (Wallerstein & Kelly, 1980). Especially, separated parents, when compared with parents in intact families, are less consistent and effective with discipline, are less nurturant, communicate less well, and make fewer demands for mature behaviors (Hetherington et al., 1978).

For the noncustodial father, single-parenting status usually means dealing with numerous losses—the loss of a familiar residence and neighborhood, daily routine, accustomed social supports, and, in many cases, the loss of a meaningful relationship with his children. This transition requires radical restructuring of his household and family roles.

Additional stress is created for these noncustodial fathers because of their lack of skills in managing a household. In fact, many fathers initially live what has been described as a "chaotic" life-style as they attempt to maintain a household, economically provide for their children, and parent their children without the support of a spouse. For example, noncustodial fathers, compared to married men, are more likely to rely on carry-out meals, eat at irregular times, have more erratic sleep patterns, and have more difficulty with household tasks (Hetherington et al., 1976).

Divorced fathers who economically support two households often experience financial problems. These problems are accentuated by remarriage as the fathers have new responsibilities and a spouse who may resent resources going to a former spouse. In addition, divorced fathers may be in continual conflict with former spouses over finances. Thus, many divorced fathers will increase their work load to compensate as well as to escape emotionally from the trauma associated with the divorce and establishment of a new life-style. This tendency of divorced fathers to increase their work load combined with an emotional instability to work effectively actually increases their level of stress (Price & McKenry, 1988).

Noncustodial fathers, like other divorced men, usually experience social isolation and loneliness. Many divorced fathers feel inept in living as single persons because they have lived much of their adult lives as married with children. These feelings of loneliness and isolation, along with a loss of social definition, contribute to the frantic social and sexual activity commonly seen in newly separated men (Myers, 1986).

Parenting Difficulties

As they move beyond the initial crisis period of separation and divorce, noncustodial fathers continue to experience difficulties in parenting. They still have trouble communicating with their children, establishing appropriate maturity demands, and remaining consistent in their discipline. Because many fathers relied heavily on their wives to initiate activities and communicate with their children, they even may lack the knowledge of how to interact with their children (Moreland & Schwebel, 1981). Divorced fathers thus often are consumed with feelings of incompetence and failure as parents. These feelings are reinforced by a society that blames men for divorce and fails to support or even acknowledge the importance of their noncustodial parenting role. In addition, some fathers experience much guilt regarding their children being deprived of both parents and thus compensate by being permissive and overly attentive to them, often in the form of providing extravagant gifts or activities—a phenomenon that some have described as the "Disneyland" or "Santa Claus" father. On the other hand, some fathers may feel that the children are the source of all their problems and thus may have hostile feelings toward them (Tedder & Scherman, 1987).

Noncustodial fathers do not parent in isolation from the former spouse, although this may be desired in many cases. Their parental relationship does not terminate with legal divorce, and the cooperation achieved in co-parenting by former spouses is highly related to positive outcomes for their children. Some men and women who have not adjusted to their divorce may not only fail to cooperate in parenting, but may, in fact, use the children as pawns to vent anger toward their former spouse. Such conflict also may serve as a way for the divorced spouse, especially men, to maintain an emotional relationship following divorce (Hetherington et al., 1989).

Most noncustodial fathers report dissatisfaction with the visitation experiences with their children. Many fathers experience the visitations with their children as painful because each visit forces them to renew the mourning process. Many begin to feel that they are no longer fathers, that they are no longer needed, and that their authority as a parent has been eroded (Atkin & Rubin, 1976). Some noncustodial fathers even reduce contact with their children because it is so painful (Hetherington et al., 1976) or in extreme cases may resort to child snatching or kidnapping. Many other fathers find visitation to be so artificial and meaningless that over time they gradually reduce contact.

Thus, noncustodial fathers increasingly socialize with their children from an emotional distance and with a great deal of laxity, becoming pals more than parents. In a national survey of children several years after divorce, it was found that fathers averaged only two visits per month, and almost half of the children had not seen their father in the past year (Furstenberg & Nord, 1985). Fathers are more likely to visit younger children and sons frequently and consistently as these relationships are perceived as easier to maintain because these children are more responsive (Wallerstein & Kelly, 1980). Noncustodial fathers' relinquishing of caregiving responsibilities after divorce also may be related to conflict with their former spouse, inability or unwillingness to maintain required financial support, barriers imposed by the legal system that fail to support fathers' rights, or merely a lack of interest in parenting.

When a father does have responsibility for his children on a frequent basis or for long periods of time, he is more likely to view his role as significant, to be less depressed, and to continue to provide emotional and financial support (Friedman, 1980; Lowery & Settle, 1985). Despite the lack of preparation for the single-parent role and the many problems associated with the noncustodial parent role, a substantial number of noncustodial fathers do report closer, more meaningful relationships with their children than existed during their marriage.

Custody Alternatives

In recent years, fathers have sought more involvement in the post-divorce parenting of their children. As a result, an increasing number of divorcing fathers now seek primary or joint custody, although this group is still a small minority. Most fathers who seek primary custody do so out of love and concern for their children, not to hurt their former spouse or because they believe their spouse is an unfit parent, as is often believed. The father who is most likely to seek custody tends to be more highly educated and financially secure, and his children are older, more often boys (Norton & Glick, 1986).

Fathers with primary custody initially report feeling confused and apprehensive about their parenting abilities, but most soon indicate feeling comfortable and competent as single fathers—regardless of their reason for seeking primary custody (Hetherington et al., 1989; Risman, 1986). These fathers clearly seem to have a more meaningful paternal role than do noncustodial fathers (Stewart, Schwebel, & Fine, 1986). In addition, it has been found that custodial fathers experience many of the same problems of custodial mothers (Mendes, 1976). However, some fathers with primary custody report feeling ostracized by the community because of their unique status.

Increasingly joint custody is being sought by parents and even advocated by courts to provide children with greater accessibility to both parents and to maintain greater equity between former spouses. Joint legal custody sometimes includes joint physical custody, but usually it is merely legal recognition of the rights of both parents to make major decisions regarding their children; under joint custody, physical custody is usually awarded to the mother with liberal visitation given the father (Flynn, 1987). Preliminary studies have reported much satisfaction with the arrangement by both parents and children; however, many of these

studies involved amicable divorces in which parents were able to make
sacrifices to maintain parental responsibilities (Hetherington et al., 1989).
The success of joint custody is contingent on parental cooperation, flexibility, mutual support, and respect—characteristics that usually do not
describe most marriages at the time of divorce (Price & McKenry, 1988).
Divorcing parents thus should be sure that they can develop and maintain such a relationship with one another if joint custody is to be beneficial
to their children.

Case Studies

The research findings on the effects of divorce on men are reflected
in the following case scenarios of three men in different stages of the
divorce process: (a) a father experiencing separation distress; (b) a man
experiencing difficulty adjusting to a single life-style; and (c) a remarried
father dealing with loyalty issues.

Lee

Lee and Elizabeth are in the process of dissolving a 28-year marriage.
They have two children, a daughter, Sue, who is married, and a son,
Don, who is a senior in high school. Lee and Elizabeth have gradually
grown apart through the years of their marriage and have very rationally
decided to divorce. They have reached a mutually satisfactory settlement
agreement out of court that will allow both to live comfortably in their
newly chosen life-styles. The pre-divorce relationship between Lee and
Elizabeth has been mature and conciliatory to the extent that Lee has
remained in the family home while searching for a suitable residence of
his own. On the morning of the day Lee moves from the home, a myriad
of unexpected feelings emerge that have been previously suppressed.
Lee goes through the typical morning routine of breakfast with his spouse
and son with intense feelings of pain, loss, and failure buried in ritual
and the stoicism of the male role. As Elizabeth leaves for work and his
son goes to school, the reality of the impending divorce is overwhelming.
As Lee moves around the house waiting for the moving van to arrive,
his mind becomes a kaleidoscope of memories. He has a need to say
good-bye to each room and attempt to capture the positive aspects of
his life reflected in each room. When Lee arrives at his new apartment,
he is struck by the significant difference between his former and his new
"home"—it is smaller, more compact, has few familiar furnishings, and
has the sound of neighbors barely audible in the background. Lee begins
putting away his belongings realizing that for the first time in his adult

life, he is truly responsible for his own life, and this feels both good and bad. He knows that the decision to divorce was right, but he also feels an enormous loss and is apprehensive about the impending changes in his life.

Doug

Doug is 28 years old and has been divorced for 1 year from his wife of 4 years, Sandra. Sandra initiated the divorce because of Doug's failure to support her career goals. Doug is now having difficulty establishing a stable life-style as a single person. He hates being alone and spends much of his free time in bars and nightclubs. Doug has had numerous superficial sexual relationships to boost his wounded ego, and he has resorted to excessive drinking and spending to ward off feelings of depression. He has been neglecting his job responsibilities as a sales representative and is progressively getting into debt. Doug is still emotionally attached to Sandra and harbors reconciliation fantasies. Sandra is sympathetic, but she is further along in the adjustment process; she is involved in a new relationship and is experiencing much satisfaction from success in graduate school. Doug sees few of his friends as he feels guilty about his divorce and new life-style and also generally feels "out of place" with them. As a result, Doug feels very isolated and lonely, and he is unable to develop the new sources of social support that would help him adjust to the divorce. Finally, his boss confronts him both about his job performance and his life-style in general and gives him the name of a counselor. Frightened and ashamed by this confrontation, Doug agrees to see the counselor. Doug is eventually referred for group counseling with individuals experiencing similar problems. After some initial reluctance to participate, Doug soon begins to trust the group and finds their insights and support very helpful.

John

John is a 38-year-old high school teacher who has been remarried for 2 years after being divorced from his first wife, Karen, for 3 years. He was involved in a highly conflictual marriage with Karen for almost 10 years prior to the divorce; they have two daughters, currently age 8 and 10. Karen has primary custody, and John has weekend visitation rights. John's current wife, Diane, also has two children, a son, 7, and a daughter, 6. Diane's husband left her early in her marriage, and she and her children have had minimal contact with him since. John and Diane are happily married, and John has a very close relationship with his stepchildren. John's relationship with his own children is not as satisfactory. Prior to his remarriage, John had begun to see his daughters less regularly. He felt that his visits were more upsetting than beneficial for him and his daughters. He felt more like a visitor than family member, he lacked confidence in his ability to interact with his children, and he began to resent giving up his weekends to child care. After meeting Diane, a secretary at the school where he was employed, his frequency of visitation further declined. He felt awkward bringing his children around his "girlfriend" and her children. After John and Diane got married, John's life became centered on his "new" family. Diane doesn't overtly discourage John's visitation with his children, but she doesn't facilitate his involvement either. Karen, his former spouse, refuses to agree to modify the visitation schedule to allow greater visitation during the summer and holidays when John has more free time. John feels guilty about the satisfaction he has found with Diane and her children and his failure to be the same kind of involved father with his own children.

Intervention

Many professionals involved with divorce are modifying traditional approaches designed to strengthen marriage (and thus prevent divorce) to include recognition of the reality of divorce and the needs of divorcing individuals. Many of these intervention approaches are gender-focused, that is, they deal specifically with issues unique to men or women. Some of these recently developed sources of assistance include divorce therapy, group approaches, mediation, services for divorced fathers and their children, and self-help materials.

Despite an increasing number of sources of assistance to divorced or divorcing individuals, men are far less likely than women to seek them out. Such reluctance is related to male socialization patterns of self-sufficiency, independent problem solving, and inhibition of feelings. As a result men are prone to use denial and avoidance in dealing with marital stress (Brown & Fox, 1978). To seek out help is to acknowledge vulnerability and weakness and thus to seem unmanly (Myers, 1986). Men's greater distress during separation and divorce may, in fact, be related to their emotional inexpressiveness and their attempt to resolve their problems independently.

Divorce Therapy

As previously mentioned, many men experience divorce as a subjective sense of abandonment and are not well prepared to deal with this narcissistic injury (Myers, 1986). For most men, their wives are their closest intimate—often the only person to whom they can express their feelings (Tamir, 1982). Thus, some men are unable emotionally to resolve their relationship on their own or with the help of familiar sources of social support, and thus are in need of some form of professional intervention. Marital crises often provide the occasion in which men who have emotional problems will seek professional assistance out of desperation. Tasks and goals for these men typically center around ventilation of feelings (especially anger, abandonment, hurt, failure, and guilt), regaining self-esteem (both sexual and social), and understanding and working through problems of trust with women, reestablishing intimacy in a new relationship, avoiding self-destructive behaviors, and learning co-parenting skills (Myers). Divorced or divorcing men will approach therapy ambivalently, and when they do, their goals may not be realistic. Because they lag behind their spouse in the mourning process and do not accept the reality of divorce as readily, many men will want to engage in marital therapy as a possible means of reconciliation as opposed to individual therapy to adjust to the divorce (Myers).

Divorce therapy per se is an increasingly popular therapeutic alternative that is designed to (a) aid those individuals considering divorce or those divorcing in determining whether their needs can be met within their present marriage or (b) assist them in the process of divorce (Brown, 1976). This form of marriage and family therapy recognizes divorce as a rational alternative and not a dysfunctional or pathological behavior as it has traditionally been viewed by marriage and family therapists.

Divorce therapy may be offered by therapists in private practice, clergy, social service agencies, conciliation counselors, or divorce mediators. Typically divorce therapy focuses on the individual although sometimes spouses as well as other family members are included. Because divorce therapy is a recently developed alternative, exact figures of use, techniques, and evaluations are only beginning to appear in the literature. It does seem that most divorce therapists utilize a grief/loss perspective and focus on helping clients "work through" or mourn the losses that divorce represents. In addition, divorce therapists typically help their clients deal with many practical issues related to divorce such as economics, family law, parent-child relationships, and establishing new relationships and social supports. Consequently, many divorce therapists are involved in both the decision to divorce as well as the litigation process.

Group Approaches

Divorce therapy may take the form of small group process to enable the divorced-divorcing man to both work through the grief process and acquire group benefits of social skill development, social support, and learning through the experiences of others. As aforementioned, for too many men, social support is minimal or an altogether deprived facet of their lives; thus group work, especially men-only membership, may prove useful and can have great worth beyond the group's ostensible purpose (Knott, 1987). Group therapy has the same goals as individual therapy, but is more short-term, problem-specific, and less expensive.

Educational groups usually focus on helping divorced individuals deal with more practical issues as well as facilitating self-esteem. These groups usually take the form of (a) short lectures followed by discussion, (b) workshops, or (c) social gatherings where information is informally shared. These groups are sponsored by churches, men's groups, various community organizations such as the YMCA, or organizations with specific interest in divorce such as Parents Without Partners. Various topics are presented including practical skill development, spiritual development, and personal growth (Tedder & Scherman, 1987). Although these groups often are based on a grief-loss model of adjustment to divorce, they stop short of formal therapy. They do, however, serve as reliable sources of information and referral for those needing more assistance.

Self-help groups also have an educational focus, but they exist primarily to offer emotional support to their members. These groups are primarily directed toward the recently separated or divorced who are most in need of encouragement, support, and enhancement of their self-esteem. Members usually take full responsibility for any program as well as for the group's leadership. Some groups emphasize dissemination of knowledge as men typically are not aware of all the community services available to them (Tedder & Scherman, 1987). Men's support groups are one popular variation of the self-help group. These are usually small groups of 6–10 members who meet without a leader to discuss whatever issues or problems are important to the members at the time. Other special interest self-help groups, such as Adult Children of Alcoholics, also deal with many divorce-related issues.

Divorce Mediation

Another recent professional response to the needs of divorcing individuals is divorce mediation. Although mediation has long been used in resolving labor-management conflicts and international disputes, it has only recently been applied to interpersonal conflicts. Mediation has been applied to the divorce process to reduce the acrimony and conflict engendered by traditional adversarial legal procedures that focus on blame and fault, thereby prohibiting rational decision making.

The mediator's goal is to assist divorcing clients in separating economic and other practical issues from emotional ones and to focus on the future and the whole family and not on individual gain. The mediator maintains a counselor's role with the couple, but if serious emotional issues arise, most mediators will refer the client to other professionals as the mediator's task is to facilitate a mutually satisfactory settlement agreement, not to practice individual or family therapy (Haynes, 1981). Divorce mediation is offered by private mediation services, therapists or attorneys in private practice, and court-affiliated family or conciliation services (in some jurisdictions couples with young children are required by courts to go through mediation). Divorce mediation has been evaluated and found to be superior to adversarial procedures in terms of ease of reaching a settlement and satisfaction with the settlement agreements (Sprenkle & Storm, 1983). It is also thought that men benefit more, both emotionally and financially, from mediation than from traditional legal procedures (Price & McKenry, 1988).

Services for Fathers and Their Children

As previously mentioned, a father's adjustment to divorce is made more difficult by the needs of his children and his need to assume greater parental involvement, if only on an infrequent basis. Many services for children also deal at least tangentially with the larger family system, but increasingly there are programs focused on the single parent and even to the single father per se.

Many of these programs are based in the public schools. Through continuing or adult education classes, fathers may find specific courses such as "Coping as a Single Parent" or course on general parent education strategies such as Systematic Training for Effective Parenting (STEP) or Parent Effectiveness Training (PET). Some schools with cooperating agencies offer behavioral management classes or groups; fathers who are experiencing difficulty in disciplining "acting out," overly aggressive, or noncompliant children might find these helpful.

Classroom teachers increasingly have been encouraged and trained to deal with divorce-related issues their students face. Many of their interventions require parental cooperation if not involvement. Teachers are also good sources of information regarding reading materials for fathers and their children, professional referrals, and general advice regarding communicating and interacting with children. Teachers frequently become very close to children during the period of their parents' separation and divorce by providing the structure, continuity, attention, and tolerance that may be lacking in the children's home environment; the classroom teachers may even become interim parent substitutes during this period (Skeen & McKenry, 1980).

Schools through their psychological services are beginning to offer direct therapeutic intervention to children and their parents, often through group experiences with the child or with the child and parents (e.g., Strauss & McGann, 1987). Such groups strive to increase self-esteem and coping skills in children, decrease behavioral problems, increase parenting skills, and decrease stress for children and parents.

Many divorced fathers complain that their children do not want to talk with them about their feelings, and therefore, they are unsure how their children feel (Tedder, Scherman, & Sheridan, 1984). Bibliotherapy can be an effective mechanism to facilitate father-child discussion of divorce and its related changes in life-style. Many excellent children's books can be read or discussed together to allow for expression of feelings and to identify problems between father and child (see listing by Pardeck & Pardeck [1987]). Teachers, as aforementioned, are also good sources of reading materials.

Divorced fathers also should be aware of various clinical services available to their children. Many counseling approaches have been specifically developed for children and their families who are experiencing divorce-related problems. These programs tend to be structured, of limited duration, and crisis-oriented or problem-specific. Divorce has been recognized as especially traumatic for children, and professional intervention is widely advocated (e.g., Wallerstein & Kelly, 1980). Such counseling is not intended to effect major personality changes and may therefore be insufficient for some particularly disturbed children; these children would need in-depth therapy that focuses on particular emotional disturbance such as guilt about anger.

Because children evidence a common pattern of reaction to divorce and are often in need of emotional support, group therapy approaches have been widely used and deemed highly successful. Like schools, the clinical community is taking a more systems, ecological approach by involving fathers and other family members in their treatment modalities.

Self-Help Materials

Numerous self-help books are available today to divorced/divorcing men that provide insight and suggestions. Some available books include the following: *Fathers Without Partners* (Rosenthal & Keshet, 1981), *Creative Divorce* (Krantzler, 1973), *Single Father's Handbook* (Gatley & Koulack, 1979), *Rebuilding: When Your Relationship Ends* (Fisher, 1981); *The Parents' Book About Divorce* (Gardner, 1977); and *Divorce: The Man's Complete Guide to Winning* (Vail, 1979). Some books provide exercises to facilitate growth and positive self-appraisal (e.g., Kessler, 1975; Kingma, 1987). Also, a variety of films, both educational and popular, deal with divorce issues; some of these include *Heartburn, Kramer vs. Kramer, Once in a Lifetime,* and *Starting Over.* Maximum benefit can be obtained from discussion of these books and films with others.

Conclusion

Although research is limited, increasing evidence suggests that men, because of their traditional sex role socialization, are particularly vulnerable to many negative consequences of divorce. Also, because of this socialization, men involved in divorce are neither able to acknowledge their symptomatology nor to seek help. Divorced fathers' participation/ involvement with their children also has been limited by this narrow socialization for instrumental roles, especially the "good provider" family role. However, with the progressive movement toward more egalitarian roles, with continuing high divorce rates, and with most women seeking opportunities outside the home, men should gradually move into more adrogynous roles and behaviors that will allow them to cope more successfully with divorce and maintain their obligations to their children. Also, society is increasingly recognizing the stress associated with divorce, and is viewing separation and divorce as a normal developmental transition in the lives of people rather than deviant behavior. As a result, more informal and formal support systems are evolving for divorcing/ divorced men and women.

*Counselors can become skillful guides for gay and bisexual men
on their journey to healthy identity formation.*

Chapter 9

GAY AND BISEXUAL MEN: DEVELOPING A HEALTHY IDENTITY

Stephen Parker and Ted Thompson

This chapter contains two linked, yet distinct sections. The first addresses the elements of healthy identity formation as specifically applied to gay and bisexual men. The second section examines approaches that might be useful to therapists and counselors when dealing with gay and bisexual men. Although the elements of healthy identity formation described in this chapter are not limited to gay or bisexual men, these particular elements are critical to these men. Likewise, the approaches to therapy described below are not meant to be an exhaustive list of therapeutic techniques, but rather attitudinal perspectives germane to gay and bisexual clients across the entire range of therapeutic technique.

During the past 7 years a substantial literature has emerged concerning psychotherapy with gay and bisexual clients. Among the best are the book-length efforts by Coleman (1988), Friedman (1988), Gonsiorek (1982), Mattison and McWhirter (1984), and Stein and Cohen (1986). To date, most of this work is built upon models of "coming out" or identity formation that describe the process of recognizing one's "gayness" as metaphorically linear (Hanley-Hagenbruck, 1989). One might be led to believe, therefore, that integrated identity is a goal, an end, or a destination. It seems more likely to us that it functions as a pathway, a means, a direction along which issues of sexual orientation flow into the broader stream of our adult development. We recognize the need for more accurate metaphors for development than a temporal line.

We also understand homosexuality to be a part of but not the sole defining characteristic of a person's identity. "There is more to having a gay heart," as one client put it, than the gender of sexual partners. Laura Brown (1988) urged us to focus on the "central understandings" of this "gay heart" and not just on homosexuality. It is important, she continued, to include in our knowledge and work the domains of human experience that tend to drop off the ends of a "normal" distribution and out of sight into the land of "special topics." She encouraged a reconstruction of psychological thought to encompass a knowledge of human experience complementary to the "scientific" facts and centered in the deeply subjective experiences of gender, race, and orientation. Simply, we will focus on the individual and cultural contexts of the gay and bisexual man.

We intend to not focus on the "why" of homosexuality (Money, 1987). The search for causes has often carried with it subtle assumptions of pathology we do not share. It is frequently a short leap from notions of cause to notions of cure, which have revealed themselves to be ineffective, shaming, or dangerous (Martin, 1984). Rather, like many things human, we suspect that causation is likely to be multiple in a way that will forever elude precise quantification or specification. E.F. Schumacher, in his *Guide for the Perplexed* (1977), made the argument that positivist science is of assistance in resolving only convergent problems, those that clarify and resolve with the generation of increasingly specific and carefully controlled information. We argue that like "pain," gender, sexual orientation, and sexuality in general belong to the class of "divergent" problems that become larger and murkier when bound to a materialistically empirical scientific method. Let us now consider elements of healthy identity formation for gay and bisexual men.

Healthy Identity Formation

Our objective is to focus on those elements that facilitate the process of healthy identity formation. In doing so we hope to touch on some intrapsychic dynamics that evolve from that process and the environmental pressures that effect those dynamics.

The dilemma we face is the ambiguity of "healthy identity formation." These words have subjective connotations. Healthy according to whom? What population of people? Identity in accordance with what cultural subgroup? What may be healthy for one group may be considered less than healthy for another. Because of this ambiguity we need to make two clarifying statements before directly listing the elements of healthy identity formation.

First, the identity of an individual depends in large measure on the cultural context within which that person develops. We tend to think in homogeneous terms as though there is no diversity within the population. Clearly a great deal of diversity exists: socioeconomic, age, race, nationality, and so on.

Second, we make the mistake of focusing on sexual development as the single most important characteristic of identity formation. Historically, discussions of healthy development have dominated the literature as though the sexual aspect of the gay individual is the principal adjustment factor. As mentioned above, the basic issues involved in identity formation are similar whether the individual be gay or heterosexual. It is the social stigma and cultural milieu within which the gay individual lives that alters the nature and focus of the formation process. Forming an identity is not intrinsically hindered by being homosexual, but rather by the labels and connotations of deviance attached to it.

With those clarifications, let us examine seven elements that affect healthy identity formation for gay and bisexual men.

First, identity formation occurs within the context of a normative heterosexual population. It is impossible to discuss the identity development of gay men without recognizing the context within which that identity is formed. The individual who is gay learns about himself in contrast to rather than as part of the larger society. Imagine learning about love and sexuality in a heterosexual world when your preference is for people of the same gender!

As a result, knowing oneself becomes an experience of duality. One develops a sense of who one is, as well as a sense of who one is not among the larger "different-than-myself" population. Minorities who live within a White majority population know this experience of duality well. The languages are different, the references are different, the sensibilities are different, the clothes can be different, and so on.

Second, because of this duality, the search for a healthy identity is a search for congruence and balance. Developing a sense of congruence between internal perceptions and images of self in contrast to external perceptions and reflections of self is essential for the gay man.. That which he is experiencing inside is either affirmed and supported or rejected and denied by the reflections and perceptions received from external sources. Balance means weighing the occassionally conflicting information that comes from the heterosexual world and the homosexual community. When a sense of congruence exists, a bridge can be built between oneself and something greater than oneself. Usually this bridge is built between the individual and the gay community. This community can provide a place in which one can more readily find congruence and balance.

Two major variables affect congruence: the social context and the notion of a continuum of "homosexuality." The larger social context is obviously heterosexual, and it is from this context that the definition of "health" is derived. Any group of people seen to be outside this normative population is by definition viewed as abnormal or unhealthy. To say out loud that one is gay is by definition an admission of unhealthiness according to the dominant society's thinking.

This has resulted in damaged identities and has been a pervasive attitude in both the psychological and psychiatric literature. Until very recently homosexuality was considered to be a psychiatric disorder. This notion of "unhealthiness" was indirectly challenged by the research conducted by Kinsey at Indiana University between 1938 and 1953. This study represents in part the single largest study in the United States that has systematically explored the incidence of homosexuality among the general population. Research subsequent to Kinsey's indicates that approximately 10% of the population describe themselves as homosexuals. Rather than seeing himself as one of the isolated few, the gay man became part of a substantial entity within the population.

The second variable affecting congruence is the change in the notion of "either-or" identification in attraction to the same sex. Kinsey described a continuum along which individuals had a range of attraction possibilities. Rather than being only homosexual or heterosexual, people have the capacity to love and nuture along the continuum. This is a dramatic example of Jung's notions of animus and anima, the male and female within each of us. Therefore, as the size of the gay population was identified and the notion of either-or was blurred, individuals were better able to find congruence and to feel a part of the normative group. The overall effect was that of sharpening the focus of congruence between internal and external perceptions.

The third element of healthy identity formation is the recognition that not all homosexuals are alike. When a gay man recognizes this, he can begin to explore his own identity with all its facets. Our metaphor for this is a prism. To the naked eye, before striking a prism, sunlight seems consistently colorless, but nothing more. After striking the prism, however, the beam breaks into a spectrum of colors. If the heterosexual majority sees gay men as only sexual beings, then regardless of individual behavior, that individual will be "gay." The single preoccupation with sexual issues omits the vision of the remaining colors in the spectrum.

The fourth element is dealing with the challenge of the inexpressive man. Gay men are brought up to be conventionally male, and thereby taught not to recognize, feel, or express their emotions. The ability to perceive, accept, and express these aspects of one's being reveals considerable information about one's identity. Recognition, acceptance, and expression of feelings become crucial steps in the formation of healthy identity. This particular element is similar for both heterosexual and gay men. Divergence occurs as the gay man begins to understand that some of his feelings are neither shared nor supported by others around him. Self-esteem must be established through contact with others like himself. In this sense the next element is particularly important.

The fifth element of healthy identity formation is finding a group, a tribe. The gay community is a valuable resource for the individual.

Because he lives in a predominantly heterosexual culture, the individual may continually experience frustration and loneliness. Because the society at large can be homophobic and punitive toward gay men, an essential feature of healthy identity formation is finding an emotional sanctuary. The salvation is to develop and utilize the support and sense of belonging one receives from the greater group that solidifies and validates an emerging identity.

Our sixth element is the necessity for the gay man to deepen his ability to be honest with himself initially, and then to be honest with others. This honesty involves looking introspectively for those parts of himself that are both pleasing and frightening, and then to acknowledge their existence. For the gay man this experience may bring a heightened sense of difference between himself and others. The tendency is to hide those facets of the self that create a sense of dissonance or anxiety.

Most difficulty may come in being honest about one's fears. The knowledge that one's feelings differ from others' creates fear. At first a gay man will grope for words to label his feelings, being unable to find a language different from the majority's. These labels are needed to help articulate and define his experience. The warnings against being different are experienced in countless verbal and nonverbal messages, all of which invoke fears of rejection. Working through the fear presents a developmental issue that is unique to minority populations within the majority culture. The question becomes, "How much of yourself do you dare to be?"

Finally, we are still left with the nagging question of "Where does sexuality fit into this picture?" In effect the process of identity development involves the integration of the individual's sense of sexuality and its associated behaviors into the larger personality structure. This includes finding a sense of balance and perspective for the sexual self so that its behaviors do not dominate nor cancel out. Burgess (1949) spoke of the conversion of sexual behavior into sexual conduct. As he described it, "conduct is behavior as prescribed or evaluated by the group . . . it is not simply external, observable behavior, but behavior that expresses a norm or evaluation" (p. 228). The idea of converting sexual behavior into sexual conduct represents a step toward gaining perspective and balance for the gay man. In this way the individual gains a value orientation that develops his ability to trust his own feelings and conduct in relation to himself as well as toward others.

These elements are not meant to be linear and were not presented in any particular order. As with the journey described in the last chapter of this book, the route can be circuitous. Each of these elements, in our experience, are necessary for healthy identity formation in gay men. Let us now look at approaches therapists can take to working with gay clients.

Therapeutic Approaches

Our first approach is conceptual. We find it helpful to assume that we are assisting our clients in a recovery process from "ego-dystonic heterosexuality," to paraphrase the *Diagnosic and Statistical Manual of Mental Disorders, Third Edition (American Psychiatric Association, 1980)*. Even though this is not an accepted diagnostic category, the phrase describes in a broad way how the normalizing development of a healthy sense of self as gay or bisexual is postponed by the environmental demand to assume a heterosexual identity dissonant with one's deepest feelings, a demand to become, as it were, invisible. To assume a heterosexual orientation, is counter to and corrosive of healthy ego functioning for a gay man.

Grace (1977) described coming out as a recovery of "lost chronological adolescence," adolescence set aside by the task of "passing" as straight or trying to become straight. Gonsiorek (1982) described the difference between genuine borderline personality organization and an "overlay" of borderline features that are generated, in part, from an intense dissonance between a person's deeply subjective sense of self and the requirements of an inauthentic heterosexual identification. Helping our clients let go of a heterosexual identification allows them and us two major freedoms.

The first freedom we gain from this conceptualization of our work is from a monolithic view of homosexuality. It becomes easier to perceive "homosexualities" when we do not take a purely heterosexual view. Bell and Weinberg (1978) identified many different life-style types for homosexuals: closed (monogamous) coupled, open coupled, functional (i.e., single people with many partners and little apparent distress), dysfunctional (the "psychiatric" population upon which most of the early pathologically based research on homosexuality was conducted), and, finally, asexual. Freedom from a monolithic view of a man's homosexuality facilitates the breakdown of stereotypes and opens the way to an understanding of his sexuality in all its considerable complexity (Klein, 1978).

Second, we are freed from the habit of pathologizing processes of normal development, a habit that has grown out of the generalized stigmatization of homosexuality in the larger culture and the resultant research bias in the direction of pathological populations. Viewed from the perspective of heterosexual expectations of development, the emotional experience of the intense "catch-up" development that occurs during coming out can easily be misunderstood. For example, developing a sense of social and sexual competence consonant with one's repressed or suppressed longings can result in an intense process of sexual exploration. Such exploration can be vulnerable to misdiagnosis as compulsive or addictive sexuality. In our clinical experience, when the developmental need is met, the high rate of sexual activity abates. Thus not pathologizing our clients increases the integrity of their own ego functioning.

The second approach to our clients underlines the importance of helping them work through grief and loss. This process heals the corrosive effects of the stigma of being labeled "different." Everyone has to face losses; gay and bisexual men face the ongoing loss of much that the larger culture says is necessary to the "good life." Potent issues of loss occur over the entire continuum of identity development and are central to healthy identity development.

"It is not enough in therapy to help gay people transform a negative self-image into a positive one because the world into which they emerge is, quite literally, 'out to get them'. . . . Not only must gay people give up attachment to what might have been but wasn't, they must also let go of what might be now and isn't and what the future might have held but won't" (Fortunato, 1982, p. 89).

Loss of membership, at least in part, in the majority culture is the first problem. It then becomes necessary to create one's own alternative vision of a "good life," that is, one that is existentially authentic, interpersonally respectful, and rewarding. This cannot occur unless these particular losses are acknowledged and grieved and cease to occupy the person's attention, consciously or unconsciously (Dorn, 1989).

Our third approach addresses the need to know intimately our own internalized homophobia and heterosexism. This may seem an obvious truism. Its tendency to drop into the background, however, prompts us to emphasize it here. To the extent that our culture operates from heterosexist values and stereotypes and to the extent that our families embody those values, it is common sense that we each have internalized those values along with the rest of our familiar behavioral inheritance. Without the ability to cultivate an awareness of its presence and operation through supervision, peer supervision, or other professional development, it is likely that our internalized heterosexism will surface unconsciously and provoke in some way a failure of empathy. Neither of the authors expects the vestiges of internalized heterosexism to disappear completely, just as is true of racism. We have found the exploration of empathic failures with clients and colleagues to be a vital component of necessary accountability. Clients often have little or no experience of this kind of relational repair, much less modeling of immediate awareness of the impact of internalized heterosexism. Among colleagues, this accountability keeps our growth alive and relieves some of people's perfectionistic fear of failure.

This sort of accountability also helps us to find the limits of our knowledge, both intellectual and experiential, and assists us in deciding when we can help and when we should refer our clients to someone else. For instance, a therapist working with a man who is just coming out needs to know the available resources in a personal enough way to fit them with a particular client's interest pattern and to assist him through forseeable barriers and objective risks. Another example is that a family with an emerging gay or bisexual member sometimes cannot get a validation of their anger at the loss of their dreams for this person by anyone else than a therapist identified as versed in gay or bisexual issues. In our experience these families have tended to stay stuck until this validation occurs. The appropriate response in this instance might well be a referral to a therapist who is "out" to the community. Another lesson of accountability has been to demonstrate in small ways that we are aware of our homophobia by keeping some gay-oriented reading materials around the office and waiting room.

The last approach that emerges from our perspective as facilitators of recovery from "ego-dystonic heterosexuality" is the need to cultivate empathic bridges. Many of us who work with this client population are gay and bisexual and have that deep subjectivity directly available in our work. It is most likely that the majority do not. Because empathy is the healing component of our work, it is essential for those who are not gay or bisexual to operate from those aspects of their experience that provide a good enough analogue.

The argument that only a gay or bisexual man can understand another is unreasonably perfectionistic and would preclude the possibility of much common understanding. A recovering alcoholic, for example, knows well the process of assuming an invisible identity that individuals stigmatized by society experience. People recovering from sexual abuse or those coming out of celibate life understand the process of discovering a new sense of sexuality and the intense "catch-up" development that is involved. Those who experienced polio or cancer in the 1950s know the irrational terror of contagion in others that gay and bisexual men infected with the human immunodeficiency virus now face. Recovering adult children of dysfunctional families of all sorts know what it is to have lost the early affirmation of one's deepest feelings by parents and to have assumed a fake identity, role-bound and oriented toward others' expectations at the expense of one's own needs and desires.

We could enumerate a long list of "good enough" analogues here. If we did, it would become clear that all of them encompass recovery from some trauma, a woundedness often inflicted by way of social stigma. It is in those parts of our lives where we have healed some significant wounds that we can look for the footings upon which to build our empathic bridges to others. We can build on those footings by coming to know gay and bisexual men and expanding our experience of empathic contact.

Lest this suggestion seem simply a nice new-age sentiment, we need to acknowledge how much this requires us to face our fear and to embrace it rather than making an enemy of it or trying to conquer or exclude it. In this way fear can become part of the "bliss," to quote mythologist Joseph Campbell (1988, p. 91), that shows us where we need to travel next in our professional journey. It becomes a sign pointing, as it were, in the direction we need to move, carefully, a step at a time, as though we were walking a narrow mountain ridge, a slender bridge, the "razor's edge" of our growth. In this way, our work becomes a journey, and the battles we encounter, in the highest spirit of aikido, become a dance (Egendorf, 1986, p. 264).

In this chapter we have reviewed our thinking and experience in helping gay and bisexual men formulate a healthy identity. We understand this process to be a journey rather than a prize. It begins in a very dark and lonely wood. But we, as counselors and therapists, can become skillful guides, grounded in our own journey, helping brothers find their way home to a tribe that mirrors and affirms their hearts and a sense of responsibility that embraces both duty and "ability to respond."

MULTICULTURAL
CONCERNS

Most social and economic indicators for Black men provide a profile of individuals whose development and quality of life are in serious jeopardy.

Chapter 10

BLACK MALE DEVELOPMENT: COUNSELING THE "NATIVE SON"

Courtland C. Lee

African-American men in contemporary society face many challenges that affect their psychosocial development. Evidence emerging from both popular and social science literature suggests that Black men in America constitute a population at risk (Gary, 1981; Louis, 1985; McGhee, 1984). Most social and economic indicators for Black men provide a profile of individuals whose development and quality of life are in serious jeopardy. Data indicate that Black men are more likely than any other ethnic/gender group in America to lack jobs or to drop out of the labor market completely, to be suspended from or drop out of the educational system, to be incarcerated, and to die from accidents or violence (Cordes, 1985; Gary; McGhee; McNatt, 1984; Poussaint, 1982). A review of such data ominously suggests that the African-American man may be an endangered species (Gibbs, 1984; Leavy, 1983).

In addition to statistics that suggest the danger of their extinction, African-American men encounter negative stereotypes about their very manhood. These stereotypes include the notions that they are socially castrated, insecure in their male identity, and lack a positive self-concept. Significantly, most of these stereotypes have stemmed from a failure to understand masculinity in an African-American sociocultural context (Staples, 1978).

From birth to death, it is apparent that Black men in America face a series of challenges to optimal academic, career, and personal-social development. These challenges take their toll at every age, but at every stage of life the toll is high and the effect is cumulative (McGhee, 1984).

Counseling professionals therefore are confronted with formidable challenges when attempting to intervene in the lives of African-American male clients. Counseling Black men requires not only an understanding of the theoretical and practical traditions of counseling and psychotherapy, but an appreciation of African-American culture and its role in shaping the development of Black men, as well as an understanding of societal forces that have historically impinged upon that development and placed them at risk.

The purpose of this chapter is to help counseling professionals develop the awareness, knowledge, and skills for proactive psychotherapeutic intervention with Black male clients. After an analysis of Black male development in a sociocultural context and an exploration of issues to consider when counseling Black men, an intervention model for promoting optimal Black male development will be offered.

Sociocultural Challenges to Black Male Development

It must be understood that manhood historically has not been a birthright for African-American man (Genovese, 1974; Hernton, 1965; Staples, 1978). Unlike their European-American counterparts, Black men have not generally been granted masculine privilege or power in the United States. Sociocultural forces throughout American history have combined to keep Black men from assuming traditional masculine roles (Staples, 1983; Wilkinson & Taylor, 1977). Whereas White American men, from boyhood, are socialized by family, school, and the dominant culture in general, with a masculine sensibility that is composed of an awareness that power and control are their birthright and that they are the primary means of ensuring personal respect, financial security, and success (Goldberg, 1976; Pleck & Sawyer, 1974), these possibilities of manhood have generally been denied to African-American men. This denial process has been an integral part of the dynamics of oppression and racism that have pervaded the Black experience in America (Grier & Cobbs, 1968; Thomas & Sillen, 1972). Beginning with the capture and selling of Africans into bondage in the Americas in the 17th century, Black men have engendered fear in the European American (Grier & Cobbs; Hilliard, 1985; Staples, 1978). Black men, and their implied physical prowess and leadership ability, have been perceived as representing the greatest threat to the social order and economic power structure so carefully constructed and controlled by White male dominance. Therefore, in order to maintain socioeconomic control, the White male-dominated power structure has ensured that African-American men have not had access to the traditional sex role values and behaviors associated with power, control, status, and achievement. Both during the era of slavery and the decades after, the White American power structure has initiated various social and economic actions that have resulted in the subordination of Black men and the cancellation of their masculine advantage in the larger society (Staples, 1978; Taylor, 1977). The racism inherent in such actions has operated to impede the sex role socialization of African-American men and has kept them in many instances from realizing even the most basic aspects of masculine privilege and power, namely life-sustaining employment and the ability to support a family (Staples, 1978).

The historical persistence of barriers to the expression of Black manhood has taken a significant toll on the psychosocial development of the African-American man. The inability to fulfill masculine roles has made rage, frustration, powerlessness, and hopelessness major forces in the Black male developmental process. These forces are manifested in the antisocial and self-destructive behavior patterns that characterize a great deal of the contemporary African-American male experience (Cordes, 1985; Gary, 1981; McGhee, 1984). Significantly, in a society where a man's worth (and ultimately his manhood) has seemingly been judged by his ability to accumulate wealth and power, the African-American man's inability to obtain little of either has had serious consequences for his psychosocial development.

Facilitating Change in the Lives of Black Men: Counseling for Optimal Development

Prelude to Counseling Practice

Before examining counseling practice for African-American male clients, it is important to consider several issues that must be understood if effective therapeutic intervention is to take place. These are: African-American culture and its relationship to optimal mental health; the barriers to effective counseling with Black men; and the importance of a proactive mental health approach to counseling with Black men.

African-American Culture: The Key to Black Mental Health

Any discipline that would seek to understand the dynamics of African-American male development must take into account the experiences that have shaped that development. Counseling strategies and techniques for Black men, therefore, must be predicated on an understanding of African-American culture and its crucial role in fostering optimal mental health. In recent years, Black educators and psychologists have concluded that several aspects of the African-American cultural experience that have evolved from African tradition have a significant relationship with Black mental health (Cross, 1974; Harper, 1973; White, 1980; Nobles, 1980; Pasteur & Toldson, 1982).

An examination of core African-American culture (i.e., the culture that has developed in relatively homogeneous Black communities where rudimentary Afrocentric ways of life have been preserved in some measure) will reveal that Americans of African descent have developed a worldview that is grounded in African-American experience and is based on African-oriented philosophical assumptions. These assumptions constitute a cultural tradition that places a high premium on harmony among people and their internal and external environments, fosters self and group development through Black expressiveness, and recognizes the need for holistic development (Nobles, 1980).

Given this, counseling professionals need to find ways to incorporate African-American cultural dimensions into the helping process with Black men. Culture-specific approaches to counseling attempt to transform basic aspects of Black male life, generally ignored or perceived as negative in a European-American psychoeducational framework, into positive developmental experiences.

In order to maximize the effectiveness of cultural specificity in the helping process, emphasis should be placed on group approaches to counseling and psychotherapy with Black men. Group-oriented counseling approaches reflect the communal nature of the African-American experience. As mentioned previously, the dynamics of socialization among Black people emphasize cooperation and a sense of community. Within this context, peer group interaction is an important means of social identification and support for Black men (Hall, 1981). Understanding and using this African-American sociocultural phenomenon in counseling intervention with Black men should be an important goal.

Barriers to Effective Counseling With Black Men

The sociocultural challenges associated with the development of Black manhood give rise to potential barriers that may block effective counseling with Black men. First, it must be understood that in most instances Black men consider seeking traditional counseling as an admission of weakness and not very "manly." Although this is a phenomenon observed in men in general, it takes on a different dimension with Black men. For them, doing anything that seems "unmanly" can threaten their masculine self-concept, already decreased by the dominant society's general view of Black manhood.

Second, more often than not, Black men are referred for counseling by some societal agent, be it teacher, school principal, judge, social worker, or probation officer. These referrals are often made after some offense against the social order. The goal of counseling, therefore, is generally rehabilitative/punitive as opposed to developmental/preventive in nature. It is not unusual, then, to find Black men approaching the counseling process with apathy or hostility. Black male resistance to the counseling process can be considered as a defense mechanism (Larrabee, 1986; Majors & Nikelly, 1983; Vontress, 1971). Black men generally view counseling as an activity that is conducted by agents of a system that has rendered them powerless. The counseling process, therefore, could be perceived as another infringement on Black manhood.

Given these barriers, if counselors want to reach Black men, they should consider alternative methods of delivering mental health services. June (1986), suggested several important methods for enhancing the delivery of counseling services to Black men. One suggestion was to offer counseling services in a seeking mode (Rappaport, 1977). Such a delivery mode generally offers counseling services outside of a tradtitional therapeutic setting and incorporates the use of nonprofessional helping resources. With Black men such a mode should include an aggressive outreach approach that makes use of indigenous helping resources available in Black churches, fraternal organizations, and other African-American communal organizations. Counseling professionals who consider a seeking mode of service delivery use an aggressive outreach approach, develop relationships with institutions and organizations in the Black community, and lay the foundations for innovative and proactive mental health intervention with Black male clients (June).

The Promise of a Proactive Perspective

As mentioned previously, the goal of counseling African-American men traditionally has been rehabilitation as opposed to development. However, if counseling is to be a comprehensive and effective discipline for helping Black men, then the scope of services offered should be proactive and preventive in nature. Counseling practice must move beyond merely assisting Black male clients to react to negative environmental forces to a point where the goal of intervention is helping them develop mastery skills. Helping Black male clients develop such skills would enable them to confront challenges in a competent and proactive manner.

Central to the emergence of a proactive approach to counseling Black men should be the advent of a developmental perspective among mental health professionals. Danish (1980), suggested that when a nondevelopmental framework is adopted by counselors, interventions are directed at remediation. Crises and problems are to be coped with or adapted to, whereas with a developmental approach, counseling practice is aimed at enhancement or optimal development.

When counseling Black men, such a perspective should emphasize facilitating normal human development and fostering manhood identity in a Black cultural context. Adopting the proactive stance inherent in a development approach can help counseling professionals promote mastery and competence in their interventions with African-American male clients.

Directions for Counseling Practice

Counseling professionals working with Black men in psychotherapeutic relationships must facilitate the process of client choice and change within an African-American cultural and developmental context. Counselors, therefore, need to be aware of intrapsychic as well as environmental factors that affect Black male development. What follows is a group intervention model for raising Black male consciousness. The overriding goal of the model is to help clients develop a positive sense of self as African-American men. This goal must serve as the basis for all counseling services and interventions with Black men. Only when Black men accept themselves and their masculine realities with a sense of understanding and pride, tangible psychotherapeutic gains are possible.

Black Male Consciousness-Raising Group Experience: "Reflections on The Native Son"

This model group experience is called **"Reflections on the Native Son"** and represents a nontraditional and innovative counseling approach designed specifically to increase awareness and promote skills associated with a positive Black masculine identity. The basis of the approach is a small group counseling experience. Significantly, the title for the group experience comes from the novel *Native Son*, the literary masterpiece by African-American author Richard Wright (1940). The book tells the story of the systematic psychological and social destruction of a young Black man by the racist American sociopolitical system. When it is considered in a mental health perspective, *Native Son* captures the powerful emotions, suffering, frustrations, and yearnings that generally typify growing up Black and male in America.

The dimensions of helping in this model evolve from the important aesthetic traditions inherent in African-American culture (Gayle, 1971; Pasteur & Toldson, 1982). Specifically, a significant feature of the model is the use of selected Black art forms as a therapeutic aid in the counseling process. Toldson and Pasteur (1972) contended that African-American art forms have important implications for the counseling process with

Black people. Using such forms of Black expressiveness as a fundamental part of the group intervention, the model stresses the strengthening of African-American male identity. It is based on a fundamental knowledge of the cultural realities of African Americans and their potential for the positive psychosocial development of Black men. This experience is a culture-specific approach to counseling African-American men that transforms Black expressiveness into positive psychotherapeutic experiences.

The model is a multisession developmental group consciousness-raising experience. It provides the opportunity for Black men to develop attitudes, insights, and skills to meet effectively environmental challenges that impinge upon African-American manhood.

In terms of general guidelines, the model has been developed in a seeking mode (Rappaport, 1977) for implementation in a variety of settings including churches, fraternal organizations, educational institutions, community mental health or social agencies, and prisons. A Black male facilitator is critical for this experience. Counselors should therefore make every effort to include competent Black men as cofacilitators whenever necessary. The experience is intended for Black men, 18 years of age or older. In forming groups, consideration should be given to making the membership as heterogeneous as possible in terms of age, socioeconomic status, occupational background, level of educational attainment, and so forth. Ideally, a group should have between 8 and 10 participants. The group experience should be conducted in an encounter format with few distractions, for as many hours as possible over a **minimum** of 3 days. In addition, during a group experience such as this, women should be discouraged from either observing or participating in the process to ensure an atmosphere conducive to optimal male bonding.

"Reflections on The Native Son"

General Purpose of the Model

The model is designed to help Black men raise their level of masculine consciousness. The experience aims to develop a supportive therapeutic atmosphere that will enable a diverse group of African-American men to explore thoughts, feelings, and behaviors associated with being Black and male in contemporary American society.

Phase I: Introducing the Group Experience

Goal: To have group members reflect on the challenges associated with being Black and male and to have them reflect on their masculinity from an African-American perspective.

Methods of Facilitation:

1. Have group members introduce themselves and discuss group ground rules. Encourage members to share of themselves and their life experiences and listen carefully to other participants as well. Emphasize that the group will be a supportive communal environment of "brothers."
2. Conduct a discussion of the participants' perceptions and possible misgivings about counseling. Ask the question, "How do you feel sitting here now with these other "brothers"?
3. Have the members listen to the song "What's Happening Brother?" by Marvin Gaye (Nyx & Gaye, 1971). Initiate a preliminary discussion of what is happening to "brothers" internationally, nationally, and locally.
4. Conduct a group exploration of the following questions:
   a) How do you see yourself as a Black man?
   b) What is important to you as a Black man?
   c) How do you feel about all those negative stereotypes of and reports about Black men? (e.g., Black men are shiftless, Black men treat Black women disrespectfully, Black men don't take fatherhood seriously, Black men are physically aggressive).

It is important to note that after this initial phase of orientation and exploration significant bonding tends to take place among the participants. The nature of the activities and questions elicits strong affect and leads to the beginning of deep levels of interpersonal sharing. These levels of sharing lead to group cohesiveness and high levels of group productivity.

Phase II: Examining the Hazards of Black Manhood

Goal: To have group members examine the psychological, social and heath hazards confronting African-American men and their personal patterns of coping with them.

Methods of Facilitation:

1. Using data from sources such as the National Urban League, National Center for Health Statistics, U.S. Department of Health and Human Services, U.S. Department of Labor, and U.S. De-

partment of Justice, have the members review the psychological, social, and health status of Black men in contemporary society.

2. Have the members listen to a recording such as "The Message" by Grand Master Flash and the Furious Five (Fletcher, Glover, Robinson, & Chase, 1982), a contemporary African-American "rap" song that graphically details the environmental challenges affecting mental and physical well-being of Black people, particularly Black men. Relate the anger and frustration in the song to the lives of the group members. Explore with the group the origin and manifestation of the hazards to Black men's health and well being.

3. Share with the group recent articles in popular periodicals (e.g., *Ebony, Time, Newsweek, Essence*, etc.) about the "plight of the Black man." Conduct a discussion of the following question: "How does it make you feel when Black men are referred to as an **endangered species**?"

4. Show the film version of *Native Son* (Wright, 1986), or excerpts if time is a factor. Have the members relate the hazards the main character, Bigger Thomas, faces to their own experience as Black men in America. Have the members compare Bigger's emotions with their own.

5. In the oral tradition of African and African-American people, encourage members to share personal experiences of struggles to overcome, or attempting to overcome, threats to Black male well-being. For example, stories of substance abuse, involvement with crime, educational failure, or chronic under- or unemployment could be shared with the group. Ask members to consider two questions when listening to these stories of struggle and triumph: "How did being Black and male contribute to the struggle?" and "How did being Black and male contribute to triumph over the struggle?" Whenever possible, get older men to share their experiences with younger group members. It is especially important for the older members to share with the group the positive ways they found to cope with the anger, frustration, and depression that often accompany the African-American male experience.

Phase III: Exploring the Soul of a Black Man

Goal: To have group members examine roles, responsibilities, and relationships in their lives in an effort to gain a better understanding of their attitudes, values, and behaviors as Black men.

Methods of Facilitation:

1. Show excerpts, the entire film version (1961), or the recent Public Broadcasting System television version (1988) of Lorraine Hansberry's play, *A Raisin in the Sun*, the quintessential artistic view of African-American family life. Conduct a discussion about the group members' feelings about the lead male character, Walter Lee Younger. Have the members focus on their feelings about Walter Lee's relationship with his wife, mother, son, sister, and the White American social system. Get members to relate aspects of Walter Lee's life to their own lives.

2. As a follow-up to feelings and insights fostered by the film, discuss the following question: "What do you as Black men feel are your proper roles, duties, responsibilities, and obligations?"

3. Explore in depth the often problematic role of Black-man-as-father. Play the song "Pappa was a Rolling Stone" by the Temptations (Whitfield & Strong, 1983) and explore feelings about the negative father images it contains. Use the following discussion questions:

   a) How do you feel about the men in your family?

   b) What are your feelings about your own father?

   c) If you have children, what kind of a father would they say you are?

   d) If you have a son(s) how do you think he sees you as a father and as a man?

   e) How do you feel about the common notion that Black men don't take fatherhood seriously?

   f) When you were growing up, who were your heroes/role models?

   g) Who are your heroes/role models now?

4. Explore the complex issue of Black male-female relationships. Have the members read or listen to taped readings of excerpts from the play "For Colored Girls Who Have Considered Suicide When the Rainbow is Enuf," by Ntozake Shange (1975). This work is a celebration of being Black and being a woman. It is a lyric and tragic exploration of Black women's awareness. Particularly useful are those parts of the play that deal with Black women's perceptions of negative relationships and interactions with Black men. Use the following discussion questions:

   a) How do you feel about the women in your family?

   b) How do you see and what do you feel about women who are lovers/friends?

    c) What are the stresses and strains in your relationships with these Black women?

    d) What are the points of solid and deep agreement between you and women who are lovers/friends?

    e) What angers you, hurts you, and brings you fulfillment in your relations with the significant women in your life?

5. To culminate the experience of self-exploration at this phase of the group process, conduct a discussion of the following questions: "As a Black man. . . . . .

    a) what brings you satisfaction?"

    b) what gives you purpose?"

    c) what role does religion play in our life?"

    d) what gives you a sense of spirituality?"

    e) what makes you fearful?"

    f) what makes you angry?"

6. As a final activity, ask each member to make a statement affirming his identity as an African-American man.

Phase IV: Concluding the Experience

Goal: To have members consolidate group cohesion and terminate the experience with a positive sense of Black manhood.

Methods of Facilitation:

1. Play the song "My Name is Man" by Grant (1972) from the African-American musical production "Don't Bother Me I Can't Cope." Discuss the meaning of the song and its relationship to members' new insights on their manhood. Explore the following questions:

    a) At this point, how do you feel about yourself as a Black man?

    b) At this point, how do you feel about each other as Black men?

    c) What forces, situations, philosophies, or values unite you as Black men?

    d) As you leave this experience, what are you going to do to make life better for yourselves and other "brothers"?

Intended Counseling Outcomes

This group experience is intended to provide a supportive therapeutic atmosphere for Black men to develop and experiment with new attitudes, behaviors, and values. The following are among the more tangible outcomes of the experience:

1. To have group members develop greater appreciation for and understanding of their Blackness *and* their masculinity through a shared community of African-American brotherhood.
2. To have group members critically analyze the image of African-American men.
3. To have group members reassess their notions of masculinity within an African-American perspective.
4. To provide group members with a forum for the healthy ventilation of feelings of anger and frustration associated with the sociocultural challenges to Black manhood.
5. To have group members develop and share proactive strategies to challenge self-destructive and high-risk behavior patterns.
6. To reinforce among participants the notion of responsible fatherhood.
7. To have members explore the nature of positive interpersonal relationships with African-American women.
8. To have members develop the attitudes and skills to make positive contributions to the optimal development of Black men.

Follow-Up Experiences

After such an experience, the participants would benefit from organized group interaction with both their Black female counterparts and their White male peers. Group experiences with Black women might include exploration of the nature and importance of positive interpersonal relationships. Such experiences should incorporate traditional African-American notions of community into the interactions to develop greater interpersonal respect, trust, and understanding between Black men and women.

Group experiences with White men should promote male interpersonal appreciation and understanding across ethnic lines. Especially important would be explorations of the commonalities and differences in male socialization and life experiences among Black and White men.

Conclusion

No counselor should attempt to conduct an experience such as this with Black men unless he is perceived as being empathic and sensitive to human diversity. The challenge for any counselor attempting to raise levels of consciousness among Black men as a developmental therapeutic experience is to have a thorough knowledge of past and contemporary African and African-American history, a complete understanding of the sociocultural challenges to Black male development, and a solid comprehension of the Black experience.

This chapter addresses three men's journeys. These journeys are particularly difficult because of the impact of sex roles as well as the press of two cultures.

Chapter 11

EXPLORING THE MACHO MYSTIQUE: COUNSELING LATINO MEN

Fernando J. Gutierrez

The purpose of this chapter is to highlight issues associated with Latino culture and Latino male development. Montalvo & Gutierrez (1984) advised that the therapist might gain a better understanding of the client by focusing on the broader processes of acculturation rather than on the client's cultural uniqueness. Valdes, Baron, and Ponce (1987) supported Montalvo and Gutierrez by stressing the need to address the uniqueness of Hispanic men in terms of degree of cultural commitment and preference for Hispanic culture versus the Anglo-American culture. Additional factors include language usage, generational level, racial/ethnic group, attitudes toward their own Hispanic group, and machismo.

Case studies of three Latino men are presented that illustrate how each of these issues affect men at different developmental stages in their lives, and to show how counselors can assist their clients in moving through this developmental process. Each of these men was seen for clinical issues. It will be important, however, to focus on their developmental process and how this process affects the resolution of clinical concerns as well as how clinical concerns affect the bicultural components of developmental processes.

Machismo

Machismo can be viewed from two different perspectives, Hispanic and non-Hispanic. Valdes et al. (1987) warned that although chauvinism and sexism exist in the Hispanic culture, there is doubt as to whether it is more prevalent among Hispanics than among men from other cultures. In fact, Cromwell and Ruiz (1979) showed that within Mexican and Chicano families, the data do not support the stereotype of macho dominance in decision making.

139

Valdes, et al. (1987) noted that the original definition of the word *machismo* included the qualities of gallantry, generosity, charity, and courage. Ruiz (1981) further identified the positive qualities of dignity in conduct, respect for others, love for the family, and affection for children.

From a non-Hispanic perspective, the definition of machismo has been syncretised to imply physical aggression, sexual promiscuity, dominance of women, and excessive use of alcohol. The source of these attitudes within Anglo society has been attributed to acute feelings of inadequacy and guilt, fear of aloneness and weakness, and the need to dominate others in order to deny one's own weakness, extreme dependence, and regressive undertow (Aramoni, 1972). This syncretism could be the result of class differences, pressures, and needs (De La Cancela, 1986).

The Hispanic perspective of machismo behavior corresponds to attributes of "knighthood" (Valdes et al., 1987). These attributes imply that a man has had a noble education and ample resources to share. The nobleman also acquires self-esteem through occupational and financial status.

The non-Hispanic perspective of machismo behavior describes a man who has not had the opportunities of the nobleman and is reacting to feelings of low self-esteem and a sense of loss of control that can only be regained by physical prowess and domination of women.

The enormous class differences among the "haves" and "have-nots" in Latin American countries and the lack of opportunities for advancement for Latinos in the United States aid to perpetuate the non-Hispanic view of machismo among Latinos. Both of these ecological phenomena contribute to feelings of low self-esteem, fear of weakness, loss of control, and extreme dependence. The result for many Latino men is dysfunctional macho adaptation.

De La Cancela (1986) advocated an analysis of machismo based on socioeconomic status that would integrate psychological, cultural, and sociopolitical views of machismo. Such an ecological approach to counseling Latino men can assist counselors in working with their clients in such a way as not to take the clients out of the context of their reality.

We will meet Andres, a young man dealing with issues of separation from the family. Next, we will see how Jose adjusts to life in the United States and the pressures that acculturation have on his family. Lastly, we will explore how Antonio adjusts to his wife's loss of health due to an industrial accident, which caused an imbalance in sex roles in their relationship.

Andres

Andres is a predominantly English-speaking 20-year-old Salvado-
rean man who is living at home and attempting to separate from his
family. Andres is the middle child in a working-class family of three. He
has one older brother, 28, who had his own apartment but recently
moved back home because of illness; and a younger sister, 17, who moved
out of the house and is living with a girlfriend. Andres's father was
physically abused as a child and has physically abused Andres in the
past. Andres's mother is a housewife and a practicing alcoholic. Andres
was referred by his physician because of panic attacks after an incident
with cocaine use. Andres must often express himself in Spanish, especially when the topic is emotionally laden. Malgady, Rogler, and Costantino (1987) found that when a client is anxious or stressed, the client
most often reverts back to his or her language of origin.

While growing up, Andres had low self-esteem. He reported that
he was always self-conscious about his facial features because they made
him look too Hispanic and they set him apart from other children. After
the age of 9, Andres's childhood pictures showed a dramatic change.
He no longer smiled. He reports that during that time, his father had
begun to abuse him physically.

Andres dropped out of high school when he was a junior. He did
not go to work; instead, he would hang out with his friends who had
also dropped out of school. They drank alcohol and smoked marijuana
together. Andres was also introduced to experimentation with cocaine.
He began to have fantasies that he was possessed by the devil and experienced panic attacks. This scared him.

From the therapist's clinical experience, panic attacks can be a way
for clients to avoid feelings of anger. The therapist's main goal was to
help Andres stabilize through emotional support and referral for medication. Andres did not like the idea of taking medication so the therapist
contracted with him to do biofeedback training. Andres's panic attacks
were reduced by the relaxation exercises. Biofeedback training is a treatment that places the therapist in an active role, which is culturally relevant
to Latino clients (Ruiz, Casas, & Padilla, 1977).

The therapist also referred Andres to Al-Anon meetings for Adult
Children of Alcoholics. Andres enjoyed the group support these meetings provided. Andres began to deal with his own issues of alcohol and
drug abuse. In AA, he also found others with similar interpersonal and
intrapsychic problems.

As trust built between Andres and the therapist, Andres felt safer
in verbalizing the anger that he had been acting out. Andres was the

scapegoat in the alcoholic family and had vowed to hurt his dad as much as his dad had hurt him in his early childhood. He was going to accomplish this by not giving his dad the satisfaction of seeing him make it in the world.

Andres was presented a chart that listed five family roles and characteristics of adult children of alcoholics outlined by Wegscheider (1981). These five roles include: (1) the responsible child; (2) the lost child; (3) the mascot; (4) the placator; and (5) the scapegoat. He immediately identified the roles that he played in his family and was also able to identify the roles that his brother and sister played.

From a Latino perspective, Andres's brother, being the oldest boy, was playing his correct role as the responsible child and placator. He would take over when dad was not able to fulfill his role as head of the household. However, Montalvo and Gutierrez, (1984) warned against the therapist's restricting attention to only certain aspects of a person's culture. This restricted attention can act as a cultural mask of dysfunctional family interactions that the therapist can misinterpret as a cultural norm, thus missing a significant treatment issue. Although the responsible-child role of Andres's older brother might seem culturally relevant, this role actually served to mask the father's lack of participation in the family as the head of the household and the dilution of his role in the family to only that of an economic provider. Andres's sister, Maria, was the lost child, and Andres held the mascot and scapegoat roles.

In a sense, he adopted these roles and behaved in such a way so as to reinforce others' perception of him in these roles. For example, Andres exhibited impulse control problems within the context of therapy. One day Andres came into a session and asked the therapist if he like the T-shirt he had just bought on the way to the session. It turned out that he had used money that his father had given him to pay for the session to purchase the shirt. He had transferred his relationship with his father to the therapist. The therapist was supposed to not only provide for Andres's needs but allow him to be irresponsible in his actions. By setting limits with him and giving him feedback about his inappropriate behavior, the therapist helped Andres learn to deal with limits.

Andres and his sister were the most acculturated of the children. They looked to their peers rather than their parents for relatedness, thus undermining their father's authority. Rather than exercising his authority, Andres's father abdicated it and allowed the household to get out of control. Andres's role was to act out in an attempt to engage his father back into the family.

At one point, Andres panicked, and he left home to go and live with his aunt and uncle in another city. This speaks to the Latino value of "familismo," a valuing of the extended family and its potential for support (Levine & Padilla, 1980). However, from a dysfunctional family perspective, this support, which was culturally appropriate, was now interfering with Andres's recovery from the dysfunctional family system because it reinforced Andres's geographic escape from his problem and transferred the dependence to the extended family.

When Andres came back, the therapist attempted to engage his family in family therapy without success. He met with Andres's father in order to bring him back into the role of the head of household. He was too defensive in denying his wife's alcoholism to want to take on this role. Perhaps it would have been better to have met with both parents. Perhaps speaking to the mother's sense of responsibility as a mother and using her concern for her children as leverage may have brought them in, and the therapist could have helped to restructure the family and place the parents back in charge, as suggested by Fishman, Stanton, and Rosman (1982), although the mother's alcoholism may have prevented the success of this approach.

Andres continued in individual therapy but began fearing that if he changed, he would be ostracized by the family. He requested to have a session with his brother in an attempt to engage his brother in recovery so that he would not be the only one. He also wanted to utilize the session to explain to his brother why he was angry and why he had been acting out in the family.

Andres began to improve after having witnessed an elderly woman become injured in a car accident. He was able to calm the woman down and provide a police officer with an accurate eyewitness report. This situation enabled Andres to see himself in a positive light.

Gutierrez (1981, 1985) discussed the need for bicultural individuals to renegotiate the identity versus identity diffusion stage from a bicultural context. In this case, Andres was working through his negative self-image, his "evil" identity, and was getting in touch with his ego ideal. He discovered that he was a likeable person who could obtain validation for doing good deeds. He did not have to act negatively in order to be validated. As Andres's self-image improved, he began to accept himself and his Hispanic features. He learned he did not have to apologize for being who he was.

This improvement scared him. He started missing his sessions and becoming irresponsible again. This coincided with the Christmas holiday, a time when his mother would drink more and the family tension escalated. The therapist was able to give feedback to Andres regarding the family dynamic and how it triggered a relapse. The therapist remained consistent and established a written contract with Andres to make it clear that Andres was financially responsible for the sessions if he did not show up, requiring that he take responsibility for his life and his sessions with the therapist.

Andres enrolled in a business college and attended classes regularly, did his homework nightly, and was well on his way to a 4.0 average. During one of the therapy sessions, he talked about the serenity he was feeling. He also talked about how he was budgeting his money so that he could move out. Suddenly he had an intrusive thought of wanting to kill the therapist because the therapist was using analogies like Andres's brother. He experienced his brother as trying to manipulate him through the use of analogies.

Andres acknowledged that he was scared of becoming intimate. Threatening the therapist was an attempt to sever the relationship with the therapist so that he could go back to his old ways. After assessing the potential danger to himself, the therapist remained consistent with Andres and reassured him that the relationship would continue. Andres was also reassured that the therapist was confident about Andres's capacity for self-control.

A month later, Andres's brother, who was ill with cancer, took a turn for the worse. Andres felt guilty that he was doing so well while his brother, the family hero, was doing badly. Andres again responded by trying to run away to his aunt's house. Unconsciously, he was reenacting his old self again, thinking that if he sacrificed himself he could spare his brother.

The therapist, using provocative therapy, confronted Andres about his continued unwillingness to accept responsibility for his behavior. (Farrelly & Brandsma, 1974). Andres was unconsciously using his brother's situation as an excuse to continue his behavior. Andres smiled at the therapist and owned his behavior. He surrendered to his powerlessness over his family. It took Andres almost a year and a half to resolve the dichotomy of trust versus mistrust. He was now ready to move into the next stage of development, autonomy versus shame and doubt.

Andres teamed up with an AA sponsor who offered him a subcontractor job in his business. Andres began to work regularly and contributed part of his income to his mother for food and a portion to his father for rent. He even began to pay for his own therapy sessions.

This case study parallels the developmental process of a 2-year-old child who is trying to separate from his parents. He runs away and comes back to make sure mommy and daddy are still there even though he is trying to accept himself as separate from his parents. In a bicultural context, as Gutierrez (1981, 1985) pointed out, this is a very difficult process. It calls for the supportive counseling of a therapist who is knowledgeable with both cultures in order to uncover the cultural masks.

Through the transference, the therapist becomes the pseudoparent, setting limits and supporting the client while the client deals with the fear of abandonment. The therapist gives the client feedback about the client's behavior and its appropriateness within the cultures in which the client is operating. The therapist allows the client to assimilate and accommodate these changes into his or her personality and allows the client to separate from the therapist, teaching the client that she or he can achieve individuation.

Jose

Jose is a 37-year-old bilingual man who came with his wife and three children to the Untied States from Puerto Rico 6 years ago. He holds a bachelor's degree in science from a university in Puerto Rico. Jose is working full-time as a department manager while going to school part-time to pursue a graduate degree. He was recently separated from his wife due to his alcoholism and a battering incident that occurred as a result of his drinking. He was referred by the alcoholism agency to work on domestic violence behavior.

Jose, the oldest child in a family of five children, was characterized as a "good" boy. He always helped with the chores around the house, did well in school, and went to college. He had the responsible and placator roles described earlier (Wegscheider, 1981).

Jose's family did not support his college attendance. They felt he should get married and start his own family. Jose married a neighbor, to whom initially he was not attracted. The pressures of college and his new marriage led Jose to start drinking as a way to relax, and thus a pattern of alcohol abuse began. This coping behavior is consistent with the findings of Panitz, McGonchie, Sauber, and Fonseca (1983), who reported that machismo behavior may generate dysphoric states that are remedied by alcohol abuse.

After graduation from college, Jose and his family moved to the mainland to find better job opportunities and create a better life for themselves. By now, Jose had two children. Because of his alcohol abuse, Jose became emotionally distant from his wife and on one occasion he battered her while he was under the influence of alcohol. He also had an affair with another woman.

Recently his wife became pregnant with their third child and had an abortion without consulting Jose. Jose felt betrayed, went on a drinking binge, and returned home to batter his wife again. She called the police and he was taken in handcuffs to jail. She went to a women's shelter with her children. This was particularly disturbing for Jose because he perceived himself as having been responsible and not having had trouble in the past, and he prided himself on his "good" image.

Jose entered an alcoholism treatment program. When he was stabilized, he entered counseling for battering. Jose's motivation to enter counseling was to get his children and his wife back. Because he was working with his alcohol problem, he felt he would be all right as long as he did not drink. Cessation of drinking, however, does not necessarily mean that a man has dealt with the way he expresses anger or the way he deals with his sense of powerlessness.

The focus of the therapy was to help Jose shift his goal of getting his family back to one of focusing on himself. This therapeutic focus is consistent with the First Step of AA, that one is powerless over people, places, and things (Alcoholics Anonymous World Services, 1976). It is also consistent with the Serenity Prayer that asks for assistance to accept things one cannot change and the courage to change the things that one can. The therapist helped Jose to see that he had power to change his own behavior.

Jose began speaking in English, even though he was more comfortable in Spanish. This was his attempt to distance himself from his feelings. He was also having difficulty understanding the therapist and would often misinterpret what his therapist was saying. The therapist intervened and asked Jose if they could switch to Spanish. This facilitated the bonding between the client and therapist.

Because Jose was college educated, the therapist was able to utilize bibliotherapy as a technique. Often counselors are so used to working with educated people that they assume that this technique is acceptable to everyone. Some Hispanics, however, have not had much education, and this technique would not be appropriate.

The therapist recommended an anger work-out book (Weisinger, 1985) to Jose. Jose faithfully completed his assignments. He was seeing options that he had not been aware of in expressing his anger.

Jose kept trying to minimize what he had done, especially in comparison to what his wife had done to their unborn child, according to Jose. He had to learn that no event justified his becoming violent with his wife and that he had options on how to deal with his wife's "betrayal."

Figueroa-Torres and Pearson (1979) explained that aggression seems to be related to skill deficits that can be addressed through behavioral approaches such as modeling alternative coping responses, reinforcing nonaggressive actions, and developing of new behaviors that result in reward.

Jose voiced feelings of loss of his children, especially his 8-year-old son, who was named after him. This is particularly significant because Jose had never really had a childhood. He had become an adult at the age of 8. Often Latino children must work at an early age in order to help support the family.

Jose lived his childhood through his son, and any nurturance he received as a "child" came through his son. The therapist assisted Jose in grieving not only the separation from his son but also the loss of the childhood that he never had. Jose began to realize how perfectionistic he was with himself and others. Because of this, Jose absorbed much stress in life.

When they came to the mainland, Jose not only had to deal with the stresses of a change in culture and a new job, but economically he also had to help his family of origin in Puerto Rico. Other relatives from his side of the family and his wife's side of the family also wanted to come to the mainland and use Jose's home as an entry point until they became settled. Because they were unfamiliar with the culture and the environment, Jose had to take the time to help them look for work.

Many of Jose's family members were also dealing drugs as a way to make money and survive on the mainland. Jose became peripherally involved in supplying drugs to two clients. The clients were not eating properly and Jose felt so badly for them that he would feed them when they came over to pick up their drug supply. Jose even adopted one of the children of a client as a foster child because he felt sorry for the child. The child was taken away by Child Protective Services because of the battering incident. Now the child's mother wanted Jose to claim that the child is his so that he could regain custody.

The reality of the scenario just presented depicts how some Latino men can lose their self-esteem and their sense of control. This results in feelings of weakness and defensiveness. The sex role demands can be particularly strong for Latino men. Rather than viewing Latino men negatively, it is important to recognize that their behavior is a function of culture, racism, and their own actions. This point was addressed by De La Cancela (1986). This understanding of the reality of Latino men enables the therapist to deal compassionately with them so that they can feel supported in their quest for healthier coping mechanisms.

The therapist introduced Jose to the concept of the child within (Whitfield, 1987). Jose had to learn that he had an inner child within him who was yearning to be taken care of and who had been abandoned. Jose needed to become assertive and set limits to the requests from his family. He had to realize that living through his son allowed his son to be nurtured but at the same time it placed a burden on his son to perform for him, as Boszormenyi-Nagy and Spark (1984) discussed. It also left Jose empty because his satisfaction was solely in giving and not in receiving.

Jose had a difficult time visualizing the child within. The therapist suggested that he go to a toy store and pick out a stuffed animal or a doll made for little boys to bring to his therapy sessions with him. This technique is powerful with men because it brings them out of their heads, their intellect, and into their hearts, their emotional center. They actually get to touch their child within, to cradle him, and care for him in vivo.

The technique works in helping the men sort out what characteristic they want in their representation of that child within, thus solidifying the identity of that child. One would think that "macho" men would be turned off by this technique. Because it is an assignment from the therapist, however, many opt to experiment with it. It has become an in-house joke for these men to see other men coming in and out of the office with paper bags because they all know what is inside.

Jose has shown dramatic improvement since he has been taking care of his inner child. He sets limits at work, with friends, and with family. He now has more time to relax and work out at the gym. He is more able to be in touch with what he feels, and reports thinking before acting on his feelings. He has learned that he has choices and that he has his own needs and desires that he can meet or have met without feeling loss of control or fear of abandonment.

Further counseling will continue, but Jose is well on his way to recovery. Whether Jose will reunite with his family is uncertain at this point, but Jose's empowerment is helping him to live his life, not react to it. He can be a macho in the original Hispanic sense of the word: a noble man.

Antonio

Antonio is a 65-year-old, monolingual Spanish-speaking Mexican-American man who has lived in the United States for 30 years. He has been married for 32 years and has six children. Six years ago, Antonio was involved in an industrial accident and had to go on disability. His wife, Marta, also worked.

Antonio worked hard while he was employed, often putting in overtime. He left the house at 5 a.m. and did not return until 8 p.m. As a result, he did not spend much time with his family. Marta, also, worked outside of the home in addition to taking care of the children and doing household chores. She sacrificed herself for her children and her family and attended to the majority of their needs.

Two years ago, Marta was also in an industrial accident, hurt her back, and was in excruciating pain much of the time. She had to be sedated in order to sleep.

Marta was referred to the therapist by her physician because she had a nervous breakdown during which she attacked her husband with a knife. She had also awakened in the middle of the night and had began to cut up her hair in front of the bathroom mirror. She does not remember the incident.

After several therapy sessions, Marta confided in the male therapist that her husband had had sexual relations with her one evening while she was asleep and sedated. She felt violated and was outraged at her husband's insensitivity.

Antonio now had to do all the housework. He had never done housework before and he did the best he could. For example, when he made the tortillas, instead of making several thin tortillas, he figured that if he made a few thick ones, he would have to make fewer of them. Marta would become frustrated with Antonio over this because the tortillas looked more like pizzas. Antonio had become her hands and she felt frustrated that Antonio could not take care of the family the way she could. The frustrations over her own and her husband's limitations caused her to take it out on her husband's inability to do housework.

Antonio was angry with Marta because of her total dependence on him. Their sexual relationship had been totally shattered and his sexual needs were not being met, so he withheld affection.

After Marta became more stable, the therapist invited the couple to begin couples therapy to address the adjustment disorder that the accident had caused in their relationship. Antonio and Marta met as a couple once, but Antonio refused to continue because Marta was "the client." He wanted her back to her original condition.

Both Antonio and Marta denied the permanence of her condition. Each wanted the other to change. Marta wanted Antonio to stop resisting the housework and to do it properly, and Antonio wanted Marta to get well so she could go back to her role of family caretaker and sexual partner.

One day the therapist talked to Antonio alone, midway through a therapy session with Marta, and confronted Antonio about his denial. The therapist explained to Antonio that he, the therapist, could not do anything about Marta's back problem, and that his role was only to assist them cope with their present condition. The therapist was supportive about Antonio's dilemma regarding the perfectionistic pressure from Marta to do the housework. He also talked with Antonio about exploring other methods of sexual relations besides penetration.

Marta felt unattractive and useless. She complained that her husband was affectionate with her only when he wanted to engage in sexual relations. Antonio confirmed this fact. The therapist worked with Antonio to change his ways, and Antonio began to demonstrate more affection to Marta.

As Marta and Antonio began to accept the accident, they stopped using each other as scapegoats for their anger at the loss of Marta's health and began to be more supportive of each other.

Marta learned to be less demanding of Antonio and not to expect him to know what her needs were. She had to learn to ask for what she needed, something she had not been used to as the caretaker who had denied her own needs throughout her life. She also had to lower her expectations about Antonio's ability to do housework according to her standards.

The therapist pointed out to Marta that the demands on Antonio were as if they were on a ship and all of a sudden a wave tipped the boat and all the cargo shifted over to his side without warning. She had become accustomed to her responsibilities gradually. In fact, she learned that she had taken on so many responsibilities because it gave her more power in the relationship. Meanwhile, she spoiled Antonio into being responsible only for the economic needs of the family.

Antonio had gladly given up his responsibilities for the affectional needs of the family. In therapy, Antonio learned that he had had this pattern since childhood. His mother died when Antonio was 7 years old, and he was raised by his grandmother and his father. His father had been emotionally unavailable, and Antonio felt isolated as he was growing up. At the age of 15, Antonio left home and took care of himself. He shut down emotionally to avoid the pain of his losses as he was growing up.

Marta's accident disrupted a dysfunctional system that had been in balance for 30 years; however, the positive outcome of this accident was that Antonio and Marta are learning how to be a couple in a more functional way, and Antonio is learning how to become more affectionate, which frees him to become more involved with his family.

Antonio's prognosis seems hopeful. Davis and Chavez (1985), found that when there is functional necessity, Hispanic men tended to accept and adjust to the househusband role.

Conclusion

The three cases just presented address three men's journeys. The specific demands of their bicultural status contributed to the stress in their journeys. A therapist's ability to understand the bicultural context as well as the dynamics of the dysfunctional family patterns helped these men cope with the realities they faced.

Andres learned to take less responsibility for his nuclear family and is developing self-esteem. He learned how to say goodbye to his parents without severing his relationship with them, to live the paradox of detachment with love. He is learning to be a man and is learning to accept his Hispanic side, which he had always associated with negative stereotypes.

Jose is learning to take less responsibility for his extended family, to set limits in his own family, and to express his anger in a more appropriate way. He is also learning to deal with his alcoholism.

Antonio is learning not to run away from his pain and his feelings. He is also learning how to share responsibility and make and respond to requests in an assertive manner.

In any culture, when people do not have balance in their life, they will become dysfunctional. It is important for counselors to assist their clients in achieving this balance.

Counselors need to be aware that differences in the way Asian-American men conceptualize problems can produce difficulties in treatment.

Chapter 12

CULTURE IN TRANSITION: COUNSELING ASIAN-AMERICAN MEN

David Sue

This article will present an overview of issues related to counseling with Asian-American men. Before we begin, however, several points have to be made. First, the Asian-American population is composed of over 25 distinct subgroups, each of which may differ in terms of values, language, religion, and customs. Second, within-group differences are large and include differences in degree of assimilation or acculturation, generational status, or native born, refugee, or immigrant status. Such diversity in groups labeled Asian-American limits the extent of generalizations that can be made. Most individuals in these groups, however, share certain common values, and these will be presented. Traditional Asian values are likely to play a continuing role for Asian men in the United States. There is a continuing arrival of immigrants and refugees from Southeast Asia. Since 1975, over 700,000 refugees from Southeast Asia have entered the United States. These populations ensure the continuation of traditional values. Also, Asian men seem to acculturate less rapidly than do Asian women. The large number of Asians who are arriving in America is changing the characteristics of the Asian-American population. For example, over 60% of the Chinese in the United States are now recent immigrants. Asian Americans constitute a highly heterogeneous population composed of fully acculturated as well as traditionally oriented individuals. With this limitation in mind, however, I will focus on: (1) the family structure and values of traditional Asian Americans, (2) counseling approaches based on these values, (3) the impact of differences in acculturation and ethnic identity in Asian Americans, (4) special problems Asian men face, and (5) treatment strategies.

Family Structure and Values

The family structure of many traditional Asian-American families is prescribed in a hierarchical manner. Older generations are given an elevated status. Men are also accorded a higher status. Within the family, the dominant member is the father, although he is subservient to his parents and grandparents. The oldest son is generally accorded the second highest status. Male family members are expected to have primary allegiance to the family of origin and are responsible for carrying on the family name. Even when they marry, their major obligation is to their family of birth—spouses and children are of secondary importance. Women are expected to assume nuturing roles and to be subservient to men. When they marry, their primary allegiance is expected to be to their husband and his family. Therefore, greater expectations are placed on men to carry on the family traditions.

A counselor with a Western orientation may encounter some difficulty dealing with a male-dominant and hierarchical family situation because personal choice and equality of relationships are often seen as positive goals in counseling. The appropriate response to cultural differences needs to be determined carefully. Kitano (1989) discussed a case of a middle-aged immigrant woman who was treated for depression. Part of the treatment involved having her become more independent and assertive. These goals fit the Western model of mental health. However, questions can be raised about the appropriateness of this approach. What impact did the treatment have on her husband and family? Would her becoming more assertive and independent interfere with the hierarchical structure of the family?

In the traditional Asian family, children are expected to be obedient and to refrain from expressing strong emotions that may be disruptive to the family process. Individual desires and wishes are less important than the survival of the family. The behavior of the individual reflects on the character of the entire family. Behaviors such as disobedience to the parents, academic failure, or mental illness reflect upon and bring shame to the entire family. Admonitions of guilt and shame are the primary means that parents use to control their children. Obligations to the parents are continually stressed. Men, especially, feel the responsibility to maintain family traditions and values.

In working with an Asian family, a counselor must be able to identify his or her own values and their impact in therapeutic interventions with Asian clients. In one case, a Chinese family was referred to a counselor because of acting-out behaviors of their teenage son. During the family session, the father seemed uncomfortable and noncommunicative. Both the son and the mother were able to talk about the conflicts at home. The counselor came to view the problem as the father's being too restrictive and controlling of the son's behavior. She addressed questions to the father about his views of child rearing. He indicated that the problem was the bad behavior of the son. The mother seemed uncomfortable with the questions the counselor raised. The family did not return for further sessions.

What could have been done in this case? Several problems interfered with the success of the counseling session. First, the father as the head of the family should have been addressed first. Because he is the representative of the family, attempts to find out his perspective of the problem would have maintained his status. In Western families, where there is more equality in relationships, having family members respond before the father is less of a problem. Second, allowing the son to voice complaints to his father was an affront. The counselor should have taken an active part in structuring the son's response in a manner that was more acceptable to the father. Jung (1984) reported a case study in which a different approach was used in dealing with an Asian family whose son had also been referred because of behavioral and school problems. During the session, Mr. and Mrs. W.'s definitions of the problem were elicited first. The father complained that his son was angry, rebellious, and stubborn. To lend a more positive note, the counselor also asked about positive aspects about the boy. The father added that his son was intelligent and could succeed if he applied himself. He also added some additional observations about his son. The son was asked if the description was accurate. He said, "Yes," and was surprised that his father knew him so well. The father was then asked what he expected of his son. The father indicated some of the problems he faced living in the United States and indicated that he was apprehensive that his son was beginning to adopt American customs. He wanted his son to succeed but also to remember his family. John, the son, was asked if he knew of the hardships that his father faced and the parents' concern that they were losing him. He said that his father had never mentioned these to him, but felt that his father was old-fashioned. The counselor gently admonished John for using this term for his father, indicating that the father's behavior reflected traditional Asian values. The counselor then asked John to relate his ideas to his parents on how the relationship could be improved. With the counselor functioning as a mediator, the father acknowledged that his son did have many good qualities. The son also understood some of the reasons his father acted the way he did and that his father did want him to succeed. During the subsequent sessions, with the appropriate respect established, both father and son indicated a willingness to make some changes. The father became more flexible in areas in which his son had demonstrated responsibility, and their relationship continued to improve.

Another case, reported by Sue and Morishima (1982), involved a family with the therapy initiated by the wife.

> Mrs. C. sought treatment at a local mental health center. She was depressed and tearful. She related that she and her

husband had recently immigrated from Hong Kong to the United States. Their marriage had gone well until her husband succeeded in bringing his parents over to live with them. Although Mrs. C. was not enthusiastic about this living arrangement, she accepted the necessity of helping his parents.

Unfortunately, Mrs. C. found out that she was expected to serve her husband's parents. She was expected to do all the cooking, washing, and other household chores. Her mother-in-law also would complain that Mrs. C. was not doing a good job. Mrs. C. would tell her husband about her unhappiness. He responded by saying, "They are my parents and they're getting old." The husband tried to avoid the conflict but would side with his parents when pressed.

From the Western perspective, the situation might seem to be patently unfair for Mrs. C. The attempts might be to try to help her develop a greater sense of personal happiness and to discuss the problem with her husband's parents directly. Such an approach might have produced unproductive family conflict. From Mr. C.'s perspective, he was fulfilling the traditional cultural expectation. He owed responsibility to his parents and was doing what was expected of a "good" son. His wife's concern was secondary to his obligation. Instead of a direct approach, the clinician decided to work through a mediator. In questioning Mrs. C. it was discovered that she thought her uncle (the mother-in-law's older brother) was a sympathetic individual. His help was enlisted. He came over for dinner and explained to his sister in private that Mrs. C. looked tired and unhappy. The mother-in-law was surprised to hear this and said that Mrs. C. was doing a good job and was a good wife. The indirect message was understood and the mother-in-law diminished her criticism and even began to help out with the chores.

When this approach is described to many counselors, they indicate some feelings of discomfort with the solution. Many feel that Mrs. C.'s personal needs were still not being met and she was merely adapting to an environment that did not allow her greater self-expression. Certainly, if Mr. C. was willing to come in for counseling, other accommodations could be made. The counselor might indicate an understanding of the conflict that Mr. C. was facing and even praise him for fulfilling his obligation. Within this framework, the counselor might ask Mr. C. his view of the problem and suggestions for improving the situation. Again, within traditional Asian families, when both spouses are present, it is very important to address the man first before the woman, even though women may be more ready to talk about personal difficulties.

Asian Americans also display a different personality pattern from Caucasian Americans. These differences seem to stem from cultural values. Studies have reported that Asian-American men as opposed to Caucasian men score lower on self-assertion (Fukuyama & Greenfield, 1983), display greater anxiety in situations requiring assertiveness (Sue, Ino, & Sue, 1983), are more likely to score higher in introversion, passivity, self-restraint, and deference (Abbott, 1987; Bourne, 1975, Conner, 1975; Sue & Kirk, 1975).

The personality characteristics Asian-American men display are thought to be a result of the cultural values that emphasize the need for control of emotional expression, self-control, sensitivity to the reaction of others, and the need not to behave in a manner that would reflect badly upon the family. Several points have to be made, however. First, not all Asian-American men fit this pattern. Large within-group differences exist. In the Sue et al. study (1983), many Asian men scored similarly to their Caucasian counterparts on personality measures. Second, Asian Americans do display a wide range of emotional reactions such as anger, insecurity, and jealousy to a number of different situations. Third, personality descriptions such as "passive" and "introvert" are considered negative in Western cultures, whereas in Asian cultures they are seen as virtues reflecting filial piety (respect and obligation to parents), modesty, and respect for authority. Certainly an individual who displays nonassertiveness because of cultural values is different from a person who is nonassertive because of insecurity or passive-aggressive tendencies. In Western culture, assertiveness and emotional expression are seen as positive characteristics. A counselor who works with an Asian man who displays emotional restraint might want the client to become more expressive. For a traditional Asian, this may lead to increased feelings of conflict.

The way people view behavior is influenced by their cultural perspective. The importance of this influence is revealed in a study by Li-Repac (1980). She studied the impact of cultural interpretation on ratings of Chinese and Caucasian clients by Chinese and Caucasian therapists. The clinicians were asked to rate both sets of videotapes of client interviews. In general, Caucasian therapists rated Caucasian clients more positively than Chinese clients. The reverse was true for Chinese clinicians. Caucasian clinicians were more likely to use term such as "anxious," "awkward," "confused," "inhibited," and "less social poise" to describe Chinese patients, whereas Chinese clinicians used terms such as "dependable," "reliable," "friendly," and "alert" to describe the same individuals. Chinese therapists also perceived Caucasian patients to be aggressive. This study certainly supports the idea that culture plays a role in how people view behaviors.

It is important for counselors to be aware that some Asian men do express a desire to become more assertive. Many experience feelings of discomfort in social situations and with authority figures. To deal with this concern, typical assertiveness training workshops can be modified. The initial focus of discussion during training is on the influence of traditional values on behavior and their positive influence. The values of respect for elders and gentleness are discussed, as is the importance of maintaining such values. Situations in which these behaviors may be nonfunctional, such as being silent in the classroom or overly modest during job interviews, are then presented. The ability to demonstrate differential nonassertiveness is discussed. In other words, the individual can choose to be deferential with parents, relatives, and in other such situations but can be assertive in others (with professors, employers, etc.). In the Sue et al. study (1983), many of the Asian-American men were not globally nonassertive but were instead situationally nonassertive. They were assertive with peers and in certain situations. Programs that help Asian men discriminate appropriate and inappropriate situations for being assertive can be an important component of a positive therapeutic intervention.

Acculturation and Ethnic Identity

Most of our discussion has revolved around individuals holding traditional values. As we mentioned earlier, Asian men are heterogeneous in terms of the degree of acculturation and commitment to cultural identity. Many third-, fourth-, and fifth-generation Asian Americans have acculturated and retain few of the values and attitudes of their ethnic groups. Kitano (1989) stated that Asian Americans vary on two important dimensions—assimilation (process of adopting the values and customs of the dominant culture) and ethnic identity (the retention of ethnic values). Individuals can be high or low on each of these dimensions. Types of problems an individual faces can vary according to these two dimensions, and a counselor should be aware of these differences. Four different patterns can be distinguished:

High Assimilation, Low Ethnic Identity

Asian men in this group may be nearly Americanized. They identify fully with American values in dress and behavior and have little or no facility with their Asian language. Many have married outside of their ethnic group and have an egalitarian relationship with their spouse and children. Problems individuals in this group display are similar to those the majority group members display. However, ethnic consciousness may remain. For example, even fourth- and fifth-generation Asian-American children have a more negative feeling about their physical characteristics than do their White peers (Pang, Mizokawa, Morishima, & Olstad, 1985). The scarcity of Asian role models will continue to result in racial self-consciousness. Although assimilation is occurring, not all values are changing at the same pace. Asian-American men of a later generation may still exhibit some hesitancy about asserting themselves, feel uncomfortable in evaluative social situations, and allow themselves more limited career choices. With this group, counselors and clinicians generally can use the same techniques and approaches that they employ with Western-oriented clients. Asians in this group are comfortable with discussing emotional issues and value self-exploration.

Low Assimilation, Low Ethnic Identity

Asian men in this group are marginal to both cultures. They are sometimes severely mentally ill. Kitano (1989) described a Japanese-American alcoholic who felt that his problem was being an Asian in a White society. He felt his Asianness would disappear when he became drunk and rejected his racial identity. However, he did not feel accepted by White society except when he was under the influence of alcohol. This category is similar to the marginal man concept in which the individual has rejected his ethnic identity. However, the individual becomes aware that he cannot quite fit in with the other cultural group and so, rejects both. Individuals in this group all tend to be dysfunctional.

High Assimilation, High Ethnic Identity

Bicultural is the best term used to describe individuals in this group. They feel comfortable with the values of both groups and move easily between them. Although the counseling approach does not have to be modified with these individuals, Kitano believes that because they possess insights from a multicultural perspective, a unicultural counselor may have too narrow a focus when working with clients with a bicultural orientation.

Low Assimilation, High Ethnic Identity

Individuals in this group include recent immigrants, refugees, those living in ethnic communities, and many second- and even third-generation Asians. Counselors working with members of this group are most likely to require information about cultural values. In working with Asian men in this group, much of what was discussed earlier for traditionally oriented individuals would apply. Physical complaints involving headaches, fatigue, and sleep disturbances are common and must be addressed. They are real concerns to these individuals. Western cultures tend to have a psychosomatic orientation—that is, they believe that physical complaints without clear organic cause are the results of psychological problems. White (1982), in a study of world cultures, stated that this conceptualization is a minority view in the world, and that if we consider the somatization of psychological problems to be a characteristic of Asian cultures, we should also study the psychologization of illness by members of Western cultures.

Kinzie (1985) outlined some possible areas in which Asian clients differ from Western clients:

Asian Beliefs	Western Beliefs
Family interdependence	Personal choice and independence
Structured, hierarchical relationships	Equality of relationships
Mental illness due to lack of willpower	Mental illness resulting from psychological or physical factors
Emotional restraint healthy	Emotional expression healthy
Problem due to bodily symptoms	Bodily symptoms a reflection of psychological problems

Differences in the way clients conceptualize problems can produce difficulties in treatment. Tsui and Schultz (1985) presented a case of a 55-year-old Asian man who was referred for counseling by the family physician. The man had complaints involving back pain and headaches that seemed to have no physical basis. The therapist was in her 30s and a Caucasian. The client complained about his back pain and indicated that he had obtained no relief from three different physicians. He stated that his cousin had recommended that he try some folk medicine and asked the therapist if he should try it. The therapist acknowledged the client's discomfort and asked if something stressful had occurred during the past year. The client said no, and then asked, "You must be a very bright woman being a doctor at such a young age as my daughter . . . How old are you, Doctor?" . . .(p. 566). The therapist responded by asking the reason for the question and if he thought that she would not be able to help him. The client became flustered and denied that interpretation. He indicated that he had not learned American customs yet and was sorry he had offended her. He shared some background information and then asked her information about her background. The therapist responded by asking him about his life in America. The client talked for the remainder of the hour, thanked her, and apologized again for being rude. He never returned for the second session.

What was wrong with the session? First, because the therapist was younger than the client and also female, she had low ascribed status. Second, the therapist adopted the Western view of physical complaints. She did not inquire about his physical problems and made the assumption that they were due to stress or other psychological factors. Thus, the communication between client and therapist was on different levels. The therapist might have inquired about the physical symptoms, found out when they occurred, and how the client had dealt with them in the past. If this had been done, the client's problem would have received attention and the therapist would have gained some idea about what the physical problems meant to the client. Her avoiding his complaints and questions were blows to his status, especially because she was female and younger than himself. Demonstrating some attention and respect to the client would have helped increase the possibility of a therapeutic alliance. However, the client still attempted to communicate with the therapist by relating some personal information and inquiring about her personal background. This was an attempt to gain commonality of background so she would not be considered a stranger and thus become an individual with whom personal material could be shared. Again, the client felt rebuffed in this attempt. If the therapist had responded to the initial physical complaints, answered the client's questions about her background directly, and demonstrated respect for the client and some understanding of his status, a therapeutic alliance could have been formed because the therapist would have obtained an achieved status.

Work with individuals in this group often will involve the use of interpreters because of poor facility with the English language. When working with Asian men, older male interpreters should be employed if possible because they have a higher status and will engender better response than would a young female interpreter. Again, the male client should be addressed first.

Special Problems With Asian Men

Educational Expectations

The pressure for Asian men to succeed academically is very high. More pressure is placed on men because they are expected to continue the family tradition. The drive to excel is great. In a study of recent Asian immigrants (Sue & Zane, 1985), good grades were the result of taking reduced course loads, and studying more hours (approximately 22 hours a week). This pressure may have been responsible for the finding that recent immigrants had high levels of anxiety and felt lonely and isolated. A male student who came in for counseling reflected this pattern. His parents expected him to do well and to earn straight As. He received no praise for Bs. Instead they indicated that he could do better. He spent most of his time in the library and had few friends or social contacts. Even his choice of a major was dictated by his parents. He became very resentful of his parents' demands but also felt guilty because he knew that his parents had sacrificed to help him enter school. Part of his conflict was the awareness that not everyone faced this type of pressure.

The client was struggling with his internalized values and his personal desire for independence. In this case, the counselor helped the client verbalize his conflict and to assess his performance realistically. The client had a 3.5 grade point average and acknowledged that he had done well academically. He also said that his parents were proud of him and that they merely wanted him to succeed. The client also wanted to be more independent, and ways of accomplishing this were discussed. He decided to talk to his mother and father about changing his major. The counselor was able to help the client understand the nature of the problem and to assess it realistically. The client also understood his need to become more independent, and was able to do it in a manner that produced the least amount of conflict.

Career Choices

As opposed to women, Asian men experience greater career restriction. They are more likely to go into the physical sciences such as engineering, chemistry, biology, and physics. This was reported in a study by Sue and Frank (1973) and is still found to be true (Sue et al., 1983; Sue & Zane, 1985). In the Sue et al. study, over 80% of the Asian men were majoring in the physical sciences, as opposed to only 35% of their Caucasian peers. Interestingly, when the study participants were asked about the reasons for the choice of field, they all answered "money." It was difficult to question this response because physical scientists do make more money than individuals in the social sciences. However, Asian men also may choose the physical sciences because they might be less subject to discrimination and prejudice in those areas than in the social sciences. Unfortunately, counselors may guide Asian men into the physical sciences unintentionally, believing them to be good in math but not good in social fields. As with any other group that has faced restricted career choices, the counselor must explore carefully all possible fields with Asian men.

Refugee Problems

Many Cambodians, Vietnamese, Khmer, and Hmong currently living in the United States have suffered severe personal losses. Many did not have time to prepare to leave their countries and fled because of danger to their lives. Because of this, a large percentage had to leave one or more family members behind. In one study of Southeast Asian refugees (Nguyen, 1985), the heads of the households complained of homesickness, loneliness, and depression. They often feel powerless to deal with these concerns, especially due to their lack of proficiency in English. Compounding the problem, many are unable to find a job. Their wives often have a more successful employment experience. In addition, their children often learn English more quickly and thus take the role of mediating between their father and the environment. Such factors have led to the loss of male status and increased feelings of powerlessness and isolation in the male head of household. Vietnamese refugees have voiced complaints that their children are displaying less respect for adults, and that the changing role of women toward greater equality is creating problems. A counselor may have to deal with problems of differential acculturation between family members and the loss of status of adult men. In addition, information about past trauma involving the loss of loved ones and reactions to this country must be explored.

In one case (Nishio & Bilmes, 1987), a Laotian couple was referred for psychotherapy. The husband had problems with alcohol abuse and would also physically abuse his wife. The psychotherapist encouraged the wife to leave her husband and to become more independent. The couple promptly left therapy and sought treatment from an Asian therapist. The counselor responded with respect to the Laotian man and established a good relationship. He reframed the notion of greater independence for the wife in terms of it allowing the husband to have more time for himself. Difficulties adjusting to the United States were brought out, and the husband was willing to discuss his feelings of inadequacy. Gradually the husband understood that his wife was trying to help him and not usurping his position. He quit beating her and also stopped drinking. In this case, the Asian counselor demonstrated an understanding of the traditional Asian family relationship, was nonjudgmental, and was able to effect change within the cultural context. A counselor must be careful, however, that he or she does not force a client to remain in an unhealthy situation. In the above case, if the wife wanted to leave the husband or become more independent, these wishes would have to be considered. However, the impact of these changes on her, her family, and her status in the community would have to be brought up so that the client would be able to consider fully the consequences of her decisions.

Treatment Strategies

In counseling traditional Asian-American men, certain guidelines can be useful in establishing a therapeutic relationship:

1. Use restraint in gathering information. Because of the stigma attached to mental illness or the seeking of help from a counselor, there will be difficulty obtaining information. The counselor might indicate that talking about their concerns might be difficult, but that they should feel good in being concerned about the well-being of the family. Sharing some personal information with the client also may be useful in establishing trust.
2. Explain to the client what occurs in counseling. Many will expect medication and not understand what psychotherapy is. Lambert and Lambert (1984) found that Asian immigrants who were provided information about counseling and the need to share information had more positive reactions to therapy, saw their therapist in a more positive light, and were more satisfied than were immigrants who did not receive such preparation regarding the counseling process.
3. Ask the client describe the problem as he sees it. If a physical complaint is brought up, allow the client to discuss it. Find out how he has dealt with similar problems in the past. Starting off with the client's perception of the problem reduces the chance that the worldview of the counselor will predominate.
4. Assume a more directive and structured role, especially during the early sessions. Counseling is a new phenomenon to many Asian men. There is an expectation that the counselor will offer the direction and answers. Some use of empathy techniques can be helpful after trust is established with the client. Do not make the assumption that discussion of feelings will not be useful, but do not begin with this approach.
5. Many of the problems of immigrants and refugees may revolve around dealing with the environment. The client may need assistance in filling out forms and interacting with different agen-

cies; such assistance addresses a major concern of the client and helps establish trust and appreciation of the counselor.

6. In working with families, assess for the possibility of intergenerational conflicts resulting from changes in status and acculturation levels. Be especially aware of the potential loss of status of adult men.

7. The therapy should be time-limited and focus on the specific resolution of the problem as identified by the individual or the family.

8. In working with families, the structured family approach may be helpful because it is consistent with the organization of Asian families, establishes the therapist as the authority figure, and focuses on the strengths rather than the weaknesses of the family. Instead of having the family members address one another as would be done with a Western-oriented family, the members address their reactions to the counselor. The structured family approach also has an advantage in that for Asians, the family is the important unit, not the individual (Jung, 1984).

Asian-American men are going through a process of acculturation and culture conflict. Many feel that their values are being eroded because of exposure to the American culture. Some desperately try to hang on to their traditions, others move rapidly toward assimilation. In both groups, the individual experiences change and often a loss of status. The counselor often must help the Asian man sort through the changes involved, being careful not to impose his or her worldview but also not assuming that the Asian man wants to maintain the status quo. Perceptiveness and flexibility on the part of the counselor is essential, as is the need for respect for the client and his cultural values.

TECHNIQUES AND TREATMENTS

A strong, grounded sense of masculine identity does more than anything else to help men be caring, nurturing, powerful, and responsible adults.

Chapter 13

A PERSONAL PERSPECTIVE ON WORKING WITH MEN IN GROUPS

Patrick Dougherty

After many years of working with men as a psychotherapist, I have become convinced that a man's participation in a men's group is very helpful for his emotional and psychological maturity and individuation. Indeed, I now see it as almost a necessity. I once viewed group therapy as just another therapeutic option to be used only occasionally for a particular client. I used to adhere to what most of the professional literature says about working with men, that is, that they prefer goal-oriented, structured therapy. But upon reflection, I wondered, doesn't this goal-oriented and structured approach merely perpetuate some of men's problems? Is it not just as important to provide a setting in which men could safely relax their often rigid boundaries and explore their feelings?

In working with men, I once preferred individual or couples therapy; in each, I could offer a structured approach. I could often see men make great strides forward in their ability to know themselves and share that knowledge with others. Over time, though, I became aware that these men had learned to function only within a limited sphere. Yes, they had learned to interact with a high degree of sophistication and maturity in one or two relationships, often with a significant other and possibly with a friend or two, but few ventured beyond that. For most, their dependence on the few relationships in which they could function narrowed their lives. Moreover, it often created an emotional burden that led to significant problems or a breakdown in these relationships, especially the significant-other relationship. Also, the men I counseled often became dependent on therapy and did not want to leave our client-therapist relationship. In short, these men were not able to sustain or build on the progress that they initially made.

Consequently, I began to ask myself some questions: What common but unspoken underlying problems bring these men to my office and why have I been blind to them? Why are these men not using what they have learned in individual and couples therapy to broaden their lives? What do they lack that seemingly makes them content to live such restricted lives?

Lack of a Strong Masculine Identity

After years of practice and reflection I think I have found an answer: Most men who come to therapy do not have a strong masculine identity. We psychotherapists are often concerned with the genderless word "self-esteem," but the concept falls far short of identifying what an individual, man or woman, needs to build a mature ego. Most men entering therapy tell me they have low self-esteem; rarely does a man tell me he doesn't feel good about being a man. Many men have left my office feeling good about their self-esteem, but I think few have left feeling grounded in their manhood. Now I ask: How strong is your masculine esteem? Most men respond with a confused look and an inarticulate answer. This led me to an obvious and rhetorical question: How grounded or relationship-healthy can a person be if he or she is not grounded in his or her gender?

So to whom does a man turn to get grounded in his masculine identity? Obviously, to other men. (I can say "obviously" now, after spending several years searching for an answer.) It astounds me how many men, and professionals who counsel men, honestly believe that a man can figure out who he is by being in a relationship with a woman. Clearly, a man needs to be with other men to learn what is unique and special about being a man. In the language of the mythopoetic arm of the men's movement, a man needs to be with other men to learn the "male mysteries."

The Absence of the Healthy Male Group

The environment most conducive to this learning is the male group. Many elements are needed to facilitate optimal male development, but perhaps none is so overlooked as the male group. Historically, "the (male) group has played a crucial role in masculine individuation and has been the single most powerful source of rites of passage in the psyche of man" (Berstein, 1987, p. 139).

Unfortunately, the importance of the male group has been eroding in Western cultures for hundreds of years. Indeed, in our culture two major events have contributed to the breakdown of what I call the healthy male group. The first was the founding of our nation, when rugged in-dividualism, self-sufficiency, and taking care of "one's own" became the ideals by which the "new man" in the New World lived and died. The

Industrial Revolution, with its emphasis on the self-made or independent man, followed. Both events placed the individual above the group. As a result, they facilitated a lessening of dependence on the group, the consequence of which was the loss of the benefits to be derived from the group.

In generations past, the healthy male group helped provide men with the three elements needed for individuation or maturity (Henderson, 1964). First, the group helped the man separate from his family or clan (which usually for the young boy was a world dominated by the feminine). Second, the group provided him with a place in which he could commit himself for a considerable time while he matured. Third, the maturing allowed him to become less attached to the safety of the group and to set out on a more individual path later in his life.

In today's culture, the first element, the need to separate, still holds true. The young man is still brought up in a world mostly dominated by the feminine because women are still the primary caregivers and nurturers of children. Obviously, a man has to leave this world, separate from it, to develop a healthy masculine ego. (As fathers become more involved in caregiving and nurturing, this process of male individuation will no doubt have to be revised.)

Given the lack of healthy male groups, the second element, the need to commit oneself to a group for a considerable time, usually goes unmet. If the adolescent or young man is fortunate enough to find a male group, it is often a peer group. He may belong to a group he has known since childhood or joined in his high school or college days, but there are usually no older men in these groups who can teach or initiate him. Thus, he is left to grow up by experimentation and guesswork and by watching his peers experiment and guess.

The third element needed for individuation and maturity, the transition of lessening the attachment to the group, goes wanting. How does a man become less dependent on a nonexistent group? From where does he embark as he steps out on his own? We now often call this transition the mid-life crisis. Most men are ill-prepared for this psychic transition, and maladaptive behaviors abound. "So pervasive has the general awareness of this phenomenon become that as we approach this time of life we almost automatically begin to brace for a psychological emergency" (Stein, 1983, p. 1). If a man had been a longtime member of a healthy group, instead of bracing himself for a psychological emergency, perhaps he would be able to embrace and welcome this transition in life.

Male Groups Today

Certainly there are group settings in which men can come together to learn. Unfortunately, most of these groups have lost the power and mystique needed to transform the male psyche. Too often the intent of group participation is to find an arena for individual advancement or a place to hide. We are left with remnants, or worse, aberrations of the healthy male group.

The military service is now a remnant, in part, because our culture has lost respect for what it traditionally offered men. Until the mid-1950s, the military service was perhaps the most universal and most powerful group for radical transformation of the male psyche. Its traditions encompassed an initiation ritual (boot camp), the requirement of commitment, competition to challenge one another to become better soldiers, and a high degree of cooperation without much focus on individual accomplishments. After the Korean War, and especially during the Vietnam War, respect for these traditions eroded drastically. Many reluctant men were drafted into the service and begrudged the time they served. Moreover, individual survival often became more important than group survival. The fear and awe that once accompanied entry into the armed forces were replaced too often by resignation and resentment. This lack of awe and respect for the military service continues today.

The male group as an aberration of its former self is quite easy to find. Many men use groups such as the Lions Club, the V.F.W., the community sports leagues, and the less formal fishing and hunting groups as a place to hide. These groups are often used as an escape from the feminine world—not for initiation or maturation as is needed, but out of fear of being dominated and engulfed by that world. Lacking a healthy male group to help him separate from the feminine world, a boy is likely to oppose or polarize against the feminine in an attempt to find his masculinity. The result is an ongoing and often unconscious fear of the feminine, which often manifests as disrespect for or even hatred of the feminine. The problem lies in the fact that a man has had no place to build a solid masculine identity by which to distinguish himself from the powerful feminine in a mature and respectful manner. Consequently, when a man is drawn to male groups as an adult, as Lionel Tiger (1970) argued in his controversial and compelling book on men's biological draw to groups, he joins groups of other men who are as emotionally stuck and confused as he is.

What Group Therapy Can Offer

Clearly, given the lack of healthy male groups in our society, group therapy can fill a significant void in a man's life. Many men who come to therapy want to straighten out their lives, but they usually want to do so in an isolated, contained manner. While in individual or couples therapy, men can often limit how much of the outside world knows of their struggles and can control the degree to which therapy influences their lives. Their desire to control and hide the fact that they have problems is an obvious consequence of our culture's emphasis on the independent man.

Because most of the men who come to me lack a sense of their masculine identity, and because individual or couples therapy is limited in responding to this problem, I now, albeit somewhat belatedly, often recommend group therapy. Men tend to balk at this suggestion initially, but consent when they are able to see how much of their struggles stem from their lack of a strong masculine identity.

Joining a therapy group can offer a man a semblance of the three elements of male maturation I have already discussed. A man joins as "the new guy on the block." He does not know what the others know about the group or the process, and thus gets a chance to be naive and innocent. This in itself is often so foreign and longed for that it opens up emotional wounds from childhood that the man may have forgotten he even had. Secondly, all of the men must make a commitment to the group. With the commitment comes a man's opportunity of being responsible for himself, to the other members of the group, and for the health of the group itself. Having to be responsible to others and also for individual growth usually flushes out more old wounds and new behaviors to work on. Finally, as a man approaches his time to leave the group, he slowly becomes less invested in the group process and the other men, who usually respond with some sadness and envy but mostly with a lot of respect and honor.

The group offers, perhaps for the first time, a place where a man can allow himself to be open and vulnerable with other men. It is not just a place where he can "get in touch with his feelings," which is often touted as the solution to men's problems. It is also a place where he can learn some of the male mysteries. In group, a man can learn what is unique and special about being a man. He finds answers to some important questions: What are the male modes of feeling and communication? How do they differ from the female modes? What does it mean to be a lover, husband, father? What is powerful and what is dangerous about being a man?

When most men figure out that they do not have much of a sense of their masculinity, they usually search relentlessly until they find it. Group therapy is a wonderful and powerful place to search out and explore it. The group can help a man define and embrace his masculine identity. Once a man feels grounded in his masculine identity, he then has the foundation from which to work as he decides how he wants to be with himself and others. I believe that a strong, grounded sense of masculine identity does more than anything else to help men be caring, nurturing, powerful, and responsible adults.

Techniques

Most men who begin therapy are quite locked into the rational and concrete, but once given the opportunity and guidance to speak about themselves in different modes, they respond quickly, albeit anxiously. One of the most effective techniques I use with men, regardless of the type of therapy (e.g., individual, couples, group) is the analogous story. Throughout history, and until recent times, in both primitive and sophisticated societies, men have formally gathered to tell stories. In our culture, men often gather informally, but not less significantly, to tell stories. Stories roll easily from men's mouths—over a drink after work, at the ball park with a friend, while playing cards, on a hunting or fishing trip. Stories have always been a man's way of telling others about himself.

Given that they have some comfort telling stories about themselves, most men quickly learn to use this technique to disclose the depth of their wounds and struggles. In the group therapy setting, it is an effective vehicle that listeners often easily relate to and learn from. In therapy, a man's story often begins when he is encouraged to find a personal metaphor, draw a picture, or write a poem trying to describe something about himself. Just this week in group men were using personal metaphors: a wolf disguised as a fox, a king accountable to no one, a passive servant harboring a lot of righteous indignation, the raging beast hidden behind the innocent child, and others.

Case Examples

Once a man begins to tell his story, it is the therapist's responsibility to help him attend to the issues that need addressing in a creative and responsible way. Rather than listing and describing all the techniques available, I will let the stories speak for themselves.

Ted and His Fear

Referred by another therapist, Ted had been in the group for several months. He needed help to grieve about his recent divorce and to explore some issues that had created problems in his marriage and contributed to its demise. He and his ex-wife had joint custody of their two young daughters. He had just been promoted to a middle-management position in a computer processing firm.

Ted came from a family of five—an older brother and sister and his parents. His father was an evangelical minister with a parish in a fairly large southwestern city. The family rules he remembered were quite rigid and usually backed by scripture. Ted did not in any way claim to have had a terrible childhood, but he knew that his fear of his father paralyzed him in many situations.

Ted had been trying for several weeks to explain why he had been scared of his father as a boy and why he was still scared of him. The other group members were totally lost; they kept telling him that they neither understood nor felt that Ted was in touch with his fear. Ted's use of evangelical theology and words such as "salvation" and "damnation" only added to the confusion. The co-leader and I were exasperated as to how to help Ted clarify this issue to himself and the group. At the end of a particularly frustrating session, I asked Ted to think of a nonverbal way to help the group understand what he was trying to tell us.

Visibly excited, Ted came to the next group with a roll of brown paper under his arm. He explained that he had drawn a picture of his father. He taped the top of the roll to the wall and let it unroll. The size (about three feet by four feet) and content of the picture left us all stunned for several minutes.

On the paper was a dark, monstrous man hanging on a cross; he had claws and fire spewed from his mouth. Next to the cross were three pictures of a boy. In the first, the boy was curled into a near-fetal position, in the second he was stooped, and in the third he stood straight with rage surging through arms pointed at the man on the cross. Ted explained that the boy in the fetal position illustrated how he had felt most of his life toward his father. The stooped boy showed how he now felt, and the upright, raging boy indicated what he felt he must be able to do to be free of his fear of his father.

Ted was never stuck for more than one session after that time. He often brought his picture and would work with it as it hung on the wall. He would stand, with tears running down his cheeks, and tell us stories about his childhood, which we now understood. For several months he tried to get angry or rage at the man on the cross, but in the end he would always sob with fear, unable to look at the picture. It wasn't until nearly a year later that he was able to stand up and angrily call down the man on the cross. To do so, Ted had to own the dark man within him. He had to admit that he was his father's son in more ways than he cared to be. Ted had learned about the dark side of himself by watching Alan.

Alan Facing His Dark Side

Alan, a single man in his mid-30s, worked as a foreman in a construction supply warehouse. He was quite shy and insecure, but most people viewed him as a competent and humble man. After several months of individual psychotherapy, we both agreed that group therapy would be more challenging and more fruitful. He had sought help because of his insecurity and his inability to maintain a long-term relationship with a woman. He was the second oldest boy in a large Catholic family. His father had worked as a superintendent for the state highway department. A stern disciplinarian, he had often physically abused his sons with his hand or a belt if they upset him.

As Alan shared his struggles with the group and spoke of his shyness and inhibition with women he dated, he also divulged that he had always had "other" women in his life while he was dating. He met most of them at work and had long-term exploitive sexual relations with them. Alan did not care about or respect these "other" women, used them for sex only when he wanted it, and had callous disregard for their feelings about his behavior. He explained that they were consenting adults; all they had to do was say no and he would be gone. The group had a hard time reconciling the shy, inhibited man with the sexually abusive and condescending man.

Alan saw the inconsistency in his behavior toward women and decided to try not to have relations with "other" women. One day in group, after Alan had had another "slip" in which he had pounded on a woman's door at 3 a.m. to wake her (and half the apartment house) so he could have some quick sex, I asked him to speak from the part of him that had pounded on the door. He sat quietly for a while, staring at the floor. Then a small, slight, hideous smirk appeared on his face, and he began to talk about women in one of the most hateful, disrespectful, and condescending manners I had ever witnessed. He went on this way for about 5 minutes. I watched as the other group members squirmed in their chairs, looking appalled and horrified. Alan broke off abruptly but continued to stare at the floor with that awful smirk on his face.

Alan had just been the first man in the group to own, in the first person, his dark side or, as the Jungians call it, his shadow. Other men had described mean or degrading behavior but always with detachment as if it were an aberration and somehow not a real part of themselves. Alan had changed all that. I asked the group to examine their own feelings before they condemned Alan. Slowly, most of the men were able to own that part of themselves that felt like Alan did, but it scared the hell out of them to see it in themselves as well as in Alan. Two of the men could not relate and remained silent.

Alan started to cry and was quickly supported for his courage, which only encouraged his sobbing. When he quit crying, Alan shared with the group what was so painful about talking from that part of himself. It wasn't remorse about his abuse of the women in his life, that would come much later. At the moment, it was the fact that he knew his feelings about women were the same as his father's, even though he had vowed to never, ever be like his father in this regard.

Of course, having clients act out the character in themselves they are trying to describe is an exercise that comes out of the psychodrama school. Just as important is the group leader's willingness and ability to act out the character if a client is stuck. This action by the leader not only gives clients permission but also serves as a model and helps lessen the feeling of foolishness.

John and His Witch

John had been in group for 3 months. His goals were to work on his anger at women and to become an active member of the group because he had never been part of a group of men. He had talked about his "snaky" behavior with women but never seemed to go far enough with it. Even after he had drawn a picture of that part of himself—a colorful and frightening witch—he remained emotionally stuck until I asked him to stand up and act out the witch.

Obviously feeling foolish and awkward, John tried to play his witch. It seemed more like a poor portrayal of the Wicked Witch of the West than of the witch in his picture. His face turned bright red with embarrassment as he became aware that it just was not working. I asked him to let me try to act out what I saw in his picture. He smiled and sat down, gratefully allowing me to take the floor. Despite my feelings of foolishness and awkwardness, I threw myself into playing the witch. After about 30 seconds I stopped, my face red with embarrassment, and asked him if I were close. The group laughed, everyone feeling awkward. John stood up and said I was close but not quite on target, and then he threw himself into it and did some excellent work with his witch. His body held a truth that his mouth could not speak.

Waiting for Dad

When a man attempts to use one of these techniques during group, the group most often responds with reverence and encouragement, even though the man may be anxious or embarrassed about what he's doing. For example, Herb, a 56-year-old Jewish man had been trying to tell the group, unsuccessfully, of his grief concerning his father's alcoholism and consequent abandonment and neglect of him during his childhood. He was asked to find a symbolic way to tell the group about his grief. He brought the following poem to the next meeting; when he finished reading his poem, he wept, as did most of the group members.

Waiting for Dad

Dad bought me a pool table
I was only 9 years old
I wanted to play with you, Dad
But you didn't even come home tonight.

I don't know why you didn't come, Dad
Mom was real quiet
No one talked about it, Dad
But I waited for you, Dad

Maybe tomorrow night, Dad
We can play pool tomorrow night
I'm real excited, Dad
My own pool table!

You usually come home around 5:30
But it's 7:00 now, and you're not home yet
Where is my Dad?
We're going to play pool tonight

Maybe tomorrow night
Sure, tomorrow night
We'll play pool tomorrow night
My dad is going to teach me to play pool
Tomorrow night

Three nights in a row, Dad
You didn't come home to play pool with me
I sat by the pool table waiting for you
What's wrong, Dad, where are you? You promised me.
Don't you like being with me, Dad?
Is something wrong with me, Dad?

It seems like we'll never play pool, Dad
I feel so sad
So sad, Dad
I can't play without you, Dad
Where are you, Dad?

I hate waiting for you, Dad
I feel so scared you'll never come home to play pool
I feel angry now, Dad
Where are you? You promised me, Dad

Come home, Dad.
I hate waiting for you, Dad
My stomach hurts and I feel sick

Where are you, Dad?
You promised me, Dad

I trusted you, Dad
You promised me, Dad
You promised me, Dad
and I believed you.

You said you'd be home at 5:30
It's 9:00 now
I have to go to bed soon
Please come home, Dad

George Getting Grounded

George was a vice president in a mid-size corporation. His career had gone well, given that he had done all the right things to make his way up the corporate ladder. Now, a few years away from retirement, he had begun to realize he did not feel close to his wife and could not communicate well with her. His problem was a classic example of the price many men (and women) pay to be part of the corporate world. Although his marriage was not threatened, as is often the case, George knew he had to do something to change his way of relating with his wife.

George's major complaint was that he did not feel very manly with his wife, children, and men outside of the business world. He would often say he just did not feel like a "solid man." The group asked George if there was anything he did that allowed him to feel manly. This always led George to the workplace. I asked him if he did anything physical that helped him feel grounded in his masculinity, if there was any tool or implement, such as a canoe paddle, shovel, or tennis racquet, that made him feel powerful. He said there was none.

A few weeks later George came to group with something wrapped in a long, brown paper bag. He explained that he had gone to a martial arts supply store to buy his son a new outfit. While in the store, he had been intrigued by several different kinds of swords made of a hard wood. He had left the store but went back the next day to buy his "grounding tool." He reported that as a boy he had been fascinated with swords and had seen them as a manly thing to own.

He began to unwrap it with some excitement plus some growing embarrassment. After all, here was a corporate vice president excited about showing off his new wooden sword. But the group's obvious excitement as they sat forward in their chairs in anticipation seemed to alleviate his hesitancy. After he had shown the group the sword, I asked him to stand up and hold it in a fashion that helped him feel grounded.

He stood up and, grasping the sword handle with both hands, held it out directly in front of him, his knees slightly bent. He stood this way for a couple of minutes, and we were amazed as George was slowing transformed. He looked totally unlike the man we had come to know. All of us felt him to be grounded and we felt grounded with him. A quiet, masculine strength emanated from the whole group, and George was on the road to claiming his masculine power.

Concerns

Certain issues continue to arise in men's groups and need to be addressed frequently so they do not become a problem. There are many issues that need to concern the therapist with any therapy group, but I will address only the issues I see specifically arising out of the fact that it is a men's therapy group.

I have found it to be extremely important while working with men's groups to set aside a specific time to talk about group process. We discuss members' feelings about being part of the group, their likes and dislikes about the group dynamics, and their efforts to ask for and give help to one another outside of the group therapy time. (I am a strong advocate of their efforts because I believe that group therapy is a contrived and artificial environment and that a man's therapy work is only effective when he can integrate it into his real life.) The group process helps to flush out men's feelings toward each other, their homophopia, those who are really working on their issues, and those who are avoiding their issues. It also keeps everyone accountable to the group.

A problem that frequently arises, and an obvious carryover from our culture, is that of "every man for himself." It astounds me how quickly a group can fall back into this mode of relating. A discernible split between some group members who are consistently working in group and those who are consistently not working, little connection among members outside of the group, and feedback that seems particularly perfunctory and dispassionate are all signs that members care mostly for themselves. When this is brought up during process time I often hear men say, "Well, if they're not working, that's their crap, not mine. It's not my job to take care of them." This mode of relating greatly reduces the benefits of group therapy and must be confronted and eradicated immediately.

Another common issue that crops up again and again is niceness or rigidity. Niceness prevails if the members seldom challenge or confront one another. I often have to encourage the men in my groups to confront one another whenever appropriate. Most men hate confrontation, giving it or receiving it, and go to great lengths to avoid another man's anger. Usually, the naive underlying hope of not confronting another group member is, "If I'm not hard on him, he won't be hard on me." Rigidity can often be seen when a group consistently tries to divide up the group time equally. Most men know how to follow rules and know that if everyone follows the rules they can avoid conflict, ambiguity, and asking for what they need. Without confrontation and with rigid rules governing the working of the group, a group quickly becomes boring and stale.

Occasionally, one of my groups goes on a "spouse hunt" or gets into their collective anger at women. This usually happens when one man is reporting the struggles he's having with a woman, and clearly is being taken advantage of or abused in the relationship. The abuse in itself does not cause the angry group reaction; rather, it usually results because the man has spoken too long as a victim and from his pain and is doing nothing to address his anger. The angry group reaction can usually be short-circuited by asking each group member to reflect on his own anger and to own it directly. The other men in the group often are quick to pick up that they are feeling the anger that the man in the abusive relationship needs to deal with and, in a sense, they are being used to act out his anger.

Conclusion

Working with men in group therapy has been one of my most profound and rewarding experiences. Most men do need some individual or couples work to get them prepared for group therapy. Once they arrive in group, however, a whole new journey begins. This journey is often a conscious and deliberate quest to find their masculinity. While on this quest, the group provides a setting in which to deal with many obstacles that come up along the way. Most of these obstacles have to do with each man's facing the grief and consequent pain and anger he has never been able to face. This grief will come when he faces his relationship with his father, who was most likely inattentive or abusive toward him when he was a boy. It will be there when he looks at his loss of innocence too early in life, at the years he has had to hide and deny his naiveté, and at the consequences to himself and others stemming from the way he learned to function in the world as a man.

For a man to understand where he is and who he is, he must understand where he has come from. For a man to look back at his life usually takes a lot of personal courage and a lot of encouragement from the words and actions of others. In his book, *The Denial of Death*, Earnest Becker discussed why men so desperately need other men. They can see

". . . in the other person the self-transcending life process that gives to one's self the larger nourishment it needs" (Becker, 1973, p. 157). Men can learn a lot as individuals and from one another, but certain issues can be explored or discovered only in the presence of a healthy male group. It is in belonging to these groups that more and more men will join in the ever-growing quiet revolution of men coming home to themselves.

This chapter outlines the process of facilitating a group for men structured to help them increase their ability to express feelings and deepen the level of intimacy in their relationships.

Chapter 14

HELPING MEN BECOME MORE EMOTIONALLY EXPRESSIVE: A TEN-WEEK PROGRAM

Dwight Moore

This chapter describes the mechanics of conducting a group for men that helps them (a) increase their ability to express their feelings, and (b) expand their relationship skills. The literature concerning men and their relationships clearly indicates that men are not taught to recognize and express emotions—only to deny, and possibly, to fear them (O'Neil, 1982; Goldberg, 1976; David & Brannon, 1976; Nichols, 1975). As men, our own experiences are replete with instances in which we were taught to hold back our feelings, to be strong and stoic, and to respond to crises in a controlled manner.

The benefits of emotional expression are many. Appropriate emotional expressiveness leads to tension reduction (Hokanson, Willers, & Koropsak, 1968) and minimizes the individual's defensive responses during conflict (Gaines, 1973). Men who increase their level of expressiveness improve their relationships with peers (Fein, 1963), as well as their marital communication (Davidson, Balswick, & Halverson, 1983). Intriguingly, there is evidence that charisma is partially accounted for by emotional expressiveness (Friedman, Prince, Riggio, & Di Matteo, 1980). Traditional male socialization has blocked the achievement of these benefits for many men. Emotional constriction is a common male experience, and there is evidence that physical and emotional health deteriorates with emotional constriction.

Background

The structured group design described in this chapter was developed by the author as part of his dissertation research (Moore, 1984). The purpose of that study was to determine if men could learn, through participation in a multimodal psychological intervention, to be more emotionally expressive. The statistical as well as clinical results provided strong support of the notion that men can learn to be more emotionally expressive. Readers interested in more detail concerning the outcome of the group are referred to Moore and Haverkamp (1989).

The group takes 10 weeks and meets once a week for 2 hours. The optimal group size is 8 to 10, and an even number of participants is required. The group combines the psychological techniques of empathy skill training, cognitive restructuring, behavioral intervention, self-monitoring, and group support. Readings and homework during the week supplement the group activities and discussions.

Because men are initially afraid to express feelings, it is difficult to get them to participate in such a group. They need to feel that they are getting something practical out of the experience. By advertising the group as "The 90s Relationship: New Skills for Men," group facilitators lead men accurately to believe that they are getting something tangible.

Each 2-week segment of the group focuses on a specific topic area:

Week 1:   Introductions
Week 2:   Basic relationship skills: listening, attending
Weeks 3&4:   Male power, control, and competition
Weeks 5&6:   Career and work
Weeks 7&8:   Family and home
Weeks 9&10:   Intimacy

Each session follows a similar format. It is useful to begin with an "experiential activity" to get the group members tuned to the "here and now" and to move them away from an intellectual encounter with the material. This experiential activity usually lasts 1 hour. The second hour of the group is process-oriented and provides a time to discuss the homework, readings, or any other concerns the group members may have that relate to the weekly topic. This section also provides the opportunity for the group members to practice skills learned in the experiential activity. Readings and homework are assigned and reviewed in each group and are selected to stimulate the men's thinking about the topics. The homework encourages men to identify feelings outside the group and to practice them in that context. What follows is a week-by-week description of the group content and suggestions for the facilitator on anticipating potential roadblocks and hurdles.

Ten Group Sessions

Week 1

Topic: Introductions

Outcomes:
This session results in the following:

- introducing members to one another;
- outlining group norms and rules;
- sharing of individual goals; and
- clarifying specific behaviors to accomplish those goals.

Experiential Activity: The facilitator welcomes the group, and then asks the men to fill out a personal banner with name, favorite food, two ways they express interest in others, and their goal for the group. The men share the first three with the group (this should take approximately 30 minutes).

The facilitator outlines the expectations of the group. The group is topic-centered, geared toward expanding relationship skills, risking own opinions and feelings, and personally sharing issues related to the topics. It is not advisable to emphasize the feelings component early on in the group. This will develop as time goes on.

The men then share their individual goals for the group, and the facilitator encourages them to clarify how they might accomplish their goals. The facilitator then addresses group mechanics: confidentiality, responsibility, taking time, right to pass, and time frames for the group.

Process:
In this first group meeting the facilitator is responsible for establishing group norms. He does so by modeling effective listening skills, focusing equally on content and feelings, and soliciting questions from the group. The group members are likely to feel nervous about how others perceive them, to feel curious about the outcome of the group, and to feel somewhat powerless and therefore uncomfortable. The facilitator should be sure to validate each member's input to encourage sharing.

The facilitator can acknowledge the feelings outlined above directly and indicate that they are appropriate feelings one might experience when beginning a relationship. The members will want to stay "intellectual" in their comments, and this should be accepted. Men tend to approach relationships in a factual manner and also may have a tendency to "show off" what they know. Comments may range from, "I don't have trouble with my relationships with men, but women baffle me" to more challenging comments such as, "What will I learn from this experience?" The facilitator should actively paraphrase both the content and feeling of these comments. For example, "You seem to feel more comfortable with men but feel somewhat confused when it comes to relating to women—is that accurate?" Or, "What do you hope to gain from this experience after the 10 weeks are over?"

Facilitators may want to refer to chapter 3 of *The Handbook of Counseling and Psychotherapy With Men* (Rabinowitz & Cochran, 1987) to prepare for the group. This chapter discusses working with men in groups.

Homework: Collect 10 articles from the newspaper and record in a journal the feelings the articles evoke in you. For example, "I feel _____ because _____." The journal should be kept for the duration of the 10 weeks. Use Table 1 as a "crib" sheet.

Readings:
Readings are assigned at the end of each session for the following week.

> Goldberg, H. (1976). *The hazards of being male*. New York: New American Library. Chapter 4: "Feelings, the real male terror."
> Nichols, J. (1975). *Men's liberation*. New York: Penguin Books. Chapter 5: "Feeling."
> David, D.S., & Brannon, R. (Eds.). (1976). *The Forty-nine percent majority*. Reading, MA: Addison-Wesley. "The inexpressive male: A tragedy of American society."

Week 2

Topic: Relationship Skills

Outcomes:
The outcomes of this session include the following:

- the skill of paraphrasing;
- the ability to separate content from feeling;
- the skill of clarifying; and
- the ability to use the levels of Carkoff's empathy scale (for advanced groups).

Experiential Activity: Using Allen Ivey's tapes or some other stimulus material, teach the men to distinguish between thoughts and feelings and to listen actively. The ability to distinguish thoughts and feelings in others and to paraphrase actively is essential to intimate relationships. Use personal examples of group members' work situations or family situations in practicing these skills. Facilitators who have access to videotape filming can tape participants and allow them to see themselves listen and reflect.

Readings are then discussed, allowing time for the men to react to the readings. The facilitator should be sure to model active listening skills and reflect an equal amount of content and feeling.

With approximately 20 minutes left in the first hour, give the following instructions: "At this time I would like you nonverbally to choose

TABLE 1

List of Feelings

Happy	Sad		Angry	Scared	Confused
Excited	Devastated	Degraded	Strangled	Fearful	Bewildered
Elated	Hopeless	Deprived	Furious	Panicky	Trapped
Exuberant	Sorrowful	Disturbed	Seething	Afraid	Immobilized
Ecstatic	Depressed	Wasted	Enraged	Shocked	Directionless
Terrific	Wounded	Abandoned	Hostile	Overwhelmed	Stagnant
Jubilant	Drained	Lost	Vengeful	Intimidated	Flustered
Energized	Defeated	Bad	Incensed	Desperate	Baffled
Enthusiastic	Exhausted	Disenchanted	Abused	Frantic	Constricted
Loved	Helpless	Deflated	Hateful	Terrified	Troubled
Thrilled	Crushed	Apathetic	Humiliated	Vulnerable	Ambivalent
Marvelous	Worthless		Sabotaged	Horrified	Awkward
Justified	Uncared for		Betrayed	Petrified	Puzzled
Resolved	Dejected		Repulsed	Appalled	Disorganized
Valued	Rejected		Rebellious	Full of dread	Foggy
Gratified	Humbled		Pissed off	Tormented	Perplexed
Encouraged	Empty		Outraged	Tense	Hesitant
Optimistic	Miserable		Exploited	Uneasy	Misunderstood
Joyful	Distraught		Throttled	Defensive	Doubtful
Proud	Deserted		Mad	Insecure	Bothered
Cheerful	Grievous		Spiteful	Skeptical	Undecided
Assured	Demoralized		Patronized	Apprehensive	Uncomfortable
Determined	Condemned		Vindictive	Suspicious	Uncertain
Grateful	Terrible		Used	Alarmed	Surprised
Appreciated	Unwanted		Repulsed	Shaken	Unsettled
Confident	Unloved		Ridiculed	Swamped	Unsure
Respected	Mournful		Resentful	Startled	Distracted
Admired	Pitiful		Disgusted	Guarded	
Delighted	Discarded		Smothered	Stunned	
Alive	Disgraced		Frustrated	Awed	
Fulfilled	Disheartened		Stifled	Reluctant	
Tranquil	Despised		Offended	Anxious	
Content	Disappointed		Displeased	Impatient	
Relaxed	Upset		Controlled	Shy	
Glad	Inadequate		Peeved	Nervous	
Good	Dismal		Annoyed	Unsure	
Satisfied	Unappreciated		Agitated	Timid	
Peaceful	Discouraged		Irritated	Concerned	
Hopeful	Ashamed		Exasperated	Perplexed	
Fortunate	Distressed		Harrassed	Doubtful	
Pleased	Distant		Anguished		
Flattered	Disillusioned		Deceived		
	Lonely		Aggravated		
	Neglected		Perturbed		
	Isolated		Provoked		
	Alienated		Dominated		
	Regretful		Coerced		
	Islanded		Cheated		
	Resigned		Uptight		
	Drained		Dismayed		
	Slighted		Tolerant		
			Displeased		

a buddy with whom you will develop a one-on-one relationship during the next 8 weeks of this group. I ask that you not talk but through nonverbal means make contact with someone else in the room and agree to develop a relationship." If people ask questions, ask them to complete the exercise first. They will be afraid, the anxiety in the room will escalate, but it is important that they not become intellectual at this point. Obviously, it is important to have an equal number of group members so that everyone can pair up.

When buddies have been chosen, process the experience:

- How do you feel?
- What was it like to choose someone?
- What are your fears about what might happen?
- What are your hopes?

The facilitator can point out that in actual interpersonal situations people initially choose others in this fashion. People usually do not ask someone to engage in a relationship, but rather send and receive subtle, nonverbal signals, and the relationship begins to be tested.

Process:
Men have been taught to "talk and tell' rather than "listen and reflect." Too often women comment that they play the role of an audience to men. The skill of listening actively has not been systematically reinforced in men. In business settings as well as in relationships, miscommunication results in hurt feelings, bad decisions, and inefficient use of talent. The facilitator can anticipate that group members believe they listen better than they actually do. Frequent role plays can illustrate this. The facilitator can model active listening skills before introducing each new skill.

Homework: 1. Call your buddy and talk about whatever you wish.
2. Choose one experience daily and write in a journal your feeling reaction to that experience utilizing your feelings list (Table 1).

Readings:

Stevens, J.O. (1971). *Awareness*. Ogden, UT: Real People Press.
Nichols, J. (1975): "Competition."
Goldberg, H. (1976): "The success trip: A fantasy portrait."

Week 3

Topic: Power, Control, and Competition

Outcomes:

The outcomes are as follows:

- learning the skills of assertiveness, "I" messages, and conflict resolution;
- practicing these skills; and
- transfering these skills to daily life.

Experiential Activity: Teach assertiveness skills, "I messages," and conflict resolution skills. One excellent resource is Robert Bolton's book, *People Skills* (1985). Again utilize group members' experiences at work and at home to illustrate power, control, and competition. Share reactions to readings and to homework. Attend specifically to the assignment of calling buddies and explore successes and difficulties that the men experienced. Reinforce appropriate behavior and explore why a particular pair might not have followed through.

Process:

The feminist revolution of the 1970s has left men in a quandary. No longer expected to be "in charge, decisive, and autonomous," men have had to learn new skills in conflict resolution and in expressing their own needs. Now some men seek equalitarian relationships in which decisions are shared, opinions are valued equally, and needs are expressed forthrightly.

The facilitator may find that men err either on the side of aggressiveness or on the side of passivity. Some men have become "men's rights" activitists and are even more aggressive in proclaiming their points of view whereas others have capitulated and feel unsure about their right to express their own needs. Assertiveness and conflict resolution skills are essential in establishing equalitarian relationships.

The facilitator should use the buddy relationships and the relationships in the group. Theoretical discussions of equity will not have as much impact on the group members as practical applications of these skills in their day-to-day relationships. For example, using a role play in which "John" expresses his disappointment that he and his buddy did not call one another one week will have more impact than an abstract discussion of assertiveness. Actually resolving a group conflict (how many breaks to take each session, one member's dominance of the group) also can be effective.

Homework: Inform the group that a panel of women will be at the group in session 4 to talk about power and control. They will be responding to the following questions:

What do you want from a relationship?
What expectations do you have of men in a relationship?

When are you aware of power in your relationships?

Ask the group to think of how they would answer these questions also.

Make another call to your buddy and share a success you had during the week.

Readings:

Nichols, J. (1975): "Dominance."

Bly, R. (1988). *Iron John and the male mode of feeling.* Seattle, WA: Limbus.

Pleck, J.H., & Sawyer, J. (Eds.). (1974). *Men and masculinity.* Englewood Cliffs, NJ: Prentice-Hall. "Why aren't we talking?" and "A visit from Uncle Macho."

Week 4

Topic: Power, Control, and Competition

Outcomes:

The outcome of this session is a demonstration of the ability to listen and process the data received from the panel of women. If the facilitator hears judgments of the womens' statements, he should ask: "And how does her opinion affect you?" Asking the men about their attempts to be equitable in relationships is appropriate. Examining how decisions are made in their lives can be helpful; for example, "Who decides to drive the car when you are together?" or "How are chores around the home divided?" The intent is to explore power, control, and competition and allow the group members to decide for themselves what styles they are comfortable with rather than prescribing a particular style.

Experiential Activity: A panel of women responds to the questions presented in Week 3. Ideally, these women should be selected from all walks of life. Choosing only PhD chemists or homemakers would not be appropriate. Diversity of opinion is desirable. Encourage the women to speak from their own experience. Panel lasts approximately 1 hour.

Process by encouraging the men to ask the women questions and to make their own comments. Keep the conversation focused on personal issues rather than "men and women in general."

The women are asked to leave after the first hour, and the processing should be continued with the men only. Because the topic focus is power and control, include these issues in the process discussion.

Process:

Male socialization focuses on competition, control, and power. From sports to academic preparation, young boys are inundated with messages to win, control, and take power. O'Neil's (1981) and Fasteau's (1975) writings will provide a background for the facilitator regarding these issues. The men in the group are likely to compete for who is the "most gentle" or who is the best listener. Some men may try and control the group process and exert power in inappropriate ways. This is to be expected and accepted. The facilitator can help men examine how this happens in group settings and explore their need to do so.

The panel of women offers the opportunity for men to listen to women's experience about men's tendency to control. The point here is to gather data, not to challenge or refute the experience of the women on the panel. Women's experiences differ from men's, and those differences should be accepted, not judged.

Homework: Chart time usage. The topic for weeks 5 and 6 is Career and Work. Using the chart in Table 2, ask the men to chart how they *actually* use their time during the week.

Buddies call one another and share a positive and negative experience that occurred that week at work.

Readings:

O'Neil, J.M. (1981). Male sex role conflict, sexism, and masculinity: Psychological implications for men, women, and the counseling psychologist. *Counseling Psychologist, 9,* 61–80.

Fasteau, M. (1975). *The male machine.* New York: Dell. "Work."

Week 5

Topic: Career and Work

Outcomes:
Examining of the role work plays in men's life and exploring alternatives.

Experiential Activity: View the movie *Men's Lives* (or whatever media you have available that address working).

If such media are not available, ask the men to complete the following sentences:

1. Success to me means. . . . .
2. At work I feel like a failure when. . . . .
3. I am most skilled at. . . . .

Review reactions to the experience, to the readings, and to the homework.

Process:
Facilitating a discussion about work is easy with men. Remember, they tend to believe that work constitutes their identity. Therefore, when they talk of work they are talking about themselves, their basic values

TABLE 2
Use of Time in Hours per Week

		2	4	6	8	10
Wednesday	Work					
	Sleep					
	Relationships					
	Recreation					
	Existential					
	Maintenance					
Thursday	Work					
	Sleep					
	Relationships					
	Recreation					
	Existential					
	Maintenance					
Friday	Work					
	Sleep					
	Relationships					
	Recreation					
	Existential					
	Maintenance					
Saturday	Work					
	Sleep					
	Relationships					
	Recreation					
	Existential					
	Maintenance					
Sunday	Work					
	Sleep					
	Relationships					
	Recreation					
	Existential					
	Maintenance					
Monday	Work					
	Sleep					
	Relationships					
	Recreation					
	Existential					
	Maintenance					
Tuesday	Work					
	Sleep					
	Relationships					
	Recreation					
	Existential					
	Maintenance					

Notes/Thoughts:

Totals:

Work
Sleep
Relationships
Recreation
Existential
Maintenance

and beliefs. The time usage exercise from their homework allows them realistically to evaluate how they are using their time. If they discover, for example, that they spend 55 hours working, 10 hours on relationships, and only 3 hours in recreation and existential activity, ask about their reactions to these findings.

It is common for work to dominate the facets of a man's life, leaving little room for spiritual, recreational, or relationship "tasks." It is true that work contains relationships and some recreation, but not the type and quality that is most beneficial. Again, it is important for the facilitator to be nonjudgmental in this exploration, allowing the group members to come to their own conclusions.

Homework: Pass out a golf counter to each group member. These can be purchased at any golf store for less than $2. Inform the group that during this week they will be counting their feelings. They should carry their counters with them at all times, and anytime they are aware of having a feeling, they should click their counter once. Develop a chart to record daily feelings.

Call buddy and discuss how counting is going.

The facilitator should be aware that the point of this exercise is to get the men to pay specific attention to their feelings at the moment they occur. If they have to count them, they will develop a hightened awareness of their emotional expressiveness.

Readings:

Pleck, J.H., & Sawyer, J. (1974). "Executives as human beings." McCoy, V.R., Ryan, C., & Lichtenberg, J.W. (1978). *The adult life cycle.* Lawrence, KS: University of Kansas. "Mid-life options." Skovholt, T.M. Chapter 4 in this volume.

Week 6

Topic: Career and Work

Outcomes:
The outcomes are:

- learning a specific method of giving feedback;
- expanding listening skills;
- practicing with a real life situation; and
- transferring these skills to life outside the group.

Experiential Activity: Teach giving feedback and listening skills (Part II). This exercise expands on what was taught in the second session. You, as facilitator, now have a clearer sense of the skills and abilities of the group in this area and can work on refining these. Your rationale is that listening skills are a fundamental component in relationships. Discuss homework and readings . . . how did it feel to chart feelings? What did the men discover about their patterns . . . more feelings in the morning? At work? With their families/friends?

Process:
Learning to give feedback is a difficult process. Men may tend to be dogmatic or passive. In either case, the skill requires that men understand their own feelings (hence the homework on charting feelings) and their own needs.

The facilitator can ask the group to choose a topic (such as feedback to one's boss about an unreasonable request, to one's partner about sexual issues, to one's children about their behavior, to one's buddy) that will be used as the content for skill acquisition. The facilitator will model the behavior desired and then the group members can practice the skills.

It should not automatically be supposed that the receiver of feedback will always accept the information. For example, explaining to one's boss that his or her last-minute requests are difficult to fulfill may not result in a stop to those requests. Feedback is respectful to both the giver and the receiver. That is, it validates the needs and feelings of the giver while respecting the right of the receiver to change his or her behavior if the receiver so chooses. Feedback should be timely, specific, and aimed at behaviors, not traits, and should include a suggestion for change.

An example of feedback to one's buddy might be: "I notice that when we talk, I spend most of the time listening. For example, last week when we met, I wanted to talk about a deadline at work that I resent, but we focused on your fight with your boss. I am willing to be more direct in asking for time, but what I would ask from you is to help me by asking directly if there are issues I need to discuss."

Men may perceive that this sort of request is "weak or wimpy." On the contrary, it is an example of a powerful process of taking charge of one's own feelings and expressing them. A man does not control the behavior of the other in this process, but rather he respects himself enough to ask for what he needs and also gives his buddy information about *his* behavior.

Homework: Pass out the interview form "Interview With Fathers" (Table 3). Explain that traditions are passed from generation to generation and that it is important to understand the "masculine" traditions in one's own family of origin. Individuals are asked to interview their fathers using the form as a guideline. Facilitators can expect a great deal of anxiety when this assignment is introduced. It may be the first time a number of the men will have had face-to-face, personal conversations with their fathers. Explore that anxiety and fear (note: leave at least ½ hour to ¾ hour for this).

TABLE 3

Interview With Fathers

1. How would you describe my way of dealing with emotions when I was a kid? e.g., surprise, joy, anticipation, anger, fear, disgust, love?
2. How would you describe how I deal with these now?
3. Who am I most like in the family re: emotional expression? Why?
4. How did other people in the family express feelings to one another? .
5. How would you describe your own style of expressing feelings?
6. How did your parents handle their emotions? (Use list above).
7. How would you describe AB, BC, DCs way of relating to one another emotionally in our family?
8. What kept people from expressing emotion in your family? In our immediate family?
9. If you could change any of this what would you change?
10. (Any other question you would like to ask your father. . . .)

Men whose fathers are deceased should choose an uncle, grandfather, older brother, or some other father-like figure for the interview. Choice of a woman is not recommended.

State that Weeks 7 and 8 will be devoted to fathers and parenting. Obtain a commitment from half of the group to be prepared to share what happened during their interview next week. This will guarantee that you have an agenda and it will help the men push through their fears.

Very important to stay in touch with buddies this week.

Readings:

David, D.S., & Brannon, R. (1976). "No sissy stuff . . . men as parents."

Berger, M., & Wright, L. (1978). Divided allegiance: Men, work, and family life. *The Counseling Psychologist 7*, 50–52.

Week 7

Topic: Family and Home

Outcomes:
Sharing the results of interviews with fathers. The most important dynamic in Weeks 7 and 8 is to embrace the perception of each man.

Experiential Activity: Divide up the 4 hours of Weeks 7 and 8 into equal sections for sharing results of the interviews with fathers. For example, if there are 8 men in the group, then each should be allocated

½ hour to share. Share results of the interview, paying attention to feelings.

Facilitator, by this point in the group your role is mostly to observe during these times of processing. Encourage the group members to respond to the speaker.

Process:
Your role as facilitator is crucial in these two sessions. Your do not have the time to do family therapy nor do you wish to solve age-old "scripts" for the group members. Your role is to encourage the group to provide a safe environment for the men to share their stories about their fathers. It is best to avoid giving advice about what one "should do next." Communicate trust that the men will find a way through the emotions they feel. This is a process experience, not a content experience.

Individual members will share the loss and pain of absent fathers, of inexpressive fathers, and of abusive fathers. They will share the joy of times spent together, of their fears that they will not be able to parent as well as their fathers did, or their fears that they will parent as their fathers did. They may grieve over the emotions that were not shared. They may rage about their losses. All are legitimate feelings. Again, the primary outcome of these sessions is to embrace the perception of each man. Discounting, minimizing, or getting too "action oriented" ("what you should do, Jim, is . . .") is not appropriate.

Homework: Group members who have not shared about their fathers should prepare to do so in Week 8. Be sure to remind buddies to stay in touch.

Readings:

Sheehy, G. (1977, March). The crisis couples face at forty." *Reader's Digest*, pp. 73–76.

Farrell, W. (1975). *The liberated man*. New York: Bantam Books. "The family: Redefining motherhood and fatherhood."

Closing: This week (or earlier if the facilitator believes the group is ready), ask the men to hold hands in a circle and share one thing they liked or appreciated about the group. The feedback should be personal and specific. The facilitator may want to model an example at first ("I appreciated Mike's willingness to share about his early family history . . . that took courage").

Week 8

Topic: Family and Home

Outcomes:
Same as for Week 7.

Experiential Activity: Continue with discussions about fathers. Process this thoroughly as suggested earlier with attention to the traditions that are carried on through the generations.

Homework: Call buddy, arrange a time to get together during the week for lunch, a walk, or to shoot pool.

Readings:

O'Neil, J.M. (1982). Gender and sex role conflict and strain in men's lives: Implications for psychiatrists, psychologists, and other human service providers. In K. Solomon & N. Levy (Eds.), *Men in transition: Theory and therapy* (pp. 5–44). New York: Plenum Press. Read pages 19–20.

Fasteau, M.F. (1975). "Friendships among men," and "Marriage and other intimate arrangements."

Goldberg, H. (1976). "The lost art of buddyship."

Ciaramella's and Levant's chapters in this volume (chapters 6 and 7, respectively).

Closing: Note to facilitator: The degree of intimacy between buddies and among group members is likely to be rising. Acknowledge and validate this for the group.

Week 9

Topic: Intimacy

Outcomes:
To provide an experience of nonsexual touching and the opportunity to talk through the feelings this may evoke.

Experiential Activity: From Stevens, J.O. (1971). *Awareness*. Ogden, UT: Real People Press, conduct the "Trust Circle" (pp. 263–266) or the "Hand Conversation" (pp. 240–242) with buddies.

Process:
The men will have an opportunity to touch and to discuss intimacy. The buddy system has modeled how an intimate relationship develops from initial nonthreatening sharing about work to more personal sharing and later on in the relationship to physical touch. The facilitator is encouraged to use examples from the buddy relationships in this discussion.

Facilitators are encouraged to read chapter 5 by Philip Colgan in this book on male sexuality. Men confuse sexuality with touch. While growing up, young boys are rarely touched in nonsexual ways. Intimacy and touch are also confused. Touch is usually associated with a progression of events toward intercourse. Learning the appropriate use of touch is essential.

The "Hand Conversation" is the better of these two exercises. After the exercise ask the following questions in the debriefing:

- What were your initial feelings before you began this exercise?
- Which emotion was the most difficult to express and why?
- What were the easiest emotions to express and why?
- In what ways are you touched in your daily relationships?

Homework: During the last session men will be giving feedback to one another. They will be asked to share their resentments and appreciations with one another. Therefore, they are asked to review any materials on feedback and to prepare notes, if they choose.

Readings:
   None

Week 10

Topic: Intimacy

Outcomes:
   This is the time to say goodbye. Resentments and appreciations of one another and the group process are shared.

Experiential Activity: Share resentments and appreciations. We suggest resentments be shared first and that the facilitator model the process. Open chair feedback process is appropriate. That is, each individual takes a turn in the "open chair," receiving resentments from the group. Something specific should be said about each participant by the facilitator, although group members may pass if they have nothing to say. We suggest that participants not respond while receiving feedback. After all members have received resentments, go on to share appreciations. This process usually takes longer than the 2 hours allocated for the group.

Process:
   This session is the culmination of the group. It utilizes all the skills learned and taps all the experiences the men have had with each other over the 10-week period. Other than modeling the process initially, the facilitator can behave as a group member during this session, although we do encourage the facilitator to have prepared a specific resentment and appreciation for each group member. Neglecting either for any group member will be noticed.

This is an opportunity for the men to be open, gentle, and compassionate. A sample resentment may be: "John, I initially resented the resistance you gave to the father interview. I found your behavior to be rigid, which seemed unlike your previous contributions. I believed that you felt particularly fearful given what we learned about your father's abusive behavior. It would have been helpful for me if you had said something like: 'I feel afraid of what might happen to me if I approach my father on this issue and am aware of strong resistance to this homework assignment.' "

Facilitator, you may observe that men in the "open chair" want to respond to the resentments or appreciations. We suggest that you clearly establish the ground rules, with the group's input, before you begin the experience.

Finally, some members may request to continue this group on their own after the 10th week. In all of the previous groups conducted by the author, such a desire was expressed. My suggestion is that you advise that they establish a time to meet and that those interested should attend. Some members may not wish to continue and this should be respected. It would be helpful for the facilitator to attend the first meeting to help establish the ground rules of the group such as focus, times to meet, frequency of meetings, and so on.

Closing: Facilitator summarizes the process and the group join hands to say goodbye.

Conclusion

This chapter outlines the process and content of facilitating a group for men structured to help them increase their ability to express feelings and deepen the level of intimacy in their relationships. Facilitators who conduct these groups ought to be trained in group process and be experienced in group work. The group combines content and process and it does ask participants to contribute personal information. It is not a therapy group, however, nor should it be treated as such.

Facilitators are reminded to gather feedback from the group members periodically so that needs of individual members can be met. Occassional reference to members' original goals is appropriate and provides content to the facilitator in giving feedback to participants in the final session.

It is crucial that a thorough intake be conducted to determine the appropriateness of fit between the group goals and an individual's goals. This is a skill-building group in which friendships may develop. Individuals seeking therapy, family-of-origin work, chemical dependency treatment, or other specific interventions are not appropriate for this group.

We suggest that a sliding scale of payment be established for fees. This will encourage the possibility of an economic cross section in the group.

Finally, the impact of the facilitator on the group cannot be underestimated. If his tone, attitude, and demeanor communicate respect for men and women, enthusiasm for change, acceptance of individual differences, an openness to suggestions, and a curiousity about the world, then the group has a strong likelihood of success. It is recommended that the facilitator read from the following bibliography before conducting this group to heighten his own awareness of the topics to be addressed.

Counseling Psychologist. (1978). Special Issue of Counseling Men, 7(4).

Moore, D., & Haverkamp, B.E. (1989). Measured increases in male emotional expressiveness following a structured group intervention. *Journal of Counseling and Development. 67*(9), 513–517.

Pleck, J.H. (1981). *The myth of masculinity*. Cambridge, MA: MIT Press.

Scher, M., Stevens, M., Good, G., & Eichenfield, G.A. *Handbook of counseling and psychotherapy with men*. (1987). New York: Sage.

Solomon, K., & Levy, N.B. (Eds.). (1982). *Men in transition, theory and therapy*. New York: Plenum Press.

The facilitator also should read all the readings that serve as homework for each session.

This chapter examines the clinical issues central to understanding and treating men who batter.

Chapter 15

TREATING MEN WHO BATTER: A GROUP APPROACH

Roger Grusznski and Gunnar Bankovics

In this chapter, we will provide an overview of treatment issues in the therapy for men who batter their female partners. The chapter is not intended to be a step-by-step process of a treatment program. Several detailed descriptions of group treatment do provide this type of information (Bankovics, 1984; Edleson, 1984; Ganley & Harris, 1978; Reilly & Grusznski, 1984). Rather, we will focus on a number of clinical issues that we see as central to group treatment programs for men who batter.

Background

Battering is the physical force, threats, and intimidation that men use to control and dominate women. Physical violence includes all forceful physical contact such as physically restraining, pushing, slapping, punching, choking, stabbing, raping, and murder. Intimidation includes physical gestures, destruction of property, yelling, name-calling, reckless driving, threats of physical violence, and threatening any of the following: to restrict finances, to kidnap children, to harm other family members, and to commit suicide. Psychological abuse includes depersonalization, social isolation, depreciation, and a general undermining of self-esteem. Most types of battering include all of these forms of abuse.

Historically, there has been little or no cultural or legal sanction against men's abuse and domination of women (Bauer & Ritt, 1983; Davidson, 1977; Jaffe, Wolfe, Telford, & Austin, 1986). Although our society is beginning to recognize and respond to the issue of male to female violence, it still remains a pervasive and central problem that is not yet resolved in the lives of most men. The recognition of battering as an issue was brought forth largely by the women's movement. The changes that need to occur, however, can only be accomplished if men begin to view it as their problem and their issue. Intervention must occur on a number of levels. Social, cultural, and legal systems all must change to make a significant impact on the safety of women (Labell, 1979; Roy, 1982; Straus, 1976).

The causes of battering are a synthesis of individual learning, cultural norms, and family experiences. Violent behavior seems to be learned. Numerous studies (Carlson, 1984; Gelles, 1980; Herman, 1986; Rosenbaum & O'Leary, 1981) show that a significant percentage of men who batter have either witnessed violence between their parents or been victims of their parents' violence. Many of these men see violence as a normal and acceptable part of family life and repeat this behavior when they have their own families. These early learning experiences, combined with cultural education and restricted male role expectations, lead many men to act violently toward those they love. Conversely, women's roles lead them to accept the abuse perpetrated by a male-dominated culture.

Men in our society are taught that they need to be strong, stoic, powerful, and in control at all costs. As a result they do not develop the qualities traditionally thought of as feminine that would allow them to express feelings and resolve conflict. Consequently, they perpetuate the intergenerational use of violence in families by modeling these roles for their children.

Our research and work with this issue has demonstrated to us and to the men we have worked with that there are alternatives to battering and that serious limitations are associated with traditional male cultural norms. For men to make changes in this area is a difficult task, and awareness is only the first step. Men who batter often engage in violence for years before they experience any consequences as a result of their behavior. Most men seek help only after their partner has left them, has threatened to leave them, or has been seriously injured. At this point, the batterer often feels overwhelming remorse and shame. Some men seek help when society, through the criminal justice system or family courts, forces them to acknowledge that their behavior is unlawful or inappropriate. This awareness is usually limited and can be seen only as a first (but crucial) step in changing this destructive pattern.

Intervention

The timing in intervention is critical; the effects of consequences are often temporary and diminish quickly. Intervention and support need to occur at the time of the perceived crisis and continue to facilitate an ongoing awareness of the problem. Legal sanctions, therapeutic support, education, and cultural change need to occur to facilitate a process of change.

In any type of intervention with batterers, the first consideration must be the protection of those that the individual may scar physically and emotionally. In assisting men to stop their violence, we have found a number of proven intervention techniques to be effective. The most effective way to help men stop battering is to instruct them to physically leave the scene when they experience an escalation of aggression. Though it sounds like a simple process, it is not. The process is composed of a number of individual steps. The first step is for the man to make a commitment to choose to be nonviolent. Once the commitment is made, we can help him make that choice. The motivation for his choice makes little difference at this level. Whether a man is trying to avoid negative consequences or has become intrinsically motivated to cease his violence does not matter. The batterer can learn new behaviors to replace violent behaviors if he wants to.

Most men are unaware of their own levels of tension and stress. So we begin by helping educate them regarding the internal and external cues that have played a role in escalating that tension and stress and the subsequent violence. As men gain experience in this area, they begin to realize that the cues generally follow a logical progression. They begin to understand when they need to exit in order to avoid a violent incident. Men are asked to develop an awareness of cues on four different levels: physical, situational, self-statements, and emotional.

In identifying the physical cues, a man is asked to think about an incident in which he has been violent and record what he experienced as well as did physically. Common physical cues are pacing, clenching of fists, tightness in the neck, raising of the voice, pointing a finger, face turning red, and so forth.

To determine situational cues, we ask men to consider the kind of situations in which they feel an escalation of aggression. These situational cues are commonly arguments about money, discipline of the children, sex, household duties, and the use of alcohol and drugs. It is also common for many men to act violently repeatedly in the same place in the house such as the kitchen or the bedroom. Additional situations may commonly occur while in the car, on vacations, and during shopping trips.

With self-statements or ruminations, many men find themselves making or rehearsing internal thoughts or phrases prior to an act of violence such as "If she says one more word about money . . ." or "If she brings up what my sister said again . . . ." This results in men's ultimately trapping themselves in negative thoughts and rehearsals in preparing to strike out.

Feeling, or emotional, cues to escalation are probably the most difficult for the men to identify. When asked how they felt prior to a violent incident, the feeling the men most commonly report is anger. Most of the men use anger to cover up other kinds of emotions that would leave them more vulnerable. It is important to help them identify the fear, hurt, and shame that they are masking.

As the men become skilled in identifying their cues, they can begin (with assistance) to develop an understanding of the point at which they can choose to exit the situation rather than risk becoming violent. In early stages of the treatment process the men are instructed to leave the situation when they become aware that their level of tension or aggression is escalating. How they leave and what they do when they exit, however, is a critical step in stopping the violence. We instruct the men to inform their partners about their intention to leave the situation as part of the therapeutic process.

Even with new awareness and skills, the men often need to deal with their own or their partners' attitudes about "leaving" an argument. They often equate leaving with losing or being cowardly and small. Partners often equate men leaving with avoidance or abandonment. What men do when they leave is as important as leaving. We instruct them to do two things—to stop ruminating on the conflict preceding the exit and to focus on relaxing and relieving their tension. We instruct them not to return until the cues have diminished or the tensions that resulted in their decision to leave have subsided. If upon their return they find that tensions are still present, they can leave again and again. If they must leave repeatedly over short periods of time, we encourage them to separate from the location until they can gain adequate control.

Considering the fact that when men leave their level of aggression is often escalated, we recommend that they do not drive or use alcohol or other drugs. We suggest that they go for a walk or find a simple task to concentrate on rather than continue dwelling on the incident.

Once a man has regained control and successfully reduced tension, we instruct him to return and discuss the situation calmly rather than ignoring the issue. "Time outs" used correctly are extremely powerful to accomplish long-term change. Although time outs will reduce the immediate threat, they will not accomplish the long-term goal of remaining violence free.

Any therapeutic program to assist men in changing their violence needs to include components for teaching the men to be assertive, release stress, decrease isolation, identify and express feelings, accept responsibility for their violence, explore remorse and shame, recognize self-talk and negative self-statements, and examine restricted male roles, family of origin (learned behavior), attitudes toward women, and sex role stereotypes.

Group Work

The acquisition of nonviolent responses to conflict is most effectively learned in a group setting. A group environment can also create a milieu in which deviation from traditional male roles can be reinforced and seen as acceptable. Groups tend to reduce the isolation and shame most of the men carry with them about their past and current violent behaviors. Though most of the men have some idea about how pervasive this problem is, they have nevertheless learned to be secretive about their violent actions.

The isolation the men experience needs specific attention in the group process. In the initial group meeting, we ask the men to disclose to the group why they are there, provide a brief history of their violence, and state their goals for participating in the group. This is generally a tense and frightening time for most participants. Additionally, we ask the men to select one other person from the group that they will communicate with on at least a one-time-per-week basis outside of the group. Though this task may seem simple, we find most of the men are resistant to developing relationships that stray from traditional male norms. We suggest to the men that the nature of their conversations include other than superficial reporting of day-to-day routine; for instance, they may discuss feelings, disappointments, or how they are integrating into their lives what they are learning about controlling their violence. Groups are also important in creating a microcosm in which the expression of aggression is neither tolerated nor reinforced regardless of the circumstances. At the beginning of every group meeting, the men are asked to report if any violence has taken place since the previous meeting. If violence has taken place it is critical to instruct the men to differentiate between the stress leading to the violence and their choice to act violently. It is important to point out that the stress does not cause the violence. Violence is only one of many possible reactions to a stressful situation. The men need to recognize that they are in full control of their behavior and that their choice to be violent is a willful one.

Many men will profess that when they are violent they have simply "lost control"; however, ample evidence suggests that they are always in full control. Generally, in any violent action, the man makes a number of choices. He chooses whether to hit with an open hand or a closed fist. He chooses the duration of the assault. He chooses to assault privately rather than publicly. He chooses to assault his female partner rather than his friends or coworkers. He chooses to interrupt the assault if there is police intervention or the presence of children. He chooses to reinitiate the assault once the intervening forces are gone. All of these factors suggest that he is in complete control. He needs to be fully aware that he is responsible for his behavior. If he is allowed to remain with the idea that the stress his partner causes results in the violence, he will forever be a victim of powerlessness and of the belief that he is unable to control his actions.

In working with the men it is important to understand that violence has clear and immediate rewards. One of these is the release of physical and emotional stress. Most episodes of violence are followed by a feeling of physical and emotional calm as in any cathartic release. If in working with the men we adapt a frustration aggression hypothesis, we do them a great disservice. If men believe the only way they can reduce their stress is to act aggressively, they will continue to do so. There are many responses to frustration and stress. For example, people who experience stress may drink, use drugs, cry, develop somatic symptoms, express their feelings verbally, repress their feelings, eat, sleep, problem-solve, or react in other ways. Violence is only one response.

In teaching the men to deal with their stress, we begin by helping them learn new ways to reduce physical stress. We ask each man to select and participate in a regular exercise program. The nature of the exercise program SHOULD NOT include aggressive forms of stress release. That is to say there should be no exercises in which an aggressive behavior is paired with feelings of relaxation, such as punching a bag, contact sports, or chopping wood while fantasizing about one's partner. The appropriate exercise program should include moderate physical exertion followed by a focus on reducing tension in the major muscle groups through deep and relaxing breathing. Regular exercise programs should effectively provide an outlet for the physical release of frustration and tension.

Eliminating physical tension is often easier than eliminating emotional stress. Learning to reduce emotional tension and developing problem-solving skills requires a greater amount of time and attention. Perhaps the most difficult task for the men is learning to recognize and express feelings other than anger. Anger is a safe emotion for men. It is accepted within the confines of male sex roles. It is external in nature—it does not require the men to expose themselves and become vulnerable. In the groups, when men are asked how they felt about a certain circumstance, their most common response is, "I was angry."

Many of the men do not possess a repertoire or vocabulary of words that describe other feeling states, particularly such feelings as fear, hurt, sadness, and inadequacy. Most of the men believe that "real men" don't experience those feelings. As part of the group process we distribute a list of feeling words that describe various feelings at different levels of intensity. It is not uncommon for the men to refer to this list when they are asked how they are feeling. It takes constant practice and reinforcement for them to become comfortable with exploring and expressing a range of feelings, particularly those they view as feminine. For most of the men, anger is a secondary feeling. Although anger serves the purpose of masking feelings that would leave the men vulnerable, it produces the consequence of leaving them distant from themselves and afraid of their internal emotions. The more they depend on anger as a defense, the more frightened they become internally, and the more controlling and abusive they become behaviorally.

The recognition and expression of feelings has to be accomplished in an assertive and clear manner. Contrary to many beliefs about men who batter, the men are not generally seen as aggressive persons. For the most part, the men fluctuate between long periods of passivity and occasional violent outbursts. Based on personality characteristics, these men cannot be distinguished from society at large. Most of the men have little idea of how to go about expressing their wants and needs. They generally possess very negative ideas about the emotion of anger. Rather than expressing any perceived displeasure or discomfort, they will ruminate on the feelings and express them as rage or violence. They need to be instructed not only how to identify their feelings but also how to express them in a timely and effective manner. This is accomplished first by instructing the men in assertiveness techniques, and, second, by conducting role plays of past and present conflicts. It is important that the use of assertiveness techniques focus not only on the men's relationship with their partner, but also on their daily interaction with people at work, family members, and other significant persons. The stress needs to be responded to where it exists. If it is not, the men may attempt to respond to their accumulated stress of their day-to-day existence by directing all their negative feelings only toward their partners. This, in fact, often occurs with men who batter.

Control

Akin to learning how to recognize, express, and resolve these feelings through assertiveness techniques is the issue of assisting the men in examining their need to control and dominate their female partners. Violent incidents always surround the issue of control. Men's violence can be seen as an attempt to stop their partners from doing something or to get them to do something.

Though the roots of the need for power and control are often seeded in feelings of powerlessness and inadequacy, they are most often detected in attempts to stifle those feelings by controlling others. For instance, feelings of sexual inadequacy might give way to unfounded suspicions and jealousies about a partner. This need for control creates a vicious cycle. The more the man attempts to control his partner, the more powerlessness and inadequacy he will experience. This can go to the extreme of calling his partner several times per day at work, monitoring her movements, accusing her of infidelity with coworkers, and serious attempts to keep her in complete social isolation.

One of the things that makes the control issue so difficult to confront is living in a society of men that has historically dominated and controlled women. Change in this area can occur only when the man begins to relinquish control and accept that fact that his feelings and inadequacies are his own. Even in the circumstances when these feelings are engendered by his female partner, the man must look at his own emotional response and find ways to resolve these issues. We attempt to instill within him the idea that the only person he can control is himself. When he realizes this, he is empowered.

When the men learn to take control of themselves as opposed to exercising control over their partners, they have taken the step of accepting responsibility for themselves. Accepting this responsibility, and acknowledging the violent behavior, is perhaps the most crucial step. When a man is able to discuss and describe his violent actions without blaming his partner, he is well on the road to using nonviolent responses. Therapeutically, this is a difficult task. By blaming his partner or circumstances for his violent actions, a man could shield himself from the intense feelings of shame and remorse for hurting someone he loves. At some point in the group process, the men are asked to record and present the most violent incident they ever perpetrated toward their partner. They are asked to present this in full and complete detail. A man's ability to do this is often a measure of how successful he will be in choosing nonviolence in his relationships. For many men, it is also the first time they have allowed others into the personal suffering and shame that they have experienced for what they have done. The emotional catharsis that occurs in this process is moving for group members and facilitators alike. It can serve to separate those men who are willing to take the risk to commit themselves to nonviolence from those who will continue to attribute the responsibility of their violent behavior to others.

The core of most deviant behavior is shame. There are two principles involved in working through behaviors that result in shameful feelings. The first is to stop the shame-producing behavior (which we have addressed: stop the violence that is the shame-producing behavior for men who batter). The second is to openly express the shame and remorse about the violent behavior. The damage inflicted upon the men's self-esteem from acting in a manner that causes them self-reproach will serve as the catalyst for future violent incidents. This is to say that the feelings of shame must be expressed or they will be acted out violently. Many men respond to their shame by keeping it isolated and secret from others. They cover it with a veneer of empty promises to be better and to cease their violence. The internal feelings of shame, however, do not have an avenue for relief and consequently create their own distress, eventually resulting in escalation and aggression. Many of the men have lost their ability to cry and grieve. Creating every opportunity for them to do that in the group is essential.

Families

A number of the issues we have discussed have their roots in the families in which the men grew up. On the face of it, most of these men will describe the homes they grew up in as normal and nonviolent. They will deny having witnessed violence between their parents and having been the recipients of their parents' violence. When asked if they were victims of violence in their own home, they will commonly say "no". However, in exploring the issue, we find that many of the men were indeed abused. To protect themselves from those earlier experiences, they tend to "normalize" them. They describe physical abuse between their parents as arguments. They describe assaults upon themselves by their parents as discipline. Men have described being hit over the head with boards, whipped with belts, punched in the face, and burned as discipline. With that definition of discipline and arguments as normative, they tend to view their own behavior also as normative rather than abusive. Early experiences of abuse also engender long-term feelings of powerlessness and the consequential need to control. There is ample support for the intergenerational existence of such familial patterns (Fitch & Papantonio, 1983; Straus, Gelles, & Steinmetz, 1098; Ulbrich & Huber, 1981).

In some instances the men have not witnessed or been subjected to abuse in their own home. They have, however, been subjected to the restricted roles men in our society experience and adhere to. When they were children and were pushed down on the playground, it was their role to come up with a handful of gravel rather than tears. Men are taught that they must be successful, consequently they have to deny feelings of inadequacy and failure. They are taught they must be strong, consequently they must deny feelings of uncertainty and ambivalence. All this results in men being pushed further away from themselves and toward an unattainable and unhealthy male stereotype. The androgenous man who can accept not only the traditionally masculine aspects of his personality but also the feminine aspects will be a healthier and happier individual.

In the group process, we refer to the deviation from traditional male roles as "breaking the rules." We heartily encourage and reinforce the men's exploration of and encounters with those new roles. Helping the men "break the rules" also serves to enlarge their support systems. Abusive men are generally extremely dependent on their female partner for recognition, reinforcement, nurturing, and validation. The nature of this dependence often reinforces the men's need to control the person who is the sole source of their emotional support. The relationship between the men and their partners, in many cases, resembles the relationship between a boy and his mother. They commonly view her as the only person who is capable of meeting their emotional needs. And not unlike a child, they expect that she will not only meet these emotional needs but recognize and respond to them as mothers often do with their children. Recognizing and breaking this dependence and learning to fulfill their needs through other people greatly reduces the stress and tension inherent in many of these relationships. Behavior and attitudes must be changed, traditional male roles must be rejected, and men's need to have power and control over women must be challenged in order to enable men to have healthy and satisfying relationships with their female partners. Any therapeutic process needs to consider and integrate all of these factors. If a man is able to stop his violent behavior yet continues to use controlling and dominating behavior in his relationship, the situation may be less dangerous physically for the victim but will be no healthier for the man. The desire and will to be nonviolent will rarely eliminate violent behavior. Even if will alone can result in a man not acting aggressively, if he has not learned to recognize and express feelings to gain support from a community of other men he will remain isolated, lonely, stressed, and at risk for violence.

Regardless of any individual man's success in remaining nonviolent and becoming more androgenous, a complete resolution of this issue cannot be accomplished without men's attempts to change the larger system that enslaves them. Personal changes are not enough. Men need to start confronting themselves and other men about how to change a system in society that has created a historical imbalance of power between men and women.

If men continue to depend exclusively on women for nurturing and recognition, they will also continue to need to exercise control and power over them. Women cannot change this. It is impossible for a healthy, intimate relationship to exist where a power imbalance exists also. For men, the escape from this rests in relinquishing the control over women that they attempt to maintain and empowering themselves with new skills, new beliefs, and new attitudes.

Conclusion

We hope that the information provided in this chapter will raise awareness about the treatment of men who batter. This treatment, if at all possible, should occur in group settings. If group treatment is unfeasible, these principles can be applied to working with men individually, although they will then not be as effective. Couples therapy is contraindicated with this population and may, in fact, be dangerous. The couple may be seen together only after the man has taken full responsibility for his violence and the woman feels safe and refuses to take responsibility for the man's violence.

Providing counseling for men who batter is difficult work. It often involves life-and-death issues. Only fully qualified professionals should p4ovide services to men who batter. Timing is crucial. Men need to be taught behavior-control skills before they are taught to express feelings that may include rage from early life abuse. Professionals need to be aware of men's resistance to give up their attempts to control women. For all of these reasons, it is important for professionals to develop and maintain a network of associates in order to counteract the emotionally draining effects of carrying out this work.

This chapter identifies means of assessing men who may be at risk of suicide and offers suggestions for counselors in responding to these men.

Chapter 16

COUNSELING SUICIDAL MEN

Dennis E. Elsenrath

Historically, suicide has proven difficult to understand and even more difficult to predict. Throughout history, philosophers and others have taken various positions of understanding and tolerance regarding suicide. A brief perspective of the diverse positions is provided by Backer, Hannon, and Russell (1982) in their excellent summary of different philosophical positions taken on suicide through the centuries. The ancient Greek philosophers were generally opposed to the act, although for different reasons. For example, Pythagoras and Plato were opposed to suicide because they felt it was God's decision when to release the soul; however, Aristotle thought suicide was a "cowardly act; contrary to the right rule of life" (Backer et al., p. 209).

By the 18th century, Voltaire, Montesquieu, Rousseau, and Hume took positions supportive of the individual's right to choose, whereas Kant believed suicide was a vice. Nineteenth-century philosophers Schopenhauer and Nietzsche agreed on the right of individuals to decide about suicide. However, they disagreed on the wisdom of the act. Durkheim's examination of suicide in late 19th-century Europe offered a sociological perspective, with a major focus on social alienation and the influence of the forces of society on the individual. Freud viewed suicide as aggression turned inward as a result of early internalization of disappointment with a loved person (object-relationship). Freud noted the ambivalence of love and anger toward this internalized object (Backer et al., 1982).

During the past 40 years the focus has shifted to prevention largely because of the leadership of Shneidman, Farberow, and Litman. In particular, Shneidman's efforts to scientifically gather and analyze data from suicide notes, psychological autopsies, and interviews with attempters and professional counselors have provided a great deal of information about characteristics of the suicidal person and strategies to prevent the suicidal act (Backer et al., 1982).

Causative Factors in Suicide

Differences by Gender

Research has provided a considerable amount of useful information about the internal and external conditions that are present for the suicidal individual. We know that suicide occurs in all age, racial, occupational, religious, and social groups, however not on an equal basis. The most obvious and consistent differences in patterns of suicide occur according to age, sex, and race (Moore & Lewis, 1986). Lester and Lester (1971, p. 88) stated that, "of all that is known about the phenomenon of suicide, there is little so clear that men and women differ in their suicidal behavior." Furthermore, "simply being born predisposes every American to the base rate of twenty men or seven women [suicides per one-hundred thousand] per year" (Cutter, 1983, p. 13). Cutter (p. 14), added that "all women are at far lesser risk than all men at every age level."

Although the rate of completed suicide is consistently higher for men than for women, women show a consistently higher rate of attempted suicide. These gender data appear to hold true for different ages, races, and nationalities; however, the ratio may change. For example, although the ratio of attempted suicide in the general population is 3:1, male-female, the ratio for adolescents is 9:1, male-female (Lester & Lester, 1971). Rich, Ricketts, Fowler, and Young (1988) cited Durkheim as providing similar data for European countries, although several British studies reported ratios closer to 1:1, but still consistently higher for men.

Various explanations for the different rates of suicide by gender have been provided. Rich, et al. (1988) posited two basic hypotheses for the differences in completion rates by men and women: (1) equal numbers of male and female attempters intend to commit suicide, but men are more successful because of their choice of methods; and (2) more men seriously intend to commit suicide.

Indeed, the evidence is overwhelming that men use more immediately fatal methods (firearms, hanging, and jumping) than do women, to the rate of 75% to 43%. In some studies, over half of male suicides involve guns, mostly handguns (Moore & Lewis, 1986; Rich et al., 1988). These authors acknowledged that many factors other than gender interact with the degree of seriousness with which individuals make attempts; they concluded, however, that being male leads to greater intentionality.

Alcohol and Drug Abuse

One of the factors identified as significantly contributing to male suicide is alcohol and other drug abuse (Cohen & Durham, 1986). Although alcohol and drug abuse is much more common in men and women who have committed suicide than in the general population, "alcoholism was . . . five times more frequent in men than women" according to a NIMH population study (Rich et al., 1988, p. 721).

"Alcoholics have extremely high rates of depression and suicide. An estimated 7% to 21% of alcoholics kill themselves, compared to about 1% of the general population" (Moore & Lewis, 1986, p. 9). Alcohol contributes to increased depression, impaired judgment, and reduced problem-solving ability, and it reduces inhibitions that are necessary to restrain individuals from their suicidal impulses. Successful treatment of suicidal men requires assessment and treatment of alcohol or other drug abuse as a first priority. In addition to the problems of reduced impulse control, individuals will usually have impaired ability to gain insight while using psychoactive substances such as alcohol. Thus, counseling efforts based on a rational exchange, insight, and understanding will be of little value while the person is under the influence.

Isolation

Another major factor that seems especially poignant in male suicide involves disrupted social relationships and isolation. Breed (1972, p. 16) succinctly made the point that ". . . isolation represents the beginning of the climax of self-destruction, because the human being is a social being, and without communication he loses his humanity." Loss of a spouse through divorce or death, on average, seems to contribute more significantly to male risk of suicide than to female risk. Maris and Lazerwitz's (1981) research suggests that men are more likely to commit suicide than women in response to divorce. The positive benefits of marriage may go beyond suicide. Married men live longer than unmarried men; however, the reverse is not true for women (Taylor, 1986). The incidence of suicide for men is lowest for married, next highest for widowed, and highest for divorced persons (Lester & Lester, 1971).

The shift from being married to being divorced is clearly more difficult for men than for women. Using measures such as suicide, violence, and debilitating diseases, Gove (1972) found men more negatively affected by divorce than women. Dreyfus (1979, p. 79) also found divorced men "frequently anxious, depressed and feeling overwhelmed." Divorced men lose not only their wives, but frequently their children, friends, home, and family life. This massive amount of change and loss of support is disruptive and contributes significantly to an increased suicide risk for men.

A critical issue at the center of these interpersonal losses involves men's ability to deal with their dependence needs. Most men have learned to deny their relationship and dependence needs largely because of the fear of being weak and losing masculinity. Frequently, men begin to address these needs for the first time during or following divorce proceedings. Unfortunately, men are frequently reluctant to seek counseling because of these same fears of dependence. The experience of major interpersonal/emotional loss, increased isolation, and resistance to counseling or other healthy sources of support leave men vulnerable and in a high-risk suicide category.

Divorce

Divorce represents a major crisis for many men, one that often results in significant psychological impairment, and, too frequently, in suicide. Counseling can be an important opportunity to help men come to terms with their emotional dependence needs in ways that will provide immediate relief and set the stage for vastly improved long-term social/emotional functioning. During counseling, men can begin to explore their values, emotional needs, quality of relationships, vulnerabilities, and life-style. They also may be encouraged to understand their own real feelings as opposed to the male role script learned well very early in life. For these men, divorce counseling can and frequently does open the door to a richer emotional life. Regrettably, many men refuse professional assistance, a fact that only emphasizes the need for primary prevention programs that teach boys from an early age how to be honest about their needs, including their relationships, while living in a society that teaches them to be self-sufficient to an excessive degree.

Family Disunity

Other studies have emphasized the importance of early disruption in family relationships as a critical factor in adolescent suicide (Joffe, Offord, & Boyle, 1988). A large proportion of young suicide attempters, in particular, have experienced this type of disruption through divorce, separation, or death of a parent (McAnarney, 1979). Many adolescents have a history of physical abuse in their families; come from families where other members have made suicide attempts; and frequently attempt suicide following some sort of family quarrel. Long-standing relationship difficulties in the family, especially with the father, also have been observed.

Hawton (1982) and McAnarney (1979) also point to evidence indicating that family disunity, multiple separations, and divorce increase the risk of suicide attempts, especially among adolescents. Conversely, a stable parental situation can be expected to reduce the likelihood of attempted suicide.

Stable, positive relationships seem to be a significant factor in reducing the risk of suicide (Hawton, 1982). When one considers the highly mobile and unstable American family, it is easy to understand the dramatic rise (estimated to be between 250% and 300%) in suicide in the 15- to 24-year-old age group over the past 30 years. The critical factor may well involve the number of persons with whom the individual can maintain meaningful communication. A decrease in the number of persons available for this type of relationship seems to be a significant factor in suicide (Reinhart & Lindea, 1983). Lester and Lester (1971) also concluded that individuals who move into a new environment or have others move into their environment are at greater risk.

Special Populations

The elderly represent a particular population at risk largely because of the increased loss of social support that in part is caused by disruption of environmental surroundings. Older persons and older men particularly constitute a disproportionate percentage of suicides. The literature suggests that among those at greatest risk are men who have lost their spouse, live alone, and receive little emotional support from their families (Wass & Meyers, 1982; Wenz, 1980). In fact, although men who live alone are at greater risk of suicide, the same is not true for women (Miller, 1979).

Other characteristics found descriptive of older Canadian men who committed suicide included physical illness; a high tendency to use lethal methods such as firearms and hanging; less likelihood of informing others in advance; and a lower tendency to be involved with alcohol or other drugs or to have been a victim of violence prior to death (Jarvis & Boldt, 1980). Men experiencing chronic illnesses are often prone to consider suicide rather than face the prospect of becoming totally dependent (McCartney, 1978).

The risk associated with widowhood seems especially great for men because of the lack of a supportive social network associated with the social and personal disorganization following the death of a spouse. The first year of widowhood for men is an especially high-risk period (Wenz, 1980).

Minorities represent another subpopulation of men with special characteristics. It would clearly be a mistake to lump all minorities together in this discussion. Differences within, as well as between, minority groups are apparent. For example, research suggests that a high rate of suicide among Native Americans may be due to living on the reservation

(Lester & Lester, 1971; McIntosh & Santos, 1981), and older Chinese immigrants have a higher suicide rate than do native born Chinese-Americans due to the loss of social support and failed expectations in the new culture (McIntosh & Santos). One of the hazards especially relevant to minorities is the issue of frustrated expectations. Lester and Lester (1971) observed that job opportunities may actually raise the suicide rate of young Black men because the expectations may exceed the reality.

Lack of social support and approval and failed expectations are themes that emerge in male suicide for minority men and nonminority men alike. Perhaps no better example can be found than the returning Vietnam soldiers. Furthermore, this group represents an anomaly, demographically, with men in their middle years experiencing the highest suicide rates as opposed to the expected higher rates for older and younger men (Cutter, 1983).

Assessment

We have learned a great deal about who is at risk and under what circumstances. Although some prevention and prediction efforts have not proven efficacious (suicide prevention centers, for example) (Cutter, 1983; Farberow & MacKinnon, 1975; Moore & Lewis, 1986), there is a great deal of information related to proper assessment, intervention, and prevention that is of considerable value especially for the professional who is working directly with the suicidal client.

Mental health professionals have a clear ethical and legal responsibility to protect suicidal clients. Most clients who express suicidal intentions are willing to cooperate with therapists to reduce the risk. In instances where clients insist that it is their right to take their own life, the professional has an obligation to intervene to protect life even when the client resists (Corey, Corey, & Callanan, 1988).

Assessing the seriousness of suicidal intent is one of the more difficult and generally stressful tasks mental health workers face. Assessment of suicidal men is frequently the most difficult for several reasons. Men tend to be reluctant to participate in any psychotherapeutic intervention, including an assessment of their emotional functioning. Even when therapists develop initial rapport with men, accurate assessment of suicidal intent may be limited by the man's willingness to divulge completely the depth of his emotional pain and felt need for support. The common male tendency to deny emotional pain and a determination to maintain the self-sufficient male role masks the seriousness of suicide risk, contributing to reduced effectiveness in the prevention of male suicide.

Over the past decade useful guidelines, checklists, and assessment scales have been developed, researched and published. Successful utilization of these assessment tools, however, requires accurate reporting of behavior, affect, and cognitions. Men frequently withhold essential information from the therapist because of fear that they might be perceived as weak or dependent. For many men, it may be more respectable to commit suicide than to disclose feelings of helplessness and need for assistance.

Sense of Hopelessness

Several approaches to the assessment of suicide risk are especially noteworthy for the mental health worker. Identification of major factors in suicide and approaches found useful in evaluating suicide risk follow. A sense of hopelessness is considered the major link between depression and suicide, and the Beck Hopelessness Scale is considered an excellent instrument for use in suicide assessment (Petrie & Chamberlain, 1983). In a 10-year longitudinal study 90% of depressed, suicidal patients who scored nine or more on Beck's Hopelessness Scale eventually killed themselves. Only one patient who had a score below nine committed suicide (Beck, Steer, Kovacs, & Garrison, 1985). Shneidman (1985b) identified feelings of hopelessness and helplessness as the common emotions in suicide. The person feels there is nothing he or she can do and that there is no one else who can help with the pain.

Psychological Pain

Psychological pain is the common stimulus in suicide (Shneidman, 1985b). Recognizing the unique meaning each individual attaches to events is imperative. It is crucial for the therapist to understand the client's unique perception and the degree of pain experienced (Bobele, 1987; Corey et al., 1988). Understanding the unique meaning of events and the degree of pain for men is difficult because of their tendency to deny the degree of emotional pain even to themselves. Because of male reluctance to disclose feelings openly, those assisting men who are contemplating suicide may need to call upon their capacity for advanced empathy to understand the particular meaning that a man attaches to an event.

A major source of pain involves the loss of something highly valued. About 10 years ago I received a call at midnight from a suicidal client who was upset and reported suicidal feelings in response to the death of a pet bird. This individual had been diagnosed as a borderline personality and had a long history of suicide attempts and hospitalizations.

Yet, for a brief moment I was tired, not yet mentally alert, and very tempted to attach my own less painful meaning to the loss of a pet bird. Fortunately, as mental alertness arrived, it became clear that this loss represented that of a "close friend." My client survived this loss, and, with continued counseling, went on to improved relationships with people.

Another example of psychological pain associated with loss occurred during my first year as a counselor in our university counseling center. In February of that year, an 18-year-old freshman, a young man who had been a straight "A" student in high school and during his first semester in college, received a "C" on a chemistry exam. That night he drank a bottle of toilet bowl cleaner containing lye and died an agonizing 24-hour death. Our psychological autopsy revealed a lonely young man who had lost what must have seemed to him like his only major source of meaning and personal worth. His psychological pain must have been enormous.

Eliciting a man's philosophy of life and the meaning he attaches to events is fundamental to the issue of suicide. Belief systems play a crucial role in suicide. Male reluctance and at times inability to disclose inner thoughts and feelings openly contribute to the difficulty in arriving at an accurate assessment of danger. Helping male clients understand that open sharing of feelings and accepting help from others is entirely congruent with being men may set the stage for the sharing of inner thoughts and feelings so essential to an accurate diagnosis of suicide risk. It also is important to treat professional men in the same manner as nonprofessional men and to avoid the mistake of undertreating people with status.

Understanding a man's lifelong coping patterns will also provide useful information in understanding the individual's reactions to threat, pain, pressure, and failure. Using this concept of lifelong coping patterns to pain, Shneidman (1985b), using background information on a group of 30 male subjects from the well-known Terman study of the gifted, was able to select accurately the 5 men who had previously committed suicide from a group of 30 profiles. Based on certain psychological consistencies such as habitual reactions to threat, pain, pressure, and failure, a determination of which men would commit suicide at about age 55 could be made before their 30th birthdays. Suicide is a movement away from internal pain that is seen as intolerable.

Constricted, Rigid Thinking

Constricted, rigid thinking is another major characteristic of individuals at high risk for suicide (Shneidman, 1985b; Cutter, 1983;

Linehan, Goodstein, Nielsen, & Chiles, 1983). A narrowing of options and reduced flexibility in perception are common cognitive qualities associated with high-risk suicide profiles. "Have to, must, should, ought to, can't, no choice, all, none, always, and never" are examples of words that characterize this rigid cognitive thought process (Lester & Lester, 1971). Furthermore, the rigidity is often negative and self-limiting. Men in our society have traditionally been taught that they need to be in control and to be the final authority. The title of the television program of the late 1950s, "Father Knows Best," is an example of the social expectation that men should be right and not make mistakes. This type of thinking contributes to the rigid, dogmatic thought process characteristic of men at high risk for suicide. Men who believe their masculinity requires that they be in control are at a great risk for depression that results from the reality that they truly cannot control the external environment, including people.

In response to failed efforts to control the external environment, a man may convince himself that the environment is in control of his emotions and may develop what Seligman (1975) described as learned helplessness. Maier and Seligman (1976) described three deficits that develop when individuals repeatedly fail in their efforts to establish control in their lives: motivational—the individual makes no effort to change the outcome; cognitive—the individual does not learn new responses; and emotional—the individual becomes depressed.

Suzanne Kobasa (1979) used the term *hardiness* to describe male executives who had high-stress jobs, yet experienced low rates of illness. Hardiness includes three factors: a *commitment* to self and to active involvement in one's surroundings; *control* (internal locus), a belief that one can influence (but not control) one's environment; and *challenge*, a willingness to change and make necessary adjustments and to see change as a challenge. In subsequent research she and her colleagues (Kobasa, Maddi, & Kahn, 1982) substantiated her early findings that individuals, especially men who possess high levels of hardiness, are more likely to remain well than individuals who have different cognitive styles. Individuals with a high level of hardiness are more likely to search for and see possibilities and are much less likely to be negative or rigid in their thought processes. Cutter (1983) described self-destructive thinking as involving a loss of flexible thinking, with less focus on positive events and more attention to negative circumstances.

Frustration of Psychological Needs

Assessing the degree of frustration of psychological needs, what Shneidman calls the perturbation level, is another important aspect of determining the level of immediate danger. "The common stressor in suicide is frustrated psychological needs" (Shneidman, 1985b, p. 11). Shneidman (1985b) believes that suicide is always a response to frustrated, highly valued needs and that frequently more than one need is not being met. Therapists need to help their clients reduce the frustration immediately, especially when this frustration is severe. In cases of high frustration/high lethality, therapists are encouraged to involve family and community to reduce the frustration level immediately. Advanced empathy skills are often necessary to understand the stoic man who conceals disappointment and frustration.

Following participation in a day-long seminar by Shneidman in 1980 (Winnebago Mental Health Series, September 12, 1980, Neenah, WI), I was presented with a suicide note written by a faculty member and discovered by a colleague. The suicidal faculty member was a single man who had dedicated his life to his discipline and was retiring at the end of the school year. Because of a shortage of office space, the university's policy was to relocate faculty from their individual offices to a large, "bull pen" type of arrangement shared by a number of retired faculty members. Adequate storage of accumulated papers and books and continuation of research under these circumstances would have been difficult at best for this faculty member, who had a strong need to continue to be actively involved in world travel, lectures, and writing. His research had been a primary source of gratification throughout his professional life. His appeals to maintain his office had been rejected and his response was to actively plan suicide. I consulted with Dr. Shneidman about the situation, and read the suicide note over the phone. Fortunately, our university administration was willing to be flexible by recognizing the special circumstances and granted this faculty member's request to maintain his individual office. This type of environmental intervention is frequently necessary to reduce the frustration level immediately, especially in severe cases.

Myths About Suicide

An important element of suicide prevention and assessment is educating professionals and lay people alike about suicide myths. The following are common myths, with a correct statement of fact following each myth.

I have found a simple handout addressing these myths to be a good tool for educating mental health professionals, student paraprofessionals, and community volunteers.

    1. *MYTH:* "People who talk about suicide or write suicide notes are not the ones who actually commit suicide."

FACT: People who commit suicide often discuss their thoughts in advance of the attempt. The suicide talk may be direct or indirect as in statements such as "I don't know if life is worth living." All suicide talk, oral or written, should be taken seriously and evaluated properly.

2. *MYTH:* "People who have attempted suicide aren't really serious."

FACT: Previous suicidal behavior is the single best predictor of future attempts. For example, one previous attempt produces a risk of one death per year per 100 people, and two previous attempts result in a risk factor of one death per year per 10 people. The risk factor for the general population is one per 5,000 per year for men and one per 15,000 per year for women (Cutter, 1983).

3. *MYTH:* "Most suicidal individuals want to die."

FACT: The vast majority of individuals who make attempts do not want to die. What they want most of all is a change, usually less pain and more hope. Death seems preferable to what seem to the individual as unresolvable and painful life circumstances.

4. *MYTH:* "All suicidal persons are mentally ill."

FACT: Although individuals with a history of depression, thought disorders, and other major emotional disorders are at higher risk, the majority of individuals who attempt and complete suicide are not emotionally disturbed. However, individuals with a strong history of emotional disorder should be monitored carefully and provided with appropriate psychotherapy and medication. The majority of individuals who attempt and commit suicide are highly frustrated, are in great emotional pain, feel helpless, and see little hope for the future.

5. *MYTH:* "Initiating direct discussion about suicide will cause the person to make an attempt."

FACT: There is no evidence that direct discussion will produce an idea that will lead to suicide. There is considerable evidence that direct discussion may prevent suicidal acts. Direct discussion is necessary to conduct a good assessment of lethality, allows meaningful interpersonal contact that is so often missing, and allows for direct intervention with the person and the environment.

6. *MYTH:* "People who are serious about suicide do not give advance warning."

FACT: Studies of a large number of psychological autopsies of suicidal deaths reveal that clear clues were present in advance in approximately 80% of the cases. Frequently, one of the last major acts of the suicidal individual is to make some interpersonal communication effort related to the suicidal act (Shneidman, 1985a).

7. *MYTH:* "Teenagers and young adults are the age group at highest risk of suicide."

FACT: Although the 15- to 24-year-old age group has experienced the most dramatic rise in suicide over the past 30 years (an increase of approximately 250% to 300%), the older age group (60 years old and older) has traditionally been most at risk. Currently, the teenage-young adult group and the older adult groups are both considered at high risk, at least in the White population. This pattern is quite different for several minority populations, where young male Blacks and young Native Americans are at much higher risk than their elders.

8. *MYTH:* "Suicidal individuals will eventually kill themselves."

FACT: Indeed, previous suicide attempts are the single best predictor of eventual suicide. Yet, only 1 out of 10 attempters will eventually kill themselves. Suicide prevention efforts that focus attention on individuals who have made previous attempts are well directed. Regular follow-up, especially in the months following an attempt, threat, or major depression involving suicidal ideation is one of the better approaches to prevention.

9. *MYTH:* "Most suicide is an impulsive act."

FACT: Suicide is much more an act of compulsion than impulsion. The vast majority of high-risk people who eventually commit suicide have given a great deal of thought and planning to the act. The major exception to this rule is the more seriously disturbed individual who is apt to act much more impulsively, randomly, and chaotically. The fact that the majority of high-risk individuals approach suicide compulsively provides mental health professionals the opportunity to intervene, providing the professionals recognize the warning signs and know how to respond.

10. *MYTH:* "The mental health professional, alone, is responsible for preventing suicide."

FACT: The mental health profession has a great deal to learn about suicide prevention. Despite efforts over many decades to prevent suicide, we are still unable to predict or prevent many suicides. However, our current knowledge suggests that effective suicide prevention requires a systems approach (Cutter, 1983). The mental health professional needs to work in concert with the medical community, family, employers, clergy, and other community members in the person's "system" to establish a prevention plan that recognizes the critical role that all people, not only professionals, can play in prevention.

Suggested Resources and Approaches for Suicide Prevention

Cutter (1983) developed an excellent compilation of assessment resources, intervention strategies, and resource materials. Furthermore, Cutter granted permission in advance to the individual reader to duplicate and use any of these materials providing the reader gives proper acknowledgment. Cutter also requested feedback from the reader regarding observations related to the use of these materials.

Cutter's core conceptual model for suicide prevention is based on the fire prevention education model that teaches that three conditions are essential for fire: oxygen, fuel, and flame (or heat). Remove any one of these and the fire will not start or will be extinguished. In suicide prevention, Cutter's model identifies the intensity of the wish to die, the kind and amount of distress, and the degree of planning as the essential ingredients in the suicide prevention triangle; remove any one or more of these, and self-injury can be deterred. Cutter believes that each of these is necessary, but is insufficient by itself, to cause suicide.

An organized, systematic approach to suicide prevention is recommended in order to mobilize an integrated and focused response from the community. Cutter's (1983) approach provides an excellent outline for mental health professionals. Cutter's comprehensive suicide prevention approach includes a flowchart of precipitating factors; data on factors that are correlated with increasing risk; a listing of suicide assessment devices; scales for rating lethality of suicide planning; a self-injury incident report form; instructions for administering and scoring a projective "draw a person committing suicide" test; a semantic differential assessment tool; Rorschach signs of suicidal intent and lethality; a satisfaction scale; a significant loss checklist; criteria for hospitalization of a high-risk person; a listing of minimal lethal doses of common prescriptions; a sample copy of a suicide prevention plan; criteria for in-patient levels of observation based on suicidal risk; checklists for forensic issues and providing optimal information to the media; a checklist of preferred methods of self-injury in the United States; and a checklist for manifestations of clinical depression in adults, adolescents, and children. Information is also provided for establishing programs for special populations including schools, colleges and universities, and the elderly. Finally, Cutter provides a quiz on knowledge about suicide and computerized assessment materials that might be used effectively as educational tools and as assessment devices when training paraprofessionals and professionals alike.

A few concrete suggestions for counselors in responding to suicidal men include:

1. Listen with empathy to the feelings of your client. Be cautious not to filter the meaning of the person's experience through your own. However, trust your feelings when you suspect your male client is masking his pain with masculine bravado or denial.
2. Ask a male client specific questions, including whether he is considering suicide, how, when, where, and so forth.
3. Give hope, if nothing else, that you will stay with the client and not abandon him.
4. Evaluate the intensity of frustration and emotional upset. Provide immediate assistance in reducing environmental barriers that are sources of frustration.
5. Listen for rigid, constricted thinking, and, when possible, begin to offer some possibilities that the individual may be willing to consider.
6. Remind the person that feelings of depression will pass. Remember that the high-risk lethality period usually lasts a matter of a few hours, although the feelings of depression may return later.
7. Evaluate suicidal potential for all depressed clients. A majority of individuals who have committed suicide have a history of serious depression (Moore & Lewis, 1986).
8. Point out that death cannot be reversed. Children and adolescents may not fully comprehend the irreversible nature of what they are about to do.
9. Never leave the person alone during an acute crisis.
10. Be supportive and caring, yet firm. If the person is out of control, take control using whatever measures are necessary including calling family, or the police or seeking involuntary hospitalization when cooperation cannot be gained from the client.

11. Remember, most suicide is not a movement toward death, rather, a movement away from pain. Much of this pain, especially for men, seems related to social isolation and lost relationships. Use the counseling relationship as a temporary source of replacement and assist the individual to develop new relationships as soon as he is able to do so. In my own practice I have assisted many men to become involved in local singles support groups with excellent results. Working with the families of these men to sensitize them to the emotional needs of their sons, brothers, husbands and fathers has also proven helpful.

12. Evaluate alcohol or other drug abuse. If chemical abuse is present, recognize the necessity to treat the drug problem as an immediate priority. Successful counseling is not possible while an individual is abusing chemicals. Men are at particular risk of alcohol abuse, which is one of the primary factors in the higher rate of male suicide. Yet, in past years, counselors were not well trained in alcohol abuse assessment and intervention.

13. Evaluate for possible medical or physiological disorders. Organic difficulties such as thyroid problems and brain tumors may be the primary cause of depression and suicidal thoughts. Work closely with the medical profession for evaluation and consultation when individuals are receiving prescription medications.

14. Take a complete history. Knowledge of previous suicide attempts is crucial. Previous attempts of suicide place individuals at greater risk.

15. Develop a no-suicide contract with every client who is thinking seriously about suicide. Keep the contract brief, usually for a period of several days or weeks, and review the contract in a timely manner.

16. Remember, you alone cannot prevent suicide. Client cooperation is ultimately the final consideration. Regrettably, we cannot always offset previous damage done to people. The good news is that much of the time we can help.

17. Remove firearms and other immediately fatal weapons and resources from the person. This is particularly important with men, who are much more prone to use firearms as the method of choice.

18. Mobilize community and family support when possible. Arranging positive, supportive relationships is one of the most important steps that can be taken to prevent suicide.

19. Develop a network of committed professionals including counselors, physicians, judges, police officers, crisis workers, clergy,

and others who communicate and who support one another toward the goal of suicide prevention.

20. Develop educational programs in the schools and community that teach young boys to disclose emotions freely and teach skills in developing and maintaining positive relationships.
21. Offer men's support and therapy groups where men can feel free to disclose feelings and offer and receive support from others.
22. Offer academic and noncredit courses and programs in men's studies. Women's studies have proliferated over the past two decades, with men's studies absent or poorly developed in most academic institutions.
23. Take every threat, gesture, and attempt seriously. Although some suicidal behavior is intentionally manipulative, only a proper evaluation will provide the basis for a sound response.

Conclusion

Although there is much to learn about counseling suicidal men, we have a great deal of valuable knowledge at the present that can be used effectively to reduce the incidence of these preventable deaths. Men represent a special challenge for the counseling profession because of their general reluctance to become involved in counseling and their adherence to the "male role," which has taught them to be self-sufficient to the point that they often commit suicide rather than seek or allow assistance from others.

In a similar manner the counselor, especially the male counselor, needs to remember the importance of seeking the assistance of others in responding to suicidal clients. Consulting with colleagues and gaining the support of key people in the client's life are examples of a shared, community approach to suicide prevention.

It is becoming increasingly apparent that the breakdown of the family and widespread drug use are major contributing factors in today's increasing risk of suicide. In a true primary prevention mode, we must seek solutions to these broad societal problems to make a true impact on suicide reduction.

Appendix A: Self-Injury Incident

Name _____ Date _____

Informant _____ Relation _____

Date of incident _____ Time _____

Place of incident (bathroom, etc.) _____

Other persons present _____

Self-injury method used _____

What became of instrument used _____

Parts of body injured _____

Substances ingested (give name, quantity, size of pills; estimate if unknown)

_____

Describe prior preparations made for this self-injury:

_____

Were prior verbalizations made about self-injury?

_____

Did the victim take steps to prevent rescue? _____ What? _____

ICAD No. (E950-959) _____ Suicide note: Yes ___ No ___
(attach copy of note if available)

Was person hospitalized as a consequence of this incident? If yes, give
details of treatment, length of stay, name of hospital, dates, etc. _____

_____

If available attach copy of law enforcement report

Give dates of prior self-injury incidents, and methods used:

_____

_____

Signature: _____

Print name and title of professional below.

_____

From *Suicide Prevention Triangle* (Report No. CG 017 875), (p. 28), by F. Cutter, 1983, Morror Bay, CA: Triangle Books. (ERIC Document Reproductive Services No. ED 251 747). Reprinted by permission.

Appendix B: The High-Risk Life Cycle

Early:

1. Bereavement before ages 13–15
2. Parental or surrogate suicide at any age
3. Unusual or premature death of parent after age 16
4. Parental psychopathology
5. Identified behavior or emotional problems before age 16
6. Maladjustment at school, work, or military
7. Marital problems
8. Older male, living alone
9. Under 35
10. History or treatment for mental disorders

Middle:

11. No meaning to life
12. Alcohol, drug dependence
13. Pain, sleep, bowel, weight problems
14. Medical compliance in long-term illnesses, e.g., diabetes
15. Onset of life-threatening illness; heart, cancer, stroke
16. Dependent-dissatisfied behavior
17. New losses
18. Two or more serious accidents including overdose
19. Institutionalization: hospital, prison
20. Self-injury behavior; low lethality, saves self

End Stage:

21. Personal resources exhausted
22. Significant losses in last two years
23. Loss of hope
24. Criteria for death approached
25. Significant others more consuming or competitive

26. Aimlessness, drifting in and out of community agencies
27. Depression, acute or recent
28. Substance addiction
29. Disabled and/or unemployed
30. One or more self-injuries with increasing lethality
31. Preferred method identifiable
32. Has plan with method available

The presence of these characteristics helps to place the client in some perspective with respect to urgency of intervention. If the majority of these identifiable conditions are in the end stage, the health professional has less margin of time for planning intervention strategies, and must mobilize these with more extremes of effort.

From *Suicide Prevention Triangle* (Report No. CG 017 875), (p. 17), by F. Cutter, 1983. Morro Bay, CA: Triangle Books. (ERIC Document Reproduction Service No. ED 251 747). Reprinted by permission.

Appendix C: Psychological Autopsy

Section A: Suggestions for the Psychological Autopsy

The traditional medical pathological conference was adapted by Shneidman and colleagues in the early fifties (1961) to evaluate ambiguous modes of death reviewed by LA Coroner's office. There is no one way to conduct an autopsy nor is it merely a collection of elicited facts. The psychological autopsy, when carried out appropriately, is really a human process where health professionals attempt to identify the motives, life-style, and feelings of the patients by reviewing their own observations, including private feelings toward the patient.

These data become available when health care teams seek to find an explanation for self-injury behavior in a client in a context of professional observations, reviews, and of searching for one or more consensuses. In this process, new facts are created coming from participants who have accumulated attitudes based on client's behavior. In the course of reviewing victim activities, one or more present begin to express these collective attitudes. Such themes become diagnostic of victim life-styles, problem solving, and intentions to die.

The user of this guideline should be aware that there are levels of observation possible and that information or attitudes surfacing in the conference will have different values depending upon what source it is perceived to rise from. These levels of observation are:

1. The fact of death or self-injury
2. The chronology of these facts
3. Inferred motivations by the observers
4. Reactions victim associates to the above
5. Collective themes observed in survivors or assembled staff

There is no set way to conduct the autopsy nor listing of acts to be obtained. It is rather a process in which the whole is greater than the sum of its parts or the isolated facts elicited.

The list attached is simply a guide to starting the process, which will proceed at its own pace and in directions never quite predictable. The guide is intended to help the chairperson keep some perspective on the events. There is no substitute for professional judgment and collegial review of ambiguous outcomes.

In addition, the facilitators should be aware that participants are experiencing a loss which varies in degree for each member of the staff, whether present or not. They will each be utilizing their own unique methods of managing these feelings. The person providing leadership to the autopsy conference needs to allow each person present sufficient psychological space to accomplish personal resolutions of grief reactions.

Section B: Guide to the Psychological Autopsy

—Prepare members for the process of reviewing a client's death.
—Elicit the facts of this death.

> Describe the self-injury incident: What happened, who was involved, where did it occur, when was behavior noticed, how did the self-injury occur. Save "why" questions until information is elicited.

—Establish the chronology of these facts, organized from remote to time of injury. Simply list information as obtained but place in a chronological framework. Include any behavior that may seem relevant. Look for all confirmed movements in the last days.
—Note behaviors and verbalizations contributed by staff members that are not part of the previous health records.
—Attempt to infer motives for the following:

1. Wish to die, extent and duration of the wish.
2. Lethality of self-injury methods and amount of the wish.
3. Meaning of death to the victim.
4. Perception of victim's existence, especially its quality by significant others.
5. Consequences of death for these others.

—Reactions of others to victim death (include staff).

1. Pre-self-injury attitudes
2. Post-self-injury reactions
3. Reactions "off" the record
4. Reactions in meetings

—Collective themes observed in meeting especially in controversies about the victim.

NB: The psychological autopsy should be separate from a medico-legal investigation. The chairperson should attempt to provide a non-judgmental and supportive atmosphere.

From *Suicide Prevention Triangle* (Report No. CG 017 875), (p. 56–57), by F. Cutter, 1983. Morro Bay, CA: Triangle Books. (ERIC Document Reproductive Service No. ED 251 747). Reprinted by permission.

Where Do We Go From Here? Ideas for the Future

The basis for the field of men's studies is, indeed, the emergence of a new paradigm for understanding men and the male role.

Chapter 17

DEVELOPING A CONTEMPORARY MEN'S STUDIES CURRICULUM

Sam Femiano

"Men's studies" describes a diversity of courses developed in colleges and universities throughout the United States and Canada over the past 15 years that have, as a common element, an exploration of notions of maleness and masculinity. The courses cover male psychological development, men's roles in society, and the evolution of the notion of masculinity in history and works of literature. In some respects, the term "men's studies" is a cognate of women's studies, and the influence of feminism and women's studies was important in the early growth of men's studies. Principally, however, the courses evolved out of the neonate men's movement, changes in society's notion of male roles, and the initiative of individual men themselves who, in response to these social changes, began to make changes in their personal lives.

The History and Development of Men's Studies

In the mid-1970s, a few scattered men's studies courses were being taught in the United States, but it was not until the beginning of the 1980s that men's studies as a distinct entity began to be noticed. In 1984, a national survey found about 40 courses in the United States. In the 6 years since that survey, however, growth has been rapid and the current number of courses has risen to at least 200.

One inspiration for the early development of men's studies was the men's movement that had begun to emerge in the early years of the 1970s. This period of the movement could be characterized as a time of growing awareness for men as they began to realize the extent to which the prescriptions of the male role influenced both their own lives and that of society at large. In response to this growing self-awareness, consciousness-raising groups appeared around the country, local and regional newsletters were begun, and men's resource centers started. The major characteristic of this first stage of the movement was a growing self-consciousness on the part of men about the realities of being male in modern society.

From this new self-consciousness gradually emerged a need for a new understanding of history. Men wanted to know how current notions of masculinity had evolved. The process of moving from a growing self-consciousness, an intrapersonal process, to a search for historical meaning, an external process, characterized the second stage of the men's movement. Emerging self-consciousness demanded a history and, in the latter half of the 1970s, writings began to appear that were historical in character (Dubbert, 1979; Filene, 1974; Katz, 1976; Pleck & Pleck, 1980). The search for a history was the second stage of the movement.

The third stage is the stage of conceptualization, and men's studies is an essential element in that part of the men's movement concerned with a deeper philosophical understanding of men and their roles. Again, it is following a pattern found in the development of the women's movement, for women's studies scholars have long been engaged in the process of conceptualizing their field of study. The 1979 meeting of the National Women's Studies Association, for example, produced a series of papers, *Theories of Women's Studies* (Bowles & Duelli-Klein, 1983), that dealt with questions concerning the role of women's studies in the academic curriculum and the development of a women's studies methodology. In the field of men's studies, such questions are now being broached.

The first men's studies courses were taught in various academic disciplines in institutions scattered around the country. Many of the teachers of these courses began to offer them because of events in their personal lives that caused them to reflect on men's roles in society. As academicians, they found it natural to investigate these events and try to understand them through the lens of their particular discipline. The result was a proliferation of men's studies courses in diverse disciplines. A national men's studies organization did not emerge until 1984, and most people who were developing courses did so independently of each other. This process of course generation out of a blend of personal and professional interest again seemed to follow the pattern for women's studies courses, which also grew in much the same way.

It is interesting that, even though the number of men's studies courses has increased fivefold in the last several years, the original diversity has remained and courses are still found in very different departments of universities. The motivation for developing courses continues to be consciousness raising but now also includes a strong research component. It is this latter element that most distinguishes current teaching from that of 6 years ago. Research in the area of men's studies has proliferated and articles now appear regularly in scholarly journals. Anthologies of articles are also appearing, and doctoral dissertations are being written with fair regularity. Today, the Men's Studies Association is a national organization linking together scholars and researchers in men's studies, and the *Men's Studies Review* is a quarterly journal of articles, book reviews, research notices, and bibliography about men's studies.

Despite this proliferation of courses and interest, the place of men's studies in the curriculum is still not clearly defined. No program of men's studies exists anywhere in the United States or Canada. Most courses are taught within the context of an already established department or, in some instances, they are interdisciplinary. The question of a final niche for men's studies seems to be awaiting further evolution of the field. Some comments regarding its right to be called an academic discipline, however, are appropriate here.

Men's Studies as an Academic Discipline

The original division of disciplines, defined in the medieval universities, has continued to furnish the basis for curriculum development. As modern science evolved in the 18th and 19th centuries, however, and as the social sciences were born in the latter decades of the 19th century, the original divisions were expanded to make room for new "disciplines." In the past several decades, we have seen science, particularly, become even more specialized so that the notion of discipline itself is often loosely equated with the specialty or subspecialty of a particular science.

At the same time, new disciplines were not always accepted immediately. The introduction of the social sciences in the latter part of the 19th century, for example, was a response to the social movements of the time and was greeted with skepticism by the more traditional and established disciplines. Thomas Kuhn suggested that the emergence of new disciplines is sometimes connected with the emergence of new paradigms and I think his suggestions, originally developed in relation to science, have a bearing on men's studies.

> When, in the development of a natural science, an individual or group first produces a synthesis able to attract most of the next generation's practitioners, the older schools gradually disappear. In part their disappearance is caused by their members' conversion to the new paradigm . . . it is sometimes just its reception of a paradigm that transforms a group previously interested merely in the study of nature into a profession or, at least, a discipline. In the sciences, the formation of specialized journals, the foundation of specialists' societies, and the claim

for a special place in the curriculum have usually been associated with a group's first reception of a single paradigm. (Kuhn, 1962, pp. 18–19)

The basis for the field of men's studies is, indeed, the emergence of a new paradigm for understanding men and the male role. Whether that fact gives it a claim to be called a discipline remains still controversial. It may be that it is too early in its development. The paradigm is not fully articulated nor does it have a consistent body of adherents (Kuhn, 1962). As the field grows, however, and gains a better sense of its own identity, it may be sufficiently coherent to be called an academic discipline.

A second consideration, however, is the role of gender studies in the evolution of the field of men's studies. It may be that both men's studies and women's studies will eventually be subsumed into a single field of gender studies that provides the philosophical underpinnings for both fields of study. Again, it is too early in the evolution of the field to know.

Despite a lack of clarity about its definitive place in the curriculum, as men's studies grows and develops, it will have an impact on the university curriculum in several ways. Its particular perspective on maleness brings a new and deeper understanding to other subject areas in the curriculum. Its emergence will also stimulate the university to grow and change as cultural contexts change. Finally, it will provide an opportunity for instructors from a variety of disciplines to work together to integrate their insights and research because men's studies offers an opportunity for integrating the university curriculum in new ways. Many men's studies courses are taught using the perspective and material of several disciplines. Such an approach to learning not only enhances students' ability to understand but also gives them a way of viewing reality that will serve them in contemporary political and social life as well. In a sense, men's studies teaches them not only about the world but about the process of learning itself.

As this evolution continues, however, certain areas of men's studies will need to be examined more closely. Men's studies, as currently practiced, is a field populated by White, middle-class men. Such a phenomenon is not surprising because White, middle-class men predominate in academic settings in the United States and other Western countries. Such a predominance of a single group, however, will create difficulties as one seeks to develop a field of study that is universal in its understanding of men and in its ability to engage a wide range of adherents. This lack needs to be remedied as the field grows.

Changes in our understanding of gender paradigms that have made men's studies possible are also important for society in general. Many of our social rituals and much of our social structure are posited on a dichotomous understanding of the relationships between men and women. This understanding is reflective of Western thought, in general, which is most comfortable with a dualistic approach to understanding the universe and human beings. Men's studies is one way to begin to change this perception of reality and to make possible more fruitful relationships between men, women, and children. The change will be slow because old habits of thought do not easily give way, even in the face of anomalous situations.

A Men's Studies Curriculum

In this section of the chapter, suggestions will be made for developing a men's studies curriculum. Such a curriculum must incorporate a number of themes, including the notion of gender as a social construct and its influence on men's psychological development, their social roles and behavior, the role of social institutions in the process of male socialization, and the historical evolution of the notion of masculinity. The role of power and dominance in men's personal lives and social relationships, particularly in their relationships with oppressed groups, also needs to be considered as well as the ways in which men's attitudes and roles are changing in the contemporary world.

Goals

The above themes can be subsumed into the following goals. The first is to define maleness and its allied concept, masculinity, through the disciplines of psychology, history, sociology, and the other social sciences. This goal is essential to the attainment of the other two. The second goal is to understand the evolution of male roles in society, both contemporary and historical, and the third is to foster a changed awareness in students of the impact of gender roles and particularly male roles on their lives and on society.

The first goal of the curriculum is to explore and understand the varied characteristics that have been attributed to men over the years. Maleness, itself, is usually seen as an innate characteristic of men whereas masculinity is defined as a set of culturally defined characteristics that have evolved through historical periods. We sometimes even speak of "masculinities" to emphasize the diverse meanings that can be attributed to this concept in different historical periods and cultures.

An understanding of the historical and cultural variability of maleness is essential for two reasons. If an adequate psychology of men is to be developed, researchers must be able to distinguish the aspects of masculinity that are subject to change from those that seem inherent to men as such. In addition, the ability of men to change and break out of their roles depends on whether or not these roles are based on innate characteristics or acquired ones. Because biological distinctions have often been the justification for male role assignments, an understanding of the interplay between biological and environmental factors in gender attribution is a part of this goal.

The second goal of the curriculum is to understand the ways in which notions of masculinity have influenced the evolution of male roles because it is society's understanding of gender roles that has guided its assignment of these roles to men and women. It is only recently, however, that sociologists, anthropologists, and other social scientists have begun to study men's roles from this viewpoint. David and Brannon (1976) commented "that the male sex role has been able to elude scientific study—or even notice—because, rather than in spite of, its enormous and pervasive influence on the knowledge, thoughts, attitudes, and assumptions of every person who has grown up under its influence" (p. 2). They explained this phenomenon by citing the adage, "The fish will be the last to discover the ocean."

This goal is important, as well, because men's roles have wide implications for society at large. Women's roles, for example, have generally been construed as complementary to men's roles, and any change in the roles men play will consequently have an effect on women and their roles as well. There is also a close correlation in society between the roles assigned to people and the power they exercise in social affairs. A study of men's roles, then, will include a study of the distribution of power in society as well as a consideration of the power allowed to the women, children, and men who belong to oppressed social classes. Recently, some men have begun to express dissatisfaction with the roles they have been acculturated to play in society. This phenomenon will also need to be studied as well as the new possibilities that are beginning to be available to men who wish to take on nontraditional roles.

Finally, the third curriculum goal is to raise students' awareness about the impact of gender roles on their own lives and society in general so that they can begin to make more informed choices about their own lives and work.

Specific Objectives

These three goals can be broken down into a number of objectives that give them more detail and clarity. In general, constructing curriculum objectives means keeping in mind both the traditional body of knowledge that needs to be handed on and the particular needs of contemporary students. Often, in curriculum development, there is a conflict between the worldview of students and their particular needs and the philosophical basis of tradition and the need for it to be understood. In men's studies, this dilemma exists in a somewhat different form, for the body of literature that constitutes the major resource for the field represents a newly emerging paradigm of masculinity and is a new tradition that has grown out of men's desire to better understand themselves and their behavior. The dilemma, then, in terms of choosing material for a curriculum, is between what one might call the new understanding of men and masculinity and the traditional view, and it can best be characterized as a clash of traditions.

Finally, curriculum objectives, if they are to be useful to the instructor, must clearly define the change they envisage in the student, whether it be in understanding or behavior, as well as the content area in which they envisage that change. Objectives in men's studies envisage changes in understanding and in behavior. Instructors in the field of men's studies have generally taken two approaches in teaching a course. Courses have been taught from a research-oriented perspective whose focus was understanding male psychology and behavior, or from a more experientially oriented perspective whose focus was on bringing about awareness and behavioral change in the students. These two approaches are not mutually exclusive and courses can incorporate both of them. The curriculum objectives, as outlined below, allow for both approaches to be used in developing courses.

1. Be able to define the meaning of maleness as a distinguishing characteristic of men. To attain this objective requires that students investigate and understand the relationship of biology to environment in the psychological development of men. It also requires them to formulate criteria for distinguishing innate characteristics from acquired ones in their investigation of men's psychology and behavior. This objective is distinguished from the following one in that it is more theoretical in nature and deals with the meaning of maleness, whereas the following objective deals with the social manifestations of maleness.

2. Be able to define and describe the notion of masculinity as a social construct. To attain this objective requires that students be familiar with the bases of gender attribution in our society and the ways in which the attribution of male gender traits is determined by social rather than individual needs. Researchers in the field of psychology, sociology, and anthropology have investigated the evolution of the concept of maleness and, although their conclusions are not always in agreement, their work needs to be analyzed and understood for the light it casts on the process of gender attribution.

This objective also requires that students be able to recognize the ways in which masculinity is understood differently by men in different social and economic classes. Attainment of this goal could also require that students use their knowledge of the concept of masculinity to analyze its influence on the choices regarding gender roles that they have made in their own lives.

3. Be able to trace the development of men's studies as a field of study and define its function in the academic curriculum. Because men's studies is a new field, it is important for students to understand the assumptions on which it is founded and its relevance to other fields of study. To attain this objective requires that students be familiar with the philosophical premises on which men's studies is based and be able to explain them. They will also be required to identify the important events in the historical development of the field, describe the relationship of men's studies to other academic disciplines, and discern the effects of male bias on their learning in other disciplines.

4. Be able to describe the historical evolution of the notion of masculinity and the male role. The ability to think historically is an important skill for students to acquire in general. To demonstrate attainment of this objective, students will need to apply this skill to showing how particular prescriptions for masculine behavior have evolved from the social contexts of different historical periods. They will also be required to trace the evolution of these ideas of masculinity. Finally, the realization of this objective requires students to describe their own historical period with its particular notions of masculinity, recognizing those that are a heritage from the past and those that are new.

5. Be able to define the function of social roles and identify the influence of the concept of masculinity in assigning men's roles. Social roles play an important part in structuring society and allowing it to function in an efficient way. To attain this objective requires that students be able to define this function and describe the ways in which notions of masculinity determine male role assignment. They will also be able to discuss the role of social institutions such as the family, the school, the military, the government, and the workplace in the socialization process. Students will be able to critique their own lives in the light of their knowledge of social roles and the process by which they have been acquired.

6. To be aware of the impact of the male role on society. To attain this goal requires that students be able to describe the hierarchical structure of society and the distribution of power according to that hierarchy. Men's roles determine the roles of other social groups because men have power and, consciously or not, determine the roles other groups play by controlling access to power. Students will also be able to discuss their own experience of power or lack of power associated with different social roles and membership in different social groups.

7. Be able to describe the nature of the changes that are happening to men's roles in contemporary society. Students will be able to identify the personal and social motivations that prompted the men's movement in its various manifestations as well as the other cultural changes of the last two decades that contributed to men's sense of a need for change. They will also be able to critique theories of male psychological development and the revised viewpoints on that development currently being discussed. Students will also evaluate the changes in their perception of their own roles or behavior that have occurred as they have studied the male role.

8. Be able to describe the harmful effects of certain aspects of the male role on men's physical and psychological health. The male role is a complex set of prescriptions that has served men well in some regards but has been detrimental to their health in others. Students will be able to describe the interrelatedness of physical and emotional health in people and the relationship of male role expectations to stress. In addition, they will be able to examine their own role functioning or that of men they know and evaluate in what ways it has been detrimental to their physical or emotional health.

9. Be able to identify and value the positive aspects of the male role. The current critique of men and the male role has sometimes portrayed men in a negative fashion. This portrayal is unwarranted because many aspects of men's functioning are positive and productive. Students will be able to identify these positive aspects and describe their value. Ideally, the attainment of this objective would stimulate students to work to create more positive roles for men and women.

Curriculum Outline

The following suggestion for a men's studies program does not list individual courses but rather areas of concentration that correspond to the goals and objectives outlines above. These areas are organized topically, and each area is capable of being further defined into several courses in various academic disciplines. For each area of concentration, there is presented a general title and a listing of topics to be included in that area. Section III is only a suggestion of special topic areas that can be developed in the field. The subject matter of these areas will be determined by the needs of particular students and the interests of teachers.

AREAS OF CONCENTRATION

SECTION I—Introductory Areas of Concentration
    The Concept of Maleness
    Men's Studies—Its History and Development
    Masculinity in a Historical Perspective
SECTION II—Applications to the Social Sciences
    The Psychological Foundations of the Notion of Masculinity
    The Male Role in Society
SECTION III—Selected Topic Areas
    Oppressed Racial Minorities, Men, and Work
    The Homosexual Tradition
    Men and Change
    Men and Maleness Portrayed in Literature
    Men's Health and Sexuality
    Men and Aggression

This curriculum is proposed as a full program in men's studies, the equivalent of a major in an academic field. It can be adapted, however, for other academic applications. Students, for example, who wish to have an understanding of men's studies but do not wish to make it their area of concentration, could develop a minor using selected courses from each section. A student in sociology, for example, might choose courses from The Concept of Maleness, Maleness in a Historical Perspective, The Male Role in Society, and The Psychological Foundations of the Notion of Masculinity as a base and add selected topical courses as needed. By the same token, courses developed from the above areas can be constructed as independent courses to be taken as social science electives in another major. Because it is unlikely that men's studies will soon become a major on most college campuses, these latter methods of implementation will most likely be the most common application of any curriculum for the immediate future.

The curriculum is proposed without distinction between undergraduate and graduate material. The goals and objectives outlined above and the areas of concentration can be implemented on either level by selecting resources appropriate to the level desired and requiring a research component as well as demonstrated mastery of the material for higher levels. The following discussion will illustrate how one of the above sections can be broken down into a course outline.

Course Title: American Masculinities: Introduction and Goals

This course will consider the concept of masculinity as it has evolved in American history and culture during the last three centuries. An understanding of this evolution is important for the student because many contemporary notions of masculinity are variations on historical themes. In this course, the historical variability and permanence of male traits will be explored.

In exploring this theme students will be made aware of the male bias in much historical work. Men have been the dominant protagonists throughout history, and their viewpoint on historical research and writing has strongly influenced our understanding of history.

This course is considered an introductory section of the curriculum because it illustrates the influence of society's needs and expectations on the definition of masculinity.

Objectives for "American Masculinities"

At the conclusion of the course, students should be able to define the characteristics of masculinity that have been prominent in various historical periods in the United States, to trace the evolution of those characteristics, and to indicate which of them continue to be evident in contemporary theory about men.

Other objectives include the ability to discuss the reasons for considering certain masculine characteristics as constant in their manifestation rather than being linked to certain historical periods. Students should also be able to trace the history of "feminist" men through the 19th and early 20th centuries.

Finally, students should be able to explain how history, its important events, and its division into periods has been defined by men from a male bias and be able to describe the notion of patriarchy as it refers to men's dominance of the social order throughout history.

Course Outline

The introductory classes (1–4) would look at the periods of American history as defined by Pleck and Pleck and the notions of masculinity that were prominent during the different historical periods. Particular attention would be paid to the end of the 19th century because of its affinity to the present period.

The next part of the course would look at cultural and racial diversity among men and the ways masculinity was understood in various social groups (5–7). This part of the course would include a study of gay men and attitudes toward them throughout the past 200 years of American history. For this section of the course, Katz's work would be used as well as Sylvia Strauss's study of feminist men. Although resources are more scarce, it would be important to include a study of Black men in this section of the course.

With the foregoing as background, students would then spend considerable time on the period since World War II (8–13). For this period, Barbara Ehrenreich's book would be a useful resource. The development of the men's movement and its current divisions would also be important to study for a better understanding of the differences in men's perceptions of the meaning of masculinity. Brod's book would also be a useful resource.

Because the required readings for the course are all books that subscribe to a new paradigm of men and masculinity, it will be important for the students to look at some traditional treatments of the period to critique the bias from which they are written. It will also be important for students to understand historical method. Degler's article is useful for this purpose.

The following books are suggested as required reading for the course:

Dubbert, J.L. (1979). *A man's place*. Englewood Cliffs, NJ: Prentice-Hall.
Ehrenreich, B. (1983). *The hearts of men*. Garden City, NY: Anchor Press/ Doubleday.
Filene, P.G. (1974). *Him/her/self: Sex roles in modern America*. New York: Harcourt Brace Jovanovich.
Katz, J. (1976). *Gay American history: Lesbians and gay men in the U.S.A.* New York: Crowell.
Pleck, E. & Pleck, J. (1980). *The American man*. Englewood Cliffs, NJ: Prentice-Hall.

The following books are suggested for additional readings:

Banner, L. (1983). *American beauty*. New York: Knopf.
Barker-Benfield, G.J. (1976). *The horrors of the half-known life: Male attitudes toward women and sexuality in nineteenth-century America*. New York: Harper & Row.
Brod, H. (Ed.). (1987). *The making of masculinities*. Boston: Allen & Unwin.
Davis, N.Z. "Women's history" in transition: The European case. (1875–1976). *Feminist Studies, 314*, 83–103.
Degler, C. (1981). What the women's movement has done to American history. In E. Langland & W. Gove, (Eds.). *A feminist perspective in the academy*. Chicago: The University of Chicago Press.
Macleod, D.I. (1983). *Building character in the American boy: The Boy Scouts, YMCA and their forerunners, 1870–1920*. Madison, WI: The University of Wisconsin Press.
Stearns, P.N. (1979). *Be a man!* New York: Holmes & Meier.
Strauss, S. (1982). *"Traitors to the masculine cause": The men's campaign for women's rights*. Westport, CT: Greenwood Press.

Personal and professional concerns of male counselors are discussed in relation to the counseling process between male counselors and male clients.

Chapter 18

A SURVEY REPORT: MEN COUNSELING MEN

Richard W. Thoreson, Stephen Cook,
Peter Shaughnessy, and Dwight Moore

The special concerns of men as men in our society relate directly to the specific issues that arise when men counsel men. The nature of the male sex role in its own right has been addressed in the literature (Thompson & Pleck, 1986; Zilbergeld, 1978), but in relation to the mental health of men and to the process of counseling the male client, the male sex role has received scant attention (see Scher, Stevens, Good, & Eichenfield, 1987; Silverberg, 1986). Consequently, there are gaps in the empirical data on how a man's internalized views of masculinity affect him personally and how these views affect the male counselor–male client counseling dyad (Kimmel, 1987).

Indications in the literature to date suggest that men who conform to the traditional heterosexual male sex role, when compared with men who display more "liberated" or "androgynous" sex role characteristics, are at greater risk for physical and mental health problems (e.g., Downey, 1984; Werrbach & Gilbert, 1987). This traditional male sex role touts the masculine values of success, status, toughness, independence, aggressiveness, and dominance to be achieved only by restricted emotionality and intellectualization and through disdain for all that is soft, compliant, effeminate, or "sissylike". It is a role that teaches men to be insensitive to their feelings, to their concerns, and to symptoms of illness (Franklin, 1984; Goldberg, 1976; Harrison, 1978; Meinecke, 1981; O'-Neil, 1981; Pleck, 1981).

Paradoxically, as the prescription to deny psychological and physical pain leads men to minimize psychological distress, traditional men may seem healthier in their self-reports of well-being than do women and nontraditional men (Gove, 1978; Thoreson, Kardash, Leuthold, & Morrow, in press; Warren 1983; Weissman & Klerman, 1977). Thus, it is difficult to determine whether the self-report by a man of his psy-

chological well-being represents the true state of his health or an artifact
of the cult of toughness and denial of pain.

Ipsaro (1986), noting the erosion of the traditional male sex role in
our society, saw changes in the roles that men are asked to play and
subsequent difficulties for men that stem from these changes. Skord and
Schumacher (1982) posed the question directly: Does the traditional male
sex role with its singular focus on the masculine components of power,
suppression, status, and success, to the exclusion of all that is feminine,
represent a kind of handicap?

The psychological characteristics associated with the traditional
male sex role have also been found to affect the counseling process.
It has been suggested that the restricted emotionality of men interferes
with the therapeutic process (O'Neil, 1981). Warren (1983) asserted
that men are socialized to be intolerant to depression. Depressive
symptomatology is incompatible with the male sex role. Therefore,
men tend to be reluctant to admit to problems or to seek help from
others. Ipsaro (1986) suggested that these concerns demand techniques such as those employed in behavior therapy that are more
direct, analytical, and educational rather than the "traditional" dynamic therapeutic approach with its focus on emotionally latent interventions and greater ambiguity.

Silverberg (1986) argued with equal persuasion that a focus on
the traditional male role in the counseling process can lead to several,
only unfavorable, outcomes. These results include the perpetuation
of traditional male stereotypes and the devaluing of the traits of emotional expressivity and tenderness. Additionally, Silverberg saw the
focus as offering but scant encouragement for the male client through
the risk of openness and emotional vulnerability to lead a fuller and
richer life.

These concerns impinge directly upon the male service provider,
and point to the need to focus specifically on the process of counseling
that occurs between male counselors and male clients. The intimate
communication characteristic of this process is especially difficult for
both male client and male counselor because the roles toward which men
are socialized are not conducive to counseling (Heppner & Gonzales,
1987; Silverberg, 1986).

The present study addresses these issues by asking male service
providers to describe (1) the concerns that they have, both professionally
and personally, and (2) the concerns of their male clients, both general
and counseling-related. The frequency and content of these two sets of
concerns are compared to each other and then related to other demographic variables. Finally, a male sex role typology based on differential
levels of endorsed concerns is developed.

Method

Subjects

Surveys were mailed to 1,000 men, randomly sampled for the membership of the American Association for Counseling and Development (AACD). Three hundred and sixty-six surveys (36.6%) were returned. Of the men who returned surveys, the average age was 44.4 (SD = 10.2) with a range from 23 to 73 years of age. The majority (n = 274; 75%) reported being married, 16% were single, 8% were divorced, and 1% widowed.

Other demographic data were gathered. In terms of ethnic background, the men in the sample identified themselves in the following manner: "White," 95%; "Black," 3%; "Hispanic," 1%; "Asian," .6%; "Native American," .3%; and "Other," .3%. According to the highest degree earned, our sample was distributed as follows: 25% PhD, 23% MA, 15% MS, 14% MEd; 10% EdD, 2% Bachelor's, and 1% PsyD. When pursuing their highest degree, 58% specialized in counseling psychology. School and clinical specializations comprised 9% and 8%, respectively. College, educational, higher education, rehabilitation and industrial/organizational personnel each made up 4% or less of our sample.

The men in our sample tended to be employed at a 4-year college/university or be in private practice (27% and 23%, respectively). Thirty-one percent were employed in other types of educational settings, 5% worked in community mental health centers, and 3% worked in hospitals. Fifty-two percent (n = 190) of those who answered the question regarding the view of their work performance indicated that it was under systematic review. Among the private practitioners, 53% worked in solo practice. The average salary for our sample was approximately $38,600.

Given the relatively low return rate (36.6%) and possible sample bias, the AACD membership office was asked to supply the current demographic data of the organization for comparison (W.M. Hamilton, personal communication, March 1, 1989). Our sample was found to be similar to the total AACD membership on those demographic characteristics gathered for comparative purposes in out study. The mean age of our respondents was 44.3 (the modal age range of AACD, of 34% of the current membership, is 39 to 48 years of age), and 95% reported their ethnic background as "White" (AACD = 90%). Twenty-five percent (25%) had received a doctoral-level degree (AACD = 19.3%). The most frequently reported work settings were 4-year collge/university, 27% (AACD = 24.2%), and private practice, 23% (AACD = 24.5%). Membership in AACD divisions was reported as follows: 30% in AMHCA

(AACD = 24%), 18% in ACPA (AACD = 15%), and 14% in ACSA (AACD = 20%).

Instrument

To fulfill the objectives of this study, a survey of AACD male members was undertaken.[1] The survey included three subparts. The first was a set of professional demographic items (e.g., employment and personal history). The second was a set of selected items taken from the Masculinity Profile (based on Tavris & Pope, 1976).

The third section, the Concerns Assessment, was developed to measure the interests and concerns of the respondents. It consisted of 36 topics that were considered to be of possible concern to male service providers of AACD. The topics were selected by an AACD committee over the course of several meetings in 1986 and 1987. The Concerns Assessment contained two columns for responses to each topic listed. In the first column, the subjects were asked to check those issues "with which you would like assistance." In the second column, respondents were asked to indicate with which issues they would like assistance relative to their male clients. The last item in this section provided space for the subjects to include any other areas of interest or concern to them.

The Masculinity Profile items, taken from Tavris and Pope (1976), address the following areas: self-rating of masculinity (e.g., "Compared to others of your sex, how masculine would you say you are?"), self-rating of femininity (e.g., "Compared to others of your sex, how feminine would you say you are?"), interpersonal relationships (e.g., "How many close friends of the same sex do you have?"), violence (e.g., "Since adolescence, have you ever struck a person of the opposite sex in anger?"), and behavioral/attitudinal measures of sex roles (e.g., "Who disciplines the children?" and "What is your attitude toward women's liberation?").

Procedures

Initial copies of the Male Counselor Development Questionnaire (MCDQ) were forwarded to faculty members, members of the AACD Committee on Men, and the current president of AACD for review and comment. From these comments, the questionnaire was revised. Mailing labels were obtained from the AACD Executive Office for a random sample of 1,000 men. The questionnaires were mailed with an outer sheet containing the cover letter to which the address labels were affixed.

---

[1]This study was part of a larger research project undertaken by the AACD Men's Committee on the nature of professional development of AACD male members.

The subjects were instructed to remove the outer sheet before mailing the questionnaire back. Self-addressed, stamped envelopes were provided inside the questionnaire for the respondents to return the survey.

The cover letter included with the questionnaire explained the purpose of the survey and included a reminder about confidentiality. The subjects were assured of the confidentiality of their responses in three ways. They were told that their responses would be completely anonymous and were reminded not to write their names anywhere on the survey. Second, professional items (such as specific place of employment) were excluded from the survey so that subjects could not be inadvertently identified. Third, subjects were reminded that their responses to any of the items were entirely voluntary.

Because there was nothing included on a questionnaire that would identify the specific respondent, follow-up to those who did not return surveys was not possible. To increase the response rate, a second mailing was made to the entire sample when the return rate of the surveys began to diminish significantly (6 weeks later). A notice was also placed in the AACD newsletter, *Guidepost*, asking those who had received a survey to return it as soon as possible if they had not already done so.

Results

The initial question asked was "What are the most frequently cited concerns of AACD male members?" Based on the respondents' endorsement the 36 concerns for themselves, the following five were seen as most important: burnout/stress, developmental issues, and again, career change, relationships, and expressing feelings. All 36 items on the Concerns Assessment were mentioned by at least 10% of the respondents. Half of the items were endorsed by at least 25% of the respondents. These data are presented in Table 1. Another important question that was to be assessed using the Concerns Assessment was "Are there groups of male members in AACD that have more concerns than other groups, and if so, what are these groups?" To assess this, the number of concerns checked by each subject for himself and for his clients was summed to produce two frequency indices. Out of 36 concerns, respondents listed an average of 9.4 concerns for themselves (SD = 7.1), and 13.6 concerns for their male clients (SD = 8.2). The difference in means between the overall concerns identified for professional development and overall concerns listed for male clients was significant, $t(320) = 5.6, p < .001$.

Characteristics of High and Low Concern Counselors

For continuous demographic variables, Pearson product-moment correlations were computed between those variables and the two fre-

TABLE 1

Item Endorsement Percentages for Self and Male Clients

	Self	Male Clients
Career Concerns		
● Career Change	33%	54%
● Retirement	32%	23%
● Leisure	29%	25%
● Dual Careers	27%	32%
● Nontraditional Career Choice	14%	26%
Men's Issues		
● Success	34%	51%
● Fathers and Parenting	33%	48%
● Changing Role of Men	31%	56%
● Power	21%	41%
● Mentoring Young Men	20%	11%
● Men's Groups	19%	17%
● Stereotypes	13%	26%
● Homosexuality	11%	33%
Physical/Emotional Health		
● Burnout/Stress	66%	58%
● Physical Health	35%	34%
● AIDS	33%	44%
● Grieving	22%	42%
● Loneliness	21%	30%
● Substance Abuse	15%	61%
● Disability	11%	24%
Counseling Concerns		
● Multicultural Issues	28%	21%
● Counselor/Client Relationship	28%	15%
● Counseling and Sex Roles	22%	34%
● Gender Differences in Counseling	22%	12%
● Touch Between Client and Counselor	18%	14%
● Male Clients	10%	8%

quency indices (see Table 2). It was found that being younger, more psychodynamically oriented, more diverse in sexual orientation, and making less money were all significantly associated with reporting more concerns for self.

Having more concerns for male clients was found to be significantly related to more diversity in sexual orientation, younger age, more phenomenological therapeutic orientation, and higher ratings of femininity.

TABLE 1 *continued*

Item Endorsement Percentages for Self and Male Clients

	Self	*Male Clients*
Relationships		
● Developmental Issues/Aging	45%	41%
● Intimacy and Friendship	39%	63%
● Relationships	37%	60%
● Self-Nurturance	34%	37%
● Expressing Feelings	31%	71%
● Love and Sexuality	29%	59%
● Moral Responsibility	27%	33%
● Divorce and Parenting	22%	57%
● Mother/Son Relationships	18%	31%
● Divorce	16%	54%

TABLE 2

Means, Standard Deviations, and Pearson Product-Moment Correlations Between Number of Concerns Indicated and Demographic/Professional Variables

	Correlations			
Concerns indicated for:	*Self*	*Clients*	*M*	*SD*
Income	−.16**	−.02	4.3	.8
Age	−.18**	−.12	44.6	10.6
Counseling Approach:				
Psychodynamic	−.11*	.14	4.6	1.4
Phenomenological	−.03	−.12*	4.3	1.7
Cognitive/ Behavioral	.07	.07	3.4	1.3
Sexual Orientation	.14**	.14**	1.4	1.0
Masculinity Rating	.08	.04	2.9	.7
Femininity Rating	−.12*	−.11*	3.0	1.0
Number of Concerns:				
For Self	—	.42***	9.4	7.1
For Clients	.42***	—	13.6	8.2

*p < .05.   **p < .01.   ***p <.001.

To further examine which groups of men were asking for help, t-tests were performed for three dichotomous, demographic variables: marital status (married vs. not married), highest degree earned (doctorate vs. nondoctorate), and ethnic background (White vs. minority). Significant differences were found on both marital status and highest degree earned. Married men listed fewer concerns for their male clients then did men who were not married ($t = -2.51$, $p < .05$). Men who had their doctorates were likely to list more concerns than did those with a master's degree or below ($t = -2.52$, $p < .05$).

Tests for analyses of variance (ANOVAs) were used to uncover any differences on the reported number of concerns based on AACD divisional membership and work setting. Significant differences in the number of concerns were indicated for male clients for division membership, $F(6,297) = 5.67$, $p < .0001$. Specifically, male members of the Association for Religious and Value Issues in Counseling (ARVIC) and the American Mental Health Counselor Association (AMHCA) listed more concerns for their clients than did members of the American College Personnel Association (ACPA) or the American School Counselor Association (ASCA). Men who worked in private practice listed more concerns for their male clients than did men who worked in university, secondary, or elementary education settings, $F(3,356) = 6.60$, $p < .001$.

We also wanted to know which of the demographic variables would predict the amount of variance in both of the frequency indices (i.e., the number of concerns indicated for self and for male clients). A stepwise regression was performed with both frequency indices separately as the dependent variables. Age, self-ratings of masculinity and femininity, the three theoretical orientation variables (phenomenological, psychodynamic, and cognitive/behavioral), sexual orientation, and income were used as independent variables. Four independent variables were found to predict the variance in the number of concerns listed for the subjects themselves: age ($F(1,325) = 6.37$, $p < .05$), sexual orientation ($F(1,325) = 4.23$, $p < .05$), and income ($F(1,325) = 5.64$, $p < .05$). Four independent variables were also found to predict the variance in the number of concerns for male clients: age ($F(1,321) = 4.80$, $p < .05$), phenomenological orientation ($F(1,321) = 4.02$, $p < .05$), psychodynamic orientation ($F(1,321) = 7.83$, $p < .01$), and sexual orientation ($F(1,321) = 4.74$, $p < .03$).

Types of Concerns

Rationally derived categories (men's issues, counseling concerns, career concerns, relationship concerns, and health concerns) were constructed by having two independent raters—both PhD's in counseling psychology with 10 or more years of post-PhD experience and each with expertise in the area of men's issues—group the 36 types of issues into "related categories." Each rater independently identified and labeled five categories of concerns within the 36 items. These categories were counseling concerns, men's issues, career concerns, physical/emotional health issues, and relationship concerns. The five scales that were constructed based on the rater's interpretations are presented in Table 1.

Scores of each of the five concern areas yielded significant Pearson product-moment correlations with several demographic variables. These correlations are displayed in Table 3. Age was found to correlate negatively with four of the scales: men's issues ($r = -.28$, $p<.001$), health ($r = -.14$, $p<.005$), counseling concerns ($r = .ms.10$, $p<.05$) and relationships ($r = -.16$, $p<.001$). Income was also found to correlate negatively with these same four scales: men's issues ($r = -.14$, $p<.01$), health ($r = -.13$, $p<.01$), counseling concerns ($r = -.15$, $p<.01$) and relationships ($r = -.14$, $p<.01$).

Pearson product-moment correlations were employed in exploring the relationship between types of concerns indicated and self-ratings of masculinity and femininity. Career concerns correlated positively with high ratings of masculinity ($r = .11$, $p<.05$). Men's concerns correlated negatively with masculinity ($r = .17$, $p<.001$). Counseling concerns correlated positively with femininity ($r = .12$, $p<.01$). Relationship issues were found to correlate negatively with masculinity ($r = -.11$, $p<.05$) and positively with femininity ($r = .15$, $p<.05$). Health concerns did not correlate significantly with either scale.

The concern areas were then used as the dependent variables in a series of ANOVAs. Work setting, divided into academic setting (48.0% of the sample), private practice (23.3%) and other (28.7%), was the in-

TABLE 3

Pearson Product-Moment Correlations Between Age, Income, Sex Role Rating, and Type of Concerns

	Correlations			
	Age	*Income*	*Masculinity*	*Femininity*
Type of Concern:				
Health	−.14**	−.12**	−.01	.03
Men's Issues	−.28***	−.14**	−.09*	.17***
Relationships	−.16*	−.14**	−.11*	.15**
Counseling	−.10*	−.15**	−.01	.12**
Career	−.02	−.04	.10*	.01

*$p < .05$.   **$p < .01$.   ***$p < .001$.

dependent variable in these ANOVAs. Career concerns were found to be significantly lower for the private practitioners as compared with the remaining groups, $F(1,358) = 6.34$, $p<.005$. No significant differences were found for the remaining concerns areas.

The grouping of issues into five categories was also applied to the concerns identified for male clients. It was found that the older the respondent, the less likely he was to identify men's concerns for his clients, $r = .11$, $p<.01$, and relationship issues, $r = -.11$, $p<.01$. The higher the respondent's self-rating of femininity, the more likely he was to identify men's issues for his clients, $r = .11$, $p<.05$, and relationship issues, $r = .18$, $p<.001$.

Table 4 provides a summary of the "masculinity" profile of the characteristics of the high- and low-concern endorser typologies among the AACD male members.

Discussion

Professional Concerns

The results of this survey indicate that male counselors can readily identify concerns for which they would like assistance. These concerns are of two varieties: those that relate to their own professional development and those that relate to their work with male clients.

TABLE 4

Characteristics of Dual Typology of AACD Male Members

Low-Concern Endorsers	High-Concern Endorsers
• Stable Marriage	• Single
• Heterosexual	• More Diverse Sexual Orientation
• Higher Income	• Lower Income
• Bachelor's or Master's Degree	• Doctoral Degree
• ASCA or ACPA Member	• ARVIC or AMHCA Member
• Older	• Younger
• Less Inclined to Phenomenological or Psychodynamic Approach	• Tend Toward Phenomenological or Psychodynamic Approach
• Employed in Secondary, Elementary, or University Setting	• Employed in Private Practice

There was a general consensus by male service providers on the five issues that most commonly relate to their own professional development. These five issues consisted of burnout and stress, developmental issues and aging, intimacy and friendships, relationships, and physical health. Each was endorsed by 35% or more of the overall sample of AACD men. Two issues, "intimacy and friendships" and "relationships," refer to often noted problem areas for men in our society. The remaining three are generic to the life of professionals of either gender. One of these three, burnout and stress, received the highest endorsement both as a personal issue and as an issue for male clients. The findings offer clear support for training programs by the counseling profession to address these concerns.

Client Concerns

From the perspective of work with male clients, clear areas of convergence and only minor divergence emerged in the concerns attributed to clients and the concerns for the respondents' own professional development. Among the five top-rated concerns, three (burnout and stress, relationships, and expressing feelings) were found common to both personal and client concerns. Two, developmental issues and aging, and career change, were seen more as professional development issues. An additional two, love/sexuality, and addictions, were reported more as client issues. The high endorsements given to the five concerns pertaining to professional development and to working with clients seem to confirm that these represent important areas for male service providers and support special programming for the AACD men to meet these concerns. Such programming could include specifically designed programs at their conventions, books on special topics, journals, workshops and, additionally, recommendations for changes in the graduate curriculum of counselor training programs.

Endorsed Concerns and Societal Expectations

This perspective, the more challenging, views relationships between level and type of endorsed concerns of AACD male service providers and identified professional-demographic variables as sources of data to test the assertion that male sex role norms play a major role in male attitudes and behaviors.

To measure the impact of normative expectations for the male role in society, we examined the relationships between the endorsed concerns and measures of masculinity, femininity, and sexual orientation. We then examined the overall intercorrelation matrix of identified concerns, masculinity ratings, femininity ratings, sexual orientation and selected professional/demographic characteristics of divisional membership, job setting, age, and counseling orientation as additional indices of normative expectations for the male role.

The results of this analysis seem to support our rationale. First, how AACD men positioned themselves on these variables relates to the level of endorsed concerns. Differences on a number of major independent variables were found to relate to differences in high- and low-concern endorsement patterns. Second, the pattern of differences offers support for the impact of normative expectations for the traditional male sex role on endorsed concerns (the more masculine the fewer the endorsed concerns for self and clients). Ettkin (1981) asserted that men operating within the traditional male role perspective **dread being known**, and this **dread of being known** deters men from admitting to weakness, vulnerability, and need for help. By the time a boy becomes a man, Ettkin claims, it is likely that he has learned to disguise himself to most other people and allow only a few to really know him.

Low-concern endorsers (LCEs) were found to be further characterized by these factors: stable marital relationships, heterosexual orientation, highest degree bachelor's or master's rather than PhDs, employed mainly in elementary or secondary schools or universities rather than in private practice or mental health settings, members of ASCA and ACPA, not inclined to have a phenomenological or dynamic counseling orientation, and likely to express career rather than relationship concerns.

High-concern endorsers (HCEs) showed the opposite pattern. They were more likely to follow nontraditional male sex role norms. They tended to be younger, more diverse in sexual orientation, more feminine and less masculine, more likely to hold the PhD degree, more likely to be members of ARVIC and AMHCA, to earn less money, and to be single. Additionally, they tended to be either psychodynamic or phenomenological in their counseling orientation, and to express relationship and counseling concerns rather than career concerns.

Thus, our findings suggest that low-concern endorsers (LCEs) have adopted the more traditional male sex role norms for masculinity and high-concern endorsers (HCEs) have adopted the nontraditional male sex role norms for masculinity. The LCE typology presents a profile of men who are more comfortable with themselves, more settled, more where they want to be in life, and more fulfilled, both in family and work.

In contrast, the HCE typology outlines a profile of men who, having adopted nontraditional sex role norms, are characterized by being more self-searching, more oriented toward growth, more fluid and less settled, more likely to espouse nontraditional societal values, and less likely to hold exact rules for living.

Implications

Both high- and low-concern endorsement typologies have implications for the counseling of male clients. Chesler (1971) warned that all male dyads may serve to reinforce traditional stereotypes without noticeable encouragement for the male client to become more vulnerable. Silverberg (1986) suggested that the potential devaluing of tenderness, sensitivity, and emotional vulnerability exists in traditional male norms. Our findings that the level of perceived concerns both for self and for client varies by typology point to differences in the valuing of the emotional side of men and the potential for reinforcing traditional male stereotypes in working with male clients.

Ehrenreich (1983), addressing the contemporary male role from a feminist perspective, further argued that change toward a less rigidly masculine male role is but one of several ongoing trends in our society. Although men are demonstrating authentic positive change, Ehrenreich noted, they also may be exhibiting only superficial change or may be changing in ways that are detrimental not only to men but to women and society in general. Our findings point to the interrelationship of masculine indentity with concern endorsement patterns and confirm the need for a positive integration of the masculine, analytical, instrumental approach of the traditional male sex role with the often devalued traits of emotional expressiveness, warmth, sensitivity, and tenderness of the nontraditional role for men in the counseling process. This position was supported by Silverberg (1986), who contended that the fundamental goal in the counseling of men is to help them to integrate the so-called masculine and feminine components of the male role.

In our study, we have identified men who are, overall, inspired to grow, to learn, and to help their male clients do likewise. However, within this overall framework of commitment to growth and personal development, the two typologies of male service providers that we have delineated constitute important benchmarks for viewing male counselor development and for counseling men. The low-concern endorsement typology includes men who are more inclined to accept life as it is and to look toward making only minor alterations in an already integrated worldview. The high-concern endorsement typology includes men who are more inclined to see growth and development as primary. Thus, it seems that how AACD men see their world affects not only their own growth pattern but also the concerns they attribute to their clients and, consequently, their work with male clients.

Both low- and high-concern endorser typologies carry with them their own particular boundary limitations in counseling men. These boundary limitations include restrictions in problem identification, awareness of issues, and views of growth for self and clients. For the traditional AACD men, issues of change and growth are more likely to be out of awareness. Traditional men are likely to be more satisfied with the status quo, with viewing life as it is, and to view it in more positive terms. For the AACD man espousing nontraditional views, change, growth and development are more central. Nontraditional men have as their Achilles' heel the likely overendorsement of a change focus for self and clients.

We wish to emphasize that the differences in the low- and high-concern endorsers were mainly differences in level, not type of concern. There was considerable consensus and only minor differences in overall types of concerns endorsed for self-development and for work with male clients by the total sample. This similarity in type of concerns endorsed, coupled with the differences in level of endorsement, has an important implication for the male service provider. It further confirms the need for the healthful integration of both traditional and nontraditional components of the male sex role to achieve optimal masculinity.

Conclusion

1. Male members of AACD share special concerns for professional development and for work with clients. Among the major concerns, stress and burnout rate the highest.

2. There is strong similarity in the concerns endorsed for professional self-development and for work with clients.

3. Level of concern endorsement by AACD men is related to differences in masculinity, femininity, and important aspects of the professional counseling role. The views that an AACD man holds about his masculinity carry with them implications both for the way he perceives himself and the way he perceives his male clients.

4. The findings of a special set of male issues support the need for special programming for professional development and counselor skill training for male service providers.

Summary

The findings in this study highlight the critical importance of the special concerns of men. Heppner and Gonzales (1987) concluded that the male socialization process profoundly affects both the male counselor and the male client. How the counselor and client view themselves as men in our culture will shape the process of counseling. The delineation in this study of concerns of AACD men for self-development and client growth sends a clear message to the counseling profession to identify and develop specific programs and professional activities pursuant with the unique concerns of men.

Educating men to choose life-styles that will facilitate health and well-being rather than life-styles that foster the potential for illness is a goal of wellness.

Chapter 19

BEING A MAN CAN BE HAZARDOUS TO YOUR HEALTH: LIFE-STYLE ISSUES

Fred Leafgren

Men's Health Hazards

American life-styles are harmful and increase men's risk of illness and premature death. Smoking and excessive alcohol consumption, lack of physical exercise, excessive weight, stress associated with relationships, work, the social environment, and lack of meaning and purpose are all factors detrimental to the well-being of men.

The focus of this chapter is men and wellness. Halbert Dunn, a public health physician in the 1950s and the first writer to introduce the high-level wellness concept, defined wellness as an integrated method of functioning that is oriented toward maximizing the potential of the individual within his or her particular environment. The goal of wellness is to achieve one's total potential by living optimally physically, spiritually, socially, occupationally, intellectually, and emotionally.

If this is our definition of wellness, it may be well to look at where we are in terms of the wellness levels for America men. Johnson (1989, pp. 62–63) provided the following facts: in 1900, U.S. women lived 48 years on the average and men 46, a difference of two years. By 1986, the difference was between 78 and 71 years respectively, or a difference of 7 years. Being a man can be hazardous to your health, with a higher risk of heart attack, lung cancer, and criminal behavior. For example, the ratio of male to female deaths from of lung cancer is 6 to 1; other bronchopulmonary disease, 5 to 1; homicide, 4 to 1; motor vehicle accidents, 2.5 to 1; suicide, 2.7 to 1; other accidents, 2.4 to 1; cirrhosis of the liver, 2 to 1; and heart disease, 2 to 1. The number of men in prison is 573,990, women, 30,834. Men diagnosed with AIDS number 68,306, women, 6,260. The number of single men who are homeless is estimated to be 165,000 to 231,000; single women who are homeless, 32,000 to 45,000.

Joseph Califano, Jr.'s, (Pelletier, 1981) report in 1969 indicated that we are killing ourselves by careless habits. We are polluting the environment and we permit harmful social conditions to persist, namely poverty, hunger, and ignorance. The Surgeon General's report observed that many Americans are apathetic and unmotivated toward better health. Ken Pelletier (1981, p. 170) noted that "psychological factors have been demonstrated to be the single most significant predator of both optimum health and longevity. Genetic and biological influences on longevity are highly dependent on the presence or absence of specific life-style influences." Ken Pelletier pointed out that "it is clearly evident that psycho-social variables and lifestyle practices established as early as adolescence are the single most significant broad vectors of adults' health and longevity, and even the timing and nature of the experience of death" (p. 171). He went on to say that ". . . psycho-social factors are of such formidable influence that they actually hold sway over the genetic and biological determinants" (p. 171). He reported that research findings indicate that stress is a major influence governing whether or not even the average life expectancy is attained, and that research also demonstrates that women live longer than men due to life-styles rather than biological variables. These trends are increasing rather than decreasing at the present.

Men may practice compensatory masculine role behavior. Such behaviors are frequently characterized by risk-taking, aggression, and violence. Forrester (1986) stated that men are socialized into a society that values achievement, power, and strength as distinctly masculine qualities. In an effort to achieve masculine status and conform to the socially prescribed male role, men frequently engage in compensatory aggressive risk-taking behaviors that predispose them to illness, injury, and even death. Furthermore, men engage in occupations that harbor risks to their health. These risks include biological, chemical, physical, and mechanical agents.

The Wellness Alternative

In a presentation at the National Wellness Association Conference at the University of Wisconsin-Stevens Point, Ken Pelletier (1989) reported data concerning longevity cited in *The Journal of the American Medical Association*. The findings in the JAMA estimate that two thirds of the deaths and disabilities prior to age 65 are preventable. Pelletier believes that two thirds of the deaths and disabilities are preventable to the age of 85.

So what are the responses then to the illnesses that we recognize among men? A powerful response that is growing in acceptance, understanding, and impact is the national wellness movement. According to Clyde Sullivan, a professor of psychology at Brigham Young University, the pattern advocated for wellness is one that is anticipatory, preventive, proactive, collaborative, and system-oriented.

Travis and Ryan (1981) talked of wellness involving breathing, communicating, eating, playing, finding meaning, moving, transcending, thinking, and feeling. This leader in the wellness movement spoke of wellness as the right and privilege of everyone and stated that the wellness paradigm calls for options, individuality, and choices freely made. Travis went on to say that the process of wellness is based on self-responsibility and love.

Self-responsibility (Travis & Ryan, 1981): means (1) tuning in on your own inner patterns, emotional and physical, and recognizing signals your body is giving you; (2) discovering your real needs and finding ways to meet them; (3) realizing that you are unique and are expert about yourself; (4) making choices; (5) creating the life you really want rather than just reacting to what seems to happen; (6) being self-assertive; (7) enjoying your body through nutrition, exercise, and physical awareness; (8) expressing emotions in ways that communicate what you are experiencing to other people; (9) creating and cultivating close relationships with others; and (10) engaging in projects that are meaningful to you, being supportive of others, and respecting your environment.

Love means: (1) trusting that your own personal resources are your greatest strengths for living and growing; (2) allowing disease to be a constructive and positive experience; (3) responding to challenges in life as opportunities to grow in strength and maturity rather than feeling beset by problems; (4) experiencing yourself as a wonderful person; (5) loving yourself and exercising compassion for your weaknesses; (6) realizing your connectedness with all things; and (7) celebrating yourself with others and the world in which you live (Travis & Ryan, p. 4).

The Wellness Journey

The wellness journey can begin with an assessment to measure current wellness levels and present health conditions. There are numerous health hazard appraisal and wellness questionnaires. A comprehensive listing of such instruments is found in the New Directions for Student Services Series entitled *Developing Campus Recreation and Wellness Programs* (Leafgren, 1986).

The data from the Health Hazard Appraisal and a wellness questionnaire provide information about the client to establish present health conditions and life expectancy. These data can serve as a stimulus to encourage experimentation with new behaviors that may result in improved wellness levels.

The remainder of this chapter will be devoted to a discussion of the wellness movement and how it can positively affect the lives of men. A model of wellness, proposed by Dr. William Hettler, cofounder of the National Wellness Institute, includes 6 dimensions: social, physical, occupational, spiritual, emotional, and intellectual. Wellness in all these dimensions is essential for well-being. Wellness in any one of these dimensions contributes positively to wellness in the other dimensions. A lack of wellness in any one of these dimensions can diminish one's well-being in other dimensions. This six-dimension model proposed by Dr. Hettler is a model that has gained national recognition and acceptance and is used in many settings.

Social Wellness

The social dimension includes contributing to one's human and physical environment to achieve the common welfare of one's community. It emphasizes the interdependence with others and with nature. It includes the pursuit of harmony in one's family, in one's relationships, in one's community.

The environmental aspect encourages environmental sensitivity and concern for cities, water, air, and earth. Government decrees alone are not likely to change the destruction of our physical environment. Individuals can contribute, take responsibility, and assist in the process. Individuals can be encouraged to learn about their environments and to accept responsibility for giving back to the earth, not only taking. When people are aware of destructive patterns, they are more likely to commit themselves to change their life-styles in ways that contribute to a more optimal, ecological way of life. People can be supportive of environmental programs.

Likewise, individuals can find ways in which they can give to their community, not only be recipients and take from it. Participating in volunteer service programs and working through agencies, religious groups, and institutions to give to one's fellow human being is a powerful way to feel productive, to feel satisfied, and to feel that one is contributing. Extending themselves to others by lending a hand, getting acquainted, and discovering others' needs and how they can assist with their needs are endeavors that provide people much satisfaction, pride, and self-esteem. The payoff is both for the recipients and the giver.

We can be socially conscious of the needs of our family and contribute to these needs also in a giving manner. Through modeling, through our life-style, through our presence, we can contribute in positive ways to the well-being of all members of our family. Again, we are the recipients or the benefactors of this giving.

Physical Wellness

The physical dimension includes cardiovascular strength and regular physical activity. Physical wellness encourages knowledge about food and nutrition and discourages the use of tobacco, drugs, and excessive alcohol consumption. It encourages consumption and activities that contribute to high-level wellness including medical self-care and appropriate use of the medical system.

Ken Pelletier (1979, p. 163) stated in his book, *Holistic Medicine*:

Physically, the human body is essentially the same that it was a half million years ago. Individuals living in the post-industrial period of only the last 100 years, however, have placed this body in the midst of a radically reshaped internal and external environment. Over thousands of years, the body was oriented through and sustained by habitual varied and extensive physical activity. Suddenly the dramatic swiftness of this functional pattern has been disrupted into one of high stress and low physical activity. The human body is built for action, not for rest. Today the struggle for survival involves the necessity of systematically reintroducing physical exercise as a preventative measure for alleviating the afflictions of civilization, and as a step toward reaching optimum health.

Pelletier (1979, p. 177) went on to say:

Benefits of a regular exercise program include 1) the replacement of intra-muscular fat leading to more efficient utilization of calories; 2) strengthening of heart and lungs and muscles throughout the body thus improving general circulation; 3) improved absorption and utilization of food, 4) increased energy and stamina; 5) more restful sleep; 6) improved appearance for positive self-image and outlook on life; 7) people who exercise regularly consume far fewer drugs, coffee, tea, alcohol, tobacco, sugar and refined carbohydrates than non-exercisers. They find these things to be antagonistic to a healthy lifestyle.

Fitness is a state of mind as well as a state of motion. There are many ways to be physically fit. Aerobic exercise in the form of cycling, running, swimming, basketball, racquetball, or handball contributes to physical well-being. It stimulates the heart and the lungs. It contributes to muscular development. When one feels physically fit, one also feels more fit emotionally and intellectually. It is recommended that people find an activity or exercise they enjoy. Suffering should be optional. If people do not engage in an activity they enjoy, it is not likely that they will continue that activity, thereby losing the positive benefits of a physical activity program.

Some individuals prefer to exercise alone. Others prefer fitness activities in groups such as in community programs, YMCA programs, or institutional programs. Many corporate and business firms are now establishing their own fitness centers and fitness programs. There are unlimited opportunities to be physically fit. One does not need to spend large sums of money to become physically active. For many, running is an excellent way to keep fit. Many who become active in running report that it does change their life. Once one becomes active in a running program, it becomes a regular habit. Regular runners feel deprived when they have not had an opportunity to run. There is also strong evidence that running has a positive impact on mental and emotional stress. For many individuals, a run after work is far more therapeutic and helpful than consumption of alcoholic beverages that are often used to bring about relaxation.

Good nutrition can be a positive path to weight control. Individuals may need professional nutrition counseling. They may need to assess their percentage of body fat and ideal weight in order to determine the need for change in this area.

It is important that individuals become aware of the food that they eat and its positive or negative effects. There are excellent recipes for low cholesterol, high wellness-oriented foods that are tasty and nutritious. In general, we know that a high intake of sugar, fat, refined flour, salt, coffee, alcohol, tobacco, and food additives is detrimental to our physical well-being. The intake of these substances needs to be reduced or replaced by other substances. In general, we consume an excess of fats and sugars today and not enough complex carbohydrates. These patterns need to be changed. People can learn about the constituency of various food products that they purchase and become aware of the amount of protein, carbohydrate, and fat in their diet. It is estimated that at the present 50% of our daily diet has no nutritional value. We consume one third cup of sugar per day, or 130 pounds per year per person in the United States. Our salt intake is about 20 times what we need on a daily basis. These are patterns that we can change and feel better as a result. There are many healthful foods too from which to select. In general, whole grain cereals, breads that contain natural grains, fresh fruits and vegetables, and fish are all nutritious and provide a balanced, healthful diet. This diet also contributes to the amount of roughage that our bodies need to function properly. In general, for good nutritional living, we need varied and balanced diets. We need to eat more slowly and more simply and consume more roughage and fiber in our diet.

Another significant area affecting physical well-being is assistance for alcohol and drug abuse. Assisting individuals to cope effectively with the abuse of drugs and alcohol is essential for optimal wellness. Alcohol and drug abuse negatively affects physical and emotional well-being. They affect the other dimensions negatively as well.

Occupational Wellness

Occupational wellness is related to our attitude about work. Occupational wellness results from participating in work or in a career in which we gain personal satisfaction and life enrichment. Job satisfaction is extremely important and relates to our careers, our expectations, and the opportunities we have to fulfill our basic personality needs.

Consistency between personality type and job expectations provides the potential for satisfaction, achievement, and persistence in that position. A mismatch between the two will often result in individuals' frustration and dissatisfaction in the work environment, leading them to seek other jobs. Today, there are almost unlimited career choices and possibilities. Helping individuals find careers they can enjoy is a significant role for counselors. Helping individuals discover how they can be fulfilled through their jobs can be a significant role for counselors as well.

Men need to be aware when the manager-subordinate relationship affects them negatively. Manager behavior that is unpredictable involves win-lose situations, which whittles away at employees' self-esteem. Tactless reprimanding and discounting ideas takes away from employees' occupational well-being. On the other hand, when employees enjoy participation, involvement, positive recognition, and support, their sense of occupational wellness is enhanced.

Intellectual Wellness

The intellectual dimension of wellness encompasses creative, stimulating mental activities. An intellectually well person uses available resources to expand his or her knowledge and improve skills, which in turn expands the potential for sharing with others. An intellectually well person uses the intellectual cultural activities as well as the human resources available to them in the community in which they live. We all need mental stimulation. This stimulation can come about through reading, involvement in the arts, study, travel, and various media. Being encouraged to participate in intellectual endeavors that are new to them can be a great source of enjoyment and satisfaction for people. Learning to play the piano, painting, or reading in a new area of interest are all activities that can be intellectually challenging, stimulating, and rewarding.

Spiritual Wellness

The spiritual dimension of wellness involves seeking meaning and purpose in human existence. It includes developing of a deep appreciation for the depth and expanse of life and the natural forces that exist in the universe. It includes values and ethics. One may find spiritual fulfillment through active involvement in an organized religious group. One may also find it through other human resources or through communing with nature. There is no specific prescription one must follow to be spiritually well—there are unlimited possibilities for involvement. Men seek out these opportunities to a much lesser degree than do women, therefore they need opportunities to explore the spiritual dimension in much greater depth. This pattern parallels the phenomena we see in counseling.

Emotional Wellness

The emotional dimension emphasizes the awareness and acceptance of one's feelings. Emotional wellness includes the degree to which one feels positive and enthusiastic about oneself and life. It includes the capacity to manage one's feelings and related behaviors including the realistic assessment of one's limitations, development of autonomy, and ability to cope effectively with stress. The emotionally well person maintains satisfying relationships with others. Men are frequently underdeveloped in the area of emotional wellness.

It is important that we do not see life as an illness for which we must seek a cure. Americans presently consume 5 million tranquilizers each year. Tranquilizers are not the way to emotional wellness. Rushing off to work every day in a frantic state of panic is not a path to emotional wellness.

Men often give themselves negative messages that take away from their sense of well-being. These messages may be fear of failure, fear of the judgments of others, fear of how others perceive them. Men also can stress themselves through overcommittment and becoming either workaholics or getting into a time trap. Men can also take away from their sense of well-being by concentrating on things that have gone wrong in their life as opposed to those that have gone right. Men need to be prepared each day for the unpredictable. Life is not always logical or predictable, and men need to have a sense of mental toughness that prepares them for the unexpected.

Many men are extremely concerned that they will be liked by others. Realistically, what they find is that some will like them, appreciate them, and respect them, and others will not. Keeping themselves highly stressed in an attempt to win over those who do not see them in positive ways is probably not going to change their opinions. To the degree that men hang on to unwarranted feelings of guilt or worthlessness that are not relevant, they undermine their sense of well-being.

Georgia Witkin-Lanoil (1986, p. 5), from a survey of over 500 men, reported that in the early warning signs of stress for men, "Men are often unaware of their stress whereas their spouses are able to identify the stress through their withdrawing, irritableness, aggressiveness or defiant manner." It is important that men learn to manage stress by developing coping skills necessary to reduce stress and to avoid stress, as well as learning to relax through meditation, exercise, or other positive activities.

It is important that men feel okay about themselves. Men need to recognize that they are victims in life when they want to be, but that they do have choices. Suffering is optional, and men need to be aware of the degree to which they create their own suffering. Numerous bio-feedback programs can give them information about their stress levels. Men need to be more sensitive to their basic feelings such as anger, sadness, fear, and joy. Negative feelings serve as warning signs to alert men that things are not going positively in their lives. They need to tune in and be more aware of such feelings. Listening to their feelings is a way of getting vital information about who they are and what is happening to them in their environments and in their life.

Men need periodically to take inventory of their personal strengths and to be aware of these strengths as gifts that they possess. They need to go with their strengths and their gifts.

All of us need positive relationships in our lives. Because we are human, there are many wonderful things we can do. Buscaglia has identified these in his books. He points out that we can sing songs, we can smell flowers, we can hold hands, we can hug, we can give to others, and we can receive from others in very positive ways. We need to be much more open to touch and hugging, caring and giving. There is nothing wrong with needing and wanting someone to like us and be a close friend to us. Most of us do not survive very long unless we hear someone say "I love you."

Women in our society are seeking opportunities for equal rights, politically and economically. Men need equal rights emotionally. They need to be permitted to experience, to express, to feel, to care, to love, to be weak, or to be strong. They need to be permitted to be all of these things.

It is probably important that we don't take ourselves too seriously. We need to permit ourselves to laugh a lot and to enjoy and participate in humor. It is probably better that we don't worry too much about tomorrow. We need to focus more on today and enjoy what life gives us, enjoy the opportunity to receive smiles, and to give smiles. We need to be glad of life because it gives us a chance to love and to work and to play and to look at the stars. We need to be aware that mental health is our greatest wealth and life can be a positive experience. When we are feeling good about life, it shows, it resonates. We have choices; we need to take responsibility for our own well-being and recognize that health is freedom. A goal of wellness is to die young as late in life as possible.

Choosing Wellness

Individuals are responsible for making choices to implement changes in their lives. Counselors can help with the process. Ardell (1977, pp. 212–213) stated:

> High level wellness is a lifestyle to be enjoyed where you consider everything that might be done. It does sound and appear overwhelming, but in fact you choose what you want to do. These choices are made one at a time and you add new wellness behaviors only when they prove more rewarding than old worseness patterns.

Wellness is seeking the best, not only avoiding disease. No matter which dimension we are involved in, we continually need to seek the best for ourselves to live optimally. The goal of wellness is to maximize our well-being and to establish life-style patterns that promote well-being throughout our lives.

Educating individuals to choose life-styles that will facilitate health and well-being rather than life-styles that foster the potential for illness is a goal of wellness. Individuals have choices for high-level wellness or low-level wellness. Wellness can be taught. It can also be modeled by those who are teaching. The greatest impact will come from good models and good teachers. Counselors can model wellness in their own lives.

When individuals take responsibility for their own health, acknowledge their own power, and recognize that they are the real authorities about their bodies, they have the potential for the positive attitude necessary for a wellness life-style. Health comes when individuals are total, whole people, when they have achieved a level of integration between mind, body, emotions, and spirit, when they allow themselves to balance.

The life of a man is a journey; a journey from the nest, to the tribe, to the woods, to standing alone, to being responsible.

Chapter 20

THE JOURNEY CONTINUES

Dwight Moore, Stephen Parker, Ted Thompson, and Patrick Dougherty

The dilemma editors face in collecting the thoughts of a number of different authors is that those thoughts may seem contradictory and disconnected when placed together in a single volume. Our authors come from many different walks of life, races, and orientations, and possess a multitude of different experiences.

Yet, these authors share the common fact of their "brotherhood." When men talk about their experiences, other men "know" what they are saying at some deep, fundamental level. This experience of "masculinity" is elusive; it is difficult to articulate; at times, it may even feel a touch fearful and powerful.

The authors of this chapter spent the winter of 1989 meeting on a regular basis to attempt to articulate the roots of this common experience, this "brotherhood." We interviewed a number of different men and asked them questions such as: "When were you first aware of being a man?" "What is the difference between someone who is a man and one who is not?" "When do you think your father became a man?" "What were major crossroads in your adult life?" "How does age affect your masculinity?" "What is dangerous about your masculinity?" We shared our findings with one another, explored these issues together, and told parts of our stories to one another in an attempt to discover the feelings, the thoughts, the spirit of men's experience that is "known."

Initially we examined developmental theory. Many authors have written about stages of male development. Piaget (1981), Dupont (1980), Loevinger (1970), Kohlberg (1969), Perry (1970), Levinson (1979), Vaillant (1977), Sheehy (1976), Neugarten (1968), Gould (1978), and, of course, Erikson (1963) all talked of the stages men go through in their development. These theories are helpful in understanding ourselves, yet we discovered that this seemingly logical approach to our own development did not capture the more circuitous route each of us seem to take in becoming men.

Although most developmental theories focus on developmental stages that seem clear-cut and linear, upon further reading, one can see complexities in male development. Each step forward is a developmental crisis and is marked by fear, trial, and error. Our conversations brought this doubt and searching into focus.

To help us maintain this focus, we have created terms to describe the emotional facets of these developmental stages. We want to conceptualize men's experience without losing the element of personal struggle, searching, and blind alleys. In a sense, men's development is like quantum physics. On an individual level, our experience is random, but on an aggregate level, it looks smooth, steplike, and progressive.

When probing our own experience and that of others, we discovered our experience to be a journey in which, although there may be an ultimate direction, the path crosses itself, doubles back, wanders, occasionally meanders, and sometimes marches directly ahead. Men's journey, the crossing of barriers, the walk, the relaxed hikes, and the mad, terrified dashes are all reflected in the chapters of this book. Our metaphor is the journey.

The Journey Begins

Most men experience at least five legs in their journey: the nest, the tribe, the woods, standing alone, and being responsible. These legs are likely to be revisited relative to one's age, culture, economic status, and relationship status. As we will see, men need to circle back periodically and meet the challenges on the journey. This journey is not linear; there are few maps. In addition, as Patrick Dougherty pointed out in his chapter, men have few elders who can help and guide them in safe ways.

The Nest

This is pre-journey, a safe place that is usually populated with women who nurture, feed, and protect. Some men did not have such a nurturing experience, and therefore, did not receive a solid sense of self-esteem and belongingness as did others.

Men were usually absent or excluded from the nest. Fathers who worked long and hard hours to provide for the family were either tired or emotionally inaccessible when they were home. They were somewhat mysterious and, although responsible and involved, somewhat distant.

Our experience is that we need to leave the nest, as early as our identity is established, not by linking with women's values, but rather by finding a group of boys to identify with. Men begin their journey by leaving the nest and venturing out into a world unknown.

The Tribe

Men seek validation from other men, although perhaps not directly. For millennia, men have hunted, prayed, played, and fought in groups. On their journey, men seek to learn how to be accepted in a group, how groups operate, and how to conform to group norms.

Formal initiation to manhood does not exist in the Western culture. Boys join Little League, Boy Scouts, military schools, or team sports as a substitute for this initiation. Neighborhood "clubs" hold initiation rites, and the growing presence of gangs speaks to the need for boys to become part of a tribe. One can argue for or against the values and norms of these different groups, but we believe the fundamental drive of men on this leg of the journey is to be included and to be protected by the tribe.

Tribe membership gives men a sense of identity. This truth repeats itself throughout their lives. Men may start with a neighborhood "club," play high school sports, join the Marines, a union, a union softball team, the Elks, and the Masons. These associations with other men in formal or semiformal groups offer rules for relationships. Intimacy in these groups is "side-by-side" intimacy as compared to "face-to-face" intimacy. That is, men engage in activities directed toward something other than the relationship between two men. For example, a guard and a center on a football team hold the mutual goal of winning, although they are not likely to talk with one another about their personal hopes and dreams.

Men express their gentleness and sensitivity through this side-by-side intimacy, although those traits may never be articulated. We believe that men express their intimacy differently than the way women express their intimacy. The dilemma for men is that group behavior, in recent history, has become increasingly competitive and has lost the flavor and power of cooperative tribal behavior. Coaches who say "Winning isn't everything; it's the only thing"; staff sergeants who continually belittle their troops; Little League coaches who berate 10-year-olds; and company presidents who pit employee against employee in a competitive environment all have lost the original power of cooperative endeavor among men.

Men need groups that find a balance between cooperation and competition, between nurturance and challenge of the individual, between quiet, reflective time and active, energetic time. In these groups, men learn about their self-esteem, their gender, their culture, their sexual orientation, their relationships, their emotions, their power, and their history. Although not all men become "true" members of the tribe, they all must struggle with the tribe's impact. Sometimes the tribe exacts too high a price for membership, whereas at other times, it will not accept certain men. Yet at some point in men's lives, each man must face the fact that the tribe is either exacting too high a price or that there is more to life than the benefits the tribe offers. It is at this time men enter the woods for the first time and begin the process of discovering and embracing their fears and grief.

The Woods

All boys at some point "go into the woods" for the first time. For some of us it occurs when we leave the world of female nurturers and begin our journey. For others it occurs after we leave our first tribe. The woods means dealing with something fearful. It is the time when we confront our own loneliness, helplessness, and terror alone. The nature of the fear is different for different people. For a Black youth it may mean coming to terms with his race; it can be making one's first career choice; it can be facing one's sexuality; it can be dealing with an abusive parent. These woods are dark, and we are alone in them. The sense is that "we can't hide out anymore."

The tools that we take on our journey into the woods primarily come from our fathers and are probably similar to those they received from their fathers. We do receive valuable tools from our mothers, yet we seem to utilize our fathers' tools in the woods. One tool we need in the woods is an answer to the question: "How do I deal with my fear?" We look to our father for the answer. What role model has he given us to deal with fear?

Sadly, as a number of the authors in this book have pointed out, fathers tend to be either absent, inexpressive, or punitive. As a result our tool bag is not particularly full when we reach the woods. How many of us, for example, heard our fathers talk about how they dealt with their fear? It seems as if they denied their own fear.

Another example of the woods is coming to terms with our sexuality. Some of us were lucky enough to receive messages of respect for ourselves and others, whereas others among us received tools of exploitation, abuse, and disrespect of our own bodies and the bodies of others.

Depending on the tools, men's experiences can differ as a result of their first trip to the woods. Sadly, however, many men end up rushing through the woods with confusion, fear, denial, and embarrassment for not having successfully dealt with the challenge. They rush back to a tribe without having faced their fears. The result is that when they go into the woods again, they are equally unprepared and at least as fearful.

On our journey, we circle back to the woods. We do so when establishing significant relationships or changing significant relationships, when changing jobs or careers, when our children arrive, when we are aging, at midlife, and at retirement. Whenever we face a hard, fearful period, we have entered the woods. Therapists and counselors who work with men are well advised to validate that experience and then closely explore the tools their clients have for walking through the woods.

Standing Alone

Learning to be self-sufficient, separate, and independent is another crucial leg of our journey. This is a particularly difficult leg of the journey. Early on in the journey we swing radically from one end of a continuum to another. Some of us become totally insulated from others, cold to the world, pleasant on the outside and distant on the inside. Some of us become dependent on the affirmation of others, are unable to assert our own will, and abdicate our power to others. Finding a balance between these two extremes is a task.

Establishing a sense of independence is a major part of our journey. Many philosophers, psychologists, and sociologists have stated this truth. Our reality, as men, is that we live some of our lives alone. Alone does not necessarily mean without a partner. Many men live with a partner and feel alone, feel insulated, feel separate from time to time. One man's father, in response to a question about his relationship, said: "You are born alone, and you will die alone."

It has been said that women establish their sense of identity within relationships. Our experience is that part of men's identity is established outside of relationships. Coming to terms with one's loneliness, with one's isolation, with one's independence is part of becoming a man. This is difficult to articulate in words, but our experience is that when we talk with one another about self-sufficiency, about separateness, about loneliness, about the sphere of isolation we each feel, there is an understanding among us.

With seeming paradox, we need to be part of a tribe, but just as fiercely need independence. It seems that connecting with the group precedes developing self-sufficiency, but ultimately both are important.

Spiritually, we "seek to cultivate our own gardens," that is, we look inward for the resources to love, grow, change, reflect, and so on. One of the great tragedies of male suicide is that these men did not have the tools to look inward, or when they did, they thought there was nothing there. Our culture so emphasizes wealth, power, prowess, determination, dominance, and competitiveness that many adolescents and older men have lost their identity and worth relative to those values. When they look inside, they believe they do not measure up and therefore leave this world. That trip back to the woods is fatal.

Even though this risk exists, some men are able to find a balance between independence, tribal time, and relationships. Our experience is that when these elements get too far out of balance, the man becomes dysfunctional. Therapists counseling men might look closely at these three elements.

Being Responsible

Taking responsibility for our family, our job, our life is an integral part of our journey. Traditional "providing" roles for the family, "protecting" our wives and children, and maintaining loyality to friendships are all part of being responsible.

All men know of the duty to be responsible. Although some of us are not able always to do so, we perceive that a fundamental part of masculinity is responsibility. We back up our buddies in a firefight, we provide food and shelter for our families, we remain loyal to company or union policies, we defend the honor of our names/culture/country.

Over and over, when responding to the question about the difference between someone who is a man and someone who is not, men answered, "Responsibility." The congruence between our behavior and our sense of responsibility is a primary clue to our mental health. When these are out of sync, we are in emotional turmoil.

During our journey we have endless opportunities to develop and act on our sense of responsibility. When entering the woods we are aware of the right thing to do (which may not be the culturally appropriate thing to do). We develop strong loyalities in groups and strive to be responsible to those groups. Men who abandon their children and families are continually and acutely aware of their violation of the contract of responsibility. Fulfilling our sense of responsibility provides immense gratification.

Conclusion

The nest, the tribe, the woods, standing alone, and being responsible are all part of our journey. All the writers have spoken directly to these legs of the journey. We will cycle through, in and out of phases.

We feel optimistic because a number of men are recognizing the importance of preparing men for this journey. Courtland Lee has developed a manhood training course for Black adolescents. Gay men are looking to one another for healthy models. Men's studies courses are growing, thus providing a sense of history. Men are becoming more active as fathers and caregivers. Groups have been developed to teach the tools of relationships. Men are exploring traditional definitions of success and reevaluating their career choices as a result. We are caring for our bodies through wellness programs.

All of this brings healthy power back to men and moves us away from destructive power. Embracing our masculinity in healthy ways and helping one another through our journeys is our task and reward.

Acknowledgment

The authors would like to thank P. Paul Heppner, Brooke Collison, and the AACD Committee on Men for their help in developing the Concerns Assessment.

REFERENCES

Chapter 1: Men on a Journey

Brannon, R.C. (1976). No sissy stuff: The stigma of anything vaguely feminine. In D. David & R. Brannon, (Eds.), *The forty-nine percent majority*. Reading, MA: Addison-Wesley.

Emerson, G. (1985). *Some American men*. New York: Simon & Schuster.

Erikson, E. (1959). *Identity and the life cycle*. New York: International Universities Press.

Fromm, E. (1955). *The sane society*. New York: Rinehart.

Hayes, L. (1988). Men in transition: Changing sex roles. *Guidepost, 30*(12), pp. 1, 3.

Houston, J. (1973, March). The varieties of postpsychedelic experience. *Intellectual Digest*, pp. 16–18.

James, W. (1890). *The principles of psychology*. Vol. 1. New York: Holt.

Jourard, S.M. (1971). *The transparent self*. New York: Van Nostrand.

Vaillant, G. (1977, September). How the best and the brightest came of age. *Psychology Today*, pp. 34–110.

Chapter 2: Finding Ourselves: Self-Esteem, Self-Disclosure, and Self-Acceptance

Arlyck, R. (Producer). (1982). *An acquired taste* [Film]. Wayne, NJ: New Day Films.

Bandura, A. (1977). *Social learning theory*. Englewood Cliffs, NJ: Prentice-Hall.

Bem, S.L. (1974). The measurement of psychological androgyny. *Journal of Consulting and Clinical Psychology, 81*, 506–520.

Berzins, J., Welling, M., & Wetter, R. (1978). A new measure of psychological androgyny based on the personal research form. *Journal of Consulting and Clinical Psychology, 46*, 126–128.

Chafetz, M.E., & Demore, H.W., Jr. (1972). *Alcoholism and society*. New York: Oxford University Press.

Chodorow, N. (1978). *The reproduction of mothering*. Berkeley: University of California Press.

Farrell, W. (1974). *The liberated man*. New York: Bantam Books.

Gilligan, C. (1982). *A different voice*. Cambridge, MA: Harvard University Press.

Goldberg, H. (1977). *The hazards of being male*. New York: New American Library.

Hanig, J., & Roberts, W. (Producers). (1974). *Men's lives* [Film]. Wayne NJ: New Day Films.

Harris, L. (1976). *The myth and reality of aging in America*. Washington, DC: National Council on the Aging.

Harrison, J. (1978). Warning: The male sex role may be hazardous to your health. *Journal of Social Issues, 34*, 65–86.

Hartley, R.E. (1959). Sex-role pressures and the socialization of the male child. *Psychological Reports, 5,* 457–468.

Herzog, J.M. (1982). On father hunger: The father's role in the modulation of aggressive drive and fantasy. In S.H. Cath, A.R. Gurwitt, & J.M. Ross (Eds.), *Father and child: Developmental and clinical perspectives* (pp. 163–174). Boston: Little, Brown.

Jourard, S. (1971). *The transparent self.* New York: Litton.

Kagan, N., & Krathwohl, D.R. (1967). *Studies in human interaction: Interpersonal process recall simulated by videotape.* ERIC Document Reproduction Service, ED 017 946.

Lapow, G. (Vocalist), & Narell, A. (Producer). (1982). *Tell it from the heart* [Record]. San Francisco: Mobius Music.

Lynn, D.B. (1966). The process of learning parental and sex-role identification. *The Journal of Marriage and Family, 28,* 466–470.

May, R. (1988). Resources for promoting change in men's lives. In R. May & M. Scher (Eds.), *Changing roles for men on campus* (pp. 91–95). San Francisco: Jossey-Bass.

May, R., & Eichenfield, G. (1989, March). *Finding our fathers.* Presented at the annual convention of the American College Personnel Association, Washington, DC.

Merton, A. (1986). Father hunger. *New Age Journal, 94,* 22–29.

Middler, B. (Vocalist), & Rothchild, P. (Producer). (1978). *The rose* [Record]. Universal City, CA: MCA.

Morgan, G. (Vocalist). (1980). *It comes with the plumbing* [Record]. Bellingham, WA: Nexus.

Morgan, G. (Vocalist). (1982). *Finally letting it go* [Record]. Chicago: Flying Fish.

Morgan, G. (Vocalist). (1985). *At the edge* [Record]. Chicago: Flying Fish.

O'Neil, J. (1982). Gender-role conflict and strain in men's lives. In K. Solomon & N.B. Levy (Eds.), *Men in transition: Theory and therapy* (pp. 5–44). New York: Plenum Press.

Organization Against Sexism and Institutional Stereotypes (Producer). (1988). *Stale roles and tight buns* [Videocassette]. Brighton, MA: O.A.S.I.S.

Osherson, S. (1986, Apr./May). Finding our fathers. *Utne Reader,* pp. 36–39.

Rogers, C. (1961). *On becoming a person.* Boston: Houghton Mifflin.

Rubin, L.B. (1983). *Intimate strangers.* New York: Harper & Row.

Satir, V. (1985). *Meditations and inspirations.* Berkeley, CA: Celestial Arts.

Satir, V., & Baldwin, M. (1983). *Satir step by step: A guide to creating change in families.* Palo Alto, CA: Science and Behavior Books.

Simon, P. (Vocalist), Garfunkel, A. (Vocalist), & Johnson, B. (Producer). (1965). *The sounds of silence* [Record]. New York: Columbia.

Spence, J.T., & Helmreich, R.L. (1972). The attitudes toward women scale. *JSAS Catalog on Selected Documents in Psychology, 2,* 66.

Spence, J.T., & Helmreich, R.L. (1978). *Masculinity and femininity: Their psychological dimensions, correlates, and antecedents.* Austin: University of Texas Press.

Spence, J.T., Helmreich, R.L., & Stapp, J. (1975). Ratings of self and peers on sex role attributes and their relation to self-esteem and conceptions of masculinity and femininity. *Journal of Personality and Social Psychology, 32,* 29–39.

Stevens, J.O. (1971). *Awareness: Exploring, experimenting, experiencing.* Lafayette, CA: Real People Press.

Travers, M. (Vocalist), & Okun, M. (Producer). (1971). *Mary* [Record]. Burbank, CA: Warner Brothers.

Weiss, J.A.M. (1974). Suicide. In S. Arieti & E.B. Brody (Eds.), *American handbook of psychiatry, Volume III* (2nd ed.) (pp. 743–765). New York: Basic Books.

Chapter 3: Assessing Men's Gender Role Conflict

Basow, S.A. (1986). *Gender stereotypes: Traditions and alternatives.* Monterey, CA: Brooks/Cole.

Beck, E.T. (1983). Self-disclosure and the commitment to social change. *Women's Studies International Forum, 6*(2), 159–163.

Boehm, F. (1930). The femininity-complex in men. *International Journal of Psycho-Analysis, 11,* 444–469.

Block, J.H. (1973). Conceptions of sex role: Some cross-cultural and longitudinal perspectives. *American Psychologist, 28,* 512–526.

Block, J.H. (1984). *Sex role identity and ego development.* San Francisco: Jossey-Bass.

Croteau, J.M., & Burda, P.C. (1983). Structured group programming on men's roles: A creative approach to change. *Personnel and Guidance Journal, 62*(4), 243–245.

David, D.S., & Brannon, R. (1976). *The forty-nine percent majority: The male sex role.* Reading, MA: Addison-Wesley.

Davis, F. (1988, August). *Antecedents and consequences of gender role conflict: An empirical test of sex role strain analysis.* Paper presented at American Psychological Association Annual Meeting, Atlanta, GA.

Doyle, J.A. (1983). *The male experience.* Dubuque, IA: Wm. C. Brown.

Doyle, J.A. (1985). *Sex and gender: The human experience.* Dubuque, IA: Wm. C. Brown.

Dubbert, J.L. (1979). *A man's place: Masculinity in transition.* Englewood Cliffs, NJ: Prentice-Hall.

Farrell, W. (1974). *The liberated man.* New York: Bantam Books.

Finkelhor, D. (1984). *Child sexual abuse: New theory and research.* New York: Free Press.

Finn, J. (1986). The relationship between sex role attitudes and attitudes supporting marital violence. *Sex Roles, 14,* 235–244.

Garnets, L., & Pleck, J.H. (1979). Sex role identity, androgyny, and sex role transcendence: A sex role strain analysis. *Psychology of Women Quarterly, 3,* 270–283.

Giele, J.Z. (1980). Adulthood as transcedence of age and sex. In N.J. Smelser & E.H. Erikson (Eds.), *Themes of work and love in adulthood* (pp. 151–173). Cambridge, MA: Harvard University Press.

Gilligan, C. (1984). *In a different voice: Psychological theory and women's development.* Cambridge, MA: Harvard University Press.

Good, G., Dell, D.M., & Mintz, L.B. (1989). Male roles and gender role conflict: Relationships to help-seeking in men. *Journal of Counseling Psychology, 3,* 295–300.

Hays, H.R. (1964). *The dangerous sex: The myth of feminine evil.* New York: Pocket Books.

Horney, K. (1967). *Feminine psychology.* New York: Norton.

Johnson, R.A. (1977). *He: Understanding masculine psychology.* New York: Harper & Row.

Jung, C.G. (1953). Animus and anima. *Collected works,* Vol. 7. New York: Pantheon.

Jung, C.G. (1954). Concerning the archetypes, with special reference to the anima concept. *Collected works,* Vol. 9, Part I. New York: Pantheon.

Kimmel, M.S. (Ed.) (1987). *Changing men: New directions in research on men and masculinity.* Newbury Park, CA: Sage.

Lederer, W. (1968). *The fear of women.* New York: Harcourt Brace Jovanovich.

Levinson, D.J., Darrow, C.N., Klein, E.B., Levinson, M.H., & McKee. (1978). *The seasons of a man's life.* New York: Ballantine Books.

Mayer, N. (1978). *The male mid-life crises: Fresh start after 40.* New York: New American Library.

Menninger, K. (1970). *Love against hate.* New York: Harcourt Brace Jovanovich.

Moreland, J.R. (1979). Some implications of life-span development for counseling psychology. *Personnel and Guidance Journal, 57,* 299–303.

Moreland, J.R. (1980). Age and change in the adult male sex role. *Sex Roles, 6,* 807–818.

O'Neil, J.M. (1981a). Patterns of gender role conflict and strain: The fear of femininity in men's lives. *The Personnel and Guidance Journal, 60,* 203–210.

O'Neil, J.M. (1981b). Male sex-role conflicts, sexism, and masculinity: Implications for men, women, and the counseling psychologist. *The Counseling Psychologist, 9,* 61–80.

O'Neil, J.M. (1982). Gender and sex role conflict and strain in men's lives: Implications for psychiatrists, psychologists, and other human service providers. In K. Solomon & N. Levy (Eds.), *Men in transition: Theory and therapy* (pp. 5–44). New York: Plenum Press.

O'Neil, J.M. (1986, May). *The gender role journey in men's lives.* Paper presented at the First National Association of Social Worker's Westchester Men's Conference, Westchester Community College, Valhalla, New York.

O'Neil, J.M. (1988, August). *Definition of gender role conflict: A study of John Lennon's life.* Paper presented at the meeting of the American Psychological Association, Atlanta, GA.

O'Neil, J.M., & Fishman, D. (1986). Adult men's career transitions and gender role themes. In Z.B. Leibowitz & H.D. Lea (Eds.), *Adult career development: Concepts, issues, and practices* (pp. 132–162). Alexandria, VA: National Career Development Association.

O'Neil, J.M., Fishman, D., & Kinsella-Shaw, M. (1987). Dual career couples' career transitions and normative dilemmas: A preliminary assessment model. *The Counseling Psychologist, 15*(1), 50–96.

O'Neil, J.M., Helms, B.J., Gable, R.K., David, L., & Wrightsman, L. (1986). Gender role conflict scale: College men's fear of femininity. *Sex Roles, 14,* 335–350.

O'Neil, J.M., & Roberts Carroll, M. (1988). A gender role workshop focused on sexism, gender role conflict, and the gender role journey. *Journal of Counseling and Development, 67,* 193–197.

Pleck, J. (1981). *The myth of masculinity.* Cambridge, MA: MIT Press.

Rebecca, M., Hefner, R., & Oleshansky, B. (1976). A model of sex-role transcendence. *Journal of Social Issues, 32,* 197–206.

Russell, D.E. (1984). *Sexual exploitation: Rape, child sexual abuse, and workplace harrassment.* Beverly Hills, CA: Sage.

Skovholt, T.M. (1978). Feminism and men's lives. *The Counseling Psychologist,* 7(4), 3–10.

Snell, W. (1986). The masculine role inventory: Components and correlates. *Sex Roles, 15,* 443–456.

Thompson, E.H., & Pleck, J.H. (1986). The structure of male role norms. *American Behavioral Scientist, 29,* 531–543.

Chapter 4: Career Themes in Counseling and Psychotherapy With Men

Bolles, R.N. (1988). *What color is your parachute? A practical manual for job hunters and career changers.* Berkeley, CA: Ten Speed Press.

Bruch, M.A., & Skovholt, T.M. (1982). Counseling services and men in need: A problem in person-environmental matching. *American Mental Health Counselors Journal, 4*(2), 89–96.

Capon, R.F. (1987). Being let go. In E. Klein & D. Erickson (Eds.), *About men.* New York: Pocket Books.

David, D.S., & Brannon, R. (Eds.). (1976). *The forty-nine percent majority: The male sex role.* Reading, MA: Addison-Wesley.

Dubois, T.E., & Marino, T.M. (1987). Career counseling with men. In M. Scher, M. Stevens, G. Good, & G.A. Eichenfield (Eds.), *Handbook of counseling and psychotherapy with men* (pp. 68–82). Newbury Park, CA: Sage.

Farrell, W. (1986). *Why men are the way they are.* New York: McGraw-Hill.

Fasteau, M. (1975). *The male machine.* New York: Dell.

Friedan, B. (1981). *The second stage.* New York: Summit Books.

Gilbert, L.A. (1987). Female and male emotional dependency and its implications for the therapist-client relationship. *Professional Psychology: Research and Practice, 18,* 555–561.

Gilbert, L.A. (1988). *Sharing it all: The rewards and struggles of two-career families.* New York: Plenum Press.

Good, G.E., Dell, D.M., & Mintz, L.B. (1989). Male roles and gender role conflict: Relationships to help-seeking in men. *Journal of Counseling Psychology, 3,* 295–300.

Hansen, L.S. (1984). Interrelationship of gender and career. In N. Gysbers & Associates (Eds.), *Designing careers*. San Francisco: Jossey-Bass.

Hansen, L.S., & Minor, C.W. (1989). Work, family, and career development: Implications for persons, policies and practices. In D. Brown & C. Minor (Eds.), *Work in America: A status report on planning and problems*. Alexandria, VA: National Career Development Association.

Hendel, D.D. (in press). Beyond babysitting: Experiences and concerns of fathers who are highly involved with their children. *Journal of Counseling and Development*.

Heppner, M.J., Johnston, J.A., & Brinkhoff, J. (1988). Creating a career hotline for rural residents. *Journal of Counseling and Development 66*, 340–341.

Kinnier, R.T., & Krumboltz, J.D. (1984). Procedures for successful career counseling. In N. Gysbers (Ed.), *Designing careers*. San Francisco: Jossey-Bass.

May, R. (1972). *Power and innocence*. New York: Dell.

Mott, G. (1987). Following a wife's move. In E. Klein & D. Erickson (Eds.), *About men*. New York: Pocket Books.

O'Neil, M. (1981). Male sex role conflicts, sexism and masculinity: Psychological implications for men, women, and the counseling psychologist. *Counseling Psychologist, 9*(2), 61–80.

O'Neil, J.M., & Fishman, D.M. (1986). Adult men's career transitions and gender-role themes. In Z.B. Leibowitz, & H.D. Lea (Eds), *Adult career development* (pp. 132–162). Alexandria, VA: National Career Development Association.

Pleck, J. (1979). Men's family work: Three perspectives and some new data. *Family Coordinator, 28*, 481–488.

Pleck, J.H. (1987). The contemporary man. In M. Scher, M. Stevens, G. Good, & G.A. Eichenfield (Eds.), *Handbook of counseling and psychotherapy with men* (pp. 16–27). Newbury Park, CA: Sage.

Skovholt, T.M., Moore, D., & Haritos-Fatorous, M. (1989). *The 180° bind for men: Trained for war, expected to nurture*. Unpublished paper.

Skovholt, T.M., & Morgan, J.I. (1981). Career development: An outline of issues for men. *Personnel and Guidance Journal, 60*, 231–237.

Wegmann, R., Chapman, R., & Johnson, M. (1989). *Work in the new economy*. Alexandria, VA: American Association for Counseling and Development.

Chapter 5: Dimensions of Pleasure: Sexuality, Men, and Counseling

Annon, J.S. (1977). The PLISSIT model: A proposed conceptual scheme for the behavioral treatment of sexual problems. In J. Fischer & H.L. Gochros, (Eds.), *Handbook of behavior therapy with sexual problems, Vol. 1* (pp. 70–83). New York: Pergamon.

Bohlen, J. (1981, September). *Sexual side effects of drugs*. Paper presented at the Family Intimacy and Chemical Dependency Training Program, University of Minnesota Medical School.

Brantner, J. (1987). Intimacy, aging, and chemical dependency. *Journal of Chemical Dependency Treatment, 1*(1), 261–268.

Brown, J.A. (1988). Shame, intimacy, and sexuality. In E. Coleman (Ed.), *Chemical dependency and intimacy dysfunction* (pp. 61–74). New York: Haworth.

Chapman, R. (1982). Criteria for diagnosing when to do sex therapy in the primary relationship. *Psychotherapy: Theory Research and Practice, 19*, 359–367.

Colgan, P. (1987). Treatment of dependency disorders in men: Toward a balance of identity and intimacy. *Journal of Chemical Dependency Treatment, 1*(1), 205–227.

Colgan, P. (1988). Assessment of boundary inadequacy in chemically dependent individuals and families. In E. Coleman (Ed.), *Chemical dependency and intimacy dysfunction* (pp. 75–90). New York: Haworth.

Cosby, P.C. (1973). Self disclosure: A literature review. *Psychological Bulletin, 79*(2), 73–91.

Derogatis, L.R., Lopez, M.C., & Zinzeletta, E.M. (1988). Clinical applications of the DSFI in the assessment of sexual dysfunctions. In A.R. Brown, & J.R. Field (Eds.), *Treatment of sexual problems in individual and couples therapy* (pp. 167–186). Baltimore: Maryland Psychological Association.

Everaerd, W. (1988). Commentary on sex research: Sex as an emotion. *Journal of Psychology and Human Sexuality, 1*(2), 3–16.

Izard, C.E., & Blumberg, S.H. (1985). Emotion theory and the role of anxiety in children and adults. In A. Husein Tuma, & J. Maser (Eds.), *Anxiety and anxiety disorders*. Hillsdale, NJ: Lawrence Erlbaum Associates.

Jung, C.A. (1959). *Aion, Collected Works 9:2*. R.F.C. Hull, (*Trans.*). New York: Pantheon.

Kail, R., & Pellegrino, J.W. (1985). Human intelligence: Perspectives and prospects. New York: Freeman.

Kaplan, H.S. (1974). The new sex therapy. New York: Brunner/Mazel.

Kinsey, A.C., Pomeroy, W.B., & Martin, C.E. (1948). *Sexual Behavior in the human male*. Philadelphia: Saunders.

Lekarezyk, D.T., & Hill, K.T. (1969). Self esteem, test anxiety, stress, and verbal learning. *Developmental Psychology, 1*, 147–154.

LoPiccolo, L. (1980). Low sexual desire. In S.R. Leiblum, & L.A. Pervin (Eds.), *Principles and practice of sex therapy* (pp. 29–64). New York: Guilford.

Maddock, J. (1975). Sexual health and health care. *Postgraduate Medicine, 58*(1).

Masters, W.H., & Johnson, V.E. (1970). *Human sexual inadequacy*. Boston: Little, Brown.

Meyer, J.K., Schmidt, C.W., Lucas, M.J., & Smith E. (1975). Short-term treatment of sexual problems: Interim report. *American Journal of Psychiatry, 132*, 172–176.

Miller, J.B. (1983). *The construction of anger in women and men*. Works in Progress #83-01. Wellesley, MA: Wellesley College.

Moore, D., & Haverkamp, B.E. (1989). Measured increases in male emotional expressiveness following a structured group intervention. *Journal of Counseling and Development, 67*(9), 513–517.

Schover, L.R., Friedman, J.M., Weiler, S.J., Heiman, J.R., & LoPiccolo, J. (1980). *A multi-axial descriptive system for the sexual dysfunctions: Categories and manual*. Stony Brook, NY: Sex Therapy Center.

Sollod, R.N. (1988). An integrated eclectic approach to psychosexual therapy. In R.A. Brown, & J.R. Field (Eds.), *Treatment of sexual problems in individual and couples therapy*. Baltimore: Maryland Psychological Association.

Stuntz, R.C. (1983). Laboratory evaluation. In J.H. Meyer, C.W. Schmidt, & T.N. Wise (Eds.), *Clinical management of sexual disorders* (2nd ed.). Baltimore: Williams & Wilkins.

Wolpe, J. (1969). *The practice of behavior therapy*. New York: Pergamon.

Additional Resource

Greimas, A.J. (1987). *On meaning: Selected writings in semiotic theory*. P.J. Perron, & F.H. Collins, (Trans.). Minneapolis: University of Minnesota Press.

Chapter 6: Men and Marriage

Bodin, A.M. The interactional view: Family therapy approaches of the Mental Research Institute. (1981). In A.S. Gurman, & D.P. Kniskern (Eds.), *Handbook of family therapy* (pp. 271–309). New York: Brunner/Mazel.

Boszormenyi-Nagy, I., & Krasner, B. (1986). *Between give and take*. New York: Brunner/Mazel.

Bowen, M. (1978). *Family therapy in clinical practice*. New York: Aronson.

Carter, E., & McGoldrick, M. (1987). *The changing family life cycle*. Boston: Allyn & Bacon.

Kerr, M., & Bowen, M. (1988). Family evaluation. New York: Norton.

Prosky, P. (1979). *Some thoughts on family life from the field of family therapy*. New York: Ackerman Institute.

Chapter 7: Coping With the New Father Role

Ambrose, P., Harper, J., & Pemberton, R. (1983). *Surviving divorce: Men beyond marriage*. Totowa, NJ: Rowman & Allenhand.

Andrews, F., & Withey, S. (1976). *Social indicators of well-being*. New York: Plenum Press.

Catalyst. (1983). *Human factors in relocation*. New York: Author.

Catalyst. (1988). Workplace policies: New options for fathers. In P. Bronstein & C.P. Cowan (Eds.), *Fatherhood today: Men's changing role in the family* (pp. 323–340). New York: Wiley Interscience.

Cowan, C.P., & Bronstein, P. (1988). Fathers' roles in the family: Implications for research, intervention, and change. In P. Bronstein & C. P. Cowan (Eds.), *Fatherhood today: Men's changing role in the family* (pp. 341–348). New York: Wiley Interscience.

Erskine, H. (1973). The polls: Hopes, tears, and regrets. *Public Opinion Quarterly, 37*, 132–145.

Farrell, W. (1986). *Why men are the way they are*. New York: McGraw-Hill.

Furstenberg, F.F., Jr., Nord, C.W., Peterson, J.L., & Zill, N. (1983). The life course of children of divorce: Marital disruption and parental contact. *American Sociological Review, 48*, 656–668.

Gilbert, L.A., & Rachlin, V. (1987). Mental health and psychological functioning of dual career families. *The Counseling Psychologist, 15*(1), 7–49.

Greif, G.L. (1985). *Single fathers.* Lexington, MA: Heath.

Juster, F. T., & Stafford, F.P. (1985). *Time, goods, and well-being.* Ann Arbor, MI: Institute for Social Research.

Kelly, J.B. (1988). Longer-term adjustment in children of divorce. *Journal of Family Psychology, 2*(2), 119–140.

LaRossa, R. (1989, Spring). Fatherhood and social change. *Men's Studies Review, 6*(2), 1–9.

Lein, L., Durham, M., Pratt, M., Schudson, M., Thomas, R., & Weiss, H. (1974). *Work and family life* (Working Paper). Wellesley, MA: Wellesley College Center for Research on Women.

Levant, R.F., & Doyle, G. (1981a). *Parent education for fathers: A personal developmental approach. Leaders' Guide.* Unpublished manuscript, Boston University.

Levant, R.F., & Doyle, G. (1981b). *Parent education for fathers: A personal developmental approach. Parents' Workbook.* Unpublished manuscript, Boston University.

Levant, R.F., & Doyle, G. (1983). An evaluation of a parent education program for fathers of school-aged children. *Family Relations, 32*, 29–37.

Lewis, R.A. (1986). Men's changing roles in marriage and the family. In R.A. Lewis (Ed.), *Men's changing roles in the family* (pp. 1–10). New York: Haworth Press.

Michaels, M., & Willworth, J. (1989, April 24). The rat race: How America is running itself ragged. *Time*, pp. 58–67.

Pleck, J.H. (1985). *Working wives/working husbands.* Newbury Park, CA: Sage.

Pleck, J.H., & Lang, L. (1978). *Men's family role: Its nature and consequences* (Working Paper). Wellesley, MA: Wellesley College Center for Research on Women.

Robinson, J. (1977). *How Americans use time: A social-psychological analysis.* New York: Praeger.

U.S. Bureau of Labor Statistics. (1985, September 19). *Labor force activity of mothers continues at record pace.* Washington, DC: U.S. Department of Labor.

Walker, K., & Woods, M. (1976). *Time use: A measure of household production of goods and services.* Washington, DC: American Home Economics Association.

Additional Resources

Aldous, J. (Ed.). (1982). *Two paychecks: Life in dual-earner families.* Newbury Park, CA: Sage.

Furstenberg, F.F., Jr. (Guest Ed.). (1980). Remarriage. *Journal of Family Issues* (Special Issue), *1*(4), 443–571.

Gilbert, L.A. (Guest Ed.). (1987). Dual career families in perspective. *The Counseling Psychologist* (Special Issue), *15*(1), 1–145.

Hanson, S.M.H., & Sporakowski, M.J. (Guest Eds.). (1986). The single parent family. *Family Relations* (Special Issue), *35*(1), 1–224.

Ihinger-Tallman, M., & Pasley, K. (1987). *Remarriage*. Newbury Park, CA: Sage.

Levant, R. (Ed.). (1986). *Psychoeducational approaches to family therapy and counseling*. New York: Springer.

Levant, R. (1988). Education for fatherhood. In P. Bronstein & C.P. Cowan (Eds.), *Fatherhood today: Men's changing role in the family* (pp. 253–275). New York: Wiley Interscience.

Levant, R., & Kelly, J. (1989). *Between father and child*. New York: Viking.

Price, S.J., & McKenry, P.C. (1988). *Divorce*. Newbury Park, CA: Sage.

Scher, M., Stevens, M., Good, G., & Eichenfield, G.A. (Eds.). (1987). *Handbook of counseling and psychotherapy with men*. Newbury Park, CA: Sage.

Spanier, G.B., & Thompson, L. (1987). *Parting*. Newbury Park, CA: Sage.

Voydanoff, P. (1987). *Work and family life*. Newbury Park, CA: Sage.

Chapter 8: Divorce: Are Men at Risk?

Ahrons, C.R. (1979). The binuclear family: Two households, one family. *Alternative Lifestyles, 2*, 449–515.

Ahrons, C.R. (1980). Divorce: A crisis of family transition and change. *Family Relations, 29*, 533–540.

Albrecht, S.L., Bahr, H.M., & Goodman, K.L. (1983). *Divorce and remarriage: Problems, adaptation, and adjustments*. Westport, CT: Greenwood.

Atkin, E., & Rubin, E. (1976). *Part-time fathers*. New York: Vanguard.

Bem, S. (1977). *Beyond sex roles*. St. Paul, MN: West.

Berman, W.H. (1985). Continued attachment after legal divorce. *Journal of Family Issues, 6*, 375–381.

Bloom B.L., & Caldwell, R.A. (1981). Sex differences in adjustment during the process of marital separation. *Journal of Marriage and the Family, 43*, 693–701.

Bloom, B.L., & Clement, C. (1984). Marital sex role orientation and adjustment to separation and divorce. *Journal of Divorce, 7*, 87–98.

Bloom, B.L., & Kindle, K.R. (1985). Demographic factors in the continuing relationship between former spouses. *Family Relations, 34*, 375–381.

Brown, E.M. (1976). Divorce counseling. In D. Olson (Ed.), *Treating relationships*. Lake Mills, IA: Graphic.

Brown, P., & Fox, H. (1978). Sex differences in divorce. In E. Gomberg & V. Frank (Eds.), *Gender and disordered behavior: Sex differences in psychopathology*. New York: Brunner/Mazel.

Buehler, C. (1987). Initiator status and the divorce transition. *Family Relations, 36*, 86–90.

Cherlin, A.J. (1981). *Marriage, divorce, and remarriage*. Cambridge, MA: Harvard University Press.

Chiriboga, D.A., & Cutler, L. (1978). Stress responses among divorcing men and women. *Journal of Divorce, 2,* 21–36.

Chiriboga, D.A., & Thurnher, M. (1980). Marital lifestyles and adjustment to separation. *Journal of Divorce, 3,* 379–390.

Daniel, R.M. (1977). Father-child intimacy in divorced families. Unpublished doctoral dissertation, California School of Professional Psychology. *Dissertation Abstracts International, 38*: 2854.

Fisher, B. (1981). *Rebuilding: When your relationship ends.* San Luis Obispo, CA: Impact.

Flynn, C. (1987). *Rethinking joint custody: Option or presumption.* Unpublished manuscript available from the author, Department of Child Development and Family Relations, University of North Carolina, Greensboro, NC.

Friedman, H.J. (1980). The father's parenting experience at divorce. *American Journal of Psychiatry, 137,* 1177–1182.

Furstenberg, F.A., & Nord, C.W. (1985). Parenting apart: Patterns of child rearing after marital disruption. *Journal of Marriage and the Family, 47,* 893–904.

Gardner, R.A. (1977). *The parents' book about divorce.* Garden City, NY: Doubleday.

Gatley, R.H., & Koulack, D. (1979). *Single father's handbook: A guide for separated and divorced fathers.* New York: Anchor Books.

Gertsel, N. (1988). Divorce and kin ties: The importance of gender. *Journal of Marriage and the Family, 50,* 209–219.

Gertsel, N., Reissman, C.K., & Rosenfield, S. (1985). Explaining the symptomatology of separated and divorced women and men: The role of material conditions and social networks. *Social Forces, 64,* 84–101.

Gove, W.R. (1973). Sex, marital status, and mortality. *American Journal of Sociology, 79,* 46–67.

Haskins, R., Dobelstein, A.W., Akin, J.S., & Schwartz, J.B. (1987). *Estimates of national child support collections potential and the income security of female-headed households.* Washington, DC: U.S. Department of Health and Human Services.

Haynes, J.M. (1981). *Divorce and mediation: A practical guide for therapists and counselors.* New York: Springer.

Hetherington, E.M., Cox, M., & Cox, R. (1976). Divorced fathers. *Family Coordinator, 25,* 417–428.

Hetherington, E.M., Cox, M., & Cox, R. (1978). The aftermath of divorce. In J.H. Stevens, Jr., & M. Matthews (Eds.), *Mother-child, father-child relations.* Washington, DC: National Association for the Education of Young Children.

Hetherington, E.M., Stanely-Hagan, M., & Anderson, E.R. (1989). Marital transitions: A child's perspective. *American Psychologist, 44,* 303–312.

Hunt, M., & Hunt, B. (1977). *The divorce experience.* New York: McGraw-Hill.

Jacobs, J.W. (1982). The effect of divorce on fathers: An overview of the literature. *American Journal of American Psychiatry, 139,* 1235–1241.

Johnson, S.M. (1977). *First person singular.* New York: Harper & Row.

Kessler, S. (1975). *The American way of divorce: Prescriptions for change.* Chicago: Nelson-Hall.

Kingma, D.R. (1987). *Coming apart: Why relationships end and how to live through the ending of yours.* New York: Fawcett Crest.

Kitson, G.C. (1982). Attachment to the spouse in divorce: A scale and its application. *Journal of Marriage and the Family, 44,* 379–393.

Knott, J.E. (1987). Grief work with men. In M. Scher, M. Stevens, G. Good, & G. Eichenfield (Eds.), *Handbook of counseling and psychotherapy with men* (pp. 97–108). Newbury Park, CA: Sage.

Krantzler, M. (1973). *Creative divorce: A new opportunity for personal growth.* New York: Evans.

Kressel, K., & Deutsch, M. (1977). Divorce therapy: An indepth survey of therapists' views. *Family Process, 16,* 413–443.

Lowery, C.R., & Settle, S.A. (1985). Effects of divorce on children: Differential impact of custody and visitation patterns. *Family Relations, 34,* 455–463.

McCubbin, H., & Dahl, B.B. (1985). *Marriage and family: Individuals and life cycles.* New York: John Wiley.

McKenry, P.C., & Price, S.J. (in press). Alternatives for support after divorce: A review of the literature. *Journal of Divorce.*

Martin, T.C., & Bumpass, L.L. (1989). Recent trends in marital disruption. *Demography, 26,* 37–49.

Mendes, H.A. (1976). Single fathers. *Family Coordinator, 25,* 439–444.

Milardo, R.M. (1987). Changes in social networks of women and men following divorce. *Journal of Family Issues, 8,* 78–96.

Moreland, J., & Schwebel, A. (1981). A gender role transcendent perspective on fathering. *Counseling Psychologist, 9,* 45–54.

Myers, M.F. (1986). Angry, abandoned husbands: Assessment and treatment. In R.A. Lewis & M.B. Sussman (Eds.), *Men's changing roles in the family.* New York: Haworth.

Norton, A.J., & Glick, P.C. (1986). One parent families: A social and economic profile. *Family Relations, 35,* 9–17.

Pardeck, J.A., & Pardeck, J.T. (1987). Using bibliotherapy to help children cope with the changing family. *Social Work in Education, 9,* 107–116.

Price, S.J., & McKenry, P.C. (1988). *Divorce.* Newbury Park, CA: Sage.

Price, S.J., & McKenry, P.C. (in press). Current trends and issues in divorce: An agenda for family scientists in the 1990s. *Family Science Review.*

Price-Bonham, S., Wright, D., & Pittman, J. (1982). *Former spouse relationships: A typology.* Presented at the Annual Meeting of the World Congress of Sociology, Mexico City, Mexico.

Risman, B.J. (1986). Can me "mother?" Life as a single father. *Family Relations, 35,* 95–102.

Roberts, T.W., & Price, S.J. (1985/1986). A systems analysis of the remarriage process: Implications for the clinician. *Journal of Divorce, 9,* 1–25.

Rosenthal, E.M., & Keshet, H.F. (1981). *Fathers without partners.* New York: Rowman & Littlefield.

Skeen, P., & McKenry, P.C. (1980). The teacher's role in facilitating a child's adjustment to divorce. *Young Children, 35,* 3–12.

Spanier, G.B., & Casto, R.F. (1979). Adjustment to separation and divorce: An analysis of 50 case studies. *Journal of Divorce, 2,* 241–253.

Spanier, G.B., & Thompson, L. (1984). *Parting: The aftermath of separation and divorce.* Beverly Hills, CA: Sage.

Sprenkle, D.H., & Storm, C.L. (1983). Divorce therapy outcome research: A substantive and methodological review. *Journal of Marital and Family Therapy, 9,* 239–258.

Stewart, J.R., Schwebel, A.I., & Fine, M.A. (1986). The impact of custodial arrangements on the adjustment of recently divorced fathers. *Journal of Divorce, 9,* 55–65.

Strauss, J.B., & McGann, S. (1987). Building a network for children of divorce. *Social Work in Education, 9,* 91–105.

Tamir, L. (1982). *Men in their forties: The transition to middle age.* New York: Springer.

Tedder, S.L., & Scherman, A. (1987). Counseling single fathers. In M. Scher, M. Stevens, G. Good, & G.A. Eichenfield (Eds.), *Handbook of counseling and pyschotherapy with men* (pp. 265–277). Newbury Park, CA: Sage.

Tedder, S.L., Scherman, A., & Sheridan, K.M. (1984). Impact of group support on divorce adjustment of single custodial fathrs. *American Mental Health Counselors Association Journal, 6,* 180–189.

U.S. Bureau of the Census. (1987). *Current population reports: Child support and alimony, 1985.* Series P-23, No. 152. Washington, DC: U.S. Government Printing Office.

Vail, L.O. (1979). *Divorce: The man's complete guide to winning.* New York: Sovereign.

Wallerstein, J.S., & Blakeslee, S. (1989). *Second chances: Men, women, and children a decade after divorce.* New York: Ticknor & Fields.

Wallerstein, J.S., & Kelly, J.B. (1980). *Surviving the breakup: How children cope with divorce.* New York: Basic Books.

Weiss, R.S. (1975). *Marital separation.* New York: Basic Books.

Weitzman, L.J. (1981). *The marriage contract: Spouses, lovers, and the law.* New York: Free Press.

Weitzman, L.J. (1985). *The divorce revolution: The unexpected social and economic consequences for women and children in America.* New York: Free Press.

Wright, D.W., & Price, S.J. (1986). Court-ordered support payments: The effect of the former spouse relationship on compliance. *Journal of Marriage and the Family, 48,* 869–874.

Chapter 9: Gay and Bisexual Men: Developing a Healthy Identity

American Psychiatric Association. (1980). *Diagnostic and statistical manual of mental disorders, Third edition.* Washington, DC: Author.

Bell, A., & Weinberg, M., (1978). *Homosexualities: A study of diversity among men and women.* New York: Simon & Schuster.

Brown, L. (1988). New voices and visions, Toward a lesbian and gay paradigm for psychology. *Division 44 Newsletter, 4*(3).

Burgess, E.W. (1949). The sociologic theory of psychosexual behavior. In P.H. Hock, & J. Zubin (Eds.), *Psychosexual development in health and disease*. New York: Grune & Stratton.

Campbell, J. (1988). *The power of myth*. New York: Doubleday.

Coleman, E. (Ed.). (1988). Chemical dependency and intimacy dysfunction. Special issue of *Journal of Chemical Dependency Treatment, 1*(1).

Dorn, W. (1989). *Let grieve and let live, The right to feel good about one's self, A final position*. Paper presented to the faculty of the Human Development Program of the Graduate Center, St. Mary's College of Winona, Minneapolis, MN, for the MA degree.

Egendorf, A. (1986). *Healing from the war, Trauma and transformation after Vietnam*. Boston: Shambhala.

Fortunato, J. (1982). *Embracing the exile*. New York: Harper & Row.

Friedman, R. (1988). *Male homosexuality, A contemporary psychoanalytic perspective*. New Haven, CT: Yale University Press.

Gonsiorek, J. (Ed.). (1982). *Homosexuality and psychotherapy, A practitioner's handbook of affirmative models*. New York: Haworth Press.

Grace, J. (1977, November). *Gay despair and the loss of adolescence: A new perspective on same sex preference and self esteem*. An address presented to the National Association of Social Workers, Las Vegas, NV.

Hanley-Hagenbruck, P. (1989). Psychotherapy and the coming out process. *Journal of Gay and Lesbian Psychotherapy, 1*(1).

Kinsey, A. (1948). *Sexual behavior in the human male*. Philadelphia: Saunders.

Klein, F. (1978). *The bisexual option*. New York: Arbor House.

Martin, A.D. (1984). The emperor's new clothes: Modern attempts to change sexual orientation. In E. Hetrick, & T. Stein (Eds.), *Psychotherapy with homosexuals* (pp. 24–57). Washington, DC: American Psychiatric Press.

Mattison, A., & McWhirter, D. (1984). *The male couple*. New York: Prentice Hall.

Money, J. (1987). Sin, sickness, or status? Homosexual gender identity and psychoneuroendocrinology. *American Psychologist, 42*(4), 384–399.

Schumacher, E.F. (1977). *A guide for the perplexed*. New York: Harper & Row.

Stein, T., & Cohen, C. (1986). *Contemporary perspectives on psychotherapy with lesbians and gay men*. New York: Plenum Press.

Chapter 10: Black Male Development: Counseling the "Native Son"

Cordes, C. (1985, January). Black males face high odds in a hostile society. *APA Monitor*, pp. 9–11, 27.

Cross, A. (1974). The Black experience: Its importance in the treatment of Black clients. *Child Welfare, 52*, 158–166.

Danish, S.J. (1980). Life-span human development and intervention: A necessary link. *Counseling Psychologist*, *9*, 40–43.

Fletcher, E., Glover, M., Robinson, S., & Chase, J. (Composers), & Grand Master Flash and the Furious Five (Recording Artists). (1982). The message, from the album *The message* (Recording No. VID-235-A-19). Englewood, NJ: Sugar Hill Records.

Gary, L.E. (1981). (Ed.). *Black men*. Beverly Hills, CA: Sage.

Gayle, A. (1971). *The Black aesthetic*. Garden City, NY: Doubleday.

Genovese, E. (1974). The slave family, women—a reassessment of matriarchy, emasculation, weakness. *Southern Voices*, *1*, 9–16.

Gibbs, J.T. (1984). Black adolescents and youth: An endangered species. *American Journal of Orthopsychiatry*, *54*, 6–21.

Goldberg, H. (1976). *The hazards of being male: Surviving the myth of masculine privilege*. New York: New American Library.

Grant, M. (Composer), & Wilkerson, A. (Recording Artist). (1972). My name is man. From the album, *Don't bother me I can't cope* (Recording No. PD-6013). New York: Polydor.

Grier, W.H., & Cobbs, P.M. (1968). *Black rage*. New York: Basic Books.

Hall, L.K. (1981). Social systems and coping patterns. In L.E. Gary (Ed.), *Black men*. Beverly Hills, CA: Sage.

Hansberry, L. (1961). *A raisin in the sun* [Film]. Burbank, CA: Columbia Pictures.

Hansberry, L. (1988). *A raisin in the sun* [Television Production]. Los Angeles, CA: NBLA Productions.

Harper, F. (1973). What counselors must know about the social sciences of Black Americans. *Journal of Negro Education*, *42*, 109–116.

Hernton, C. (1965). *Sex and racism in America*. New York: Grove.

Hilliard, A.G. (1985). A framework for focused counseling on the African American man. *Journal of Non-White Concerns in Personnel and Guidance*, *13*, 72–78.

June, L.N. (1986). Enhancing the delivery of mental health and counseling services to Black males: Critical agency and provider responsibilities. *Journal of Multicultural Counseling and Development*, *14*, 39–45.

Larrabee, M.J. (1986). Helping reluctant Black males: An affirmation approach. *Journal of Multicultural Counseling and Development*, *14*, 25–38.

Leavy, W. (1983, August). Is the Black male an endangered species? *Ebony*, pp. 40–49.

Louis, E.T. (1985, March). Black male unemployment. *Essence*, pp. 99–100, 103, 138, 140.

McGhee, J.D. (1984). *Running the gauntlet: Black men in America*. New York: National Urban League.

McNatt, R. (1984, January). The first annual economic outlook for Black America. *Black Enterprise*, pp. 28–39.

Majors, R., & Nikelly, A. (1983). Serving the Black minority: A new direction for psychotherapy. *Journal of Non-White Concerns in Personnel and Guidance*, *11*, 142–151.

Nobles, W.W. (1980). African philosophy: Foundations for Black psychology. In R.L. Jones (Ed.), *Black psychology* (2nd ed.) (pp. 23–26). New York: Harper & Row.

Nyx, J., & Gaye, M. (Composers), & Gaye, M. (Recording Artist). (1971). What's happening brother? From the album, *What's going on?* (Recording No. Hs-1867). Detroit: Motown Record Corp.

Pasteur, A.B., & Toldson, I.L. (1982). *Roots of soul: The psychology of Black expressiveness.* Garden City, NY: Anchor Press/Doubleday.

Pleck, J.H., & Sawyer, J. (Eds.). (1974). *Men and masculinity.* Englewood Cliffs, NJ: Prentice-Hall.

Poussaint, A.F. (1982, August). What every Black woman should know about Black men. *Ebony,* pp. 36–41.

Rappaport, J. (1977). *Community psychology: Values, research, and action.* New York: Holt, Rinehart & Winston.

Shange, N. (1975). *For colored girls who have considered suicide when the rainbow is enuf.* New York: Macmillan.

Staples, R. (1978). Masculinity and race: The dual dilemma of Black men. *Journal of Social Issues, 34,* 169–183.

Staples, R. (1983). *Black masculinity: The Black male's role in American society.* San Francisco: Black Scholar Press.

Taylor, R.L. (1977). Socialization to the Black male role. In D.Y. Wilkinson, & R.L. Taylor (Eds.), *The black male in America: Perspectives on his status in contemporary society* (pp. 1–6). Chicago: Nelson-Hall.

Thomas, A., & Sillen, S. (1972). *Racism & psychiatry.* Secaucus, NJ: The Citadel Press.

Toldson, I., & Pasteur, A. (1972). Soul music: Techniques for therapeutic intervention. *Journal of Non-White Concerns in Personnel and Guidance, 1,* 31–39.

Vontress, C.E. (1971). *Counseling Negroes.* New York: Houghton Mifflin.

White, J.L. (1980). Toward a Black psychology. In R.L. Jones (Ed.), *Black psychology* (2nd ed.) (pp. 5–12). New York: Harper & Row.

Whitfield, N., & Strong, B. (Composers), & The Temptations (Recording Artists). (1983). Pappa was a rolling stone. From the album, *The Motown story* (Recording No. 6048ML5). Hollywood, CA: Motown Record Corp.

Wilkinson, D.Y., & Taylor, R.L. (1977). *The Black male in America: Perspectives on his status in contemporary society.* Chicago: Nelson-Hall.

Wright, R. (1940). *Native son.* New York: Harper & Row.

Wright, R. (1986). *Native son.* [Film]. Hollywood CA: Diane Silver Productions.

Chapter 11: Exploring the Macho Mystique: Counseling Latino Men

Alcoholics Anonymous World Services, Inc. (1976). *Alcoholics anonymous.* New York: Author.

Aramoni, A. (1972, January). Machismo. *Psychology Today,* pp. 69–72.

Boszormenyi-Nagy, I., & Spark, G. (1984). *Invisible loyalties*. New York: Brunner/Mazel.

Cromwell, R., & Ruiz, R. (1979). The myth of macho dominance in decision making within Mexican and Chicano families. *Hispanic Journal of Behavioral Sciences, 1*(4), 355–373.

Davis, K., & Chavez, V. (1985). Hispanic househusbands. *Hispanic Journal of Behavioral Sciences, 7,* 317–322.

De La Cancela, V. (1986). A critical analysis of Puerto Rican machismo: Implications for clinical practice. *Psychotherapy, 23*(2), 291–296.

Farrelly, F., & Brandsma, J. (1974). *Provocative therapy*. San Francisco: Shields.

Figueroa-Torres, J., & Pearson, R. (1979). Effects of structured learning therapy upon self-control of aggressive Puerto Rican fathers. *Hispanic Journal of Behavioral Sciences, 1*(4), 345–354.

Fishman, H.C., Stanton, M.D., & Rosman, B. (1982). Treating families of adolescent drug abusers. In M.D. Stanton, T. Todd, & Associates (Eds.), *The family therapy of drug abuse and addiction* (pp. 335–357). New York: Guilford Press.

Gutierrez, F. (1985). Bicultural personality development: A process model. In E. Garcia, & R. Padilla (Eds.), *Advances in bilingual education research* (pp. 96–124). Tucson: University of Arizona Press.

Gutierrez, F. (1981). *A process model of bicultural personality development*. Unpublished dissertation, Boston University, Boston, MA.

Levine, E., & Padilla, A. (1980). *Crossing cultures in therapy: Pluralistic counseling for the Hispanic*. Monterey, CA: Brooks/Cole.

Malgady, R., Rogler, L., & Costantino, G. (1987). Ethno-cultural and linguistic bias in mental health evaluation of Hispanics. *American Psychologist, 42*(3), 228–234.

Montalvo, B., & Gutierrez, M. (1984, July/August). The mask of culture. *Family Therapy Networks*, pp. 42–46.

Panitz, D., McGonchie, R., Sauber, S., & Fonseca, J. (1983). The role of machismo and the Hispanic family in the etiology and treatment of alcoholism in Hispanic American males. *American Journal of Family Therapy, 11*(1), 31–44.

Ruiz, R. (1981). Cultural and historical perspective in counseling Hispanics. In D.W. Sue (Ed.), *Counseling the culturally different: Theory and practice* (pp. 186–214). New York: Wiley.

Ruiz, R., Casas, J.M., & Padilla, A. (1977). *Culturally relevant behavioristic counseling*. Spanish Speaking Mental Health Research Center, Occasional Paper Number 5. Los Angeles: University of California at Los Angeles.

Valdes, L., Baron, A., & Ponce, F. (1987). Counseling Hispanic men. In M. Scher, M. Stevens, G. Good, & G. Eichenfield (Eds.), *Handbook of counseling & psychotherapy with men* (pp. 203–217). Newbury Park, CA: Sage.

Wegscheider, S. (1981). *Another Chance: Hope and health for the alcoholic family*. Palo Alto, CA: Science and Behavior Books.

Weisinger, H. (1985). *Dr. Weisinger's anger work-out book*. San Francisco: Volcano Press.

Whitfield, C. (1987). *Healing the child within: Discovery and recovery for adult children of dysfunctional families*. Pompano Beach, FL: Health Communications.

Chapter 12: Culture in Transition: Counseling Asian-American Men

Abbott, K.A. (1976). Culture change and the persistence of the Chinese personality. In G. DeVos (Ed.), *Responses to change: Society, culture, and personality* (pp. 87–119). New York: Van Nostrand.

Bourne, P.G. (1975). The Chinese student: Acculturation and mental illness. *Psychiatry, 38,* 269–277.

Conner, J.W. (1975). Value changes in third generation Japanese-Americans. *Journal of Personality Assessment, 39,* 597–600.

Fukuyama, M.A., & Greenfield, T.K. (1983). Dimensions of assertiveness in an Asian-American student population. *Journal of Counseling Psychology, 30,* 429–432.

Jung, M. (1984). Structural family therapy: Its application to Chinese families. *Family Process, 23,* 365–374.

Kinzie, J.D. (1985). Overview of clinical issues in the treatment of Southeast Asian refugees. In T.C. Owan (Ed.), *Southeast Asian mental health* (pp. 113–136). Washington, DC: NIMH.

Kitano, H.H.L. (1989). A model for counseling Asian Americans. In P.B. Pedersen, J.G. Draguns, W.L. Lonner, & J.E. Trimble (Eds.), *Counseling across cultures* (pp. 139–151). Honolulu: University of Hawaii Press.

Lambert, R.G., & Lambert, M.T. (1984). The effect of role preparation for psychotherapy on immigrant clients seeking mental health in Hawaii. *Journal of Community Psychology, 12,* 263–275.

Li-Repac, D. (1980). Cultural influences on clinical perception: A comparison between Caucasian and Chinese-American therapists. *Journal of Cross-Cultural Psychology, 11,* 327–342.

Nishio, K., & Bilmes, M. (1987). Psychotherapy with Southeast Asian American clients. *Professional Psychology: Research and Practice, 18,* 342–346.

Nguyen, S.D. (1985). Mental health services for refugees and immigrants in Canada. In T.C. Owan (Ed.), *Southeast Asian mental health: Treatment prevention, services, training, and research* (pp. 261–281). Washington, DC: NIMH.

Pang, V.O., Mizokawa, D.T., Morishima, J.K., & Olstad, R.G. (1985). Self concepts of Japanese-American children. *Journal of Cross-Cultural Psychology, 16,* 99–109.

Sue, D., Ino, S., & Sue, D.M. (1983). Nonassertiveness of Asian-Americans: An inaccurate assumption? *Journal of Counseling Psychology, 30,* 581–588.

Sue, D.W., & Frank, A.C. (1973). A typological approach to the psychological study of Chinese and Japanese American college males. *Journal of Social Issues, 29,* 129–148.

Sue, D.W., & Kirk, B.A. (1973). Differential characteristics of Japanese-American college students. *Journal of Counseling Psychology, 20,* 142–148.

Sue, S., & Morishima, J.K. (1982). *The mental health of Asian Americans.* San Francisco: Jossey-Bass.

Sue, S., & Zane, N.W.S. (1985). Academic achievement and socioemotional adjustment among Chinese university students. *Journal of Counseling Psychology, 32,* 570–579.

Tsui, P., & Schultz, G.L. (1985). Failure of rapport: Why psychotherapeutic engagement fails in the treatment of Asian clients. *American Journal of Orthopsychiatry, 55,* 561–569.

White, G.M. (1982). The role of cultural explanations in "somatization" and "psychologization." *Social Science and Medicine, 16,* 1519–1530.

Chapter 13: A Personal Perspective on Working With Men in Groups

Becker, E. (1973), The denial of death. New York: The Free Press.

Berstein, J. (1987). In L. Mahdi, S. Foster, & M. Little (Eds.), *Betwixt & between.* La Salle, IL: Open Court.

Henderson, J. (1964). Thresholds of initiation. Middletown, CT: Wesleyan University Press.

Stein, M. (1983). In midlife. Dallas: Spring Publications.

Tiger, L. (1970). Men in groups. New York: Vintage Books.

Chapter 14: Helping Men Become More Emotionally Expressive: A Ten-Week Program

Bly, R. (1988). *Iron John and the male mode of feeling.* Seattle, WA: Limbus.

Bolton, R. (1985). *People skills.* New York: Bantam Books.

David, D.S., & Brannon, R. (1976). *The forty-nine percent majority: The male sex role.* Reading, MA: Addison-Wesley.

Davidson, B., Balswick, J., & Halverson, C. (1983). Affective self-disclosure and marital adjustment: A test of equity theory. *Journal of Marriage and the Family, 45,* 93–102.

Fasteau, M.F. (1975). *The male machine.* New York: Dell.

Fein, L.G. (1963). The use of psychodrama to strengthen self concepts of student nurses. *Group Psychotherapy, 16,* 161–163.

Friedman, H.S., Prince, L.M., Riggio, R.E., & Di Matteo, M.R. (1980). Understanding and assessing nonverbal expressiveness: The affective communication test. *Journal of Personality and Social Psychology, 39,* 333–351.

Gaines, R. (1973). *The effects of two types of anger expression on target person's subsequent aggression.* Unpublished doctoral dissertation, University of North Carolina, Chapel Hill.

Goldberg, H. (1976). *The hazards of being male.* New York: New American Library.

Hokanson, J.R., Willers, K.R., & Koropsak, R. (1968). The modification of autonomic responses during aggressive interchange. *Journal of Personality, 36,* 186–404.

Moore, D. (1984). *An investigation of changes in affective expressiveness in men as a result of participation in a multimodal psychological intervention.* Unpublished doctoral dissertation, University of Minnesota, Minneapolis.

Moore, D., & Haverkamp, B.E. (1989). Measured increases in male emotional expressiveness following a structured group intervention. *Journal of Counseling and Development, 67*, 513–517.

Nichols, J. (1975). *Men's liberation: A new definition of masculinity.* New York: Penguin Books.

O'Neil, J.M. (1981). Male sex-role conflicts, sexism, and masculinity: Psychological implications for men, women, and the counseling psychologist. *Counseling Psychologist, 9*, 61–80.

O'Neil, J.M. (1982). Gender and sex role conflict and strain in men's lives: Implications for psychiatrists, psychologists, and other human service providers. In K. Solomon & N. Levy (Eds.), *Men in transition: Theory and therapy* (pp. 5–44). New York: Plenum Press.

Rabinowitz, F.E., & Cochran, S.V. (1987). Counseling men in groups. In M. Scher, M. Stevens, G. Good, & G.A. Eichenfield. *Handbook of counseling and pychotherapy with men* (pp. 51–67). New York: Sage.

Stevens, J.O. (1971). *Awareness.* Ogden, UT: Real People Press.

Additional Resources

Karsk, R., & Thomas, B. (1987). *Working with men's groups.* Duluth, MN: Whole Person Associates.

Osherson, S. (1987). *Finding our fathers.* New York: Fawcett.

Pruett, K. (1987). *The nurturing father: Journey toward the complete man.* New York: Warner.

Chapter 15: Treating Men Who Batter: A Group Approach

Bankovics, G. (1984). *A manual for the group treatment of batterers.* Unpublished manuscript.

Bauer, C., & Ritt, L. (1983). Wife-abuse, late Victorian English feminists, and the legacy of Frances Power Cobbe. *International Journal of Women's Studies, 6*, 195–207.

Carlson, B.E. (1984). Children's observations of interpersonal violence. In A.R. Roberts (Ed.), *Battered women and their families.* New York: Springer.

Davidson, T. (1977). Wifebeating: A recurring phenomenon throughout history. In M. Roy (Ed.), *Battered women: A psychological study of domestic violence.* New York: Van Nostrand Reinhold.

Edleson, J.L. (1984). Working with men who batter. *Journal of Social Work, 29*, 237–242.

Fitch, F.J., & Papantonio, A. (1983). Men who batter: Some pertinent characteristics. *The Journal of Nervous and Mental Disease, 171*, 190–192.

Ganley, A.L., & Harris, L. (1978, August). *Domestic violence: Issues in designing and implementing programs for male batterers.* Paper presented at the meeting of the American Psychological Association, Toronto.

Gelles, R.J. (1980). Violence in the family: A review of research in the seventies. *Journal of Marriage and the Family, 42,* 873–885.

Herman. J.L. (1986). Histories of violence in an outpatient population: An exploratory study. *American Journal of Orthopsychiatry, 56,* 137–141.

Jaffe, P., Wolfe, D.A., Telford, A., & Austin, G. (1986). The impact of police charges in incidents of wife abuse. *Journal of Family Violence, 1,* 37–49.

Labell, L.S. (1979). Wife abuse: A sociological study of battered women and their mates. *Victimology, 4,* 258–267.

Reilly, P., & Grusznski, R. (1984). A structural didactic model for men for controlling family violence. *International Journal of Offender Therapy and Comparative Criminology, 28*(3), 223–235.

Rosenbaum, A., & O'Leary, K.D. (1981). Children: The unintended victims of marital violence. *American Journal of Orthopsychiatry, 51*(4), 692–699.

Roy, M. (Ed.). (1982). *The abusive partner. An analysis of domestic battering.* New York: Van Nostrand Reinhold.

Straus, M.A. (1976). Sexual inequality, cultural norms and wife-beating. *Victimology, 1*(1), 54–70.

Straus, M.A., Gelles, R.J., & Steinmetz, S.K. (1980). *Behind closed doors: Violence in the American family.* Garden City, NY: Doubleday.

Ulbrich, P., & Huber, J. (1981). Observing parental violence: Distribution of effects. *Journal of Marriage and the Family, 43,* 623–631.

Chapter 16: Counseling Suicidal Men

Backer, B.A., Hannon, N., & Russell, N.A. (1982). *Death and dying: Individuals and institutions.* New York: Wiley.

Beck, A.T., Steer, R.A., Kovacs, M., & Garrison, B. (1985). Hopelessness and eventual suicide: A 10-year study of patients hospitalized with suicidal ideation. *American Journal of Psychiatry, 142,* 559–563.

Bobele, M. (1987). Therapeutic interventions in life-threatening situations. *Journal of Marital and Family Therapy, 13*(3), 225–239.

Breed, W. (1972). Five components of a basic suicide syndrome. *Life-Threatening Behavior, 2,* 3–13.

Cohen, F.L., & Durham, J.D. (1986). Men's health. *The Nursing Clinics of North America, 21*(1), 15–83.

Corey, G., Corey, M.S., & Callanan P. (1988). *Issues and ethics in the helping professions* (3rd ed.). Pacific Grove, CA: Brooks/Cole.

Cutter, F. (1983). *Suicide prevention triangle* (Report No. CG 017 875). Morro Bay, CA: Triangle Books. (ERIC Document Reproduction Service No. ED 251 747)

Dreyfus, E.A. (1979). Counseling the divorced father. *Journal of Marital and Family Therapy, 5*(4), 79–85.

Farberow, N.L., & MacKinnon, D. (1975). Prediction of suicide: A replication study. *Journal of Personality Assessment, 39,* 497–501.

Gove, W.R. (1972). Sex, marital status, and suicide. *Journal of Health and Social Behavior, 13,* 204–213.

Hawton, K. (1982). Attempted suicide in children and adolescents. *Journal of Child Psychology and Psychiatry and Allied Disciplines, 23*(4), 497–503.

Jarvis, G.K., & Boldt, M. (1980). Suicide in later years. *Essence, 4*(3), 145–158.

Joffe, R.T., Offord, D.R., & Boyle, M.H. (1988). Ontario child health study: Suicidal behavior in youth aged 12–16 years. *American Journal of Psychiatry, 145*(11), 1420–1423.

Kobasa, S.C. (1979). Stressful life events and health: An inquiry into hardiness. *Journal of Personality and Social Psychology, 37,* 1–11.

Kobasa, S.C., Maddi, S.R., & Kahn, S. (1982). Hardiness and health: A prospective study. *Journal of Personality and Social Psychology, 42,* 168–177.

Lester, G., & Lester, D. (1971). *Suicide: The gamble with death.* Englewood Cliffs, NJ: Prentice-Hall.

Linehan, M.M., Goodstein, J.L., Nielsen, S.L., & Chiles, J.A. (1983). Reasons for staying alive when you are thinking of killing yourself: The reasons for living inventory. *Journal of Consulting and Clinical Psychology, 51*(2), 276–286.

Maier, S.F., & Seligman, M.E.P. (1976). Learned helplessness: Theory and evidence. *Journal of Experimental Psychology: General, 195,* 3–46.

McAnarney, E.R. (1979). Adolescent and young adult suicide in the United States—A reflection of societal unrest? *Adolescence, 14*(56), 765–774.

McCartney, J.R. (1978). Suicide vs. right to refuse treatment in the chronically ill. *Psychosomatics, 19,* 548–551.

McIntosh, J.L., & Santos, J.F. (1981). Suicide among minority elderly: A preliminary investigation. *Suicide and Life-Threatening Behavior, 11*(3), 151–166.

Miller, M. (1979). A review of the research on geriatric suicide. *Death Studies, 3,* 283–296.

Moore, P.S., & Lewis, D.B. (Ed.). (1986). *Suicide. Useful information on . . .* (Report No. CG 019 962). Rockville, MD: National Institute on Alcohol and Alcoholism. (ERIC Document Reproduction Service No. ED 283 073)

Petrie, K., & Chamberlain, K. (1983). Hopelessness and social desirability as moderator variables in predicting suicidal behavior. *Journal of Consulting and Clinical Psychology, 51*(4), 485–487.

Reinhart, G.R., & Lindea, L.L. (1983). Suicide by industry and occupation: A structural-change approach. *Suicide and Life-Threatening Behavior, 12*(1), 34–45.

Rich, C.L., Ricketts, J.E., Fowler, R.C., & Young, D. (1988). *American Journal of Psychiatry, 145*(6), 718–722.

Seligman, M.E.P. (1975). *Helplessness: On depression, development, and death.* San Francisco: Freeman.

Shneidman, E.S. (1985a). *Definition of suicide.* New York: Wiley.

Shneidman, E.S. (1985b, August 23). *Ten commonalities of suicide and some implications for public policy* (Report No. CG 018 734). Los Angeles, CA: 93rd Convention of the American Psychologicl Association. (ERIC Document Reproduction Service No. ED 264 506)

Taylor, S.E. (1986). *Health psychology*. New York: Random House.

Wass, H., & Myers, J.E. (1982). Psychosocial aspects of death among the elderly: A review of the literature. *The Personnel and Guidance Journal, 61*(3), 131–137.

Wenz, F.V. (1980). Aging and suicide: Maturation or cohort effect? *International Journal of Aging and Human Development, 11*(4), 297–305.

Additional Resources

Bailey, B.E., and Others. (1984, April 21). *Suicidal ideation across populations.* (Report No. CG 017 907). Austin, TX: Texas University, Hogg Foundation for Mental Health. (ERIC Document Reproduction Service No. ED 251 778)

Bogdaniak, R.C., & Coronado, M.G. (1987, May). *Suicide prevention in special populations* (Report No. CG 1020 558). San Francisco, CA: 20th Annual Meeting of the American Association of Suicidology and International Association for Suicide Prevention. (ERIC Document Reproductive Service No. ED 291 026)

Burger, J.V. (1987). Alan: A case history of a troubled adolescent and his family. *The Pointer, 31*(4), 46–49.

Corsini, R.J., & Wedding, D. (1989). *Current psychotherapies* (4th ed.). Itasca, IL: Peacock.

Crase, D. (1981). *Selected resources on suicide: Causes and prevention* (Report No. CG 016 081). (ERIC Document Reproductive Service No. ED 219 658)

Davis, R. (1982). Black suicide and social support systems: An overview and some implications for mental health practitioners. *Phylon, 43*(4), 307–314.

Domino, G., Moore, D., Westlake, L., & Gibson, L. (1982). Attitudes toward suicide: A factor analytic approach. *Journal of Clinical Psychology, 38*(2), 257–262.

Fyer, M.R., Frances, A.J., Sullivan, T., Hunt, S.W., & Clarkin, J. (1988). *American Journal of Psychiatry, 145*(6), 737–739.

Hendin, H. (1982). *Suicide in America*. New York: Norton.

Holinger, P.C. (1987). Violent death rates, United States, 1900–1984, by type of mortality, sex and race. In P.C. Holinger (Ed.), *Violent deaths in the United States* (pp. 207–218). New York: Guilford Press.

Holinger, P.C., & Klemen, E.H. (1987). Violent deaths as reflecting self-destructive tendencies. In P.C. Holinger (Ed.), *Violent deaths in the United States* (pp. 123–137). New York: Guilford Press.

Holinger, P.C. & Sandlow J. (1987). Suicide. In P.C. Holinger (Ed.), *Violent deaths in the United States* (pp. 41–55). New York: Guilford Press.

Ishisaka, H.S. (1987). Mental health education: Depression prevention. *Contemporary Education, 59*(1), 42–43.

Leenaars, A.A. (1987). An empirical investigation of Shneidman's formulations regarding suicide: Age and sex. *Suicide and Life-Threatening Behavior, 17*(3), 233–250.

Maris, R.W., & Lazerwitz, B. (1981). *Pathways to suicide: A survey of self-destructive behaviors.* Baltimore, MD: Johns Hopkins University Press.

Mills, R.C., Dunham, R.G., & Alpert, G.P. (1988). Working with high-risk youth in prevention and early intervention programs: Toward a comprehensive wellness model. *Adolescence, 23*(91), 643–660.

Perrone, P.A. (1987). Counselor response to adolescent suicide. *The School Counselor, 35*(1), 51–57.

Rich, C.L., Fowler, R.C., Young, D., & Blenkush, M. (1986). San Diego suicide study: Comparison of gay to straight males. *Suicide and Life-Threatening Behavior, 16*(4), 448–457.

Scheftner, W.A., Young, M.A., Endicott, J., Coryell, W., Fogg, L., Clark, D.C., & Fawcett, J. (1988). Family history and five-year suicide risk. *British Journal of Psychiatry, 153*, 805–809.

Scher, M., Stevens, M., Good, G., & Eichenfield, G.A. (Eds.). (1987). *Handbook of counseling & psychotherapy with men.* Newbury Park, CA: Sage.

Schwartz, A.J., & Reifler, C.B. (1988). College student suicide in the United States: Incidence data and prospects for demonstrating the efficacy of preventive programs. *Journal of American College Health, 37*(2), 53–59.

Seiden, R.H. (1981). Mellowing with age: Factors influencing the nonwhite suicide rate. *International Journal of Aging and Human Development, 13*(4), 265–284.

Snipe, R.M. (1988). Ethical issues in the assessment and treatment of a rational suicidal client. *The Counseling Psychologist, 16*(1), 128–138.

Trout, D.L. (1980). The role of social isolation in suicide. *Suicide and Life-Threatening Behavior, 10*(1), 10–23.

Vandivort, D.S., & Locke, B.Z. (1979). Suicide ideation: Its relation to depression, suicide and suicide attempt. *Suicide and Life-Threatening Behavior, 9*(4), 205–218.

Wenz, F.V. (1984). Household crowding, loneliness, and suicide ideation. *Psychology, A Quarterly Journal of Human Behavior, 21*(2), 25–29.

Willings, D., & Arseneault, M. (1986). Attempted suicide and creative promise. *Gifted Education International, 4*(1), 10–13.

Zeiss, A.M., Zeiss, R.A., & Johnson, S.M. (1980). Sex differences in initiation of and adjustment to divorce. *Journal of Divorce, 4*(2), 21–33.

Chapter 17: Developing a Contemporary Men's Studies Curriculum

Bowles, G., & Duelli-Klein, R. (Eds.) (1983). *Theories of women's studies.* Boston: Routledge & Kegan Paul.

David, D.S., & Brannon, R. (Eds.). (1976). *The forty-nine percent majority: The male sex role.* Reading, MA: Addison-Wesley.

Dubbert, J.L. *A man's place.* (1979). Englewood Cliffs, NJ: Prentice-Hall.

Filene, P.G. (1974). *Him/her/self: Sex roles in modern America.* New York: Harcourt Brace Jovanovich.

Katz, J. *Gay American history: Lesbians and gay men in the U.S.A.* (1976). New York: Crowell.

Kuhn, T.S. (1962). *The structure of scientific revolutions.* Chicago: The University of Chicago Press.

Pleck, E., & Pleck, J. (1980). *The American man.* Englewood Cliffs, NJ: Prentice-Hall.

Chapter 18: A Survey Report: Men Counseling Men

Chesler, P. (1971). Patient and patriarch: Women in the psychotherapeutic relationship. In V. Gornick & B.K. Moran (Eds.), *Woman in sexist society: Studies in power and powerlessness.* New York: Basic Books.

Downey, A.M. (1984). The relationship of sex-role orientation to self-perceived health status in middle-aged males. *Sex-Roles, 11*(3–4), 211–225.

Ehrenreich, B. (1983). *The hearts of men.* Garden City, NY: Doubleday.

Ettkin, L. (1981). Treating the special madness of men. In R.A. Lewis (Ed.), *Men in difficult times: Masculinity today and tomorrow.* Englewood Cliffs, NJ: Prentice-Hall.

Franklin, C. (1984). *The changing definition of masculinity.* New York: Plenum Press.

Goldberg, H. (1976). *The hazards of being male: Surviving the myth of masculinity.* New York: New American Library.

Gove, W.R. (1978). Sex differences in mental illness among adult men and women: An evaluation of four questions raised regarding the evidence on the higher rates of women. *Social Science and Medicine, 12,* 187–198.

Harrison, J. (1978). Warning: The male sex role may be dangerous to your health. *Journal of Social Issues, 34,* 65–86.

Heppner, P.P., & Gonzales, D.S. (1987). Men counseling men. In M. Scher, M. Stevens, G. Good, & G.A. Eichenfield (Eds.), *Handbook of counseling and psychotherapy with men* (pp. 30–38). Newbury Park, CA: Sage.

Ipsaro, A.J. (1986). Male client-male therapist: Issues in a therapeutic alliance [Special Issue: Gender issues in psychotherapy]. *Psychotherapy, 23*(2), 257–266.

Kimmel, M.S. (Ed.). (1987). *Changing men: New directions in research on men and masculinity.* Newbury Park, CA: Sage.

Meinecke, C.E. (1981). Socialized to die younger? Hypermasculinity and men's health. *The Personnel and Guidance Journal, 60,* 241–245.

O'Neil, J.M. (1981). Male sex role conflicts, sexism and masculinity: Psychological implications for men, women and the counseling psychologist. *The Counseling Psychologist, 9,* 61–80.

Pleck, J.H. (1981). *The myth of masculinity.* Cambridge, MA: MIT Press.

Scher, M., Stevens, M., Good, G., & Eichenfield, G.A. (Eds.). (1987). *Handbook of counseling and psychotherapy.* Newbury Park, CA: Sage.

Silverberg, R.A. (1986). *Psychotherapy for men.* Springfield, IL: Charles C Thomas.

Skord, K.G., & Schumacher, B. (1982). Masculinity as a handicapping condition. *Rehabilitation Literature, 43,* 9–10.

Tavris, C., & Pope, D. (1976, March). Masculinity: What does it mean to be a man? *Psychology Today*, pp. 59–67.

Thompson, E.H., & Pleck, J.H. (1986). The structure of male role norms. *American Behavioral Scientist, 29*(5), 531–543.

Thoreson, R.W., Kardash, C.A., Leuthold, D.A., & Morrow, K. (in press). The academic career: Sources of stress, sources of satisfaction. *Higher Education Abstracts*.

Warren, L.W. (1983). Male intolerance of depression: A review with implications for psychotherapy. *Clinical Psychology Review, 3*, 147–156.

Weissman, M.M., & Klerman, G.L. (1977). Sex differences and the epidemiology of depression. *Archives of General Psychiatry, 34*, 98–11.

Werrbach, J., & Gilbert, L.A. (1987). Men, gender, stereotyping, and psychotherapy: Therapists' perceptions of male clients. *Professional Psychology: Research and Practice, 18*(6), 562–566.

Zilbergeld, B. (1978). *Male sexuality: A guide to sexual fulfillment*. Boston: Little, Brown.

Chapter 19: Being a Man Can Be Hazardous to Your Health: Life-Style Issues

Ardell, D. (1977). *High level wellness*. Emmaus, PA: Rodale Press.

Forrester, D. A. (1986). Myths of masculinity. *Nursing Clinics of North America, 21*(1), 15–23.

Johnson, D. (1989, Jan.–Feb.). The loneliness of the male body. *American Health*.

Leafgren, F. (Ed.) (1986). *Developing campus recreation and wellness programs*. San Francisco: Jossey-Bass.

Pelletier, K.R. (1979). *Holistic medicine*. New York: Delacorte Press.

Pelletier, K.R. (1981). *Longevity*. New York: Delacorte Press.

Travis, J.W., & Ryan, S.R. (1981). *The wellness workbook*. Berkeley, CA: Ten Speed Press.

Witkin-Lanoil, G. (1986). Male stress syndrome. *Men's Health, 2*(7), 5.

Additional Resources

Foreman, M.D. (1986). Cardiovascular disease. *Nursing Clinics of North America, 21*(1), 65–73.

Matteson, M.T., & Ivancevich, J.M. (1987). *Controlling work stress*. San Francisco: Jossey-Bass.

Pelletier, K.R. (1978). *Toward a science of consciousness*. New York: Dell.

Siegel, B.S. (1989). *Peace, love, and healing*. New York: Harper & Row.

Chapter 20: The Journey Continues

Dupont, H. (1980). Affective development: Stage and sequence. In R.L. Mosher, (Ed.), *Adolescent development in education*. Berkeley: McCutchan.

Erikson, E.H. (1963). *Childhood and society*. (2nd ed.). New York: Norton.

Gould, R. (1978). *Transformations: Growth and change in adult life*. New York: Simon & Schuster.

Kohlberg, L. (1969). Stage and sequence: The cognitive developmental approach to socialization. In D. Goslin (Ed.), *Handbook of socialization theory and research*. Chicago: Rand McNally.

Levinson, D. (1979). *The seasons of a man's life*. New York: Knopf.

Loevinger, J. (1970). *Ego development*. San Francisco: Jossey-Bass.

Neugarten, B.L. (Ed.). (1968). *Middle age and aging: A reader in social psychology*. Chicago: University of Chicago Press.

Perry, W.G. (1970). *Forms of intellectual and ethical development in the college years*. New York: Holt, Rinehart & Winston.

Piaget, J. (1981). *Intelligence and affectivity: Their relationship during child development*. Palo Alto, CA: Annual Review.

Sheehy, G. (1976). *Passages*. New York: Bantam Books.

Vaillant, G.E. (1977). *Adaptation to life*. Boston: Little, Brown.

MEN'S ISSUES:
A
BIBLIOGRAPHY

**Prepared by
American Association for
Counseling and Development
Committee on Men**

This bibliography was prepared cooperatively by the AACD Committee on Men. We see this bibliography as an evolving document.

Thanks go to the committee members for their work and creativity, to Dave Capuzzi and Brooke Collison for their support, and to Greg Eichenfield and Gary Neal for their cooperation.

Members of the Committee:

Fred Leafgren	Earl Geissler
Richard Thoreson	Vince Ciaramella
Gini Cooper-Watts	Dwight Moore, Chair

CONTENTS

(Note: RIE refers to *Resources in Education*)

General Readings

August, E. (1985). *Men's studies: A selected and annotated interdisciplinary bibliography*. Littleton, CO: Libraries Unlimited.

David, D.S., & Brannon, R. (1976). *The forty-nine percent majority: The male sex role*. Reading, MA: Addison-Wesley.

Farrell, W. (1975). *The liberated man*. New York: Bantam.

Farrell, W. (1986). *Why men are the way they are*. New York: McCraw-Hill.

Fasteau, M.F. (1975). *The male machine*. New York: Dell.

Goldberg, H. (1976). *The hazards of being male*. New York: Signet.

Goldberg, H. (1979). *The new male: From self-destruction to self-care*. New York: Morrow.

Grady, K.E., Brannon, R., & Pleck, J.H. (1979). *The male sex role: A selected and annotated bibliography*. Washington, DC: U.S. Department of Health, Education, and Welfare. NIMH, PLD-07401-77.

Kimmel, M.S. (1987). *Changing men: New directions in research on men and masculinity*. Beverly Hills, CA: Sage.

Maccoby, E., & Jacklin, C. (1974). *The psychology of sex differences*. Stanford, CA: Stanford University Press.

Nichols, J. (1975). *Men's liberation*. New York: Penguin.

O'Neil, J.M. (1981). Male sex role conflicts, sexism, and masculinity: Psychological implications for men, women and the counseling psychologist. *Journal of Counseling Psychology*, *9*, 61–80.

Pleck, J.H. (1982). *The myth of masculinity*. Cambridge, MA: MIT Press.

Pleck, J., & Sawyer, J. (1974). *Men and masculinity*. Englewood Cliffs, NJ: Prentice-Hall.

Scher, M., Stevens, M., Good, G., & Zichenfield, G.A. (1987). *Handbook of counseling and psychotherapy with men*. Beverly Hills, CA: Sage.

Scher, M. (Ed.). (1981). Counseling males [Special issue]. *Personnel and Guidance Journal*, *60*(4).

Solomon, K. and Levy, N.B. (Eds.). (1982). *Men in transition, theory and therapy*. New York: Plenum Press.

Special issue on counseling men. (1978). *Counseling Psychologist*, *7*(4).

Zilbergeld, B. (1978). *Male sexuality*. New York: Bantam Books.

Periodicals

Achilles Heel, 7 St. Mark's Rise, London E8.

Brother, Newsletter of the National Organization for Changing Men, P.O. Box 93, Charleston, IL 61920-0093. For information about NOCM call (815) 432-3010.

Changing Men: Issues In Gender, Sex and Politics, VW YMCA Community Center, 306 N. Brooks, Madison, WI 53715.

Homosexual Counseling Journal.

Men's Studies Review: Contact Martin Acker, 1761 Alder Street, Eugene, OR 94703, (503) 343-1937 or Jim Doyle, P.O. Box 32, Harriman, TN 37748.

Nuturing Today, Nuturing Press, 187 Caselli Avenue, San Francisco, CA 94114, (415) 861-0847.

Sex Roles.

The Men's Journal, P.O. Box 545, Woodacre, CA 94973.

Transitions, Coalition of Free Men, P.O. Box 129, Manhasset, NY 11030.

Black Men

Boyer, J. (1988). The other side of gender equity: Black males in America. *Educational Considerations*, 15–17.

Davis, G., & Watson, G. (1982). *Black life in corporate America.* New York: Anchor Press.

Davis, R. (1981). A demographic analysis of suicide. In L.E. Gary (Ed.), *Black men.* (pp. 179–196). Beverly Hills, CA: Sage.

Gardner, W.E. (1985). Hope: A factor in actualizing the young adult black male. *Journal of Multicultural Counseling and Development, 13*(3).

Gunnings, T.S., & Lipscomb, W.D. (1986). Psychotherapy for black men: A systematic approach. *Journal of Multicultural Counseling and Development, 14*, 17–24.

Johnson, J. (1982, March). Why Black men have the highest cancer rate. *Ebony,* pp. 69–72.

Jones, K. (1986). The black male in jeopardy: A crisis report on the status of the Black American male. *The Crisis, 93*(3).

Lawrence, G.E. (Ed.). (1981). *Black Men.* Beverly Hills, CA: Sage.

Lee, C.C., & Lindsey, C.R. (1985). Black consciousness development: A group counseling model for Black elementary students. *Elementary School Guidance & Counseling, 19,* 228–236.

Majors, R.G. *Cool posse: A new approach toward a systematic understanding and study of black male behavior.* PhD dissertation, Dept.of Education, University of Illinois at Urbana Champaign.

McGhee, J.D. (1984). *Running the gauntlet: Black men in America.* New York: National Urban League.

Patton, J.M. (1981). The Black male's struggle for an education. In L.E. Gary (Ed.), *Black men* (pp. 199–214). Beverly Hills, CA: Sage.

Smith, E.J. (1977). Counseling Black individuals: Some stereotypes. *Personnel and Guidance Journal, 55,* 390–396.

Staples, R. (1982). *Black masculinity.* San Francisco: Black Scholar Press.

Burnout and Stress

Bloom, B.L., Asher, S.J., & White, S.W. (1978). Marital disruption as a stressor: A review and analysis. *Psychological Bulletin, 85,* 867–894.

Brim, O. (1976). Theories of the male mid-life crisis. *The Counseling Psychologist, 6,* 2–9.

Burnett, E.C., & Daniels, J. (1985). The impact of family of origin and stress on interpersonal conflict resolution skills in young adult men. *American Mental Health Counselors Association Journal, 7*(4), 162–171.

Chiampi, J.D. (1982). An investigation of anxiety, depression and family role involvement of adolescent males whose fathers have cardiovascular disability. *Dissertation Abstracts International, 43,* (3-A), 671.

Coddington, R.D., & Troxell, J.R. (1980). The effect of emotional factors on football injury rates: A pilot study. *Journal of Human Stress, 6*(4), 3–5.

Denny, D.R., & Rupert, P.A. (1977). Desensitization and self-control in the treatment of test anxiety. *Journal Counseling Psychology, 4,* 272–280.

Friedman, M., & Rosenman, R. (1974). *Type A behavior and your heart.* Greenwich, CT: Fawcett.

Gary, L.E. & Berry, G.L. (1985). Depressive symptomatology among Black men. Special issue: The Black male: Critical counseling, developmental, and therapeutic issues: II. *Journal of Multicultural Counseling and Development, 13*(3), 121–129.

Gatchel, R.J., Hatch, J.P., Watson, P.J., et al. (1977). Comparative effectiveness of voluntary heart rate control and muscular relaxation as active coping skills for reducing speech anxiety. (1977). *Journal of Consulting Clinical Psychology, 45,* 1093–1100.

Glass, D.C. (1977). *Behavior patterns, stress, and coronary disease.* Hillsdale, NJ: Lawrence Erlbaum Associates.

Hacker, H.M. (1957). The new burdens of masculinity. *Marriage and Family Living, 19,* 227–233.

Hartley, R.E. (1959). Sex role pressures and the socialization of the male child. *Psychological Reports, 5,* 457–468.

Hendin, H., Pollinger, A., Singer, P., & Ulman, R.B. (1981). Meanings of combat and the development of posttraumatic stress disorder. *American Journal of Psychiatry, 138*(11), 1490–1493.

Hurvitz, N. Marital strain in the blue-collar family. In A. Shostak, & W. Gomberg (Eds.), *Blue collar world* (pp. 92–109). Englewood Cliffs, NJ: Prentice-Hall.

James, S.A., LaCroix, A.Z., Kleinbaum, D.G., & Strogatz, D.S. (1984). John Henryism and blood pressure differences among Black men: II. The role of occupational stresssors. *Journal of Behavioral Medicine, 7*(3), 259–275.

Kolodny, R.L. (1984). Get'cha after school: The professional avoidance of boyhood realities. *Social Work With Groups, 7*(4), 21–37.

Krause, N., & Stryker, S. (1984). Stress and well-being: The buffering role of locus of control beliefs. *Social Science & Medicine, 18*(9), 783–790.

Mayer, N. (1978). *The male mid-life crises: Fresh start after 40.* New York: New American Library.

Meichenbaum, D.H., & Cameron, R. (1972). *Stress inoculation: A skills training approach to anxiety management.* Unpublished manuscript, University of Waterloo, Ontario.

Meinecke, C.E. (1981). Socialized to die younger? Hypermasculinity and men's health. *Personnel and Guidance Journal, 60*(4), 241–245.

Robinson, N., & Heller, R.F. (1980). Experience with the Bortner Questionnaire as a measure of Type A behaviour in a sample of UK Families. *Psychological Medicine, 10*(3), 567–571.

Roskies, E. (1980). Considerations in developing a treatment program for the coronary-prone (Type A) behavior pattern. In P. Davidson (Ed.), *Behavioral medicine: Changing health lifestyles* (pp. 299–334). New York: Brunner/Mazel.

Schumacher, S., & Lloyd, C.W. (1981). Physiological and psychological factors in impotence. *Journal of Sex Research, 17*(1), 40–53.

Scott, D.W., Oberst, M.T. & Bookbinder, M.I. (1984). Stress-coping response to genitourinary carcinoma in men. *Nursing Research, 33*(6), 325–329.

Selye, H. (1950). *The physiology and pathology of exposure to stress.* Montreal: Acta.

Siegrist, J. (1984). Threat to social status and cardiovascular risk. 77th World Congress of the International College of Psychosomatic Medicine: Psychosomatic Research and Practice (1983, Hamburg, West Germany). *Psychotherapy & Psychosomatics, 42*(1–4), 90–96.

Sime, W.E., Buell, J.C., & Eliot, R.S. (1980). Cardiovascular responses to emotional stress (quiz interview) in post-myocardial infarction patients and matched control subjects. *Journal of Human Stress, 6*(3), 39–46.

Suinn, R.M. (1975). The cardiac stress management program for Type A patients. *Cardiac Rehabilitation, 5*, 13–16.

Suinn, R.M., & Richardson, F. (1971). Anxiety management training: A nonspecific behavior therapy program for anxiety control. *Behavior Therapy 2*, 498–510.

Suls, J., Becher, M.A., & Mullen, B. (1981). Coronary-prone behavior, social insecurity and stress among college-aged adults. *Journal of Human Stress, 7*(3), 27–34.

Syrotuik, J., & Darcy, C. (1984). Social support and mental health: Direct, protective and compensatory effects. *Social Science & Medicine, 18*(3), 229–236.

Turner, R. (1970). *Strains of masculinity. Family interaction.* New York: Wiley.

Waldron, I. (1976). Why do women live longer than men? *Journal of Human Stress, 2*, 1–13.

Warr, P., & Jackson, P. (1984). Men without jobs: Some correlates of age and length of unemployment. *Journal of Occupational Psychology, 57*(1), 77–85.

Career Change

Bolles, R.N. (1977). *What color is your parachute?* Berkely, CA: Ten Speed Press.

Brim, O. (1976). Theories of the male mid-life crisis. *The Counseling Psychologist, 6*, 2–9.

Gysbers, N.C., & Moore, E.J. (1975). Beyond career development—life career development. *Personnel and Guidance Journal, 53*, 647–652.

Parkinson, T., Bradley, R., & Lawson, G. (1980). Career counseling revisited. *Vocational Guidance Quarterly, 28*, 121–218.

Thomas, L.E. (1980). A typology of mid-life career changes. *Journal of Vocational Behavior, 6*, 173–182.

Changing Roles of Men

Abramowitz, S.I., Abramowitz, C.V., & Moore, D. (1977). Masculine, male, and human: Implementing and evaluating a men's conference. *Professional Psychology, 8*(2), 185–191.

Bly, R. (1982). What men really want, *New Age Journal, 31*.

Bly, R. (1986). *Little book of the human shadow*. Seattle, WA: Limbus.

Brenton, M. (1966). *The American male*.

Brod, H. (1988). *The making of masculinities: The new men's studies*. Winchester, MA: Allen & Unwin.

Chesler, P. (1978). *About men*. New York: Simon & Schuster.

Cohen, J.F. (1979). Male roles in mid-life. *Family Coordinator, 28*, 465–471.

Cooke C. (1978). *The men's survival resource book: On being a man in today's world*. Minneapolis: M.S.R.B. Press.

Diamond, J. (1983). *Inside out: Becoming my own man*. Fifth Wave Press, P.O. Box 9355, San Rafael, CA 94912.

Dittes, J.E. (1985). *The male predicament: On being a man today*. New York: Harper & Row.

Druck, K., & Simmons, J. (1985). *The secrets men keep*. Garden City, NY: Doubleday.

Firestone, R. (Ed.) (1975). *A book of men: Visions of the male experience*. New York: Stonehill.

Foxley, C.H. (1979). *Nonsexist counseling: Helping women and men redefine their roles*. Dubuque, IA: Kendal/Hunt, TX.

Gerzon, M. (1982). *A choice of heroes: The changing face of American manhood*. Boston: Houghton Mifflin.

Hartley, R.E. (1959). Sex role pressures and the socialization of the male child. *Psychological Reports, 5*, 452–468.

Holahan, C.K., & Spence, J.T. (1980). Desireable and undesireable masculine and feminine traits in counseling clients and unselected students. *Journal of Consulting and Clinical Psychology, 48*(2), 300–302.

Hurd, H.T., & Allred, H.F. (1978). Interest in and stereotyping of the secretarial position for males. *Vocational Guidance Quarterly, 26*(3), 255-259.

Kimmel, M. (Ed.) (1986). *Researching male roles*. Beverly Hills, CA: Sage.

Kriegel, L. (1978). *The myth of American manhood*. New York: Dell.

Lewis, R.A. (1981). Men's liberation and the men's movement: Implications for counselors. *Personnel and Guidance Journal, 60*(4), 256–259.

Lewis, R., & Sussman, M. (Eds.). (1986). *Men's changing roles in the family*. New York: Haworth Press.

Lewis, R.A., & Solt, R.E. (1986). *Men in families, Vol. 76*. Beverly Hills, CA: Sage.

Lofaro, G.A., & Reeer, C.W. (1978). Male competition: An issue in counselor training. *Counseling Psychologist, 7*(4), 20–22.

Lyon, H.C. (1977). *Tenderness in strength: From machismo to manhood*. New York: Harper & Row.

Mangan, J., & Walvin, J. (1987). *Manliness and morality: Middle-class masculinity in Britain and America, 1800-1940*. New York: St. Martin's Press.

McCabe, B. (1980, January 27). *Taming macho man: A more sensitive male comes to the screen*. *Boston Globe*.

Montemayor, R. (1978). Men and their bodies: The relationship between body type and behavior. *Journal of Social Issues, 34*(1), 48–64.

Nasper, E.D. (1969). The role of gender in the perception of therapist nurturance and authority: An analogue study. *Dissertation Abstracts International, 46*(5-B).

Olarte, S.W. (1985). Changing gender stereotyped behavior: Role of therapist's personal disclosure. *Journal of the American Academy of Psychoanalysis, 13*(2), 259–269.

Pleck, J.H. (1975). Man to man: Is brotherhood possible? In N.G. Malbin (Ed.), *Old family/ new family: Interpersonal relationships*. New York: Van Nostrand.

Pleck, J.H. (1976). The male sex role: Definitions, problems, and sources of change. *Journal of Social Issues, 32*(3).

Pleck, J.H. (1976). The psychology of sex roles: Traditional and new views. In L.A. Carter & A.F. Scott (Eds.), *Women and men: Changing roles, relationships and perceptions*. New York: Aspen Institute for Humanistic Studies.

Pleck, J.H. (1977). Men's power with women, other men and society: A men's movement analysis. In L.A. Carter & A.F. Scott (Eds.), *Women and men: The consequences of power*. Cincinnati: Office of Women's Studies, University of Cincinnati.

Pleck, J.H., & Brannon, R. (Eds.). (1978). Male roles and the male experience. *Journal of Social Issues, 34*, 155–164.

Pietropinto, A., & Simenaver, J. (1977). *Beyond the male myth*.

Steinmann, A., & Fox, D.J. (1974). *The male dilemma*. New York: Aronson.

Steinmetz, S.K. (1985). Battered husbands: A historical and cross-cultural survey. In, F. Baumli (Ed.), *Men freeing men: Exploding the myth of the traditional male* (pp. 201–213). Jersey City, NJ: New Atlantis Press.

Tavris, C. (1977, January). Men and women report their views on masculinity. *Psychology Today, 10*(8).

Thompson, K. (1982). What men really want: A new age interview with Robert Bly. *New Age, 7*(12).

Wade, L.A., Wade, J.E., & Croteau, J.M. (1983). The man and the male: A creative outreach program on men's roles. *Journal of College Student Personnel, 24*(5), 460–461.

Whitley, B.E. (1979). Sex roles and psychotherapy: a current appraisal. *Psychological Bulletin, 86*(6), 1309–1321.

Counseling and Sex Roles

Averswald, E. (1986). Response to the problem of gender in family therapy theory. *Family Process, 26*(1), 29–31.

Banikiotes, P.G., & Merluzzi, T.V. (1981). Impact of counselor gender and counselor sex role orientation on perceived counselor characteristics. *Journal of Counseling Psychology, 28*(4), 342–348.

Baumli, F. (1985). *Men freeing men: Exploding the myth of the traditional male*. Jersey City, NJ: New Atlantis Press.

Billingsley, D. (1977). Sex bias in psychotherapy: An examination of the effects of client sex, client pathology and therapist sex on treatment planning. *Journal of Consulting and Clinical Psychology, 45*, 250–256.

Broverman, I.K., Broverman, D.M., Clarkson, P.S., Rosenkrantz, S., & Vogel, S.R. (1970). Sex role stereotypes and clinical judgments of mental health. *Journal of Cousulting and Clinical Psychology, 34*(1), 1–7.

Butler, M. (1983). Survey on the professional development of male counseling psychologists. *Counseling Psychologist, 11*(2), 97–99.

Campion, J. (1985). Sexism and the educational psychologist. *Educational Psychology in Practice, 1*(3), 118–119.

Ephraim, N. (1984). Sex role consciousness in male psychologists working with men: A phenomenological inquiry. *Dissertation Abstracts International, 44*(12-B), 3976.

Fong, M.L., & Borders, L.D. (1985). Effect of sex role orientation and gender on counseling skills training. *Journal of Counseling Psychology, 32*(1), 104–110.

Hare-Mustin, R. (1987). The problem of gender in family therapy theory. *Family Process, 26*(1), 15–28.

Hayes, M.M. (1985). Counselor sex-role values and effects on attitudes toward, and treatment of non-traditional male clients. *Dissertation Abstracts International, 45*(9-B), 3072.

Hull, M.B. (1980). Counselors' perceptions of sex role stereotypes. *Dissertation Abstracts International, 41,* 106.

Johnson, R. (1977). *HE: Understanding masculine psychology.* New York: Perennial Library.

Kabacoff, R.I., Marwit, S.J., & Orlofsky, J.L. (1985). Correlates of sex role stereotyping among mental health professionals. *Professional Psyhcology: Research and Practice, 16*(1), 98–105.

Mitchack, J.A. (1978). Occupational sex role stereotypes and social desirability among counselor trainees. *Journal of Counseling Psyhcology, 25*(2), 172–175.

Myhr, R.P. (1977). Sex-role and counselor evaluation. *Dissertation Abstracts International, 38*(6-B), 2873–2874.

Phillips, R.D. (1985). The adjustment of men and women: Mental health professionals' views today. Special issue: Gender roles. *Academic Psychology Bulletin, 7*(2), 253–260.

Phillips, R.D., & Gilroy, F.D. (1985). Sex-role stereotypes and clinical judgments of mental health: The Broverman's findings reexamined. *Sex Roles, 12*(1-2), 179–193.

Pleck, J. (1976). The male sex role: Definitions, problems and sources of change. *Journal of Social Issues, 32,* 155–164.

Ray, D.C., Raciti, M.A., & Ford, C.V. (1985). Ageism in psychiatrists: Associations with gender, certification, and theoretical orientation. *Gerontologist, 25*(5), 496–500.

Ricker, P., & Carmen, E. (Eds.). (1987). *The gender gap in psychotherapy, social realities and psychological processes.* New York: Plenum Press.

Silverberg, R. (1986). *Psychotherapy for men: Transcending the masculine mystique.* Springfield, IL: Charles C Thomas.

Snell, W. J. (1986). The masculine role inventory: Components and correlates. *Sex Roles, 15,* 445–456.

Solomon, K. (1979). Sexism and professional chauvinism in psychiatry. *Psychiatry, 42,* 374–377.

Subich, L.M. (1984). Ratings of counselor expertness, attractiveness, and trustworthiness as a function of counselor sex role and subject feminist orientation. *Sex Roles, 11*(11-12), 1033–1043.

Towson, S.M., Zanna, M.P., & MacDonald, G. (1984–85). Fulfilling prophesy: Sex role stereotypes as expectations for behavior. *Imagination, Cognition, & Personality, 4*(2), 149–160.

Walker, P.W. (1983). Sex-role stereotyping as a factor influencing counselors' advising of black male students to investigate selected allied health professions. *Dissertation Abstracts International, 44*(2-A), 445.

Wentworth, V.R. (1977). An investigation of sex-role stereotype in student counselors' descriptions of the healthy adult man and the healthy adult woman and their responses to hypothetical male and female clients. *Dissertation Abstracts International, 38*(5-A), 2570.

Yogev, S., & Shadish, W.R. (1982). A method for monitoring the impact of sex-role stereotypes on the therapeutic behavior of beginning psychotherapists. *American Journal of Orthopsychiatry, 52*(3), 545–548.

Counselor/Client Relationships

Alexander, J.F., & Abeles, N. (1969). Psychotherapy process: Sex differences and dependency. *Journal of Counseling Psychology, 16*(3), 191–196.

Carlson, N.L. (1981). Male client—female therapist. *Personnel and Guidance Journal, 60*(4), 228–231.

Cayleff, S.E. (1986). Ethical issues in counseling gender, race, and culturally distinct groups. Special issue: Professional ethics. *Journal of Counseling and Development, 64*(5), 345–347.

Daddario, L.J., (1978). Sexual relations between female clients and male therapists. *Dissertation Abstracts International, 38*(10-B), 5007.

Delk, J.L., & Ryan T.T. (1977). A-B status and sex stereotyping among psychotherapists and patients. Toward a model for maximizing therapeutic potential. *Journal of Nervous and Mental Disease, 164*, 253–262.

Edelwich, J., & Brodsky, A. (1984). Sexual dynamics of the client-counselor relationship. Special issues: Alcoholism and sexual dysfunction: Issues in clinical management. *Alcoholism Treatment Quarterly, 1*(3), 99–117.

Ephraim, N. (1984). Sex role consciousness in male psychologists working with men: A phenomenological inquiry. *Dissertation Abstracts International, 44*(12-B), 3976.

Feldstein, J.C. (1979). Effects of counselor sex and sex role and client sex on clients' perceptions and self-disclosure in a counseling analogue study. *Journal of Counseling Psychology, 26*(5), 437–443.

Geer, C.A., & Hurst, J.C. (1976). Counselor-subject sex variables in systematic desensitization. *Journal of Counseling Psychology, 23*(4), 296–301.

Janda, L.H., & Rimm, D.C. (1977). Type of situation and sex of counselor in assertive training. *Journal of Counseling Psychology, 24*(5), 444–447.

Johnson, D.H. (1978). Students' sex preferences and sex role expectancies for counselors. *Journal of Counseling Psychology, 25*(6), 557–562.

McClernan, J.L. (1973). Implications of sexual attraction (feeling) in the counselor-client relationship. *Dissertation Abstracts International, 33*(9-A), 4844.

Moreland, J.R. (1976). Facilitator training for consciousness raising groups in an academic setting. *The Counseling Psychologist, 6*, 66–68.

Morison, J.K., Layton, B., & Newman, J. (1982). Values, ethics, legalities and the family therapist: V. Ethical conflict in clinical decision making: A challenge for family therapists. *Family Therapy Collections, 1*, 75–86.

Nasper, E.D. (1985). The role of gender in the perception of therapist nurturance and authority: An analogue study. *Dissertation Abstracts International, 46*(5-B), 1696.

O'Leary, V.E., & Donoghue, J.M. (1976). Latitudes of masculinity: Reactions to sex-role deviance in men. *Journal of Social Issues, 32*, 155–164.

Peabody, S.A., & Gelso, C.J. (1982). Countertransference and empathy: The complex relationship between two divergent concepts in counseling. *Journal of Counseling Psychology, 29*(3), 240–245.

Robbins, J.H. (1983). Complex triangles: Uncovering sexist bias in relationship counseling. Special issue: Women changing therapy: New assessments, values and strategies in feminist therapy. *Women & Therapy, 2*(2-3), 159–169.

Russell, M.S. (1985). The relationship among sex, sex role and therapist response to client hostility. *Dissertation Abstracts International, 46*(5-B), 147–158.

Sturdivant, S. (1980). *Therapy with women. A feminist philosophy of treatment*, New York: Springer.

Swenson, E.V., & Ragucci, R. (1984). Effects of sex-role stereotypes and androgynous alternatives on mental health judgments of psychotherapists. *Psychological Reports, 54*(2), 475–481.

Thoresen, C.E., Krumboltz, J.D., & Varenhorst, B. (1967). Sex of counselors and models: Effect of client career exploration. *Journal of Counseling Psychology, 14*(6), 503–508.

Walker, E.F., & Stake, J.E. (1978). Changes in preferences for male and female counselors. *Journal of Consulting and Clinical Psychology, 46*(5), 1153–1154.

Zachary, I.G. (1978). The effects of male threat from female competence (MTFC) and client sex-role on empathy levels and clinical judgments of male counselor-trainees. *Dissertation Abstracts International, 39*(2-A), 686.

Developmental Issues and Aging

Brim, O. (1976). Theories of the male mid-life crisis. *The Counseling Psychologist, 6*, 2–9.

Cohen, J.F. (1979). Male roles in mid-life. *Family Coordinator, 28*, 465–471.

Collison, B.B. (1987). Counseling aging men. In M. Scher et al. (Eds.). *Handbook of counseling and psychotherapy with men*. Beverly Hills, CA: Sage.

Drake, C.T. (1977). Effects of the absence of a father and other male models on the development of boys' sex roles. *Developmental Psychology, 13*(5), 537–538.

Foley, J.M., & Murphy, D.M. (1977, November 20). *Sex role identity in the aged*. Presented at the 30th annual meeting of the Gerontological Society, San Francisco, CA.

Fred, B. (1976). *The middle age crisis*. New York: Harper & Row.

Garfinkel, R. (1975). The reluctant therapist. *Geriatrics, 18*, 296–301.

Goldfarb, A. (1971). Group therapy with the old and aged. In H.I. Kaplan, & B.J. Sadock (Eds.), *Comprehensive group therapy* (pp. 623–642). Baltimore: Williams & Wilkins.

Gould, R. (1978). *Transformations*. New York: Simon & Schuster.

Gutmann, D. (1976). Individual adaptation in the middle years. Developmental issues in the masculine mid-life crisis. *Journal of Geriatric Psychiatry, 9*, 41–77.

Gutmann, D. (1987). *Reclaimed powers: Toward a psychology of men and women in later life*. New York: Basic Books.

Gutmann, D., Grunes J., & Griffin B. (1979, November 29). *The clinical psychology of later life: Developmental paradigms*. Presented at the 32nd annual meeting of the Gerontological Society, Washington, DC.

Gysbers, N.C., & Moore, E.J. (1975). Beyond career development-life career development. *Personnel and Guidance Journal, 53*, 647–652.

Hobson, K.G. (1984). The effects of aging on sexuality. *Health and Social Work, 9*(1), 25–35.

Keith, P.M. (1977). An exploratory study of sources of stereotypes of old age among administrators. *Journal of Gerontology, 32*(4), 463–469.

Keith, P.M., & Brubaker, T.H. (1979). Male household roles in later life: A look at masculinity and marital relationships. *Family Coordinator, 28*, 497–502.

Levinson, D.J. (1978). *The seasons of a man's life*. New York: Ballantine.

Mayer, N. (1978). *The male mid-life crises: Fresh start after 40*. New York: New American Library.

McGill, M. (1980). *The 40 to 60 year old male*. New York: Simon & Schuster.

Neugarten, B.L. (1979). Time, age, and the life cycle. *American Journal of Psychiatry, 136*, 887–894.

Peterson, B.H. (1983). Counselling for growth in mid-life. *Australian Journal of Sex, Marriage and Family, 4*(3), 133–141.

Sacher, G.A. (1978). Longevity, aging and death: An evolutionary perspective. *Gerontologist, 18*, 112–119.

Sheely, G. (1977). *Passages*. New York: Bantam Books.

Solomon, K. (1981). The depressed patient: Social antecedents of psychopathologic changes in the elderly. *Journal of the American Geriatrics Society, 29*, 14–18.

Solomon, K. (1984). Psychosocial crises of older men. *Hillside Journal of Clinical Psychiatry, 6*(1), 123–134.

Sparacino, J. (1978–1979). Individual psychotherapy with the aged: A selective review. *International Journal of Aging and Human Development, 9*, 197–220.

Talley, W.M. (1981). Sensitizing counselors to mid-life counselling. *International Journal for the Advancement of Counselling, 4*(2), 101–110.

Thomas, L.E. (1980). A typology of mid-life career changes. *Journal of Vocational Behavior, 16*, 173–182.

Thompson, D. (1980). *As boys become men: Learning new male roles*. Washington, DC: U.S. Department of Education.

Woods, S.M. (1976). Some dynamics of male chauvinism. *Archives of General Psychiatry, 33*, 63–65.

Disabled Client

Balswick, J.O., & Peek, C.W. (1971). The inexpressive male: A tragedy of American society. *The Family Coordinator, 20*, 363–368.

Greenblatt, R.B. (1974). Casanova, Med Aspects Hum. *Sexuality, 8,* 78, 82–84.

Grimes, J.W. (1980). The effects of assertion training on severly disabled students/clients. *Journal of Applied Rehabilitation Counseling, 11,* 36–39.

LeShan, L., & LeShan, E. (1961). Psychiatry and the patient with a limited life span. *Psychiatry, 24,* 318–323.

McKusick, V.A. (1968). Simply inherited disorders. In A.M. Harvey, L.E. Cluff, R.J. Johns, et al. (Eds)., *The principles and practice of medicine* (pp. 447–469). New York: Appleton-Century-Crofts.

Power, P.W. (1979). The chronically ill husband and father: His role in the family. *The Family Coordinator, 28,* 616–621.

Solomon, K. (1981). The depressed patient: Social antecedents of psychopathologic changes in the elderly. *Journal of the American Geriatrics Society, 29,* 14–18.

Wilson, R.N. (1970). *The sociology of health: An introduction.* New York: Random House, pp. 13–32.

Divorce

Ambrose, P., Harper, J., & Pemberton, R. (1983). *Surviving divorce: Men beyond marriage.* Rowman & Allanheld.

Barenbaum, N.B., & Bursik, K. (1985, September). Parental acrimony and children's post-separation adjustment. *RIE.*

Baden, C. (Ed.). *Parenting after divorce.* Wheelock College Center for Parenting Studies, 200 The Riverway, Boston, MA 02215.

Brody, J., & Osborne, G.B. (1980). *The 20-year phenomenon: Men and women talk about the breakup of their long-term marriages.* New York: Simon & Schuster.

Cauhape, E. *Fresh starts: Men and women after divorce.* New York: Basic Books.

Changing family lifestyles: Their effect on children. (1982). Washington, DC: Association for Childhood Education International.

Darling, S. (1980, August). Young women's phenomenological sense of father and parental marital relationship and their relation to paternal loss. *RIE.*

Felton, B.J., Lehmann, S., & Brown, P. & Liberators, P. (1980). The coping function of sex-role attitudes during marital disruption. *Journal of Health & Social Behavior, 21*(3), 240–248.

Galper, M. (1979, August). Co-parenting: Sharing your child equally. A source book for the separated or divorced family. *RIE.*

Gersick, K.E. *Divorced men who receive custody of their children.* New York: Basic Books.

Glick, P.C., & Norton, A.J. (1973). Perspectives on the recent upturn in divorce and remarriage. *Demography, 10,* 301–314.

Honeyman, N.S. (1985). Self-concept incongruence and adjustment in divorced men. *Dissertation Abstracts International, 45*(12-B, Pt 1), 3995.

Jansen, L.S., & Michaels, G.Y. (1985, September). Children's perceptions of their parents: Relationship to child adjustment following divorce. *RIE.*

Katz, R., & Pesach, N. (1985). Adjustment to divorce in Israel: A comparison between divorced men & women. *Journal of Marriage and the Family, 47*(3), 765–771.

Keith, P.M. (1985). Financial well-being of older divorced/separated men & women: Findings from a panel study. *Journal of Divorce, 9*(1), 61–72.

Kerpelman, L. (1983). *Divorce: A guide for men.* South Bend, IN: Icarus.

Keshet, H.F., & Rosenthal, K.M. (1978). Fathering after marital separation. *Social Work, 23*(1), 8–11.

Laufer, R.S., & Gallops, M.S. (1985). Life-course effects of Vietnam combat & abusive violence: Marital patterns. *Journal of Marriage and Family, 47*(4), 839–853.

Levin, R.J. (1980). Toward a developmental theory of the first ten years of marriage, and a strategy of divorce prevention: Perceptions by divorced individuals and married couples about stressors in marriage. *Dissertation Abstracts International. 40*(12): 5842-B. (University Microfilms No. 8013329).

Maxwell, J.W., & Andress, E.L. (1982). Marriage role expectations of divorced men and women. *Journal of Divorce, 5*(4), 55.

Metz, C.V. *Divorce and custody for men.* Garden City, NY: Doubleday.

Mitchell-Flynn, C.L. Problems and coping strategies of urban divorced men at the time of divorce and six months later. *Dissertation Abstracts International,* V46, 09, Sec A, P2570.

Sexton, T.L., Hingst, A.G., & Regan, K.R. (1985). The effect of divorce on the relationship between parental bonding and sexrole identification of adult males. *Journal of Divorce, 9*(1), 17–31.

Snyder, L.M. (1979, November). The deserting nonsupporting father: The scapegoat of family nonpolicy. *RIE.*

Woolley, P. (1980, February). The custody handbook. *RIE.*

Wylder, J. (1982). Including the divorced father in family therapy. *Social Work, 27*(6), 479–482.

Divorce and Parenting

Ambert, A.M. (1982). Differences in children's behavior toward custodial mothers and custodial fathers. *Journal of Marriage and the Family,* 44, 73–86.

Bowman, M.E., & Ahrons, C.R. (1985). Impact of legal custody status on fathers' parenting postdivorce. *Journal of Marriage and the Family, 47*(2), 481–488.

Briggs, B.A., & Walters, C.M. (1985, June). Single-father families: Implications for early childhood educators. *CIJ.*

Dail, P.W. (1986, October). Can fathers "mother"? The nurturing characteristics of single parent fathers. *RIE.*

DeFrain, J.D. (1975, June). A father's guide to parent guides: Review and assessment of the paternal role as conceived in the popular literature. *RIE.*

Gladding, S., & Huber, C. (1984). The position of the single-parent father. *Journal of Employment Counseling, 21*(1), 13.

Greif, G.L. (1985). Single fathers rearing children. *Journal of Marriage and the Family, 47*(1), 185–191.

Guisinger, S., & Schuldberg, D. (1985). *Divorced fathers describe their current and former spouses: An investigation of "splitting."*

Hanson, S.M.H. (1983, April). Single custodial fathers. *RIE.*

Jansen, L.S., & Michaels, G.Y. (1985). *Children's perceptions of their parents: Relationships to child adjustment following divorce.*

Koch, M.A.P., & Lowery, C.R. (1984). Visitation and the noncustodial father. *Journal of Divorce, 8*(2), 47–65.

Leavitt, S.E., & Davis, M. (1981, June). Evaluating the effectiveness of a training program for single-parents. *RIE.*

Melli, M.S. (1986). The changing legal status of the single parent. *Family Relations, 35*(1), 31–35.

Moore, R.T. (1986, August). The androgynous black parent: One answer to the single parent dilemma. *RIE.*

Moreland, J.R. (1983). *Nuclear family break-up as an impetus for male change.*

New Relations: A Film About Fathers & Sons. Fanlight Productions, 47 Halifax St., Boston, MA 02130.

Pichitino, J.P. (1983). Profile of the single father: A thematic integration of the literature. *Personnel and Guidance Journal, 61*(5), 295–299.

Single parent families, Parts 1-4.: U.S. District of Columbia. (1981, May). *RIE.* Eric Doc. #ED19563.

Woody, R.H. (1978). Fathers with child custody. *The Counseling Psychologist, 7*(4), 60–63.

Dual Careers

Arkin, W., & Dobrofsky, L.R. (1978). Shared labor and love: Job sharing couples in academia. *Alternative Lifestyles*, *1*, 492–512.

Astrachan, A. (1986) *How men feel: Their response to women's demands for equality and power.* Garden City, NY: Anchor Press.

Baer, D., & Spicer, C.H. (1984, April). Communication and the dual-career couple: A literature assessment. *RIE*.

Berman, E., Sacks, S., & Lief, H. (1975). The two profession marriage: A new conflict syndrome. *Journal of Sex and Marital Therapy*, *1*, 242–253.

Booth, A. (1977). Wife's employment and husband's stress: A replication and refutation. *Journal of Marriage and the Family*, *39*, 645–650.

Burke, R., & Weir T. (1976). Relationships of wives' employment status to husband, wife and pair satisfaction and performance. *Journal of Marriage and the Family*, *38*, 279–287.

Gappa, J.M. (1981, May). The dual careers of faculty and family: Can both prosper. *RIE*.

Gilbert, L.A. (1985). *Men in dual career families: Current realities and future prospects.* Hillsdale, NJ: Erlbaum.

Hardesty, S.A., & Betz, N.E. (1980). The relationships of career salience, attitudes toward women, and demographic and family characteristics to marital adjustment in dual-career couples. *Journal of Vocational Behavior*, *17*(2), 242–250.

Heckman, N.A., Bryson, R., & Bryson J.B. (1977). Problems of professional couples : A content analysis. *Journal of Marriage and the Family*, *39*, 323–330.

Hood, J., & Golden, C. (1979). Beating time/making time: The impact of work schedules on men's family roles. *Family Coordinator*, 575–582.

Horner, M. (1972). Toward an understanding of achievement related conflicts in women. *Journal of Social Issues*, *28*, 157–175.

Jump, T.L. (1984, August). Dual career families: The interfaces of work, family and the home. *RIE*.

Kassner, M.W. (1981). Will both spouses have careers? Predictors of preferred traditional or egalitarian marriages among university students. *Journal of Vocational Behavior*, *18*(3), 340–355.

Keith, P.M., & Brubaker, T.H. (1979). Male household roles in later life: A look at masculinity and marital relationships. *Family Coordinator*, *28*, 497–502.

Keith, P.M., & Schafer, R.B. (1980). Role strain and depression in two-job families. *Family Relations*, *29*(4), 483–488.

Knowles, E.C. (1980, April 11–12). Dual career couple relationships. An annotated bibliography, for conference presented by the Women's Resources and Research Center, University of California, Davis. UCD-Women's Resources and Research Center Working Paper Series No. 20. *RIE*.

Matthews, J.R., & Matthews, L.H. (1981, April). A survey of dual-career couples in psychology. *RIE*.

Nadelson, T., & Eisenberg L. (1977). The successful professional woman: On being married to one. *American Journal of Psychiatry*, *134*, 1071–1076.

Papenek, H. (1973). Men, women and work: Reflections on the two-person career. *American Journal of Sociology*, *78*, 852–872.

Pleck, J. (1979). Men's family work: Three perspectives and some new data. *Family Coordinator*, *28*, 481–488.

Pleck, J.H. (1985). *Working wives/working husbands.* Newbury Park, CA: Sage.

Rallings, E.M., & Pratto, D.J. (1985). *Two clergy marriages: A special case of dual careers.* Lanham, MD: University Press of America.

Rappoport, R. (1971). *Dual career families.* New York: Penguin Books.

Rice, D.G. (1979). *Dual career marriages.* New York: Free Press.

Skinner, D.A. (1980). Dual-career family stress and coping: A literature review. *Family Relations*, *29*(4), 473–480.

Tauss, V. (1976). Working wives and house husbands. *Journal of Family Counseling*, *4*, 52–55.

Zimmerman, K.W. (1980). Career involvement and job satisfaction as related to job strain and marital satisfaction of teachers and their spouses. *Home Economics Research Journal,* *8*(6), 421–427.

Expressing Feelings

Alberti, R.E., & Emmons, M.L. (1970). *Your perfect right: A guide to assertive behavior.* San Luis Obispo: Impact.

Alberti, R.E., & Emmons, M.L. (1975). *Stand up, speak out, talk back: The key to self-assertive behavior.* New York: Pocket Books.

Allen, J., & Haccoun, D. (1976). Sex differences in emotionality: A multidimensional approach. *Human Relations, 8,* 711–722.

Anderton, C.H., & Heckel, R.V. (1985). Touching behaviors of winners and losers in swimming races. *Perceptual & Motor Skills, 60*(1), 289–290.

Baer, S., Berger, M., & Wright, L. (1979). Even cowboys sing the blues: Difficulties experienced by men trying to adopt nontraditional sex roles and how clinicians can be helpful to them. *Sex Roles, 5,* 191–197.

Balkwell, C., Balswick, J.O., & Balkwell, J. (1978). On black and white family patterns in America: Their impact on the expressive aspect of sex-role socialization. *Journal of Marriage and the Family, 40,* 743–747.

Balswick, J. (1974). Why husbands can't say "I love you." *Woman's Day, 64,* 66, 67, 160.

Balswick, J. (1979). The inexpressive male: Functional conflict and role theory as contrasting explanations. *Family Relations, 28,* 331–336.

Balswick, J. (1980). Types of inexpressive male roles, In R.A. Lewis (Ed.), *Men in difficult times.* New York: Prentice-Hall.

Balswick, J.O., & Avertt, C. (1977). Differences in expressiveness: Gender, interpersonal orientation, and perceived parental expressiveness as contributing factors. *Journal of Marriage and the Family, 38,* 121–127.

Balswick, J.O., & Balkwell, J. (1978). Religiosity, orthodoxy, emotionality. *Review of Religious Research, 19,* 282–286.

Balswick, J.O., & Peek, C.W. (1971). The inexpressive male: A tragedy of American society. *The Family Coordinator, 20,* 363–368.

Barras, J.A. (1985). Male responses to female sexual assertiveness and nonassertiveness in casual and committed relationships. *Dissertation Abstracts International, 45,* (9-B), 3060.

Beck, J.G., & Barlow, D.A. (1986). The effects of anxiety and attentional focus on sexual responding: II. Cognitive and affective patterns in erectile dysfunction. *Behaviour Research and Therapy, 24*(1), 19–26.

Bem, S.L. (1976). Probing the promise of androgyny. In A.G. Kaplan & Bean (Eds.), *Beyond sex-role stereotypes: Readings toward a psychology of androgyny.* Boston: Little, Brown.

Bem, S.L., & Lenney, E. (1976). Sex-typing and avoidance of cross-sex behavior. *Journal of Personality and Social Psychology, 33,* 48–54.

Bem, S.L., Martyna, W., & Watson C. (1976). Sex-typing and androgyny: Further exploration of the expressive domain. *Journal of Personality and Social Psychology, 34,* 1006–1023.

Berman, P.W., & Smith, V.L. (1984). Gender and situational differences in children's smiles, touch, and proxemics. *Sex Roles, 10*(5–6), 347–356.

Berman, S.A. (1985). Men and romantic relationships: A qualitative study of men and intimacy. *Dissertation Abstracts International, 46,* (6-A), 1516.

Blanchard, R., & Steiner. B.W. (1983). Gender reorientation, psychological adjustment, and involvement with female partners in female-to-male transsexuals. *Archives of Sexual Behavior, 12*(2), 149–157.

Booth, A. (1972). Sex and social participation. *American Sociological Review, 37,* 183–193.

Brannon, R., & Juni, S. (1984). A scale for measuring attitudes about masculinity. *Psychological Documents, 14*(1), 6–7.

Brenton, M. (1966). *The American male.* Greenwich, CT: Fawcett.

Brooks-Gunn, J., & Lewis, M. (1979). Why mama and papa? The development of social labels. *Child Development, 50*(4), 1203–1206.

Brooks-Gunn, J., & Matthews, W.S. (1979). *He and she: How children develop their sex-role identify.* Englewood Cliffs, NJ: Prentice-Hall.

Broverman, I.K., Broverman, D.M., Clarkson, P.S., Rosenkrantz, S., & Vogel, S.R. (1970). Sex role stereotypes and clinical judgments of mental health. *Journal of Consulting and Clinical Psychology, 34*(1), 1–7.

Carrier, J.M. (1985). Mexican male bisexuality. Special issue: Bisexualities: Theory and Research. *Journal of Homosexuality, 11*(1–2), 75–85.

Cazenave, N.A. (1984). Race, socioeconomic status, and age: The social context of American masculinity. *Sex Roles, 11*(7–8), 639–656.

Chafetz, J.S. (1974). *Masculine/femine or human.* Itasca, IL: Peacock.

Chelune, G.J. (1978). Nature and assessment of self-disclosing behavior. In P. McReynolds (Ed.), *Advances in psychological assessment IV* (pp. 278–320). San Francisco: Jossey-Bass.

Chesney, N. (1979, September 4). *Cultural and sex differences in the type "A" pattern.* Presented at the annual meeting of the American Psychological Association, New York.

Clark, P.E., & Clark, M.J. (1984). Therapeutic touch: Is there a scientific basis for the practice? *Nursing Research, 33*(1), 37–41.

Cohen, J.F. (1979). Male roles in mid-life. *Family Coordinator, 28*, 465–471.

Cooke, C. (1978). *The men's survival resource book: On being a man in today's world.* Minneapolis: M.S.R.B. Press.

Daher, D. (1981). The loss and search for the peer: A consideration of inferiority feelings in certain male adolescents. *Adolescence, 16*(61), 145–158.

David, D.S., & Brannon, R. (1976). The male sex role: Our culture's blueprint of manhood, and what it's done for us lately. In D.S. Brannon, & R. Brannon (Eds.), *The forty-nine percent majority* (pp. 1–48). Reading, MA: Addison-Wesley.

Davitashvili, D. (1984). The hands, health and healing. *PSI Research, 3*(3–4), 83–87.

Deethardt, J.F., & Hines, D.G. (1983). Tactile communication and personality differences. *Journal of Nonverbal Behavior, 8*(2), 143–156.

Derlaga, V.J., & Chaikin, A.L. (1976). Norms affecting self-disclosure in men and women. *Journal of Consulting and Clinical Psychology, 44*, 376–380.

Donlou, J.N., Wolcott, D.L., Gottlieb, M.S., & Landsverk, J. (1985). Psychosocial aspects of AIDS and AIDS-Related complex: A pilot study. *Journal of Psychosocial Oncology, 3*(2), 39–55.

Dosser, D.A., & Balswick, J.O. (1978, October 19). *Expressive training for emotionally inexpressive males.* Presented at the annual meeting of the National Council on Family Relations, Philadelphia, PA.

Downs, A.C., & Engleson, S.A. (1982). The attitudes toward men scale (AMS): An analysis of the role and status of men and masculinity. *Catalog of Selected Documents in Psychology, 12*(4), 45.

Drescher, V.M., Whitehead, W.E., Morrill, C.E.D., & Cataldo, M.F. (1985). Physiological and subjective reactions to being touched. *Psychophysiology, 22*(1), 96–100.

Dubbert, J.L. (1979). *A man's place: Masculinity in transition.* Englewood Cliffs, NJ: Prentice-Hall.

Duberman, L. (1975). *Explanations for sex role development. Gender and sex in society.* New York: Praeger.

Dunn, C., Bruggen, P., & O'Brian, C. (1982). Touch and action in group therapy of younger adolescents. *Journal of Adolescence, 5*(1), 31–38.

Earls, F. (1976). The fathers (not the mothers): Their importance and influence with infants and young children. *Psychiatry, 39*, 209–226.

Edwards, D.J. (1984). The experience of interpersonal touch during a personal growth program: A factor analytic approach. *Human Relations, 37*(9), 769–780.

Ekman, P. (1972). Universals and cultural differences in facial expressions of emotion, In J.K. Cole (Ed.), *Nebraska Symposium on Motivation* (pp. 207–283). Lincoln: University of Nebraska Press.

Ellis, L.J., & Bentler, P.M. (1973). Traditional sex-determined role standards and sex stereotypes. *Journal of Personality and Social Psychology, 25*(1), 28–34.

Fetsch, R.J., & Sprinkle, R.L. (1982). Stroking treatment effects on depressed 'males.' *Transactional Analysis Journal, 2*, 57–78.

Fensterheim, H., & Baer, J. (1975). *Don't say yes when you want to say no*. New York: Dell.

Fisher, W.A. (1984). Predicting contraceptive behavior among university men: The role of emotions and behavioral intentions. *Journal of Applied Social Psychology, 14*(2), 104–123.

Forisha, B. (1978). *Sex roles and personal awareness*. Morristown, NJ: General Learning Press.

Freund, K., & Blanchart, R. (1983). Is the distant relationship of fathers and homosexual sons related to the sons' erotic preference for male partners, or to the sons' atypical gender identity, or to both? *Journal of Homosexuality, 9*(1), 7–25.

Gaddis, A., & Brooks-Gunn, J. (1985). The male experience of pubertal change. *Journal of Youth & Adolescence, 14*(1), 61–69.

Galassi, M.D., & Galassi, J.P. (1977). *Assert yourself: How to be your own person*. New York: Human Sciences Press.

Gearing, J. (1978). Facilitating the birth process and father-child bonding. *The Counseling Psychologist, 7*(4), 53–56.

Gibson, J.T., Wurst, K.K., & Cannonito, M. (1984). Observations on contact stimulation provided young children in selected areas of Greece, USA, and USSR. *International Journal of Psychology, 19*(3), 233–243.

Giella, P. (1983). Obsessive-compulsiveness and depression in men: Their effects on a stoic worldview. *Dissertation Abstracts International, 43*, (9-B), 3014.

Gillin, S.M. (1984). I 'love' her, I 'love' her not: Male ambivalence in initmate adult relationships. *Dissertation Abstracts International, 45*, (3-B), 1014.

Glass, L.L. (1984). Man's man/ladies' man: Motifs of hypermasculinity. *Psychiatry, 47*(3), 260–278.

Gould, R. (1974). Measuring masculinity by the size of the paycheck. In J. Pleck & J. Sawyer (Eds.), *Men and masculinity*. Englewood Cliffs, NJ: Prentice-Hall.

Grady, K., Brannon, R., & Pleck, J. (1979). *The male sex role: A selected and annotated bibliography*. Rockville, MD: National Institute of Mental Health.

Grand, H.T. (1982). The uncommitted male and his female counterpart. *American Journal of Psychoanalysis, 42*(4), 283–292.

Green, R., Neuberg, D.S., & Finch, S.J. (1983). Sex-typed motor behaviors of 'feminine' boys, conventional masculine boys, and conventionally feminine girls. *Sex Roles, 9*(5), 571–579.

Halle, E. (1979). The abandoned husband: When wives leave. *Psychiatric Opinion, 16*, 18–19, 22–23.

Harford, T.D., Willis, C.H., & Deabler, H.L. (1967). Personality correlates of masculinity-femininity. *Psychological Reports, 21*, 881–884.

Harrigan, J.A. (1985). Self-touching as an indicator of underlying affect and language processes. *Social Science & Medicine, 20*(11), 1161–1168.

Hartley, R.E. (1959). Sex-role pressures and the socialization of the male child. *Psychological Reports, 5*, 457–468.

Heiman, J.R., & Hatch, J.P. (1980). Affective and physiological dimensions of male sexual response to erotica and fantasy. *Basic & Applied Social Psychology, 1*(4), 315–327.

Heiss, J.S. (1962). Degree of intimacy and male-female interaction. *Sociometry, 25*, 197–208.

Heller, M.A., & Boyd, M.E. (1984). Touching with a wand. *Perceptual and Motor Skills, 58*(2), 390.

Hewitt, J., & Lewis, G. (1985). Observers' reaction to touchers. *Perceptual & Motor Skills, 60*(2), 452–454.

Heyman, S.R. (1977). Dogmatism, hostility, aggression, and gender role. *Journal of Clinical Psychology, 33*, 694–698.

Highlen, P.S., & Gillis, S.F. (1978). Effects of situational factors, sex, and attitude on affective self-disclosure and anxiety. *Journal of Counseling Psychology, 25*, 270–276.

Highlen, P.S., & Johnson, B. (1979). Effects of situational variables on affective self-disclosure with acquaintances. *Journal of Counseling Psychology, 26*, 255–258.

Hoffman, M.L. (1977). Sex differences in empathy and related behaviors. *Psychological Bulletin*, 1977, 84:712–722.

Holly, P.M., Trower, T.L., & Chance, D.R. (1984). Wall-to-wall hugging and counseling. *Elementary School Guidance & Counseling, 19*(2), 147–151.

Holmes, C.S., Hayford, J.T., & Thompson, R.G. (1982). Personality and behavior differences in groups of boys with short stature. *Children's Health Care, 11*(2), 61–64.

Howe, F. (1971, October 16). Sexual stereotypes start early. *Saturday Review*.

Jackubowski, P., & Lange, A.J., (1976). *The assertive option: Your rights and responsibilities*. New York: Research.

Jones, S.E., & Yarbrough, A.E. (1985). A naturalistic study of the meanings of touch. *Communication Monographs, 52*(1), 19–56.

Jourard, S.M. (1961). Age trends in self-disclosure. *Merrill-Palmer Quarterly, 7*, 191–197.

Jourard, S.M. (1971). *The transparent self*. New York: Van Nostrand.

Kagan, J. (1964). Acquisition and significance of sex typing and sex role identity. In M.M. Hoffman, & L. Hoffman (Eds.), *Review of Child Development, Vol. I.* (pp. 137–168). New York: Russell.

Kaplan, A.G., & Bean, J.P. (1976). *Beyond sex-role stereotypes: Readings toward a psychology of androgyny*. Boston: Little, Brown.

Keith, P.M., & Brubaker, T.H. (1979). Male household roles in later life: A look at masculinity and marital relationships. *Family Coordinator, 28*, 497–502.

Klein, A.R., & Bates, J.E. (1980). Gender typing of game choices and qualities of boys' play behavior. *Journal of Abnormal Child Psychology, 8*(2), 201–212.

Kohlberg, L.A. (1966). Cognitive-developmental analysis of children's sex-role concepts and attitudes. In E. Maccoby, (Ed.), *The Development of Sex Differences* (pp. 82–173). Stanford: Stanford University Press.

Komarovsky, M. (1973). Cultural contradictions and sex roles: The masculine case. *American Journal of Sociology, 78*, 873–884.

Korda, M. (1972). *Male chauvinism: How it works and how to get free of it*. New York: Berkley.

Kriegel, L. (1978). *The myth of American manhood*. New York: Dell.

Krodel, L.F. (1981). The effectiveness of sensitivity training in all-male groups to facilitate self-disclosure and emotional expressiveness in men. *Dissertation Abstracts International, 42*, (6-A), 2574.

L'Abate, L. (1980). Inexpressive males or overexpressive females? A reply to Balswick. *Family Relations, 29*, 229–230.

Lafrance, M. (1985). The school of hard knocks: Nonverbal sexism in the classroom. *Theory Into Practice, 24*(1), 40–44.

Lamb, M.E. (Ed.) (1976). *The role of the father in child development*. New York: Wiley.

Larsen, K.S., & Leroux, J. (1984). A study of same sex touching attitudes: Scale development and personality predictors. *Journal of Sex Research, 20*(3), 264–278.

LaTorre, R.A. (1980). Devaluation of the human love object: Heterosexual rejection as a possible antecedent to fetishism. *Journal of Abnormal Psychology, 89*(2), 295–298.

Lederer, W. (1979). The decline of manhood: Adaptive trend or temporary confusion? *Psychiatric Opinion, 16*, 14–17.

Leik, R.K. (1963). Instrumentality and emotionality in family interaction. *Sociometry, 26*, 131–145.

Leon, M., Adels, L., & Coopersmith, R. (1985). Thermal limitation of mother-young contact in Norway rats. *Developmental Psychobiology, 18*(2), 85–105.

Levinger, L., & Senn, P. (1967). Disclosure of feelings in marriage. *Merrill-Palmer Quarterly, 13*, 237–249.

Lewis, R.A. (1978). Emotional intimacy among men. *Journal of Social Issues, 34*, 101–121.

Locksley, A., & Colten, M.E. (1979). Psychological androgyny: A case of mistaken identity? *Journal of Personality and Social Psychology, 37*, 1017–1031.

Lutz, D.J., Roback, H.B., & Hart, M. (1984). Feminine gender identity and psychological adjustment of male transsexuals and male homosexuals. *Journal of Sex Research, 20*(4), 350–362.

Lynn, D.B. (1974). *The father: His role in child development*. Monterey, CA: Brooks Cole.

Lyon, H.C. (1977). *Tenderness in strength: From machismo to manhood.* New York: Harper & Row.

Maccoby, E.E., & Jacklin, C.M. (1974). *The psychology of sex differences.* Stanford: Stanford University Press.

Mallen, C.A. (1983). Sex role stereotypes, gender identity and parental relationships in male homosexuals and heterosexuals. *Journal of Homosexuality, 9*(1), 55–74.

Marlowe, M. (1981). Boyhood sex-role development: Implications for counseling and school practices. *Personnel and Guidance Journal, 60*(4), 210–214.

Mayo, P.R. (1968). Self disclosure and neuroses. *British Journal of Sex and Clinical Psychology, 1*, 140–148.

Mazur, A., & Lamb, T.A. (1980). Testosterone, status, and mood in human males. *Hormones & Behavior, 14*(3) 236–246.

Mills, C.J., & Bohannon, W.E. (1983). Personality, sex-role orientation, and psychological health in stereotypically masculine groups of males. *Sex Roles, 9*(12), 1161–1169.

Moore, D. (1985). An investigation of changes in affective expressiveness in men as a result of participation in a multimodal psychological intervention. *Dissertation Abstracts International, 46*, (4-B), 1316.

Moore, D., & Nuttall, J.R. (1981). Perceptions of the male sex role. *Personality & Social Psychology Bulletin, 7*(2), 320–325.

Mosher, D.L., & Sirkin, M. (1984). Measuring a macho personality constellation. *Journal of Research in Personality, 18*(2), 150–163.

Naffziger, C.C., & Naffziger, K. (1974). Development of sex-role stereotypes. *The Family Coordinator, 23*, 251–259.

Nichols, J. (1975). *Men's liberation: A new definition of masculinity.* New York: Penguin.

O'Leary, V.E., & Donoghue, J.M. (1978). Latitudes of masculinity: Reactions to sex-role deviance in men. *Journal of Social Issues, 34*, 17–28.

Olson, K. (1978). *Hey man! Open up and live.* New York: Fawcett.

Orlofsky, J.L., & Ginsburg, S.D. (1981). Intimacy status: Relationship to affect cognition. *Adolescence, 16*(61), 91–100.

Paulsell, S., & Goldman, M. (1984). The effect of touching different body areas on prosocial behavior. *Journal of Social Psychology, 122*(2), 269–273.

Paulson, M.J. (1980). Self-disclosure patterns of maladjusted male adolescents. *Canadian Counsellor, 14*(4), 206–211.

Payne, F.D., & Futterman, J.R. (1983). Masculinity, femininity, and adjustment in college men. *Journal of Research in Personality, 17*(1) 110–124.

Pelletier, K.R. (1977). *Mind as healer, mind as slayer.* New York: Dell.

Penick, E.C., Powell, B.J., & Read, M.R. (1984). Sex-role affiliation among male alcoholics. *Journal of Clinical Psychology, 40*(1), 359–363.

Penick, E.C., Powell, B.J., Read, M.R., & Mahoney, D. (1980). Sex-role typing: A methodological note. *Psychological Reports, 47*(1), 143–146.

Pleck, J.H. (1975). Male-male friendship: Is brotherhood possible? In M. Blazer (Ed.), *Old family/new family: Interpersonal relations* (pp. 229–234). New York: Van Nostrand Reinhold.

Pleck, J.H. (1975). Men's response to changing consciousness of women, In E.L. Zuckerman (Ed.), *Women and men: Roles, attitudes, and power relationships* (pp. 102–112). New York: The Radcliff Club of New York.

Pleck, J.H., & Brannon, R. (Eds.). (1978). Male roles and the male experience. *Journal of Social Issues. 34*, 1–4.

Quinn, J.F. (1984). Therapeutic touch as energy exchange: Testing the theory. *Advances in Nursing Science, 6*(2), 42–49.

Roberts, M.K. (1982). Men and women: Partners, lovers, friends. *Advances in Descriptive Psychology, 2*, 57–78.

Robinson, B.E. (1979). Men caring for the young: An androgynous perspective. *Family Coordinator, 28*, 553–560.

Robinson, R.J. (1981). Self-disclosure, friendship, and emotional intimacy among men. *Dissertation Abstracts International, 42*, (2-B), 785.

Roy, A. (1981). Vulnerability factors and depression in men. *British Journal of Psychiatry, 138*, 75–77.

Sattel, J.W. (1976). The inexpressive male: Tragedy or sexual politics? *Social Problems, 23*, 469–477.

Sawin, D.B., & Park, R.D. (1979). Fathers' affectionate stimulation and caregiving behaviors with newborn infants. *Family Coordinator, 28*, 509, 513.

Scanzoni, J. (1979). Strategies for changing male family roles: Research and practical implications. *Family Coordinator, 28*, 435–442.

Scher, M. (1979). The little boy in the adult male client. *Personnel and Guidance Journal, 57*, 537–539.

Scher, M. (1979). On counseling men. *Personnel and Guidance Journal, 57*, 252–254.

Schuckit, M.A. (1982). Prevalance of affective disorder in a sample of young men. *American Journal of Psychiatry, 139*(11), 1431–1436.

Shatan, C.F. (1978). Bogus manhood, bogus honor: Surrender and transfiguration in the United States Marine Corps. In G.D. Goldman, & D.S. Milman, (Eds.), *Psychoanalytic perspectives on aggression* (pp. 77–100). Dubuque IA: Kendall/Hunt.

Skord, K.G., & Schumacher, B. (1982). Masculinity as a handicapping condition. *Rehabilitation Literature, 43*(9–10), 284–289.

Skovholt, T.M., & Hansen, A. (1980). Men's development: A perspective and some themes. In T.M. Skovholt, P.G. Schanble, & R. David, (Eds.), *Counseling men*. Menlo Park, CA: Brooks/Cole.

Smith, M.J. (1975). *When I say no, I feel guilty*. New York: Dial Press.

Smith, S.G. (1983). A comparison among three measures of social sex-role. *Journal of Homosexuality, 9*(1), 99–107.

Solomon, K. (1979). Viewpoint: Do men have better relationships with each other than women do with other women? *Medical Aspects of Human Sexuality, 13*, 39, 43.

Stein, N., & Sanfilipo, M. (1985). Depression and the wish to be held. *Journal of Clinical Psychology, 41*(1), 3–9.

Steinem, G. (1974). The myth of masculine mystique, In J.H. Pleck, & J. Sawyer, (Eds.), *Men and masculinity* (pp. 134–139). Englewood Cliffs, NJ: Prentice-Hall.

Stevens, B. (1974). The sexually oppressed male. *Psychotherapy: Theory, Research and Practice, 11*, 16–21.

Stier, D.S., & Hall, J.A. (1984). Gender differences in touch: An empirical and theoretical review. *Journal of Personality and Social Psychology, 47*(2), 440–459.

Stokes, J., Fuehrer, A., & Childs, L. (1980). Gender differences in self-disclosure to various target persons. *Journal of Counseling Psychology, 27*, 192–198.

Stoller, R.J., & Herdt, G.H. (1982). The Development of masculinity: A cross-cultural contribution. *Journal of the American Psychoanalytic Association, 30*(1), 29–59.

Suiter, R.L., & Goodyear, R.K. (1985). Male and female counselor and client perceptions of four levels of counselor touch. *Journal of Counseling Psychology, 32*(4), 645–648.

Suls, J., Becker, M.A., & Mullen, B. (1981). Coronary-prone behavior, social insecurity and stress among college-aged adults. *Journal of 'Human' Stress, 7*(3), 27–34.

Syrotuik, J., & Darcy, C. (1984). Social support and mental health: Direct, protective and compensatory effects. *Social Science & Medicine, 18*(3) 229–236.

Tolson, A. (1977). *The limits of masculinity: Male identity and women's liberation*. New York: Harper & Row.

Ward, D., & Balswick, J. (1978). Strong men and virtuous women. A content analysis of sex roles stereotypes. *Pacific Sociological Review, 21*, 45–53.

Warren, N.J., & Gilner, F.H. (1978). Measurement of positive assertive behaviors: The behavioral test of tenderness expression. *Behavior Therapy, 9*, 178–184.

Washington, C. (1979). Men counseling men: Redefining the male machine. *Personnel and Guidance Journal, 57*, 462–463.

Weitsman, L.J., et al. (1972). Sex-role socialization in picture books for pre-school children. *American Journal of Sociology, 77*(6), 1125–1149.

Willison, B.G., & Masson, R.L. (1986). The role of touch in therapy: An adjunct to communication. *Journal of Counseling and Development, 64*(8), 497–500.

Witkin, H.A. (1974). Social conformity and psychological differentiation. *International Psychology, 9,* 11–29.

Wolchik, S., et al. (1980). The effect of emotional arousal on subsequent sexual arousal in men. *Journal of Abnormal Psychology, 89*(4), 595–598.

Worell, J. (1978). Sex roles and psychological well-being: Perspectives on methodology. *Journal of Consulting and Clinical Psychology, 46,* 298–313.

Fathers and Parenting

Axelson L. (1960). Personal adjustment in the postparental period. *Marriage and Family Living, 22,* 66–68.

Balswick, J., & Avrett, C.P. (1977). Differences in expressiveness: Gender, interpersonal orientation, and perceived parental expressiveness as contributing factors. *Journal of Marriage and the Family, 39,* 121–127.

Bannon, J.A., & Southern, M.L. (1980). Father-absent women: Self-concept and the modes of relating to men. *Sex Roles: A Journal of Research, 6*(1), 75–84.

Barnett, R.C., & Baruch, G.K. (1984). *Determinants of father's participation in family work.* Working Paper No. 136. Wellesley, MA: Wellesley College Center for Research on Women.

Barret, R.L., & Robinson, B.E. (1982). A descriptive study of teenage expectant fathers. *Family Relations, 31*(3), 349–352.

Bartemeier L. (1953). The contribution of the father to the mental health of the family. *American Journal of Psychiatry, 110,* 277–280.

Barton, K. (1981). Six child rearing dimensions common to both fathers and mothers. *Multivariate Experimental Clinical Research, 5*(3), 91.

Bartz, K.W., & Witcher, W.C. (1978). When father gets custody. *Children Today, 7*(5), 2–6, 35.

Baruch, G.K., & Barnett, R.C. (1983). *Correlates of father's participation in family work: A technical Report.* Working Paper No. 106 and 126. Wellesley, MA: Wellesley College Center for Research on Women.

Baruch, G.K., & Barnett, R.C. (1985, March). *Fathers' participation in family work: Effects on children's sex role attitudes.* Working Paper No. 126. *RIE.*

Bell, Alan P. (1969). Role modeling of fathers in adolescence and young adulthood. *Journal of Counseling Psychology, 16*(1), 30–39.

Benson, L. (1968). *Fatherhood: A sociological perspective.* New York: Random House.

Bigner, J.J. (1970). Fathering: Research and practice implications. *Current Index to Journals in Education.*

Biller, H.B. (1969). Father dominance and sex-role development in kindergarten-age boys. *Developmental Psychology,* 87–94.

Biller, H.B. (1971). Father absence, perceived maternal behavior and masculinity of self-concept among junior high school boys. *Developmental Psychology,* 178–181.

Block, C.R. (1981). Husband gatekeeping in childbirth. *Family Relations, 30*(2), 197–204.

Bowman, M.E., & Ahrons, C.R. (1985). Impact of legal custody status on fathers' parenting postdivorce. *Journal of Marriage and the Family, 47*(2), 481–488.

Bozett, F.W. (1980). Gay fathers: How and why they disclose their homosexuality to their children. *Family Relations, 29*(2), 173–179.

Cath, S., Gurwitt, A., & Ross, J. (1982). *Father and child.* Boston: Little, Brown.

Coley, S.B., Jr., & James, B.E. (1976). Delivery: A trauma for fathers. *Family Coordinator, 25*(4), 351–356.

Dail, P.W., & Way, W.L. (1985). What do parents observe about parenting from prime time television. *Family Relations, 34*(4), 491–499.

DeFrain, J.D. (1975, June). A father's guide to parent guides: Reviews and assessment of the paternal role as conceived in the popular literature. *RIE.*

Earls, F. (1976). The fathers (not the mothers): Their importance and influence with infants and young children. *Psychiatry, 39,* 209–226.

Emihovich, C.A. (1984). Sex-role expectations changes by fathers for their sons. *Sex Roles*, *11*(9-10), 861–868.

Entwisle, D., & Doering, S. (1988). The emergent father role. *Sex Roles*, *18*(3/4), 119–41.

Fein, R. (1974). *Men's experiences before and after the birth of the first child: Dependence, marital sharing and anxiety.* Unpublished doctoral disseration, Harvard University, Cambridge, MA.

Fein, R.A. (1978). Research on fathering: Social policy and an emergent perspective. *Journal of Social Issues, 34,* 122–135.

Figueroa-Torres, J., & Pearson, R.E. (1979). Effects of structural learning therapy upon self-control of aggressive Puerto Rican fathers. *Hispanic Journal of Behavioral Sciences, 1*(4), 345–354.

Filsinger, E.E., & Lamke, L.K. (1983). The lineage transmission of interpersonal competence. *Journal of Marriage and the Family, 45*(1), 75–80.

Gagnon, J.H., & Roberts, E. (1982). Men vs. fathers. *Television & Children, 5*(2), 9–15.

Galper, M. (1979, August). Co-parenting: Sharing your child equally. A source book for the separated or divorced family. *RIE.*

Gershenson, H.P. (1983). Redefining fatherhood in families with white adolescent mothers. *Journal of Marriage and the Family, 45*(3), 591–599.

Gold, H. (1967). *Fathers.* New York: Random House.

Gordon, T. (1970). *PET: Parent effectiveness training.* New York: Wyden.

Grando, R., & Ginsberg, B.G. (1976). Communication in the father-son relationship: The parent-adolescent relationship development program. *Family Coordinator, 25*(4), 465–472.

Greif, G. (1985). *Single fathers.* Lexington, MA: Lexington Books.

Hanson, S., & Bozett, F. (Eds.). (1985). *Dimensions of fatherhood.* Beverly Hills, CA: Sage.

Hawkins, L.F. (1974). Child rearing learning interests of fathers of first grade children. *Home Economics Research Journal, 2*(3), 194–199.

Hendricks, L.E., & Montgomery, T. (1983). A limited population of unmarried adolescent fathers: A preliminary report of their views on fatherhood and the relationship with the mothers of their children. *Adolescence, 18*(69), 201–210.

Herzog, J. (1983). *Father and child.*

Hillman, L., et al. (1978). The liberated husband—Father or babysitter. *Intellect, 106*(2397), 462–465.

Hodgman, C.H. (1975, April). Talks between fathers and sons. *Human Sexuality.*

Kellerman, J. (1974). Sex role stereotypes and attitudes toward parental blame for the psychological problems of children. *Journal of Consulting and Clinical Psychology, 42*(1), 153–154.

Kendall, E.D. (Ed.). (1981, December). Effects of changed family structures on children: A review of the literature. *RIE.*

Kimball, G. (1988). *50/50 Parenting.* Lexington, KY.

Kurland, M.L. (1981). Child rearing by lone fathers. *Society, 17,* 149–166.

Lamb, M.E. (Ed.). (1976). *The role of the father in child development.* New York: Wiley.

Lein, L. (1979). Male participation in home life: Impact of social supports and breadwinner responsibility on the allocation of tasks. *Family Coordinator, 28,* 489–495.

Levine, J. (1976). *Who will raise the children? New options for the fathers and mothers.* New York: Lippincott.

Lewis, C. (1986, February). Men's involvement in fatherhood: Historical and gender issues. *RIE.*

Lewis, C., & O'Brien, M. (1987). *Reassessing fatherhood.* Beverly Hills: Sage.

Lewis, R., Freneau, P., & Roberts, C. (1979). Fathers and the postparental transition. *Family Coordinator, 28,* 514–520.

Lewis, R., & Salt, R. (Eds.). (1986). *Men of families.* Beverly Hills, CA: Sage.

Lewis, R., & Sussman, M. (Eds.). (1986). *Men's changing roles in the family.* New York: Haworth Press.

Lewis, R.A., & Pleck, J.H. (1979). Men's roles in the family. *Family Coordinator, 28,* 429–646.

Lynn, D.B. (1974). *The father: His role in child development.* Monterey, CA: Brooks Cole.

Matthews, D.B., & Quinn, J.L. (1982, September). Congruence of parental behavior as perceived by parents and their middle school children. *RIE*.

May, K.A. (1982). Factors contributing to first-time fathers' readiness for fatherhood: An exploratory study. *Family Relations, 31*(3), 353–361.

Maxwell, J.W., & DeLissovoy, V. (1976). The keeping fathers of America. *Family Coordinator, 25*(4), 387–395.

McBride, A.B., & Black, K.N. (1984). Differences that suggest female investment in, and male distance from, children. *Sex Roles; A Journal of Research, 10*(3-4), 231–246.

McCall, R.B. (1985, February). Early education and alternative childcare in the context of the family and society. *RIE*.

McCall, R.B. (1985). Stresses and relationships in the families of the 1980s. *PTA Today, 10*(6), 9–10.

McCord, J. (1979). Some child-rearing antecedents of criminal behavior in adult men. *Journal of Personality and Social Psychology, 37*(9), 1477–1487.

Merton, A. (1986). Father hunger: The secret wound of American men. *New Age Journal, 2*(13), 22.

Nelson, M., & Nelson, G.K. (1982). Problems of equity in the reconstituted family: A social exchange analysis. *Family Relations, 31*(2), 223–231.

Ogg, E. (1978). What about the prospective father. *Today's Education, 67*(1), 77–79.

Osherson, S. (1986). *Finding our fathers: The unfinished business of manhood*. New York: Free Press.

Patterson, R. (1985, March). A father's role in his child's development. Unit for child studies. Selected Papers Number 20. *RIE*.

Pedersen, F.A. (1976). Does research on children reared in father-absent families yield information on father influences. *Family Coordinator, 25*(4), 459–563.

Phillips, R.A. (1978). Men as lovers, husbands and fathers: Explorations of male socialization and implications for marriage and family therapy. In C.H. Simpkinsen, & L.J. Platt (Eds.), *Synopsis of family therapy practice* (pp. 142–147). Olney: Family Therapy Practice Network.

Pleck, J.H. (1985). *Paternity leave: Current status and future prospects*. Working Paper No. 157. Wellesley, MA: Wellesley College Center for Research on Women.

Radin, N. (1972, April). Father-child interaction and the intellectual functioning of four-year-old boys. *Journal of Developmental Psychology, RIE*.

Robinson, B.D. (1979). Men caring for the young: An androgynous perspective. *Family Coordinator, 28*, 553–560.

Rosenfeld, J.M., Rosenstein, E., & Raab, M. (1973). Sailor families: The nature and effects of one kind of father absence. *Child Welfare, 52*, 33–44.

Sawin, D.B., & Park, R.D. (1979). Father's affectionate stimulation and caregiving behaviors with newborn infants. *Family Coordinator, 28*, 509, 513.

Scanzoni, J. (1979). Strategies for changing male family roles: Research and practical implications. *Family Coordinator, 28*, 435–442.

Scheck, D.C., & Emerick, R. (1976). The young male adolescent's perception of early child-rearing behavior: The differential effects of socioeconomic status and family size. *Sociometry, 39*(1), 39–52.

Schwarz, J.C., Barton, H., Marianne, L., & Pruzinsky, T. (1985). Assessing child-rearing behaviors: A comparison of ratings made by mother, father, child, & sibling on the CRPBI. *Child Development, 56*(2), 462–479.

Single Dad's Lifestyle Magazine. P.O. Box 4842, Scottsdale, AZ 85261.

Smith, R., & Smith, C. (1981). Child rearing and single-parent fathers. *Family Relations, 30*, 411–417.

Snyder, L.M. (1979, November). The deserting nonsupporting father: The scapegoat of family nonpolicy. *RIE*.

Snarey, J., Son, L., & Kuehn, V. (1986). *How husbands cope when pregnancy fails: A longitudinal study of infertility and psychosocial generativity*. Wellesley, MA: Wellesley College Center for Research on Women.

Tauss, V. (1976). Working wives and house husbands. *Journal of Family Counseling, 4*, 52–55.

Wente, Arel S., & Crockenberg, S.B. (1976). Transition to fatherhood: Lamaze preparation, adjustment difficulty and the husband-wife relationship. *Family Coordinator*, 25(4), 351–356.

Woolner, R.B. (1979, January). What do we do today, daddy? (Father's perception of his role and responsibilities). *RIE*.

Vijatrasil K. The relationship between gender, socioeconomic status, sex-typing, sex-role attitudes, self-esteem and attitudes toward child-rearing among fathers and mothers. *Dissertation Abstracts International*, 42(02), Sec B, PO571.

Yablonsky, L. (1982). *Fathers and sons*. New York: Simon & Schuster.

Gender Differences in Counseling

Abramowitz, C.V., Abramowitz, S.I., & Weitz, L.J. (1976). Sex related effects on clinicians' attributions of parental responsibility for child psychopathology. *Journal of Abnormal Child Psychology*, 4, 129–138.

American Psychological Association. (1975). Report of the Task Force on Sex Bias and Sex-Role Stereotyping in Psychotherapeutic Practice. *American Psychologist*, 30, 1169–1175.

Berzins, J.I. (1971). Therapist-patient matching. In A.S. Gurman, & A.M. Razin (Eds.), *Effective psychotherapy, A handbook of research* (pp. 222–251). New York: Pergamon.

Birk, J. (1980, September 5). *Sexism, relevancy, and training in counseling psychology*. Paper presented at the 88th annual meeting of the American Psychological Association, Montreal, Que.

Broverman, I.K., Broverman, D.M., Clarkson, P.S., Rosenkrantz, S., & Vogel, S.R. (1970). Sex role stereotypes and clinical judgments of mental health. *Journal of Consulting and Clinical Psychology*, 34(1), 1–7.

Carter, C.A. (1971). Advantages of being a woman therapist. *Psychotherapy: Theory, Research, and Practice*, 8, 297-300.

Cicone, M., & Ruble, D. (1978). Beliefs about males. *Journal of Social Issues*, 34, 5–16.

Clayton, V., & Jellison, J.M. (1975). Preferences for the age and sex of advisors: A life span approach. *Developmental Psychology*, 11, 861–862.

Collin, S.A., & Sedlacek, W. (1974). Counselor ratings of male and female clients. *Journal of the National Association of Women Deans, Administrators and Counselors*, 37, 128–132.

Davies, P.S. (1978). Attributions of sex role and competency characteristics to male and female transcript therapists as a function of sex of subject and therapy involvement. *Dissertation Abstracts International*, 38(7-B), 3387–3388.

Dewey, C. (1974). Exploring interests: A non-sexist method. *Personnel and Guidance Journal*, 52, 311–315.

Feldstein, J.C. (1979). Effects of counselor sex and sex role and client sex on clients' perceptions and self-disclosure in a counseling analogue study. *Journal of Counseling Psychology*, 26(5), 437–443.

Feldstein, J.C. (1982). Counselor and client sex pairing: The effects of counseling problem and counselor sex role orientation. *Journal of Counseling Psychology*, 29(4), 418–420.

Freimuth, M., & Hornstein, G. (1982). A critical examination of the concept of gender. *Sex Roles*, 8, 514–532.

Fuller, F. (1963). Influence of sex of counselor and of client on client expression of feeling. *Journal of Counseling Psychology*, 10, 34–40.

Goldstein, M.Z. (1982). Dominance and sex bias in the therapy relationship: A comparison of male therapists with male and female clients. *Dissertation Abstracts International*, 43(6-B), 2006.

Greenberg, R.P., & Zeldow, P.B. (1980). Sex differences in preferences for an ideal therapist. *Journal of Personality Assessment*, 44(5), 474–478.

Greene, L.R. (1980). On terminating psychotherapy: More evidence of sex-role related countertransference. *Psychology of Women Quarterly*, 4(4), 548–557.

Haring, M., Beyard-Tyler, K., & Gray, J. (1983). Sex biases attitudes of counselors: The special case of nontraditional careers. *Counseling and Values, 27*(4), 242–247.

Hill, C.E. (1976). Sex of clients and sex and experience level of counselor, *Journal of Counseling Psychology, 22*, 6–11.

Hoffman, M. (1977). Sex differences in empathy and related behavior. *Psychological Bulletin, 84*, 712–72.

Kahn, S.E., & Schroeder, A.S. (1980). Counselor bias in occupational choice for female students. *Canadian Counsellor, 14*(3), 156–159.

Lerner, H.E. (1978). Adaptive and pathogenic aspects of sex-role stereotypes: Implications of parenting and psychotherapy. *American Journal of Psychiatry, 135*, 48–52.

Lobaro, G.A., & Reeder, C.W. (1978). Male competition: An issue in counselor training. *Counseling Psychologist, 7*, 20–22.

MacDonald, A. (1974). The importance of sex role to gay liberation. *Homosexual Counseling Journal, 1*, 169–180.

Morgan, J.I., Skovholt, T.M., & Orr, J.M. (1979). Career counseling with men: The shift in focus. In S.G. Weinroch (Ed.), *Career counseling: Theoretical and practical perspectives* (pp. 260–266). New York: McGraw-Hill.

O'Neil, J.M. (1981). Male sex role conflicts, sexism, masculinity: Psychological implications for men, women and the counseling psychologist. *Journal of Counseling Psychology, 9*, 61–80.

Orcutt, M.A., & Walsh, W.B. (1983). Recognition of sex-biased counseling interactions. *Professional Psychology: Research and Practice, 14*(4), 462–472.

Packer, J. (1983). Sex stereotyping in vocational counseling of blind/visually impaired persons: A national study of counselor choices. *Journal of Visual Impairment & Blindness, 77*(6) 261–268.

Padronaggio, J.A. (1977). Sex-role stereotyping of male clients by counselors-in-training. *Dissertation Abstracts International, 38*(6-B), 1895–1896.

Pleck, J.H. (1975). Men's response to changing consciousness of women. In E.L. Zuckerman (Ed.), *Women and men roles, attitudes, and power relationships* (pp. 102–112). New York: The Radcliff Club of New York.

Robyak, J.E. (1981). Effects of gender on the counselor's preference for methods of influence. *Journal of Counseling Psychology, 28*(1), 7–12.

Ross, M.W. (1985). Actual and anticipated societal reaction to homosexuality and adjustment in two societies. *Journal of Sex Research, 21*(1), 40–55.

Scher, M. (1979). On counseling men. *Personnel and Guidance Journal, 57*, 252–254.

Scher, M. (1981). Counseling males. *Personnel and Guidance Journal, 60*, 199–202.

Scher, M. (1981). Gender issues in psychiatric supervision. *Comprehensive Psychiatry, 22*(2), 179–183.

Skovholt, T. (1980, September 5). *Psychological services and male clients: How wide is the gap?* Paper presented at the 88th annual meeting of the American Psychological Association, Montreal, Que.

Smith, M.L. (1980). Sex bias in counseling and psychotherapy. *Psychological Bulletin, 87*(2), 392–407.

Solomon, K. (1971). Sex roles and group therapy dropouts. *American Journal of Psychiatry, 136*, 727–728.

Solomon, K. (1979). Sexism and professional chauvinism in psychiatry, *Psychiatry, 42*, 374–377.

Solomon, M.D. (1981). Therapist sex-role orientation, sex-role attitudes and response to male and female client affect. *Dissertation Abstracts International, 42*(4-B), 1665–1666.

Sturdivant, S. (1980). *Therapy with women. A feminist philosophy of treatment.* New York: Springer.

Tinsley, E.H., & Harris, D.J. (1976). Client expectations for counseling. *Journal of Counseling Psychology, 23*, 173–177.

Unger, R. (1979). Toward a redefinition of sex and gender. *American Psychologist, 34*, 1085–1094.

Washington, C.S. (1979). Men counseling men: Redefining the male machine. *Personnel and Guidance Journal, 59*, 462–463.

Wetmore-Foshay, A.A., O'Neill, P., & Foster, J.A. (1981). Sex role stereotyping among school counsellors. *Canadian Counsellor, 15*(4), 180–184.
Wittkower, E.D., & Robertson, B.M. (1977). Sex differences in psychoanalytic treatment. *American Journal of Psychotherapy, 31*, 66–75.

Grieving

Allen, J., & Haccoun, D. (1976). Sex differences in emotionality: A multidimensional approach. *Human Relations, 8*, 711–722.
Arieti, S., & Bemporad, J. (1978). *Severe and mild depression*. New York: Basic Books.
Balswick, J. (1980). Types of inexpressive male roles. In R.A. Lewis (Ed.), *Men in difficult times*. New York: Prentice-Hall.
Egendorf, A. (1985). *Healing from the war: Trauma transformation after Vietnam*. Boston: Houghton Mifflin.
Freud, S. (1934). Mourning and melancholia (1917). In *Collected papers, Vol IV*. London: Hogarth Press, pp. 152–170.
Wolff, C.T. (1977). Loss, grief, and mourning in adults. In R.C. Simons, & H. Pardes (Eds.), *Understanding human behavior in health and illness*. Baltimore: Williams & Wilkins, pp. 378–386.

Homosexuality (see also Love and Sexuality)

Adair, N., & Adair C. (1978). *Word is out, Stories of some of our lives*. New York: Dell.
Boswell, J. (1980). *Christianity, social tolerance, and homosexuality*. Chicago: University of Chicago Press.
Brown, H. (1976). *Familiar faces. Hidden lives: The story of homeosexual men in America today*. New York: Harcourt Brace Jovanovich.
Clark, Don. (1978). *Loving someone gay*. New York: Simon & Schuster.
Fisher, P. (1972). *The gay mystique: The myth and reality of male homosexuality*. New York: Stein & Day.
Freedman, M. (1975). Homosexuals may be healthier than straights. *Psychology Today, 8*, 28–32.
Garner, B., & Smith, R.W. (1976, June). *Are there really any gay athletes?* Paper presented at the Society for the Scientific Study of Sex, San Diego, CA.
Gochros, H.L. (1978). Counseling gay husbands. *Journal of Sex Education and Therapy, 4*, 6–10.
Green, R. (1978). Sexuality identity of 37 children raised by homosexual or transsexual parents. *American Journal of Psychiatry, 135*, 692–697.
Hatterer, L.J. (1970). *Changing homosexuality in the male: Treatment for men troubled by homosexuality*. New York: McGraw-Hill.
Hyman, R. (1980, April). *Working with the gay client: Methods of eliminating counselor homophobia*. Paper Presented at the annual meeting of the American Personnel and Guidance Association, Atlanta.
Jay, K., & Young, A. (1972). *Out of the closets: Voices of gay liberation*. New York: Pyramid Books.
Jay, K., & Young, A. (1975). *After you're out, Personal experiences of gay men and lesbian women*. New York: Links Brooks.
Jay, K., & Young A. (1979). *The gay report*. New York: Summit Books.
Journal of Gay and Lesbian Psychotherapy. New York: Haworth Press.
Karlen, A. (1971). *Sexuality and homosexuality: A new view*. New York: Norton.
Katz, J. (1976). *Gay American history, Lesbians and gay men in the U.S.A.* New York: Crowell.
Kelly, J. (1977). The aging male homosexual, Myth and reality. *Gerontologist, 17*, 328–332.

Lauritson, J., & Thorstad, D. (1974). *The early homosexual rights movement.* New York: Times Change Press.

Masters, W.S., & Johnson, V. (1979). *Homosexuality in perspective.* Boston: Little, Brown.

Morin, S., & Garfinkle, E.M. (1978). Male homophobia. *Journal of Social Issues, 34,* 29–47.

Morin, S.F. (1974). Educational programs as a means of changing attitudes toward gay people. *Homosexual Counseling Journal, 1*(4).

Morin, S.F. (1978). Psychology and the gay community: An overview. *Journal of Social Issues, 34,* 1–5.

National Gay Task Force. (1978). *About coming out.* New York: Author.

Reid, J. (Pseud.). (1977). *The best little boy in the world.* New York: Ballantine Books.

Riddle, D.I. (1978). Relating to children: Gays as role models. *Journal of Social Issues, 34,* 38–58.

Rossman, P. (1976). *Sexual experiences between men and boys.* New York: Associaton Press.

Silverstein, C. (1977). *A family matter: A parent's guide to homosexuality.* New York: McGraw-Hill.

Silverstein, C. (1987). *Man to man - Gay couples in America.* New York: Morrow.

Silverstein, C., & White, E. (1977). *The joy of gay sex.* New York: Crown.

Spada, J. (1979). *The Spada report, The newest survey of gay male sexuality.* New York: New American Library.

Teal, D. (1971). *The gay militants.* New York: Stein & Day.

Walker, M. (1977). *Men loving men.* San Francisco: Gay Sunshine Press.

Weinberg, M.S., & Williams, C.J. (1974). *Male homosexuals, Their problems and adaptations.* New York: Oxford University Press.

West, D.J. (1968). *Homosexuality.* (3rd ed.). London: Duckworth.

West, D.J. (1977). *Homosexuality re-examined.* Minneapolis: University of Minnesota Press.

Intimacy and Friendship

Berman, S.A. (1985). Men and romantic relationships: A qualitative study of men and intimacy. *Dissertation Abstracts International, 46*(6-A), 1516.

Bly, R. *Loving a woman in two worlds.* New York: Doubleday.

Burns, D.D. (1985). *Intimate connections.* New York: New American Library.

Crider, W.E. (1982). A comparison of verbal intimacy and verbal control levels of males and females. *Dissertation Abstracts International, 42*(12-B, PT 1) 4968-4969.

Devlin, P.K., & Cowan, G.A. (1985). Homophobia, perceived fathering, and male intimate relationships. *Journal of Personality Assessment, 49*(5), 467–473.

Gilder, G. (1974). *Naked nomads: Unmarried men in America.* New York: Quadrangle.

Gillin, S.M. (1984). I love her, I love her not: Male ambivalence in intimate adult relationships. *Dissertation Abstracts International, 45*(3-B) 1014.

Harry, J. (1976). Evolving sources of happiness for men over the life cycle: A structural analysis. *Journal of Marriage and the Family, 38*(2), 289–296.

Kahn, S., Zimmerman, G., Csikszentmihalyi, M., & Getzels, J. W. (1985). Relations between identity in young adulthood and intimacy at midlife. *Journal of Personality and Social Psychology, 49*(5), 1316–1322.

Kimball, G. (1983). *50/50 marriage,* Boston: Beacon Press.

Leonard, L. (1988). *On the way to the wedding.* Boston, MA: Shambhala.

Levenson, R. (1984). Intimacy, autonomy and gender: Developmental differences and their reflection in adult relationships. *Journal of the American Academy of Psychoanalysis, 12*(4), 529–544.

Lewis, R.A. (1978). Emotional intimacy among men. *Journal of Social Issues, 34,* 108–121.

Macklin, E.D. (1983). Effect of changing sex roles in the intimate relationships of men and women. *Marrige & Family Review, 6*(3), 97–113.

Madden, M.E. (1986). A study of a male bonding ritual and its impact on adolescent males. *Dissertation Abstracts International, 46*(10-A) 2973.

Mannarino, A.P. (1976). Friendship patterns and altruistic behavior in preadolescent males. *Developmental Psychology*, *12*(6), 555–556.

Mark, E.W., & Alper, T.G. (1985). Women, men, and intimacy motivation. *Psychology of Women Quarterly*, *9*(1), 81–88.

Matson, J. (1986). *An analysis of the effect of feminism on intimate male-female relationships*. PhD dissetation, United States International University, School of Human Behavior.

McAdams, D.P., & Vaillant, G.E. (1982). Intimacy motivation and psychosocial adjustment: A longitudinal study. *Journal of Personality Assessment*, *46*(6), 586–593.

Merchant, D.C. (1985). Father-son intimacy: Its relationship to self-esteem, academic achievement, and psychological well-being in college males. *Dissertation Abstracts International*, *46*(3-B) 1000.

Miller, S. (1986). *Men and friendship*. Boston: Houghton Mifflin.

Rubin, L. (1983). *Intimate strangers, men and women together*. New York: Harper & Row.

Rutter, E.R. (1982). An exploration of intimacy between gay men. *Dissertation Abstracts International*, *42*(12-B, Pt 1) 4940.

Scher, M. (1980, September 5). *Men and intimacy: Implications for the counseling psychologist*. Paper presented at the 88th annual meeting of the American Psychological Association, Montreal, Que.

Shotland, R.L., & Craig, J. (1988). Can men and women differentiate between friendly and sexually interested behavior? *Social Psychology Quarterly*, *51*(1), 66–73.

Swain, S.O. (1986). Male intimacy in same-sex friendships. *Dissertation Abstracts International*, *46*(10-A) 3167.

Tesch, S.A. (1984). Sex-role orientation and intimacy status in men and women. *Sex Roles*, *11*(5-6), 451–465.

Wagner, R. (1975). Complementary needs, role expectations. interpersonal attraction, and the stability of working relationships. *Journal of Personality and Social Psychology*, *32*(1), 116–124.

Wall, S.M., Pickert, S.M., & Pardise, L.V. (1984). American men's friendships: Self reports on meaning and changes. *Journal of Psychology*, *116*(2), 179–186.

Welwood, J. (1985). *Challenge of the heart: Love, sex and intimacy in changing times*. Boston MA: Shambhala.

Wortman, C., Adesman, P., Herman, E., & Greenberg, R. (1976). Self-disclosure: An attributional perspective. *Journal of Personality and Social Psychology*, *33*(2), 184–191.

Leisure

Allen, L.R. (1980). Leisure and its relationship to work and career guidance. *Vocational Guidance Quarterly*, *28*, 257–262.

Winters, R.A., & Hanse, J.C. (1976). Toward an understanding of work-leisure relationships. *Vocational Guidance Quarterly*, *24*, 238–243.

Loneliness

Burgess, J. (1980). *Men in crises: The widower*.

Hacker, T.A., et al. (1984). *Social skills, attractiveness and gender: Factors in perceived social support*.

Inderbitzen, H.M., & Clark, M.L. (1986). *The relationship between adolescent loneliness and perceptions of controllability and stability*.

Nerviano, V.J., & Gross, W.F. (1976). Loneliness and locus of control for alchoholic males: Validity against Murray need and Cattell trait dimensions. *Journal of Clinical Psychology*, *32*(2), 479–484.

Stokes, J., & Levin, I. (1985). *Gender differences in predicting loneliness from social network variables*.

Vinick, B.H. (1981). *Three years after bereavement: Lifestyles of elderly men.*
Vinick, B.H. (1983). *Loneliness among elderly widowers.*

Love and Sexuality

Babl, J.D. (1979). Compensatory masculine responding as a function of sex role. *Journal of Consulting and Clinical Psychology, 47*, 330–335.

Bancroft, J. (1984). Interaction of psychosocial and biological factors in marital sexuality: Differences between men and women. *British Journal of Guidance & Counseling, 12*(1), 62–71.

Barlow, D.H. (1986). Causes of sexual dysfunction: The role of anxiety and cognitive interference. *Journal of Consulting and Clinical Psychology, 54*(2), 140–148.

Basu, A. (1982). Sexual dysfunctions in males: A psychoanalytic point of view. *Samiksa, 36*(3), 78–87.

Beck, J.G., & Barlow, D.H. (1986). The effects of anxiety and attentional focus on sexual responding: I. Physiological patterns in erectile dysfunction. *Behaviour Research and Therapy, 24*(1), 9–17.

Beck, J.G., & Barlow, D.H. (1986). The effects of anxiety and attentional focus on sexual responding: II. Cognitive and affective patterns in erectile dysfunction. *Behaviour Research and Therapy, 24*(1), 19–26.

Bieber, I., Dain, H.J., Dince, P.R., et al. (1962). *Homosexuality: A psychoanalytic study of male homosexuals.* New York: Basic Books.

Broughton, J. (1983). *Broughton's ecstasies: Poems 1975–1983.* Syzygy.

Brown, M., & Amoroso, D.M. (1976). Behavioral effects of viewing pornography. *Journal of Social Psychology, 98*(2), 235–245.

Campagna, A.F. (1985–86). Fantasy and sexual arousal in college men: Normative and functional aspects. *Imagination, Cognition & Personality, 5*(1), 3–20.

Decker, J., Dronkers, J., & Staffeleu, J. (1985). Treatment of sexual dysfunctions in male-only groups: Predicting outcome. *Journal of Sex & Marital Therapy, 11*(2), 80–90.

Dermer, M., & Pyszczynski, T.A. (1978). Effects of erotica upon men's loving and liking responses for women they love. *Journal of Personality and Social Psychology, 36*(11), 1302–1309.

Dias, P.L. (1983). The long-term effects of vasectomy on sexual behaviour. *Acta Psychiatrica Scandinavica, 67*(5), 333–338.

Dinnerstein, D. (1977). *The mermaid and the minotaur. Sexual arrangements and human malaise.* New York: Harper & Row.

Donnerstein, E., & Berkowitz, L. (1981). Victim reactions in aggressive erotic films as a factor in violence against women. *Journal of Personality and Social Psychology, 41*(4) 710–724.

Everaerd, W., & Dekker, J. (1985). Treatment of male sexual dysfunction: Sex therapy compared with systematic desensitization and rational emotive therapy. *Behavior Research and Therapy, 23*(1), 13–25.

Finkel, M.L., & Finkel, D.J. (1983). Male adolescent sexual behavior, the forgotten partner: A review. *Journal of School Health, 53*(9), 544–547.

Fox, L.S. (1983). Adolescent male reproductive responsibility. *Social Work in Education, 6*(1), 32–43.

George, W.H., & Marlatt, G.A. (1986). The effects of alcohol and anger on interest in violence, erotica, and deviance. *Journal of Abnormal Psychology, 95*(2), 150–158.

Gillin, S.M. (1984). I love her, I love her not: Male ambivalence in intimate adult relationships. *Dissertation Abstracts International, 45*(3), 1014.

Grady, K., Brannon, R., & Pleck, J. (1979). *The male sex role: An annotated research bibliography.* Washington, DC: U.S. Government Printing Office.

Gray, S.H. (1982). Exposure to pornography and aggression toward women: The case of the angry male. *Social Problems, 29*(4), 387–398.

Green, R. (1978). Sexual identity of 37 children raised by homosexual or transsexual parents. *American Journal of Psychiatry, 135*, 692–697.

Green, R. (1985). Gender identity in childhood and later sexual orientation: Follow-up of 78 males. *American Journal of Psychiatry, 142*(3), 339–341.

Hawton, K. (1984). Sexual adjustment of men who have had strokes. *Journal of Psychosomatic Research, 28*(3), 243–249.

Heiman, J.R., & Hatch, J.P. (1980). Affective and physiological dimensions of male sexual response to erotica and fantasy. *Basic & Applied Social Psychology, 1*(4), 315–327.

Henley, N.M. (1977). *Body politics: Power, sex, and nonverbal communication.* Englewood Cliffs, NJ: Prentice-Hall.

Hunt, M. (1974). *Sexual behavior in the 1970's.* Chicago: Playboy Press.

Jay, K., & Young, A. (1972). *Out of the closets: Voices of gay liberation.* New York: Pyramid Books.

Julien, E., & Over, R. (1984). Male sexual arousal with repeated exposure to erotic stimuli. *Archives of Sexual Behavior, 13*(3), 211–222.

Lauritson, J., & Thorstad, D. (1974). *The early homosexual rights movement.* New York: Times Change Press.

Lee, J.A. (1978). *Getting sex, a new approach: More fun, less guilt.* Don Mills, Ontario, Canada: General Publishing.

Leonard, K.E., & Taylor, S.P. (1983). Exposure to pornography, permissive and nonpermissive cues, and male aggression toward females. *Motivation & Emotion, 7*(3), 291–299.

Lester, D. (1984). Pornographic films and unconscious homosexual desires: An hypothesis. *Psychological Reports, 54*(2), 606.

Lewis, R., Casto, R., Aquilino, W., & McGuffin, N. (1978). Developmental transitions in male sexuality. *The Counseling Psychologist, 7*(4).

Lewittes, D.J., & Simmons, W.L. (1975). Impression management of sexually motivated behavior. *Journal of Social Psychology, 96*(1), 39–44.

Lloyd, R. (1976). *For money or love, boy prostitution in America.* New York: Vanguard Press.

Lo Presto, C.T., Sherman, M.F., & Sherman, N.C. (1985). The effects of a masturbation seminar on high school males' attitudes, false beliefs, guilt, and behavior. *Journal of Sex Research, 21*(2), 142–156.

Malamuth, N.M. (1986). Predictors of naturalistic sexual aggression. *Journal of Personality and Social Psychology, 50*(5), 953–962.

Malamuth, N.M., & Check, J.V. (1985). The effects of aggressive pornography on beliefs in rape myths: Individual differences. *Journal of Research in Personality, 19*(3), 299–320.

Money, J. (1962). Factors in the genesis of homosexuality, In G. Winokur, (Ed.), *Determinants of human sexual behavior.* Springfield, IL: Charles C Thomas.

Money, J. (1980). *Love and love sickness: The science of sex, gender differences, and pair bonding.* Baltimore: Johns Hopkins Press.

Money, J., & Ehrhardt, A. (1972). *Man and woman, boy and girl.* Baltimore: Johns Hopkins University Press.

Money, J., & Tucker, P. (1975). *Sexual signatures.* Boston: Little Brown.

Morton, R.A., & Hartman, L.M. (1985). A taxonomy of subjective meanings in male sexual dysfunction. *Journal of Sex Research, 21*(3), 305–321.

Nelson, J. (1983). *Between two gardens: Reflections on sexuality and religious experiences.* Pilgrim Press.

Nielsen, T. (1983). Sexual abuse of boys: Current perspectives. *Personnel and Guidance Journal, 62*(3), 139–142.

Nutter, D.E., & Condron, M.K. (1985). Sexual fantasy and activity patterns of males with inhibited sexual desire and males with erectile dysfunction versus normal controls. *Journal of Sex & Marital Therapy, 11*(2), 91–98.

Rapaport, K., & Burkhart, B.R. (1984). Personality and attitudinal characteristics of sexually coercive college males. *Journal of Abnormal Psychology, 93*(2), 216–221.

Reading, A.E. (1983). A comparison of the accuracy and reactivity of methods of monitoring male sexual behavior. *Journal of Behavioral Assessment, 5*(1), 11–23.

Reading, A.E., & Wiest, W.M. (1984). An analysis of self-reported sexual behavior in a sample of normal males. *Archives of Sexual Behavior, 13*(1), 69–83.

Safilios-Rothschild, C. (1977). *Love, sex, sex roles.* Englewood Cliffs, NJ: Prentice-Hall.

Sakheim, D.K., Barlow, D.H., Beck, J.G., & Abrahamson, D.J. (1984). The effect of an increased awareness of erectile cues on sexual arousal. *Behaviour Research and Therapy, 22*(2), 151–158.

Sakheim, D.K., Barlow, D.H., Beck, J.G., & Abrahamson, D.J. (1985). A comparison of male heterosexual and male homosexual patterns of sexual arousal. *Journal of Sex Research, 21*(2), 183–198.

Silverstein, C., & White, E. (1977). *The joy of gay sex.* New York: Crown.

Spada, J. (1979). *The Spada report, the newest survey of gay male sexuality.* New York: New American Library.

Steven, B.S. (1974). The sexually oppressed male. *Psychotherapy: Theory, Research and Practice, 11*, 16–21.

Tuber, S., & Coates, S. (1985). Interpersonal phenomena in the Rorschachs of extremely feminine boys. *Psychoanalytic Psychology, 2*(3), 251–265.

Wayson, P.D. (1985). Personality variables in males as they relate to differences in sexual orientation. Special issue: Bisexualities: Theory and research. *Journal of Homosexuality, 11*(1–2), 63–73.

Weaver, J.B., Masland, J.L., & Zillmann, D. (1984). Effect of erotica on young men's aesthetic perception of their female sexual partners. *Perceptual and Motor Skills, 58*(3), 932–930.

Welwood, J. (Ed.). (1985). In *Challenge of the heart: Love, sex, and intimacy in changing times.* Boston, MA: Shambhala.

West, D.J. (1977). *Homosexuality re-examined.* Minneapolis: University of Minnesota Press.

White, L.A. (1979). Erotica and aggression: The influence of sexual arousal, positive affect, and negative affect on aggressive behavior. *Journal of Personality and Social Psychology, 37*(4), 591–601.

Wilson, G.T., & Niaura, R. (1984). Alcohol and the disinhibition of sexual responsiveness. *Journal of Studies on Alcohol, 45*(3), 219–224.

Wilson, G.T., Niaura, R.S., & Adler, J.L. (1985). Alcohol, selective attention and sexual arousal in men. *Journal of Studies on Alcohol, 46*(2), 107–115.

Wilson, K., Faison, R., & Britton, G.M. (1983). Cultural aspects of male sex aggression. *Deviant Behavior, 4*(3–4), 241–255.

Love and Sexuality (Addendum)

Broude, G.J. (1983). Male-female relationships in cross-cultural perspective: A study of sex and intimacy. *Behavior Science Research, 18*(2), 154–181.

Cohen, D.D. (1983). Male adolescent psychosexual development: The influence of significant others on contraceptive behavior. *Dissertation Abstracts International, 43*(11-A) 3514.

Isaacs-Giraldi, G.J. (1980). Influences of frequency of visitation by the divorced natural father on the self-concept and sexual identity of the male child. *Dissertation Abstracts International, 41*(3-B), 1111–1112.

Kleinman, C., et al. (1978, April). Secrets of the new male sexuality. *Ms., 6*(10).

Nelson, J. (1983). *Between two gardens: Reflections of sexuality and religious experiences.* Pilgrim Press.

Pietropinto, A., & Simenauer, J. (1978). *Beyond the male myth: What women want to know about men's sexuality.* New York: New American Library (Signet).

Talefman, J., & Brender, W. (1984). An analysis of the effectiveness of two components in the treatment of erectile dysfunction. *Archives of Sexual Behavior, 13*(4), 321–340.

Tiefler, L. (1986). In pursuit of the perfect penis: The medicalization of male sexuality. *American Behavioral Scientists, 29*, 579–599.

Male Clients

Abramowitz, C.V., Abramowitz, S.J., & Weitz, L.J. (1976). Are men therapists soft on empathy? Two studies in feminine understanding. *Journal of Clinical Psychology, 32*, 434–437.

American Psychological Associaton. Council of Representatives. (1981). Ethical principles of psychologists. *American Psychologist, 36*(6), 633–638.

Berger, M. (1979). Men's new family roles—Some implications for therapists. *Family Co-ordinator, 28*, 638–646.

Berzins, J.I. (1971). Therapist-patient matching. In A.S. Gurman, & A.M. Razin (Eds.), *Effective psychotherapy. A handbook of research* (pp. 222–251). New York: Pergamon.

Billingsley, D. (1977). Sex bias in psychotherapy: An examination of the effects of client pathology, and therapist sex on treatment planning. *Journal of Consulting and Clinical Psychology, 45*, 250–256.

Birk, J.M. (1980, September 5). *Relevancy and alliance: Cornerstones in training counselors of men*. Presented at the annual meeting of the American Psychological Association, Montreal, Quebec.

Coleman, E. (1981). Counseling adolescent males. *Personnel and Guidance Journal, 60*(4), 249–252.

Collin, S.A., & Sedlacek, W. (1974). Counselor ratings of male and female clients. *Journal of the National Association of Women Deans, Administrators and Counselors, 37*, 128–132.

Delk, J.L., & Ryan, T.T. (1977). A-B status and sex stereotyping among psychotherapists and patients. Toward a model for maximizing therapeutic potential. *Journal of Nervous and Mental Disease, 164*, 253–262.

Friedrich, W., Beilke, R., & Urquiza, A. (1988). Behavior problems in young sexually abused boys. *Journal of Interpersonal Violence, 3*, 21–28.

Holpern, J. (1987). Family therapy in father-son incest. *Social Casework, 68*, 88–94.

Isparo, A.J. (1986). Male client-male therapist: Issues in a therapeutic alliance. *Psychotherapy, 23*(2).

Lewis, R.A. (1978). Emotional intimacy among men. *Journal of Social Issues, 34*, 108–121.

Lofaro, G.A., & Reeder, C.W. (1978). Male competition: An issue in counselor training. *Counseling Psychologist, 7*, 20–22.

Morgan, J.I., Skovholt, T.M., & Orr, J.M. (1979). Career counseling with men: The shifting focus. In S.G. Weinroch (Ed.), *Career counseling: Theoretical and practical perspecives* (pp. 260–266). New York: McGraw-Hill.

O'Neil, J.M. (1981). Male sex-role conflicts, sexism, and masculinity: Psychological implications for men, women and counseling psychologists. *The Counseling Psychologist, 8*.

O'Neil, J.M. (1982). Gender and sex role conflict and strain in men's lives: Implications for psychiatrists, psychologists, and other human service providers. In K. Solomon, & N. Levy (Eds.), *Men in transition: Changing male roles, theory, and therapy*. New York: Plenum Press.

Pierce, L. (1987). Father-son incest: Using the literature to guide practice. *Social Casework, 68*, 67–75.

Scher, M. (1979). The little boy in the adult male client. *Personnel and Guidance Journal, 57*, 537–539.

Scher, M. (1979). On counseling men. *Personnel and Guidance Journal, 57*, 252–254.

Scher, M. (1980, September 5). *Men and intimacy. Implications for the counseling psychologist*. Paper presented at the 88th annual meeting of the American Psychological Association, Montreal, Que.

Scher, M. (1981). Counseling males: Introduction. *Personnel and Guidance Journal, 60*, 199–202.

Scher, M., & Stevens, M. (1987). Men and violence. *Journal of Counseling and Development, 65*(7), 351–356.

Skovholt, T. (1980, September 5). *Psychological services and male clients: How wide is the gap?* Paper presented at the 88th annual meeting of the American Psychological Association, Montreal. Que.

Skovholt, T., Gormally, J., & Schauble, P. (1978). Counseling men. *Counseling Psychologist* 7(2).

Skovholt, T., & Hansen, A. (1980). Men's development: A perspective and some themes. In T. Skovholt, P. Schauble, & R. Davis, (Eds.), *Counseling men* (pp. 1–29). Menlo Park, CA: Brook/Cole.

Solomon, K. (1979). Therapeutic aspects of changing masculine role behavior. *World Journal of Psychosynthesis, 11*, 13–16.

Toomer, J.E. (1978). Males in psychotherapy. *Counseling Psychologist, 7*, 22–25.

Washington, C. (1979). Men counseling men: Redefining the male machine. *Personnel and Guidance Journal, 57*, 462–463.

Wong, M.R., David, J., & Conroe, R.M. (1976). Expanding masculinity: Counseling the male in transition. *Counseling psychologist, 6*, 58–61.

Men's Groups

Aries, E. (1976). Interaction patterns and themes of male, female and mixed groups. *Small Group Behavior, 7*, 7–18.

Barkley, H., Wilborn, B., & Towers, M. (1984). Social interest in a peer counseling training program. *Individual Psychology: Journal of Adlerian Theory, Research & Practice, 40*(3), 295–299.

Bernardez-Bonesatti, T., & Stein, T.S. (1979). Separating the sexes in group therapy: An experiment with men's and women's groups. *International Journal of Group Psychotherapy, 29*, 493–502.

Bly, R. (1986). Men's initiation rights. *Utre Reader, 15*, 42–49.

Croteau, J.M., & Burda, P.C. (1983). Structured group programming on men's roles: A creative approach to change. *Personnel and Guidance Journal, 62*(4), 243–245.

Follingstad, D., Kilmann, P.R., Robinson, E., et al. (1976). Prediction of self-actualization in male participants in a group conducted by female leaders. *Journal of Clinical Psychology, 32*, 706–712.

Heppner, P.P. (1981). Counseling men in groups. *Personnel and Guidance Journal, 60*(4), 249–252.

Heppner, P. (1983). Structured group activities for counseling men. *Journal of College Student Personnel, 24*, 275–277.

Karsk, R., & Thomas B. (1979). *Working with men's groups.* Columbia, MO: New Community Press.

Lewis, R.A. (1981). Men's liberation and the men's movement: Implications for counselors. *Personnel and Guidance Journal, 60*(4), 256–259.

Lyon, D.A. (1973, September 14–15). *Experiences with men's awareness groups.* Invited paper at the conference of the International Psychiatric Research Society, Eau Claire, WI.

Moore, D. (1985). An investigation of changes in affective expressiveness in men as a result of participation in a multimodal psychological intervention. *Dissertation Abstracts International, 46*, (4-B), 1316.

Moreland, J. (1976). A humanistic approach to facilitating college students' learning about sex roles. *Counseling Psychologist, 6*, 61–64.

Page, R.C., & Miehl, H. (1982). Marathon groups: Facilitating the personal growth of male illicit drug users. *International Journal of the Addictions, 17*(2), 393–397.

Pittman, J.F., & Gerstein, L.H. (1984). Graduated levels of group therapy for substance abusers. *Journal for Specialists in Group Work, 9*(1), 7–13.

Schonbar, R.A. (1973). Group co-therapists and sex-role identification. *American Journal of Psychotherapy, 27*, 539–547.

Smith, T.E. (1985). Groupwork with adolescent drug abusers. *Social Work With Groups, 8*(1), 55–64.

Solomon, K. (1979). Sex roles and group therapy dropouts. *American Journal of Psychiatry, 136*, 727–728.

Stein, T.S. (1983). An overview of men's groups. *Social Work With Groups. 6*(3-4), 149–161.

Tiger, L. (1970). *Men in groups*, New York: Vintage.

Wade, L.A., Wade, J.E., & Croteau, J.M. (1983). The man and the male: A creative outreach program on men's roles. *Journal of College Student Personnel*, *24*(5), 460–461.

Washington, C. (1979). Men counseling men: Redefining the male machine. *Personnel and Guidance Journal*, *57*, 462–463.

Washington, C.S. (1982). Challenging men in groups. *Journal for Specialists in Group Work*, *7*(2), 132–136.

Wong, M.R. (1978). Males in transition and the self-help group. *Counseling Psychologist*, *7*, 46–50.

Mentoring Younger Men (see also Intimacy and Friendship)

Coleman, E. (1981). Counseling adolescent males. *Personnel and Guidance Journal*, *60*(4), 215–218.

Levinson, D. (1979). *The seasons of a man's life*. New York: Ballantine Books.

Mahdi, L.C., (Ed.). *Betwixt and between: Patterns of masculine and feminine initiation*. Open Court.

Pierce, C.A. (1984). Mentoring, gender, and attainment: The professional development of academic psychologists. *Dissertation Abstracts International*, *45*(3-A), 793.

Possick, S. (1983). The therapist as mentor: An aspect of clinical work with schizophrenic outpatients. *Journal of Nervous and Mental Disease*, *17*(5), 314–317.

Moral Responsibilities

American Psychological Association. (1975). Report of the Task Force on Sex Bias and Sex Role Stereotyping in Psychotherapeutic Practice. *American Psychologist*, *30*, 1169–1175.

Birk, J. (1980, September 5). *Sexism, relevancy and training in counseling psychology*. Paper presented at the 88th annual meeting of the American Psychological Association, Montreal.

Block, J.H. (1976). Debatable conclusions about sex differences. *Contemporary Psychology*, *21*, 517–522.

Bolen, J.S. (1989). *Gods in every man*. New York: Harper & Row.

Denmark, F.L. (1977). Growing up male. In C.A. Carney, & S.L. McMahon (Eds.), *Exploring contemporary male/female roles: A facilitator's guide* (pp. 125–138). LaJolla, CA: University Associates.

Fuller, F.F. (1963). Influence of sex of counselor and of client on client expressions of feeling. *Journal of Counseling Psychology*, *10*, 34–40.

Hallenbeck, A.R. (1978). Problems of reliability in observational research. In G.P. Sackett, (Ed.), *Observing behavior II: Data collection and analysis methods* (pp. 79–98). Baltimore: University Park Press.

Hansen, L.S. (1980). Born free: change process evaluation of a psychological intervention to promote sex fair career development. *Pupil Personnel Services Journal*, *9*, 35–47.

Kaplan, A.G. (1979). Toward an analysis of sex role related issues in the therapeutic relationship. *Psychiatry*, *42*, 112–120.

Morgan, J.I., Skovholt, T.M., & Orr, J.M. (1979). Career counseling with men: The shifting focus. In S.G. Weinroch (Ed.), *Career counseling: Theoretical and practical perspectives* (pp. 260–266). New York: McGraw-Hill.

O'Leary, V.E., & Donoghue, J.M. (1976). Latitudes of masculinity: Reactions to sex-role deviance in men. *Journal of Social Issues*, *32*, 155–164.

Pleck, J.H. (1976). Sex role issues in clinical training. *Psychotherapy: Theory, Research and Practice*, *13*, 17–19.

P.L. 92–318: The Education Amendment of 1972, Title IX, Prohibition of Sex Discrimination, 20 USC, 1681.

Scanzoni, J. (1979). Strategies for changing male family roles; Research and practical implications. *Family Coordinator, 28*, 435–442.

Sondgrass, J. (1977). *A book of readings for men against sexism.* New York: Times Change Press.

Sue, D.W. (1978). Eliminating cultural oppression in counseling. Toward a general theory. *Journal of Counseling Psychology, 25*, 419–428.

Worrell, J. (1978). Sex roles and psychological well-being: Perspectives on methodology. *Journal of Consulting and Clinical Psychology, 46*, 298–313.

Mother/Son Relationships

Brook, J.S., Whiteman, M., Gordon, A.S., & Brook, D.W. (1983). Paternal correlates of adolescent marijuana use in the context of the mother-son and parental dyads. *Genetic Psychology Monographs, 108*(2), 197.

Genshaft, J.L. (1978). The empirical study of mother-son interactions. *Social Behavior & Personality 6*(2), 235.

Gjerde, P.F. (1986). The international structure of family interaction settings: Parent-adolescent relations in dyads & triads. *Developmental Psychology, 22*(3), 297–304.

Kenemore, T.K., & Wineberg, L.D. (1984). The tie that binds: A clinical perspective on divorced mothers and adolescent sons. *Clinical Social Work Journal, 12*(4), 332–346.

Kitahara, M. (1978). Social contact versus bodily contact: A qualitative difference between father and mother for the son's masculine identity. *Behavior Science Research, 13*(4), 273–287.

Margolis, M. (1984). A case of mother-adolescent son incest: A follow-up study. *Psychoanalytical Quarterly, 53*(3), 355–385.

Phelps, R.E., & Slater, M.A. (1985). Sequential interactions that discriminate high & low-problem single mother-son dyads. *Journal of Consulting and Clinical Psychology, 53*(5), 684–692.

Sitgraves, M.E. (1981). Recent life event stress and patterns of mother-son interaction in high risk versus low risk black mothers. *Dissertation Abstracts International*, 40(12), 5832-B. (University Microfilms No. 8013300).

Solomon, J.G., Fernando, T.G., & Solomon, S.M. (1978). Mother-son folie a deux: A case report. *Journal of Clinical Psychiatry, 39*, 11.

Tucker, L.S., & Cornwall, T.P. (1977). Mother son folie-a-deux: Case of attempted patricide. *The American Journal of Psychiatry, 134*(10), 1146.

Vandell, D.L. (1979). Effects of a playground experience on mother-son and father-son interaction. *Developmental Psychology, 15*(4), 379–385.

Nontraditional Career Choice

Bear, S., Berger, M., & Wright, L. (1979). Even cowboys sing the blues: Difficulties experienced by men trying to adopt nontraditional sex roles. *Sex Roles 5*, 191–198.

Bem, S. (1975). Sex roles adaptability: One consequence of psychological androgyny. *Journal of Personality and Social Psychology, 31*, 634–643.

Boles, J., & Tatro, C. (1980). The new male model: Traditional or androgynous? *Psychoanalysis, 40*(3), 227–237.

Dewey, C. (1974). Exploring interests: A non-sexist method. *Personnel and Guidance Journal, 52*, 311–315.

Farrell, W. (1975). *The liberated man.* New York: Bantam Books.

Gould, R. (1974). Measuring masculinity by the size of the paycheck. In J. Pleck, & J. Sawyer (Eds.), *Men and masculinity.* Englewood Cliffs, NJ: Prentice-Hall.

Guttentag, M., & Bray, H. (1976). *Undoing sex role stereotypes.* New York: McGraw-Hill.

Hasen, L.S. (1980). *Born Free*: Change process evaluation of a psychological intervention to promote sex fair career development. *Pupil Personnel Services Journal, 9*, 35–47.

Howe, F. (1971, October 16). Sexual stereotypes start early. *Saturday Review.*

Lunneborg, P.W. (1979). Service vs. technical interests—biggest sex difference of all? *Vocational Guidance Quarterly, 28,* 146–153.

Morgan, J.I., Skovholt, T.M., & Orr, J.M. (1979). Career counseling with men: The shift in focus. In S.C. Weinrich (Ed.), *Career counseling: Theoretical and practical perspectives.* New York: McGraw-Hill.

O'Leary, V.W., & Donoghue, J.M. (1976). Latitudes of masculinity: Reactions to sex-role deviance in men. *Journal of Social Issues, 32,* 155–164.

Yanico, B.J. (1978). Sex bias in career information. Effects of language on attitudes. *Journal of Vocational Behavior, 13,* 26–34.

Physical Health

American Heart Association. (1974). *Heart facts.* New York: Author.

Anderson, M.B., & MacNair, N.C. (1983). Herpes: Coping and caring: A total college health program. *Journal of American College Health, 32*(3), 128–129.

Bayer, R., Levine, C., & Murry, T.H. (1974). Guidelines for confidentiality in research on AIDS. *IRB: A review of human subjects research, 6*(6), 1–7.

Bennett, S.M., & Dickinson, W.B. (1980). Student parent rapport and parent involvement in sex, birth control, and venereal disease education. *Journal of Sex Research, 16*(2), 114–130.

Chass, M. (1974, August 18). A gut issue: Who shapes up best, athletes or dancers? *New York Times,* Sec. 2, pp. 1, 25.

Chng-Chwee, L. (1983). The male role in contraception: Implications for health education. *Journal of School Health, 53*(3), 197–201.

Coates, T.J., Temoshok, L., & Mandel, J. (1984). Psychosocial research is essential to understanding and treating AIDS. *American Psychologist, 39*(11), 1309–1314.

Deabler, H., Fidel, E., Dillenkoffer, R., et al. (1973). The use of relaxation and hypnosis in lowering high blood pressure. *American Journal of Clinical Hypnosis 16,* 75–83.

Donlou, J.N., Wolcott, D.L., Gottlieb, M.S., & Landsverk, J. (1985). Psychosocial aspects of AIDS and AIDS-related complex: A pilot study. *Journal of Psychosocial Oncology, 3*(2), 39–55.

Downey, A.M. (1984). The relationship of sex-role orientation to self-perceived health status in middle-aged males. *Sex Roles, 11,* (3–4) 211–225.

Drob, S. (1985). Psychotherapy with patients suffering from genital herpes. *Psychotherapy in Private Practice, 3*(4), 129–137.

Drob, S., & Bernard, H.S. (1985). Herpes in dyadic relationships: Patterns and treatment. *Journal of Marital & Family Therapy, 11*(4), 391–397.

Drob, S., & Bernard, H. (1985). Two models of brief group psychotherapy for herpes sufferers. *Group, 9*(3), 14–20.

Edwards, L.D. (1982). What a counselor needs to know about sexually transmitted diseases. *Journal of Psychology & Christianity, 1*(4), 47–52.

Felman, Y.M., & Nikitas, J.A. (1983). Sexually transmitted diseases and child sexual abuse: II. *New York State Journal of Medicine, 83*(5), 714–716.

Ferrara, A.J. (1984). My personal experience with AIDS. *American Psychologist, 39*(11), 1285–1287.

Fluker, J.L. (1983). The perils of promiscuity. *Journal of Psychosomatic Research, 27*(2), 153–156.

Frances, R.J., Wikstrom, T., & Alcena, V. (1985). Contracting AIDS as a means of committing suicide. *American Journal of Psychiatry, 142*(5), 656.

Friedman, M. (1969). *Pathogenesis of coronary artery disease.* New York: McGraw-Hill.

Fullerton, T.F., & Britton, J.O. (1976). Collegiate persistence of vocationally undecided males. *Journal of Educational Research, 69*(8), 300–304.

Goedert, J.J. (1984). Recreational drugs: Relationship to AIDS. *Annals of the New York Academy of Sciences, 437,* 192–199.

Gould, S.S., Tissler, D.M. (1984). The use of hypnosis in the treatment of herpes simplex II. *American Journal of Clinical Hypnosis. 26*(3), 171–174.

Greenwood, R., Bhalla-Ashok, G.A., & Roberts, J. (1983). Behavior disturbances during recovery from herpes simplex encephalitis. *Journal of Neurology, Neurosurgery & Psychiatry, 46*(9), 809–817.

Harrison, J.W. (1978). The male sex role may be dangerous to your health. *Journal of Social Issues, 34,* 65–86.

Hays, L.R., & Lyles, M.R. (1986). Psychological themes in patients with acquired immune deficiency syndrome. *American Journal of Psychiatry, 143*(4), 551.

Hillard, J.R., et al. (1984). Knowledge and attitudes of university health service clients about genital herpes: Implications for patient education and counseling. *Journal of American College Health, 33*(3), 112–117.

Hirsch, D.A., & Enlow, R.W. (1984). The Effects of the acquired immune deficiency syndrome on gay lifestyle and the gay individual. *Annals of the New York Academy of Sciences, 437,* 273–282.

Howard, M. (1985). Postponing sexual involvement among adolescents: An alternative approach to prevention of sexually transmitted diseases. *Journal of Adolescent Health Care, 6*(4), 271–277.

Jenkins, C.D. (1976). Recent evidence supporting ecologic and social risk factors for coronary disease. *New England Journal of Medicine, 294,* 987–994, 1033–1038.

Khan, M., & Sexton, M. (1983). Sexual abuse of young children. *Clinical Pediatrics, 22*(5), 369–372.

Kimball, C.P. (1975). Psychological aspects of cardiovascular disease. In M.F. Reiser (Ed.), *American handbook of psychiatry,* Vol IV (2nd ed.) (pp. 609–617). New York: Basic Books.

Krause, N., & Stryker, S. (1984). Stress and well-being: The buffering role of locus of control beliefs. *Social Science & Medicine, 18*(9), 783–790.

Lairson, D., Lorimor, R., & Slater, C. (1984). Estimates of the demand for health: Males in the pre-retirement years. *Social Science & Medicine, 19*(7), 741–747.

Lipkin, B. (1984). Fear of Aids. *British Journal of Psychiatry, 147,* 210.

Lopez, D.J., & Getzel, G.S. (1984). Helping gay AIDS patients in crisis. *Social Casework, 65*(7), 387–394.

Malinow, K. (1980, March 6). *Doc, my meth isn't holding me: An analysis of the narcotic withdrawal syndrome.* Presented at a scientific meeting of the Maryland Psychiatric Society, Towson, MD.

Manne, S., Sandler, I., & Zautra, A. (1986). Coping and adjustment to genital herpes: The effects of time and social support. *Journal of Behavioral Medicine, 9*(2), 163–177.

Marmor, M., et al. (1984). The epidemic of acquired immunodeficiency syndrome (AIDS) and suggestions for its control in drug abusers. *Journal of Substance Abuse Treatment, 1*(4) 237–247.

McPherson, A., & Hall, W. (1983). Psychiatric impairment, physical health and work values among unemployed and apprenticed young men. *Australian & New Zealand Journal of Psychiatry, 17*(4), 335–340.

McPherson, B.D., & Guppy, N. (1979). Pre-retirement life-style and the degree of planning for retirement. *Journal of Gerontology, 34*(2), 254–263.

Meinecke, C.E. (1981). Socialized to die younger? Hypermasculinity and men's health. *Personnel and Guidance Journal, 60*(4), 241–245.

Morin, S.F., Charles, K.A., & Malyon, A.K. (1984). The psychological impact of AIDS on gay men. *American Psychologist, 39*(11), 1288–1293.

Navarro, V. (1976). The underdevelopment of health in working America: Causes, consequences and possible solutions. *American Journal of Public Health, 66,* 538–547.

Nichols, S.E. (1983). Psychiatric aspects of AIDS. *Psychosomatics, 24*(12), 1083–1089.

O'Reilly, K.R., & Aral, S.O. (1985). Adolescence and sexual behavior: Trends and implications for STD. *Journal of Adolescent Health Care, 6*(4) 262–270.

Owen, W.F. (1985). Medical problems of the homosexual adolescent. *Journal of Adolescent Health Care, 6*(4), 278–285.

Phillips, S., & Spence, M.R. (1983). Medical and psychosocial aspects of gonococcal infection in the adolescent patient: Epidemiology, diagnosis, and treatment. *Journal of Adolescent Health Care, 4*(2), 128–134.

Roseman, R.H., & Friedman, M. (1974). Neurogenic factors in pathogenesis of coronary heart disease. *Medical Clinics of North America, 58*, 269–279.

Roseman, R.H., Friedman, M., Straus, R., et al. (1964). A predictive study of coronary heart disease. *Jama, 189*, 103–110.

Sacher, G.A. (1978). Longevity, aging and death: An evolutionary perspective. *Gerontologist, 18*, 112–119.

Sandholzer, T.A. (1980). Physician attitudes and other factors affecting the incidence of sexually transmitted diseases in homosexual males. *Journal of Homosexuality, 5*(3), 325–327.

Schmidt, D.D., et al. (1985). Stress as a precipitating factor in subjects with recurrent herpes labialis. *Journal of Family Practice, 20*(4), 359–366.

Shoemaker, J., & Tasto, D. (1975). Effects of muscle relaxation on blood pressure of essential hypertensives. *Behavior Research and Therapy, 13*, 29–43.

Silber, T.J. (1981). Gonorrhea in adolescence: Its impact and consequences. *Adolescence, 16*(63), 537–541.

Silber, T.J. (1982). Ethical consideration in the medical care of adolescents who consult for treatment of gonorrhea. *Adolescence, 17*(66), 267–271.

Simon, K.J., & Das-Anima. (1984). An application of the health belief model toward educational diagnosis for VD education. *Health Education Quarterly, 11*(4), 403–418.

Solomon, K. (1979). Is there a genetic basis to aging? *Gerontologist, 19*, 226–228.

Solomon, K. (1981). The masculine gender role and its implications for the life expectancy of older men. *Journal of the American Geriatrics Society, 29*, 297–301.

Stein, P.J., & Hoffman, S. (1978). Sports and male role strain. *Journal of Social Issues, 34*, 136–150.

Tripathi, A.D., & Aurora, S. (1976). A study of need patterns of adolescents facing different behavioural problems. *Psycho-Lingua, 6*(1–2), 41–44.

Vaillant, G.E. (1972). Why men seek psychotherapy: I. Results of a survey of college graduates. *American Journal of Psychiatry, 129*(6), 645–651.

Vaillant, G.E. (1978). Natural history of male psychological health: VI. Correlates of successful marriage and fatherhood. *American Journal of Psychiatry, 135*(6), 653–659.

Vaillant, G.E., & McArthur, C.E. (1972). Natural history of male psychologic health: I. The adult life cycle from 18–50. *Seminars in Psychiatry, 4*(4), 415–427.

Waldron, I. (1976). Why do women live longer than men? *Social Science Medicine, 10*, 349–362.

William, D.C. (1984). The prevention of AIDS by modifying sexual behavior. *Annals of the New York Academy of Sciences, 437*, 283–285.

Power

American Psychological Association. (1978). *Principles for counseling and psychotherapy for women.* (Division 17).

Bowen, D.D. (1985). Were men meant to mentor women? *Training and Developmental Journal, 39*(2), 31–34.

Brodsky, A., & Hare-Mustin, R. (1980). *Women and psychotherapy: An assessment of research and practice.* New York: Gilford.

Cooke, M., & Kipnis, D. (1986). Influence tactics in psychotheraphy, Special issue: Psychotherapy research. *Journal of Consulting and Clinical Psychology 54*(1), 22–26.

Dutton, D., & Strachan, C. (1987). Motivational needs for power and spouse-specific assertiveness in assaultive and non-assaultive men. *Violence and Victims, 2*(3), 145–156.

Gannon, L. (1982). The role of power in psychotherapy. *Women & Therapy, 1*(2), 3–11.

Grauerholz, E. (1986). Power and intimacy: Power relationships between men and women. *Dissertation Abstracts International, 46*(9-A), 2824.

Journal of Counseling and Development, (1987). Special issue: Counseling and violence, *65*(7).

May, R. (1972). *Power and innocence.* New York: Dell.

Pleck, J.H. (1977). Men's power with women, other men and society: A men's movement analysis, In D. Hiller, & R. Sheets (Eds.), *Women and men: the Consequences of power.* Cincinnati, OH: University of Cincinnati Office of Women's Studies.

Reynolds, L. (1984). Rape: A social perspective. Special issue: Gender issues, sex offenses, and criminal justice: Current trends. *Journal of Offender Counseling, Services & Rehabilitation, 9*(1-2), 149–160.

Robyak, J.E., Goodyear, R.K., Prange, M.E., & Donham, G. (1986). Effects of gender, supervision, and presenting problems on practicum students' preference for interpersonal power bases. *Journal of Counseling Psychology, 33*(2), 159–163.

Roy, M. (1982). *The abrasive partner: An analysis of domestic battering.* New York: Van Nostrand Reinhold.

West, C. (1984). When the doctor is a "lady": Power, status and gender in physician-patient encounters. *Symbolic Interaction, 7*(1), 87–106.

Zuckerman, E.L. (1975). *Women and men's roles, attitudes, and power relationships.* New York: The Radcliff Club of New York.

Relationships

Abbott, M.W., & Koopman-Boyden, P.G. (1981). Expectations and predictions of the divisions of labour within marriage. *New Zealand Psychologist, 10*(1), 24–32.

Aries, E. (1977). Male-female interpersonal styles in all male, all female, and mixed groups. In A.G. Sargent (Ed.), *Beyond sex roles* (pp. 292–299). St. Paul, MN: West.

Balswick, J., & Avertt, C. (1977). Differences in expressiveness: Gender, interpersonal orientation, and perceived parental expressiveness as contributing factors. *Journal of Marriage and the Family, 38,* 121–127.

Brown, D.G. (1957). Masculinity-femininity development in children. *Journal of Counseling Psychology, 21,* 197–203.

Canavan, P., & Haskell, J. (1977). The American male stereotype. In C.G. Carney, & S.L. McMahon (Eds.), *Exploring contemporary male/female roles: A facilitator's guide.* La Jolla, CA: University Associates.

Geis, F.L., Brown, V., Jennings, J., & Corrado-Taylor, D. (1984). Sex vs. status in sex-associated stereotypes. *Sex Roles, 11*(9-10), 771–785.

Gray, S.W. (1957). Masculinity-femininity in relation to anxiety and social acceptance. *Child Development, 28,* 203–214.

Harford, T.D., Willis, C.H., & Deabler, H.L. (1967). Personality correlates of masculinity-femininity. *Pychological Report, 21,* 881–884.

Heiss, J.S. (1962). Degree of intimacy and male-female interaction. *Sociometry, 25,* 197–208.

Jenkins, N., & Vroegh, K. (1969). Contemporary concepts of masculinity and femininity. *Psychological Reports, 25,* 679–697.

Jones, W.E., Chernovetz, O.C., & Hansson, R. (1978). The enigma of androgyny: Differential implications for males and females. *Journal of Consulting and Clinical Psychology, 46,* 298–313.

Keith, P.M., & Brubaker, T.H. (1979). Male household roles in later life: A look at masculinity and marital relationships. *Family Coordinator, 28,* 497–502.

L'Abate L. (1980). Inexpressive males or overexpressive females? A reply to Balswick. *Family Relations, 29,* 229–230.

Lein, L. (1979). Male participation in home life: Impact of social supports and breadwinner responsibility on the allocation of tasks. *Family Coortdinator, 28,* 489–495.

Lewis, R.A., & Pleck, J.H. (Eds.). (1979). Special issue: Men's roles in the family. *Family Coordinator, 28,* 425–652.

Stein, P.J. (1984). Men in families. Special issue: Women and the family: Two decades of change. *Marriage & Family Review*, 7(3-4), 143–162.

Swensen, C.H., & Trahaug, G. (1985). Commitment and the long-term marriage relationship. *Journal of Marriage and the Family*, 47(4), 939–945.

Retirement

Brecher, E.M., & The Editors of Consumer Reports Books. (1986). *Love, sex and aging.* New York: Atlantic Institute, Atcom Publishing.

Colburn, E.D. Psychological adjustment to loss of work due to retirement: A study of retired men 60 years old & older. *Dissertation Abstracts International*, 43, 09, Sec A, P2890.

Fillenbaum, G.G., George, L.K., & Palmore, E.G. (1985). Determinants and consequences of retirement among men of different races and economic levels. *Journal of Gerontology*, 40(1), 85–94.

Friedmann, E.A., & Orbach, H.L. (1974). Adjustment to retirement. In S. Arieti (Ed.), *American handbook of psychiatry*, Vol I (2nd ed.) (pp. 609–645). New York: Basic Books.

Hayward, M.D., & Hardy, M.A. (1985). Early retirement processes among older men: Occupational differences. *Research on Aging*, 7(4), 491–516.

Keith, P.M. (1985). Work, retirement and well-being among unmarried men and women. *The Gerontologist*, 25(4), 410–416.

Keith, P.M. (1986). Isolation of the unmarried in later life. *Family Relations*. 35(3), 389–395.

Longino, C.G., & Lipman, A. (1981). Married and spouseless men and women in planned retirement communities: Support network differentials. *Journal of Marriage and The Family*, 43(1), 169–177.

Orand, A.M., & Landerman, R. (1984). Women's and men's retirement income status. Early family role effects. *Research on Aging*, 6(1), 25.

Osgood, N.J. (1982). *Life after work: Retirement, leisure, recreation, and the elderly.* New York: Praeger.

Parnes, H. (1981). *Work and retirement: A longitudinal study of men.* Cambridge, MA: MIT Press.

Parnes, H.S., Crowley, J.E., Haurin, R.J., Less, L.J., Morgan, W.R., Mottfrank, L., & Nestel, G. (1985). *Retirement among American men.* Lexington, MA: Lexington Books.

Sheppard, H.L. (1976). Work and retirement. In R.M. Binstock, & E. Shanas (Eds.), *Handbook of aging and the social sciences* (pp. 286–309). New York: Van Nostrand Reinhold.

Sinick, D. (1976). Counseling older persons: Career changes and retirement. *Vocational Guidance Quarterly*, 25, 18–25.

Solomon, K. (1980, May 7). *Psychosocial crises of older men.* Presented at the 133rd annual meeting of the American Psychiatric Association, San Francisco, CA.

Self-Nurturance

Cook, E.P. (1984). Students' perceptions of personal problems, appropriate help sources, and general attitudes about counseling. *Journal of College Student Personnel*, 25(2), 139–145.

Goldberg, H. (1979). *The new male: From self-destruction to self-care.* New York: Morrow.

Halpern, T.P. (1977). Degree of client disclosure as a function of past disclosure, counselor disclosure, and counselor facilitativeness. *Journal of Counseling Psychology*, 24(1), 41–47.

Hotaling, M.W. (1981). The effect of progrssive relaxation training on male self-reported past self-disclosure and anticipated willingness to self-disclosure. *Dissertation Abstracts International*, 4(12-B, PT 1), 4668.

Lewis, R.A. (1978). Emotional intimacy among men. *Journal of Social Issues, 34*, 108–121.

Petros, J.W. (Ed). (1974). *Sex, male, gender, masculine.* New York: Alfred.

Rhoads, D.L. (1983). A longitudinal study of life stress and social support among drug abusers. *International Journal of the Addictions, 18*(2), 195–222.

Scher, M. (1981). Men in hiding: A challenge for the counselor. *Personnel and Guidance Journal, 60*(4), 199–202.

Selby, J.W., Calhoun, L.G., & Parrott, G. (1978). Attitudes toward seeking pastoral help in the event of the death of a close friend of relative. *American Journal of Community Psychology, 6*(4), 399–403.

(See also resources on massage, stress reduction, play, and relaxation.)

Stereotypes

Abrahams, B., Feldman, S.S., & Nash, S.C. (1978). Sex role self-concept and sex role attitudes: Enduring personality characteristics or adaptations to changing life situations? *Developmental Psychology, 14*(4), 393–400.

Babladelis, G., Deaux, K., Helmreich, R.L., & Spence, J.T. (1983). Sex-related attitudes and personal characteristics in the United States. *International Journal of Psychology, 18*(1-2), 111–123.

Barry, R.B., & Barry, A. (1976). Stereotyping of sex roles in preschool kindergarten children. *Psychological Reports, 38*, 948–950.

Bell, D. (1982). *Being a man: The paradox of masculinity.* Lexington, MA: Lewis.

Bem, S.L. (1976). Probing the promise of androgyny. In A.G. Kaplan, & Bean (Eds.), *Beyond sex-role stereotypes: Readings toward a psychology of androgyny.* Boston: Little, Brown.

Bem, S.L., & Lenney, E. (1976). Sex-typing and avoidance of cross-sex behavior. *Journal of Personality and Social Psychology, 33*, 48–54.

Broverman, I.K., Broverman, D.M., Clarkson, P.S., Rosenkrantz, S., & Vogel, S.R. (1970). Sex role stereotypes and clinical judgements of mental health. *Journal of Counseling and Clinical Psychology, 34*(1), 1970.

Canavan, P., & Haskell, J. (1977). The American male stereotype. In C.A. Carney, & S.L. McMahon (Eds.), *Exploring contemporary male/female roles: A facilitator's guide* (pp. 150–166). LaJolla, CA: University Associates.

Duberman, L. (1975). *Explanations for sex role development. Gender and sex in society.* New York: Praeger.

Ellis, L.J., & Bentler, P.M. (1973). Traditional sex-detemined role standards and sex stereotypes. *Journal of Personality and Social Psychology, 25*(1), 28–34.

Fausto-Sterling, A. (1985). *Myths of gender.* New York: Basic Books.

Feingold, A. (1988). Cognitive gender differences are disappearing. *American Psychologist, 43*, 95–103.

Guttentag, M., & Bray, H. (1976). *Undoing sex role stereoptypes.* New York: McGraw-Hill.

Harris, V.L. (1983). The effects of perceived sex-appropriateness of a task on performance of selected sports skills. *Dissertation Abstracts International, 44*(5-A), 1375–1376.

Joesting, J. (1982). Sex-role attitudes of Australian and United States women's rights activists. *Psychological Reports, 51*(3, PT 1), 839–842.

Kaplan, A.G., & Bean, J.P. (1976). *Beyond sex-role stereotypes: Readings toward a psychology of androgyny.* Boston: Little, Brown.

King, M. (1973). The politics of sexual stereotypes. *The Black Scholar,* 4–12.

Maccoby, E.E., & Jacklin, C.N. (1975). *The psychology of sex differences.* Stanford, CA: Stanford University Press.

Mallen, C.A. (1983). Sex role stereotypes, gender identity and parental relationships in male homosexuals and heterosexuals. *Journal of Homosexuality, 9*(1), 55–74.

Miller, K.A. (1984). The effects of industrialization on men's attitudes toward the extended family and women's rights: A cross-national study. *Journal of Marriage and The Family, 46*(1), 153–160.

Monick, E. (1987). *Phallos, sacred images of the masculine*. Toronto: Inner City Books.

Naffziger, C.C., & Naffziger, K. (1974). Development of sex-role stereotypes. *Family Coordinator 23*, 251–259.

Nordstrom, B.C. (1983). Men's lives. *Dissertation Abstracts International, 44*(1-A) 296.

Peterson, G.W., Rollins, B.C., Thomas, D.L., & Heaps, L.K. (1982). Social placement of adolescents: Sex-role influences on family decisions regarding the careers of youth. *Journal of Marriage and the Family, 44*(3), 647–658.

Rao, V.P., & Rao, V.N. (1985). Sex-role attitudes: A comparison of sex-race groups. *Sex Roles, 12*(9–10), 939–953.

Salazar, D. (1979). A cross-cultural analysis of Chicano and Anglo undergraduates' perceptions of sex-role characteristics: Masculine, feminine, androgynous, and undifferentiated. *Dissertation Abstracts International, 40*(4-A), 1940.

Steinmann, A. (1975). Studies in male-female sex role identification. *Psychotherapy: Theory, Research and Practice, 12*(4), 412–417.

Taylor, A. (1983). Conceptions of masculinity and femininity as a basis for stereotypes of male and female homosexuals. *Journal of Homosexuality, 9*(1), 37–53.

Weitsmsan, L.J., et al. (1972). Sex-role socialization in picture books for preschool children. *American Journal of Sociology, 77*(6), 1125–1149.

Substance Abuse

Altman, L.S., & Plunkett, J.J. (1984). Group treatment of adult substance abusers. *Journal for Specialists in Group Work, 9*(1), 7–13.

Baumrind, L. (1983). Psychologists' attitude toward patients with a history of drug abuse. *Dissertation Abstracts International, 43*(12-A), 3843.

Bissell, L., Fewell, C.H., & Jones, R.W. (1980). The alcoholic social worker: A survey. *Social Work in Health Care, 5*, 421–432.

Bissell, L., & Haberman, P.W. (1984). *Alcoholism in the professions*. New York: Oxford University Press.

Braukmann, C.J. (1985). Effects of community-based group-home treatment programs on male juvenile offenders' use and abuse of drugs and alcohol. *American Journal of Drug & Alcohol Abuse, 11*(3-4), 249–278.

Cahalan, D. (1970). *Problem drinkers*. San Francisco: Jossey-Bass.

Carway, J.P. (1983). A study of the effects of a goal oriented counseling program on the self-concept and perception of environment and the association of dogmatism with these variables among a male incarcerated substance abuse population. *Dissertation Abstracts International*, (10-A), 3213–3214.

Chalmers, D.G. (1984). Evaluation research. In R.W. Thoreson, & E.P. Hosokawa (Eds.), *Employee assistance programs in higher education: Alcohol, mental and professional development: Programming for faculty and staff* (pp. 285–310). Springfield, IL: Charles C Thomas.

Collins, R.L., & Carlin, A.S. (1983). Case study: The cognitive behavioral treatment of a multiple-drug abuser. *Psychotherapy: Theory, Research and Practice, 20*(1), 101–106.

Cooper, S.E. (1982). The relation of interpersonal behavior, sex-role attitudes, and severity of dependency on outcomes of intensive treatment for alcoholism. *Dissertation Abstracts International, 42*(12-B, PY 1), 4926–4927.

Duehn, W.D. (1978). Covert sensitization in group treatment of adolescent drug abusers. *International Journal of the Addictions, 13*(3), 485–491.

Exo, K.J. (1981). *Substance abuser among professionals: Weaving the fabric of partnership*. (CSEP Occasional Papers No. 5). Chicago: Illinois Institute of Technology, Center for the Study of Ethics in the Professions.

Jordan, K.S., Roszell, D.K., Calsyn, D.A., & Chaney, E.F. (1985). Perception of treatment needs: Differences between patients and staff of a drug abuse treatment program. *Intrnational Journal of the Addictions, 20*(2), 345–351.

Keane, T.M., et. al. (1983). Substance abuse among Vietnam veterans with post-traumatic stress disorders. *Bulletin of the Society of Psychologists in Addictive Behaviors, 2*(2), 117–122.

Kliner, D.J., Spicer, J., & Barnett, B.S. (1980). Treatment outcome of alcoholic physicians. *Journal of Studies on Alcohol, 41*, 1217–1220.

Laliotis, D.A., & Grayson, J.H. (1985). Psychologist heal thyself: What is available for the impaired psychologist? *American Psychologist, 40*, 84–96.

Madsen, W. (1983). Reaching the alcoholic academic: An anthropological perspective. In R.W. Thoreson, & E.P. Hosokawa (Eds.), *Employee assistance programs in higher education: Alcohol, mental health and professional development programming for faculty and staff* (pp. 145–158). Springfield, IL: Charles C Thomas.

Miller, W.R., Hedrick, K.E., & Taylor, C.A. (1983). Addictive behaviors and life problems before and after behavioral treatment of problem drinkers. *Addictive Behaviors, 8*(4), 403–412.

Murphy, M. (1983). Music therapy: A self-help group experience for substance abuse patients. *Music Therapy, 3*(1), 52–62.

Newlove, D. (1981). *Those drinking days: Myself and other writers.* New York: Horizon.

Pittman, J.F., & Gerstein, L.H. (1984). Graduated levels of group therapy for substance abusers. *Journal for Specialists in Group Work, 9*(1), 26–31.

Rhoads, D.L. (1983). A longitudinal study of life stress and social support among drug abusers. *International Journal of the Addictions, 18*(2), 195–222.

Skorina, J. (1982). Alcoholic psychologists: The need for humane and effective regulations. *Professional Practice of Psychology, 3*, 33–41.

Smith, T.E. (1985). Groupwork with adolescent drug abusers. *Social Work With Groups, 8*(1), 55–64.

Solomon, K. (1982). *Counseling the drug dependent woman: Special issues for men.* N.I.D.A.— Treatment Research Monograph Series: Treatment Services for Drug Dependent Women Vol 2. ADM 82-1219, 572–612.

Sommer, B. (1984). The troubled teen: Suicide, drug use, and running away. *Women & Health, 9*(2–3), 117–141.

Steindler, E.M. (1975). *The impaired physician: An interpretive summary of the AMA conference on the disadvantaged challenge of the profession.* Chicago: American Medical Association.

Sweeney, T.T., & Foote, J.E. (1982). Treatment of drug and alcohol abuse in spinal cord injury veterans. *International Journal of the Addictions, 17*(5), 897–904.

Tarter, R.E., Alterman, A.I., & Edwards, K.L. (1985). Vulnerability to alcoholism in men: A behavioral-genetic perspective. *Journal of Studies on Alcohol, 46*, 329–357.

Thorarinsson, A.A. (1979). Mortality among men alcoholics in Iceland, 1951–1974. *Journal of Studies on Alcohol, 40*, 704–718.

Thoreson, R.W. (1976). Current views on alcoholism: Their implication for treatment. *Addictions, 23*, 58–59.

Thoreson, R.W. (1981). Alcohol problems in academia: The renaissance man, the inscrutable scholar and other myths. In J. Johnston, & E.P. Hosokawa (Eds.), *Employee assistance programs in higher education. Conference proceedings.* Columbia, MO: University of Missouri, Office of the Provost.

Thoreson, R.W. (1981). Alcoholism in the profession: The dilemma of reaching the chemically dependent or alcoholic psychologist. In P. Nathan (Chair.), *Psychologists in distress.* Symposium conducted at the meeting of the American Psychological Association, Los Angeles, CA.

Thoreson, R.W. (1984). The professor at risk: Alcohol abuse in academe. *Journal of Higher Education, 55*, 56–72.

Thoreson, R.W., Budd, F.C., & Krauskopf, C.J. (1986). Perception of alcohol misuse and work behavior among professionals: Identification and intervention. *Professional Psychology: Research and Practice, 17*, 210–226.

Thoreson, R.W., Budd F., & Krauskopf, C. (in press). Alcoholism among psychologists: Work related bahavior and patterns in recover. *Professional Psychology: Research and Practice.*

Thoreson, R.W., Nathan, P., Skorina, J., & Kilburg, R. (1983). The alcoholic psychologist: Issues, problems and implications for the profession. *Professional Psychology: Research and Practice. 14*, 670–684.

Weiner, H., & Fox, S. (1982). Cognitive-behavioral therapy with substance abusers. *Social Casework, 63*(9), 564–567.

Weiss, R.W., & Russakoff, S. (1978). The sex role identity of male drug abusers. *Journal of Clinical Psychology, 34*(4), 1010–1013.

Success

Balswick, J.O. (1970). The effect of spouse companionship support on employment success. *Journal of Marriage and the Family, 32*, 212–215.

Feather, N.T., & Simon, J.G. (1975). Reactions to male and female success and failure in sex-linked occupations: Impressions of personality, causal attributions, and perceived likelihood of different consequences. *Journal of Personality and Social Psychology, 31*, 20–31.

Gould, R. (1974). Measuring masculinity by the size of the paycheck. In J. Pleck, & J. Sawyer (Eds.), *Men and masculinity.* Englewood Cliffs, NJ: Prentice-Hall.

Touch Between Client and Therapist

Dye, L.W. (1983). Effects of counselor touch on perceived counselor expertness, attractiveness and trustworthiness. *Dissertation Abstracts International, 44*(2-B), 604.

Pope, K.S., Keith, S.P., & Tabachnick, B.G. (1986). Sexual attraction to clients: The human therapist and the (sometimes) inhuman training system. Special issue: Psychotherapy research. *American Psychologist, 4*(12), 147–158.

Stier, D.S., & Hall, J.A. (1984). Gender differences in touch: An empirical and theoretical review. *Journal of Personality and Social Psychology, 47*(2), 440–459.

Suiter, R.L., & Goodyear, R.K. (1985). Male and female counselor and client perceptions of four levels of counselor touch. *Journal of Counseling Psychology, 32*(4), 645–648.

Working

Craig, J.M., & Jacobs, R.R. (1985). The effect of working with women on male attitudes toward female firefighters. *Basic & Applied Social Psychology, 6*(1), 61–74.

Gaesser, D.L., & Whitbourne, S.K. (1985). Work identity and marital adjustment in blue-collar men. *Journal of Marriage and the Family, 47*(3), 747–751.

Golding, J.M., Resnick, A., & Crosby, F. (1983). Work satisfaction as a function of gender and job status. *Psychology of Women Quarterly, 7*(3), 286–290.

Gottfredson, L.S. (1979). Aspiration-job match: Age trends in a large nationally representative sample of white men. *Journal of Counseling Psychology, 26*, 319–328.

Gould, R. Measuring masculinity by the size of the paycheck. In J. Pleck, & J. Sawyer (Eds.), *Men and masculinity.* Englewood Cliffs, NJ: Prentice-Hall.

Haber, L.D. (1970). Age and capacity devaluation. *Journal of Health & Social Behavior, 11*(3), 167–182.

Hansen, G.R. (1980). *Early childhood sex role socialization and the career choices of men.* Presented at the 88th annual convention of the American Psychological Association, Montreal.

Hansen, L.S. (1980). BORN FREE; Change process evaluation of a psychological intervention to promote sex fair career development. *Pupil Personal Services Journal, 9*, 35–47.

Harrison, J. (1978). Warning: The male sex role may be dangerous to your health. *Journal of Social Issues, 34*, 65–86.

Hill, R.E., & Miller, E.L. (1981). Job change and the middle seasons of a man's life. *Academy of Management Journal, 24*(1), 114–127.

LaBier, D. (1986). *Modern madness: The Emotional fallout of success*. Reading, MA: Addison-Wesley.

Miller, Jr. (1980). Relationship of fear of success to perceived parental attitudes toward success and autonomy in men and women. *Psychological Reports, 47*(1), 79–86.

Morgan, J.I., Skovholt, T.M., & Orr, J.M. (1979). Career counseling with men: The shifting focus. In S.G. Weinrech (Ed.), *Career counseling: Theoretical and practical perspectives*. New York: McGraw-Hill.

Pleck, J.H. (1985). *Working wives, working husbands*. Newbury Park, CA: Sage.

Powell, G.N. (1988). *Women and men in management*. Newbury Park, CA: Sage.

Powell, G.N., & Butterfield, D.A. (1984). If "good managers" are masculine, what are "bad managers"? *Sex Roles, 10*(7-8), 477–484.

South, S.J., Bonjean, C.M., Markham, W.T., & Corder, J. (1983). Female labor force participation and the organizational experiences of male workers. *Sociological Quarterly, 24*(3), 367–380.

Terkel, Studs. (1974). *Working*. New York: Ballantine Books.

Thomas, L.E. (1979). Causes of mid-life change from high-status careers. *Vocational Guidance Quarterly, 27*(3), 202–208.

Wooleat, P.A., & Skovholt, T.M. (1978). Sculpting roles for men and women: The symmetry option. *Journal of Career Education, 5*, 78–89.

Workaholic. (1981). *Family Relations, 30*(1), 131–136.